PEOPLES' TRIBUNALS AND INTERNATIONAL LAW

Edited by

ANDREW BYRNES

University of New South Wales

GABRIELLE SIMM

University of Technology Sydney

CAMBRIDGE
UNIVERSITY PRESS

CAMBRIDGE
UNIVERSITY PRESS

University Printing House, Cambridge CB2 8BS, United Kingdom

One Liberty Plaza, 20th Floor, New York, NY 10006, USA

477 Williamstown Road, Port Melbourne, VIC 3207, Australia

314–321, 3rd Floor, Plot 3, Splendor Forum, Jasola District Centre, New Delhi – 110025, India

79 Anson Road, #06–04/06, Singapore 079906

Cambridge University Press is part of the University of Cambridge.

It furthers the University's mission by disseminating knowledge in the pursuit of education, learning, and research at the highest international levels of excellence.

www.cambridge.org
Information on this title: www.cambridge.org/9781108421676
DOI: 10.1017/9781108368360

First published 2018

Printed in the United Kingdom by Clays, St Ives plc

A catalogue record for this publication is available from the British Library.

Library of Congress Cataloging-in-Publication Data
Names: Byrnes, Andrew, editor. | Simm, Gabrielle, editor. | Australian Human Rights Centre, sponsoring body. | Permanent Peoples' Tribunal, sponsoring body.
Title: Peoples' tribunals and international law / edited by Andrew Byrnes, University of New South Wales, Sydney and Gabrielle Simm, University of Technology, Sydney.
Description: Cambridge, United Kingdom ; New York, NY, USA : Cambridge University Press, 2018. | Includes papers presented at the expert seminar of people's tribunals and international law on 27-28 September 2013 in Rome at the Permanent Peoples' Tribunal under the sponsorship of the Australian Human Rights Centre of the University of New South Wales, Sydney, Australia. | Includes bibliographical references and index.
Identifiers: LCCN 2017042294 | ISBN 9781108421676 (hardback)
Subjects: LCSH: International law–Citizen participation–Congresses. | International courts–Citizen participation–Congresses. | International criminal law–Citizen participation–Congresses. | Human rights and international law–Citizen participation–Congresses.
Classification: LCC KZ1240 .P46 2018 | DDC 341/.04–dc23 LC record available at https://lccn.loc.gov/2017042294

ISBN 978-1-108-42167-6 Hardback

CONTENTS

CONTRIBUTORS

ANDREW BYRNES is Professor of Law at the Faculty of Law, University of New South Wales (UNSW) Sydney, Australia, where he also served as Chair of the Steering Committee of the Australian Human Rights Centre from 1995 to 2017. He researches and teaches in the fields of international law and human rights.

SARA DEHM is Lecturer at the Faculty of Law, University of Technology Sydney, Australia. She researches and writes on topics of international law and institutions, migration politics and governance and legal theory. She is also a doctoral candidate at the Institute for International Law and the Humanities, University of Melbourne, Australia, and an associate with the Australian Human Rights Centre, UNSW.

USTINIA DOLGOPOL is Associate Professor of Law at Flinders University, Adelaide, Australia. She has published in the fields of human rights, children's rights, women's rights, the interplay between human rights law and international criminal law, the gender dynamics of issues before the International Criminal Court and the search for redress by the 'Comfort Women'. During December 2000, she was one of the chief prosecutors for the Women's International War Crimes Tribunal held in Tokyo. She has served on a number of domestic and international boards including the Advisory Board of the Women's Initiatives for Gender Justice.

NICOLA EDWARDS is a Research Assistant and PhD student at the Sydney Southeast Asia Centre at the University of Sydney, Australia. She was awarded the Sydney University medal for Arts (Languages) for her undergraduate thesis on the movement towards sustainable agriculture in Indonesia, and the university medal for Law (Juris Doctor) at the University of New South Wales. Her research on human rights and social activism has been published in *Social Activism in Southeast Asia*

(Routledge, 2013), *The Australian Journal of Asian Law, Court of Conscience and Inside Indonesia.*

SIMONA FRAUDATARIO has worked with the Permanent Peoples' Tribunal since 2006 as coordinator of its activities, closely involved with the organising committees of the main sessions held in Latin America and Asia (Colombia, Mexico, India, Cambodia, Indonesia). Due to her activities and investigations, she participated in international conferences in Colombia, Argentina and Brazil. She edited the second edition of François Rigaux's volume on the Universal Declaration of the Rights of Peoples (*La Carta di Algeri*) and was co-editor and co-author of the volume *Colombia entre violencia y derecho: Implicaciones de una sentencia del Tribunal Permanente de los Pueblos.* She was also co-author of *Memorie di repressione resistenza e solidarietà in Brasile e in America Latina.* She took part as researcher on the role of peoples' participation in the Second Russell Tribunal on Latin America in a project concluded by the Fondazione Lelio and Lisli Basso ISSOCO in agreement with the Ministry of Justice of the Brazilian government.

ROSALBA ICAZA is Senior Lecturer in Governance and International Political Economy at the International Institute of Social Studies, Erasmus University Rotterdam, in the Netherlands. She served as a senior researcher in the University of Amsterdam's Diversity Commission to conduct research on the state of epistemic justice and pedagogical diversity. She researches and teaches in the fields on international studies, feminism, social movements and epistemic justice.

BELÉN OLMOS GIUPPONI is Senior Lecturer in EU and International Law at Liverpool Hope University, England. Her research interests include EU law, general international law, international economic law, human rights and environmental law.

GABRIELLE SIMM is Chancellor's Postdoctoral Research Fellow, Faculty of Law, University of Technology Sydney, and a visiting fellow and formerly a research associate at the Australian Human Rights Centre, UNSW Law. Her research interests include international law and migration law. She has worked as a government lawyer advising on international law, a diplomat and a refugee lawyer.

GIOVANNI TOGNONI is a doctor of medicine and surgery and since 1969 has undertaken basic, clinical, epidemiological and public health research in some of the most critical fields of medicine, such as cardiology, intensive therapy, neurology, psychiatry and oncology, publishing results in more than 600 articles in leading international journals. He has also served as the director of research in various departments of the Mario Negri Institute in Milan. Among his activities, he has served as a World Health Organization (WHO) consultant for the selection of essential medicines, as a founding member of the international society for independent information on pharmaceuticals and as a coordinator of projects on community epidemiology in countries in Central and Latin America and Africa. From his collaboration with the Second Russell Tribunal to scientific activities, he has actively worked in the fields of human rights, right to health and rights of peoples. He has been the secretary-general of the Permanent Peoples' Tribunal since its establishment in 1979.

SASKIA WIERINGA is Emeritus Professor of Anthropology at the University of Amsterdam. She occupied the chair of Gender and Women's Same-Sex Relations Crossculturally. She has published widely on sexual politics in Indonesia, women's empowerment and women's same-sex relations, and heteronormativity globally. She chairs the Foundation International People's Tribunal on the Mass Crimes against Humanity in Indonesia and is working on two books on the Indonesian genocide.

ACKNOWLEDGEMENTS

The research project in the context of which this book was developed was largely funded by an Australian Research Council Discovery grant, DP11 110101594 ('Whose Law Is It, Anyway? Citizens' and Peoples' Challenges to State Dominance in the Making and Application of International Law') (2011–13) awarded to Andrew Byrnes and administered through the Australian Human Rights Centre at UNSW where Gabrielle Simm worked as a co-researcher on the project from 2012 to 2013. That funding concluded at the end of 2013, and work on the project continued with the support of UNSW Law, the Macquarie Law School and the University of Technology Sydney Law Faculty. We are most grateful for that support.

We acknowledge the assistance of the Lelio and Lisli Basso Foundation, which hosts the Permanent Peoples' Tribunal (PPT) in Rome. In particular, Secretary-General of the PPT, Dr Gianni Tognoni, and Research Officer, Simona Fraudatario, have been patient and consistently generous in their support of this project despite its having taken much longer than was originally envisaged. They facilitated a visit in 2011 by Andrew Byrnes to carry out research into the archives of the PPT at the Basso Foundation in Rome, and his attendance at the PPT Session on Agrochemical Transnational Corporations in Bangalore in December 2011.

Gianni Tognoni and Simona Fraudatario undertook a great deal of work in organising, hosting and presenting at the workshop held on 27–28 September 2013 in the PPT in Rome at which many of the papers collected here were presented. The workshop was conducted in English, Spanish and Italian, and we are indebted to the interpreters provided by the PPT for facilitating communication. Salvatore Senese, the former president of the PPT, and Franco Ippolito, the current president, also participated. Without the assistance of the PPT and the guidance they have so generously and patiently provided, much of our research would not have been possible.

We would also like to thank the participants at the 2013 workshop. They include Gill Boehringer, Javier Bogantes, Brid Brennan, Harold Cook, Sara Dehm, Soledad Castro Vargas, Ayça Çubuçku, Tina Dolgopol, Daniel Feierstein, Dianne Otto, Antoni Pigrau Solé, Sarojeni Rengam, Claudia Torrelli, Ramon Vera Herrera and Sarah Williams. While not all the papers presented at the workshop are included in this volume, a number of these contributions have been published elsewhere.

We would like to thank colleagues at UNSW. Diane Macdonald, administrator of the Australian Human Rights Centre, played a key role in supporting the project website and assisting with arrangements for the workshop. The director of the centre, Andrea Durbach, and its deputy director, Justine Nolan, have been very supportive of the project and always willing to be enlightened as to the many virtues of the peoples' tribunal format. Leanne Palmer in her role as research administrator in the Faculty of Law provided enthusiastic and efficient support for the project, as did other colleagues in the faculty. We are grateful to Lucas Lixinski for his advice on a number of translation matters.

We owe a significant debt to several UNSW students who provided research support and translation assistance at various stages of the project, in some cases in their role as interns with the Australian Human Rights Centre. We would like to thank Amy Rogers, Gabriela Cuadrado Quesada, Alba Boer Cueva, Monique Dam, Uzma Sherieff, Joanna Lee and Ruby Lew.

Gabrielle Simm would like to acknowledge former president of the Permanent Peoples' Tribunal, the late François Rigaux, who provided fascinating insights into the history of the PPT in an interview shortly before his death in November 2013. She also thanks Dianne Otto and Christine Chinkin for the opportunity to participate in a panel on peoples' tribunals, which was part of a workshop at Melbourne Law School in 2013.

Andrew Byrnes would like to thank the students in the different versions of the course on Peoples' Tribunals and International Law that he has taught at UNSW, the University of Zurich and the University of Vienna for their engagement with this topic and their critical feedback. Thanks are also due to Professor Christine Kaufmann at the University of Zurich and Professor Christina Binder then of the University of Vienna for facilitating the offering of courses at their institutions in 2013 and 2015 respectively. Andrew would like to thank the Centre for Human Rights Research at the University of Vienna – in particular its then Director Professor Manfred Nowak and Anna Müller

Funk – and Professors August Reinisch and Ursula Kriebaum and the staff of the International Law Department of the Faculty of Law, University of Vienna, where he spent a productive period of sabbatical in late 2015.

We are grateful to Palgrave Communications for permission to include in this collection a revised version of Rosalba Icaza's article, 'The Peoples' Permanent Tribunals and Indigenous People's Struggles in Mexico: Between Coloniality and Epistemic Justice' (2015, 1 *Palgrave Communications*, www.palgrave-journals.com/articles/palcomms201520), and to Cambridge University Press for its willingness to permit us to include a revised version of Belén Olmos Giupponi's article, 'Transnational Environmental Law and Grass-Root Initiatives: The Case of the Latin American Water Tribunal' (2016, 5[1] *Transnational Environmental Law* 145–74).

We thank Finola O'Sullivan and Rebecca J. Roberts at Cambridge University Press for their patience and assistance with the publication process.

And we acknowledge the support and patience of our families throughout the process of this project.

NOTE ON REFERENCES

The material contained in the various chapters is up to date as of May 2017. References to websites were also current as of that date. The websites of a number of peoples' tribunals that were active at the time the tribunals were held are no longer available online at the original web address. However, some or all of the documents from those websites are available through the internet archive, Wayback Machine (http://archive.org/web/), and we have included citations to those archived versions where available, or to the documents on other websites. We have also done this for other sources where the original version is no longer available but the material is available through the Internet Archive.

Introduction

ANDREW BYRNES AND GABRIELLE SIMM

From 10 to 13 November 2015, in the seventeenth-century Niuewe Kerk (New Church) in The Hague, an international people's tribunal took place to examine the suppression of the Indonesian Communist Party and those presumed to be associated with it that was carried out by the Sukarno government in 1967.[1] During this crackdown, tens and probably hundreds of thousands of people were killed and many more were subjected to enslavement, imprisonment, torture, sexual violence, persecution and forced disappearances.

This tribunal, held fifty years after the occurrence of events that it examined, was a response to the continuing failure of the Indonesian state over that period to fully acknowledge the systematic violations of human rights that had taken place. The violations had been the subject of a 2012 report by the Indonesian National Human Rights Commission (Komnas HAM) as well as of other national and international examinations. The Indonesian government had failed to provide justice to survivors and the families of those who had not survived. The Final Report adopted by the judges found that the allegations of systematic violations of human rights amounting to crimes against humanity had been established and that the Indonesian government should take concrete steps to acknowledge the wrongs, correct the historical record and ensure justice and reparation to survivors and the families of victims.[2]

This tribunal, significant in itself, was only one of several major international peoples' tribunals that have been held or instituted in the last few years. Others have included an international people's tribunal

[1] International People's Tribunal 1965, www.tribunal1965.org/en/. See Lena Bjurström, 'Indonésie: juger l'histoire' (9 November 2015) 1398 (1) *Politis* 21–22, www.politis.fr/Indonesie-juger-l-histoire,33057.html, and Wieringa, Chapter 5 in this volume.

[2] *Final Report of the IPT 1965: Findings and Documents of the IPT 1965*, 20 July 2016, http://www.tribunal1965.org/en/tribunal-1965/tribunal-report/.

into alleged crimes against the Filipino people[3] and into systematic violations committed in Iran in the 1980s,[4] a number of tribunals engaging with historical and current Israel-Palestine issues,[5] issues relating to the 2003 Iraq war,[6] on the Canadian mining industry in Latin America,[7] international tribunals for nature,[8] on water and environmental rights in Latin America,[9] on minimum wage for garment workers in Asia,[10] violations of labour rights,[11] violations of women's rights,[12] the situation of human rights in Mexico and Central America,[13] the role of

[3] The International People's Tribunal (IPT) on Crimes against the Filipino People by Pres. Benigno S. Aquino III and the US Government represented by Pres. Barack Obama, Washington, DC, 16–18 July 2015, http://internationalpeoplestribunal.org/.

[4] Payam Akhavan, 'Is grassroots justice a viable alternative to impunity? The case of the Iran People's Tribunal' (2017) 39(1) *Human Rights Quarterly* 73.

[5] Russell Tribunal on Palestine (2010–2014) [RtoP], www.russelltribunalonpalestine.com/en/; Kuala Lumpur War Crimes Tribunal Hearing on Palestine (2012–2014), www.legal-tools.org/en/browse/ltfolder/0_28267/ (the official website of the KL War Crimes Tribunal is no longer available). See also Frank Barat and Daniel Machover, 'The Russell Tribunal on Palestine' in Chantal Meloni and Gianni Tognoni (eds.), *Is There a Court for Gaza?: A Test Bench for International Justice* (T. M. C. Asser Press, 2012) 527–43. For a critical view of the RToP, see NGO Monitor, 'Russell Tribunal on Palestine', 3 October 2012, www.ngo-monitor.org/article/russell_tribunal_on_palestine. The NGO Monitor's work critiquing the work of the Russell Tribunal on Palestine is part of its overall work of responding to actions taken by state, UN organs and groups and individuals in relation to alleged human rights committed by Israel, in particular the use of 'lawfare' by some of these bodies.

[6] See Müge Gürsöy Sökmen (ed.), *World Tribunal on Iraq: Making the Case against War* (Olive Branch Press, 2008); Kuala Lumpur War Crimes Tribunal, *Chief Prosecutor of the Kuala Lumpur War Crimes Commission v. George W. Bush and Anthony L. Blair*, Judgment, 22 November 2011, www.globalresearch.ca/chief-prosecutor-of-the-kuala-lumpur-war-crimes-commission-v-george-w-bush-anthony-l-blair/27821.

[7] Permanent Peoples' Tribunal, *Session on the Canadian Mining Industry in Latin America*, 29 May-1 June 2014, www.tppcanada.org/a-propos-du-tpp/session-canada.

[8] International Rights of Nature Tribunal, www.therightsofnature.org/rights-of-nature-tribunal/.

[9] Tribunal Latinoamericano del Agua (Latin American Water Tribunal), 'Ciudad de Guatemala, 2015', http://tragua.com/audiencias/ciudad-de-guatemala-2015/ (7 cases throughout Latin America).

[10] National People's Tribunals on Living Wage for Garment Workers in Asia. See Matthew Burnett-Stuart, 'Transnational Advocacy Networks as Counter Hegemonic Actors: The Asia Floor Wage Alliance and the Living Wage People's Tribunals', www.academia.edu/7276015/The_Asia_Floor_Wage_Alliance_and_the_Living_Wage_Peoples_Tribunals.

[11] Tribunal Internacional de Libertad Sindical (International Tribunal on Trade Union Freedoms), www.tribunaldelibertadsindical.blogspot.no/.

[12] www.hartford-hwp.com/archives/51/002.html.

[13] Tribunal Hearings on the Human Rights Crisis in Mexico and Central America International Tribunal of Conscience of Peoples in Movement, http://internationaltribunalofconscience.org/.

transnational corporations and international organisations in the commission of human rights violations[14] and the human rights impacts of the global trade regime[15] and of international financial institutions.

While the number of such tribunals and the variety of topics they address may have increased over the years, the phenomenon of the international peoples' tribunal is not a recent one.[16] In this book we bring together a series of essays examining the phenomenon of international peoples' tribunals, their history and political justification, the types of issues with which they engage, the criticisms commonly made of them and the different roles that they can perform. Our focus is on international peoples' tribunals rather than on domestic peoples' tribunals.[17] Peoples' tribunals are diverse in their subjects and forms; we are interested in those that place the forms of legal process, and the standards of international law, at the centre of their activities. For our purposes, an international peoples' tribunal is a process initiated by civil society that involves the presentation to a body of eminent persons of evidence and arguments that seek to establish whether a state, international organisation,

[14] Permanent Peoples' Tribunal, *The European Union and Transnational Corporations in Latin America: Policies, Instruments and Actors Complicit in Violations of the Peoples' Rights, Deliberating Session*, Madrid, 14–17 May 2010, the Judgement (2010); Permanent Peoples' Tribunal, *Session on Agrochemical Transnational Corporations*, Bangalore, 3–6 December 2011, Verdict.

[15] Global People's Tribunal on WTO and Free Trade Agreements (2013), www.popularresistance.org/global-peoples-tribunal-on-wto-free-trade-agreements/.

[16] See generally Arthur Jay Klinghoffer and Judith Apter Klinghoffer, *International Citizens' Tribunals: Mobilising Public Opinion to Advance Human Rights* (New York: Palgrave, 2002). In his 1992 article on the subject, Blaser lists dozens of tribunals held since the late 1960s: Arthur Blaser, 'How to advance human rights without really trying: An analysis of nongovernmental tribunals' (1992) 14 *Human Rights Quarterly* 339, 366–70.

[17] There are many examples of peoples' tribunals at the national level. Standing tribunals include the Indian People's Tribunal on Environment and Human Rights, www.iptindia.org/. There are also many instances of ad hoc peoples' tribunals inquiring into one situation or series of events: see, e.g., farmers' tribunals in India (Muzaffar Assadi, 'Seed Tribunal: Interrogating farmers' suicides' (21 October–3 November, 2000) 35 (43/44) *Economic and Political Weekly* 3808–10; the New Zealand People's Inquiry into the Impacts and Effects of Aerial Spraying Pesticide over Urban Areas of Auckland, 2006, https://web.archive.org/web/20130214091720/http://www.peoplesinquiry.co.nz/; El Tribunal de Conciencia contra la Violencia Sexual hacia las Mujeres en Guatemala durante del Conflicto Armado Interno [The Tribunal of Conscience on Sexual Violence against Women in Guatemala during the Internal Armed Conflict], 2010, www.cicig.org/index.php?page=tribunal-de-conciencia-contra-la-violencia-sexual-hacia-las-mujeres. See Alison Crosby and M. Brinton Lykes, 'Mayan women survivors speak: The gendered relations of truth telling in postwar Guatemala' (2011) 5(3) *International Journal of Transitional Justice* 456.

corporations or, less frequently, specified individuals have committed breaches of international law or of another body of law or norms. It may evaluate the adequacy of existing international law, institutions or structures with broader notions of law or justice including 'peoples' law'.

While individual peoples' tribunals have been examined – and the last decade has seen a burgeoning literature – there has been only limited attention to the phenomenon as a whole. We seek to provide a framework for understanding the significance of these institutions within a broader context of international advocacy by civil society groups and to explore the common elements, as well as the diversity, of different peoples' tribunals.

The first part of the book, setting out the history and theory of peoples' tribunals, opens with a chapter by the editors in which we provide a *tour d'horizon* of the phenomenon of international peoples' tribunals from their emergence on the stage in the late 1960s to the present. We explore the nature, composition, normative frameworks, legitimacy, impact and special contributions that peoples' tribunals have made to the development of a just international order and the implementation of human rights guarantees.

In Chapter 2, Gianni Tognoni, Secretary-General of the Permanent Peoples' Tribunal (PPT), describes and analyses its role. This institution has been influential, not just in its own work of holding more than forty tribunals since its founding in the late 1970s, but in providing a model and support for many other peoples' tribunals. Tognoni explores the origins of the PPT, tracing its history from the First Russell Tribunal and its conceptual foundation in the rights of peoples. The chapter examines the different types of cases that the PPT has examined and shows its evolution as a body that engages with a wide range of issues, including international power structures and the role of international law in resisting or reinforcing them.

In Part 2 the focus moves to the role of peoples' tribunals in relation to international criminal law and violence against women. In Chapter 3 Gabrielle Simm compares peoples' tribunals with women's courts, focusing on international crimes of sexual violence. International criminal law has been the focus of much feminist activism and contestation to the extent that it has been claimed that 'feminism rules'. At the same time, unofficial or peoples' tribunals and women's courts – civil society initiatives – continue to proliferate. This chapter examines the treatment of international crimes of sexual violence by peoples' tribunals through a focus on the former Yugoslavia. It explores two key questions. First, what do peoples' tribunals offer to victim-survivors of international crimes of sexual violence that is lacking in official courts? Second, to what extent do 'mainstream' peoples' tribunals suffer from the same defects as official courts, thereby rendering 'women's tribunals' necessary? In addressing these questions, she analyses the Berne and Barcelona hearings of the Permanent Peoples' Tribunal and the Women's Court feminist approach to justice against the backdrop of the International Criminal Tribunal for the former Yugoslavia.

In Chapter 4 Ustinia Dolgopol explores these and related issues in her revisiting of the Women's International War Crimes Tribunal for the Trial of Japan's Military Sexual Slavery held in Tokyo in 2000. This is one of the most important peoples' tribunals of the last twenty years and one at which Dolgopol was a prosecutor. Better known as the Tokyo Women's Tribunal, it resulted from civil society's perceptions about the shortcomings of the state system and a desire to influence how the international community understands state violence. For many of the participants, law was seen as a way of presenting their efforts as 'neutral' – that is, not based on political ideology. However, law is not neutral. Its power to exclude those not conversant with its language or rituals can exclude the very people for whom such a tribunal is created. This chapter addresses ethical issues about the use of law for organisers of and participants in people's tribunals. Ultimately peoples' tribunals cannot provide full accountability. In this context, the chapter raises questions about the extent to which organisers are accountable and whether they sufficiently acknowledge the limits of what peoples' tribunals can offer those in whose name they are established.

In Chapter 5 Saskia Wieringa outlines the establishment of the International Peoples' Tribunal on 1965 crimes against humanity in Indonesia. The surviving victims are haunted by stigma and the perpetrators live with impunity. The government of Indonesia has never taken any judicial steps to deal with this period and it seems unlikely to do so in the near future. The chapter discusses the author's role in organising the tribunal and assesses the significance of the tribunal both inside and outside Indonesia. The chapter also deals with some ethical and practical concerns and concludes with reflections on this tribunal in the light of other peoples' tribunals.

Part 3 addresses how peoples' tribunals can contribute to the development of a more participatory, fairer international law. In Chapter 6 Fraudatario and Tognoni expand on the discussion in Chapter 2 by outlining the way in which the PPT has sought to involve peoples in the critique and development of international law. Peoples' tribunals document and judge gaps in international law, a process that underlines the centrality of peoples as alternative subjects capable of thinking of themselves as judging the delays, absences and ambiguity of international law. This chapter presents the history and experience of the PPT as an example of an experimental laboratory of the possible paths that are increasingly necessary when aiming for a law for and by peoples. It explains how the Tribunal formulates a framework of rules that see peoples as subjects and holders of rights and not just as victims of breaches unpunished by an international law that has abdicated its role as an effective instrument for promoting and protecting the self-determination and dignity of peoples.

In Chapter 7 Sara Dehm examines Tribunal 12, an international peoples' tribunal held in Stockholm in 2012 that explored the liability of 'Europe' for the systematic violations of the rights and dignity of refugees, asylum seekers and migrants. The Tribunal, as an internationalised articulation of migrant justice, adopted a legal and aesthetic framework in order to put 'Europe' on trial. This chapter unpacks the Tribunal 12 project as an international civil society initiative ambivalently situated within a legacy of peoples' tribunals and their entanglement with international law and institutions. The Tribunal differed significantly from many other international peoples' tribunals in that it did not hear any witness testimonies from migrants themselves. Nonetheless the Tribunal 12 project can be read as contributing to a 'popular' form of international law, that is, a form of law belonging to the people.

In Chapter 8 Rosalba Icaza problematises the work of peoples' tribunals, taking as her case study the PPT and the struggle of indigenous people in Mexico. The chapter investigates the potential of the PPT to contribute to epistemic justice in Mexico by focusing on indigenous people communities' long-term struggle for legal pluralism and autonomy. It analyses the coloniality of international human rights law operating in non-governmental mechanisms such as the PPT, a perspective that has remained absent in critical international and global studies. In particular, the article argues that the PPT in Mexico overlaps with Eurocentric modes of legal production but that it nonetheless has the potential to contribute, in a relevant but fragile way, to epistemic justice.

In Chapter 9 Nicola Edwards analyses a tribunal held in Sydney in 2013 that sought to bring about accountability for a massacre that took place on 6 July 1998 on the island of Biak, in the disputed Indonesian region of West Papua. This chapter evaluates the importance of the Biak Tribunal in the broader context of scholarly activism about human rights violations in West Papua. It addresses the argument that West Papuans have been denied the right to self-determination and the related accusations that Indonesia is committing genocide in the region. It assesses the contribution of this tribunal to the broader struggle for human rights in West Papua.

In Chapter 10 Belén Olmos Giupponi examines another major international repeat player in the field of peoples' tribunals, the Latin American Water Tribunal (LAWT). This chapter analyses the role played by the LAWT in resolving environmental disputes over water resources. Since its inception in 1998, the LAWT has emerged as a non-governmental body with a multidisciplinary composition and a mandate based on both formal and informal sources of law that holds public hearings to address water-related complaints. Whereas the traditional model of interstate dispute settlement offers only limited possibilities of redress to non-state actors (mainly individuals and groups), the LAWT provides them with the opportunity to present their demands before an environmental justice forum.

In Chapter 11 the editors draw together the major themes of the essays and reflect on the future of peoples' tribunals. The chapter engages with three substantive questions. First, to what extent are the peoples' tribunals discussed here representative of international peoples' tribunals more generally? Second, what is the relationship between peoples' tribunals, social movements and international law? Third, what impact do peoples' tribunals have on the implementation and development of international law?

We conclude that, despite all the criticism of the lack of legitimacy of peoples' tribunals, they continue to offer a valuable means of social activism for those whose rights have been violated and who, despite the proliferation of formal institutions and mechanisms for redress, still frequently fail to achieve recognition of and redress for violations of their rights. The possibilities and the limitations of this form of juridically oriented activism are illustrated by the case studies presented in this book.

PART I

Introduction

History of Peoples' Tribunals

1

International Peoples' Tribunals

Their Nature, Practice and Significance[1]

ANDREW BYRNES AND GABRIELLE SIMM

1.1 Introduction

The conventional history of modern international peoples' tribunals traces their origins in the post–World War II era to the Russell Tribunals held in the late 1960s and early to mid-1970s.[2] These were the brainchild of the British philosopher and mathematician Bertrand Russell who, together with Jean-Paul Sartre and other like-minded leftist intellectuals, wished to hold the United States and its allies to account for their actions in prosecuting the war in Vietnam. This was the subject of the first Russell Tribunal, modelled on the Nuremberg Tribunal and held in Sweden and Denmark in 1967.[3]

[1] Sections of this chapter draw on Gabrielle Simm and Andrew Byrnes, 'International Peoples' Tribunals in Asia: political theatre, juridical farce or meaningful intervention?' (2014) 4 *Asian Journal of International Law* 103, and Andrew Byrnes and Gabrielle Simm, 'Peoples' tribunals, international law and the use of force' (2013) 36 (2) *University of New South Wales Law Journal* 711.

[2] For a view that they begin earlier, see Arthur Jay Klinghoffer and Judith Apter Klinghoffer, *International Citizens' Tribunals: Mobilising Public Opinion to Advance Human Rights* (New York: Palgrave, 2002) 3 (referring to the Joint Commission of Inquiry [Dewey Commission] held in the United States in 1937 to respond to Moscow show trials alleging that Trotsky had engaged in conspiracy against the USSR and to an earlier 'countertrial' held in London to the 1933 Reichstag fire in Berlin). Andersson argues that there are more differences than similarities between these earlier inquiries and the Russell Tribunal: Stefan Andersson, 'International Citizens' Tribunals [review of Arthur Jay Klinghoffer and Judith Apter Klinghoffer, *International Citizens' Tribunals*' (2002) 22 *Russell: Journal of Bertrand Russell Studies* 83, 85. For another example of a pre-war tribunal, see Louis Anthes, 'Public deliberative drama: The 1934 Mock Trial of Adolf Hitler for "Crimes against Civilization"' (1998) 42 *American Journal of Legal History* 391, and the American Jewish Congress, *The Case of Civilization against Hitlerism* (R. O. Ballou, 1934). We thank Frédéric Mégret for drawing our attention to this example.

[3] See Peter Limqueco and Peter Weiss (eds.), *Prevent the Crime of Silence: Reports from the Sessions of the International War Crimes Tribunal founded by Bertrand Russell* (Allen Lane, 1971).

The Tribunal was justified as necessary to 'prevent the crime of silence', given that relatively little was known about the violations taking place and that there was no formal international court before which allegations of violations could be brought. A mass of primary and secondary evidence was presented to the Tribunal in relation to alleged violations by the United States and its allies of international law on the use of force, international humanitarian law and human rights law.[4] The members of the Tribunal comprised a mix of prominent intellectuals – it was not a panel comprised solely of legal experts.

The Tribunal found that the United States and its allies had committed a range of violations of international law in the initiation and conduct of the war and sought to place these violations of positive law within a broader narrative of US imperialist expansion. The Tribunal was criticised by many as partisan, procedurally flawed and illegitimate and assessments of its contemporary impact and subsequent legacy vary.[5] The Russell Tribunal itself subsequently held sessions in relation to repression in Latin America (1973–76),[6] freedom of opinion and public sector employment in West Germany (*Berufsverbot*) (1978–79)[7] and the rights of the Indians of the Americas (1980),[8] followed some twenty years later by a

[4] See generally Stefan Andersson, 'A secondary bibliography of the international war crimes tribunal: London, Stockholm and Roskilde' (2011) 31 *Russell: Journal of Bertrand Russell Studies* 167 (wide-ranging bibliography of secondary sources in English, Swedish and French).

[5] Richard Falk, 'War, war crimes, power, and justice: Toward a jurisprudence of conscience' (2013) 21(3) *Transnational Law & Contemporary Problems* 667, 682–84.

[6] See Bertrand Russell Peace Foundation (ed.), *The Bertrand Russell Tribunal on Brazil and Repression in Latin America* (Bertrand Russell Peace Foundation, 1973) and other sources referred to in the Bibliography. See also Julio Cortázar, *Fantomas contra los vampiros multinacionales* (1975); *Fantomas Versus the Multinational Vampires: An Obtainable Utopia* (translated by David Kurnick, 2015) (Semiotexte, 1975), and Jaume Peris Blanes, 'Cortázar entre la cultura *pulp* y la denuncia política' ['Cortázar between pulp culture and political protest'] (2012) 50 *Estudios Filológicos* 95.

[7] Hugh Mosley, 'Third International Russell Tribunal on Civil Liberties in West Germany' (Spring, 1978) 14 *New German Critique* 178, www.jstor.org/stable/488068. See also Internationales Russell Tribunal and Internationales Russell Tribunal Deutscher Beirat (eds.), *Zur Situation der Menschenrechte in der Bundesrepublik Deutschland/3. Internat. Russell-Tribunal* [*On the Situation of Human Rights in the Federal Republic of Germany/Third International Russell Tribunal*] (Rotbuch-Verlag, 1978), and the documentation at '3. Russell-Tribunal über die Situation der Menschenrechte in der BRD (1977–1979): Materialien zur Analyse von Opposition' ['The Third Russell Tribunal on the Situation of Human Rights in the Federal Republic of Germany (1977–1979): Materials for the Analysis of Opposition'], www.mao-projekt.de/BRD/REP/Russell-Tribunal.shtml.

[8] *Report of the Fourth Russell Tribunal on the Rights of the Indians of the Americas: Conclusions* (Rotterdam, November 1980); Julien Louvrier, 'Le *Tribunal Russell II pour l'Amérique latine* (1973–1976): Mobiliser les intellectuels pour sensibiliser l'opinion

tribunal on the rights of psychiatric patients (2001)[9] and, most recently, by the Russell Tribunal on Palestine (2009–2014).[10]

Whatever its problems, the Russell Tribunal did, however, provide inspiration, a model and theoretical justification for the holding of such tribunals – fora in which the actions of governments and others were subjected to scrutiny against international legal standards, as well as against other legal and non-legal norms. It is this category of peoples' tribunal that is of particular interest to international lawyers: tribunals that seek to harness the power and legitimacy of law and claim for themselves a role in interpreting it and holding its addressees accountable in a public albeit informal way. It is this emphasis on law, international law in particular, and a deliberative process of evaluation of evidence in the light of law that distinguishes these tribunals, for example, from a speech at a public rally denouncing violations of international law by states, or a political show trial. The difference lies in the extent to which the forms and procedure of a legal proceeding are observed, as well as in the cogency of the analysis and reasoning that is adopted, although not all tribunals designated as peoples' tribunals aspire to or achieve this.

The major successor to the Russell Tribunal and one of the small number of repeat institutional players in the field of peoples' tribunals is the Permanent Peoples' Tribunal (PPT) based in Rome.[11] The PPT was established by the Italian leftist senator, Lelio Basso (who was himself involved in the Russell Tribunals), in conjunction with the International League for the Rights and Liberation of Peoples. The PPT has held more than forty hearings since it commenced its work in 1979.[12] In its founding documents and orientation it represents the two strands of legal authority that have been drawn on at different times by international peoples' tribunals: the positive law of nations and the law of

publique internationale' ['The Second Russell Tribunal on Latin America: Mobilising intellectuals to influence public opinion']. www.academia.edu/166082/Le_Tribunal_Russell_II_pour_l_Am%C3%A9rique_latine_1973-1976_Mobiliser_les_intellectuels_pour_sensibiliser_l_opinion_publique_internationale.

[9] Ian Parker, 'Russell Tribunal on Human Rights in Psychiatry & *"Geist gegen Genes"*, 30 June–2 July 2001' (2001) 27 *PINS (Psychology in Society)* 120.

[10] www.russelltribunalonpalestine.com/en/.

[11] See, generally, Tognoni, Chapter 2 in this volume. The Latin American Water Tribunal (*Tribunal Latinoamericano del Agua*) is another important example of a repeat player.

[12] http://tribunalepermanentedeipopoli.fondazionebasso.it/category/sessioni-e-sentenze-it/. A list of the sessions of the PPT appears in the Bibliography in this volume. All the final verdicts or judgments of the PPT's sessions may be found on the PPT website, though not all the verdicts are available there in English. The titles of all sessions are given here in English.

peoples – a body of law that claims its validity as grounded in the sovereignty of peoples that exists outside and independently of the Westphalian system. The latter is represented in particular by the Universal Declaration of the Rights of Peoples adopted in Algiers in 1976 by the International League for the Rights and Liberation of Peoples.[13]

This chapter considers three major sets of questions that arise in respect of many peoples' tribunals. The chapters that follow generally engage with one or more of these issues in the context of particular tribunals. The first set of questions relates to the definition of peoples' tribunals, the types of cases they take on and the roles played by judges-jurors, victim-witnesses and, almost invariably, absent defendants. The second set of questions addresses the relationship of peoples' tribunals to international law: the standards that peoples' tribunals apply and the types of liability and responsibility with which they engage. Third, this chapter sets out the main types of critiques levelled at peoples' tribunals and discusses the extent to which they are justified. It deals with questions of legitimacy and authority, bias and whether peoples' tribunals are representative of those in whose name they claim to speak.

1.2 What Are Peoples' Tribunals?

As already noted, we understand an international peoples' tribunal to be a civil society initiative establishing a forum for a body of eminent persons and/or experts to consider allegations of violations of specific standards of international law (and possibly also other bodies of law such as national law, indigenous law or 'peoples' law') in the light of documentary and other forms of evidence presented to them in formal proceedings. The tribunal presents a reasoned set of findings based on its evaluation of that material. The process is thus a formal deliberation characterised by the public presentation of material and the delivery of reasoned conclusions by the adjudicative or evaluating body, whose members are sometimes termed 'judges', at other times 'jurors'. While this description captures nearly all of the bodies that would describe themselves as peoples' tribunals, there is nonetheless considerable variation in the emphasis and practices of such tribunals.

Various terms have been used to refer to peoples' tribunals. Isaac Deutscher, who was involved in the original Russell Tribunal, thought

[13] Universal Declaration of the Rights of the Peoples, Algiers (adopted 4 July 1976), www.algerie-tpp.org/tpp/en/declaration_algiers.htm.

the term 'commission of inquiry' was an appropriate term for such proceedings, as it connoted moral and political independence and fair representation of both sides. Bertrand Russell privately referred to it as an 'international investigation commission', while publicly preferring the term 'tribunal' due to its Nuremberg antecedents.[14] A more legal 'governmentally coercive image' is projected by use of the term 'tribunal'.[15] Other terms used include court of inquiry,[16] people's hearing, tribunal of opinion (*tribunal d'opinion*),[17] civil society tribunal,[18] ethical tribunal (*tribunal ético*) and jury or tribunal of conscience (*tribunal de consciencia*; *Gewissenstribunal*).[19]

Peoples' tribunals do not just respond to a technical failure in the system of existing state and state-sponsored institutions. They reflect a broader claim that asserts the rights of peoples (and people) to claim for themselves the benefit of international and other forms of law, and to interpret and develop international law. They assert the right of peoples themselves to articulate law that is not dependent on endorsement by states for its legitimacy but that derives its status from the choice of those whom it affects. Peoples' tribunals critique the content of existing international law in some areas, where that law embodies and perpetuates oppressive power relations.

14 Klinghoffer and Klinghoffer, n. 2, 114.

15 Richard Falk, 'Keeping Nuremberg Alive' in Giuliano Amato, Antonio Cassese, José Echeverria, Valentino Gerratana, Georges Haupt, Leo Matarasso, Oskar Negt, François Rigaux, Stefano Rodotà and Albert Soboul (eds.), *Marxismo, democrazia e diritto dei popoli: Scritti in onore di Lelio Basso* [*Marxism, Democracy and the Rights of Peoples: Essays in Honour of Lelio Basso*] (Franco Angeli Editore, 1979) 811, 814. On 'tribunality', see Judith Shklar, *Legalism: Law, Morals and Political Trials* (Harvard University Press, 1964) 143–221.

16 Klinghoffer and Klinghoffer, above n. 2, 113.

17 Louis Joinet, 'Les tribunaux d'opinion. Bilan et perspective' ['Opinion tribunals: Assessment and perspective'] in Giuliano Amato et al., above n. 15, 821; Janine Odink, 'The Permanent Peoples' Tribunal' (1993) 11 *Netherlands Quarterly of Human Rights* 229, 231.

18 Ayça Çubukçu, 'On cosmopolitan occupations' (2011) 13(3) *Interventions: International Journal of Postcolonial Studies* 422.

19 See, e.g., Tribunal ético sobre la intervención militar de Estados Unidos de América en América Latina y el Caribe [Ethical Tribunal on the Military Intervention of the United States of America in Latin America], Buenos Aires 2007, www.apdh-argentina.org.ar/sites/default/files/TribunalEtico.pdfwww.apdh-argentina.org.ar/sites/default/files/TribunalEtico.pdf; Javier Bogantes Díaz, 'Tribunales Éticos: Un acercamiento filosófico y práctico a la justicia ambiental' ['Ethical Tribunals: A Philosophical and Practical Approach to Environmental Justice'], *Ediciones del Tribunal Latinoamericano del Agua*, Colección Ecología Política, 2012, www.tragua.com/wp-content/uploads/2012/04/tribunales_eticos.pdf. See further, Fraudatario and Tognoni, Chapter 6 in this volume.

At the same time peoples' tribunals are well aware that, even in those cases when they state their conclusion as a 'verdict' that involves 'findings' of liability or guilt, their decisions have no legal validity within positivist systems of international and national law. The formality and juridical form of such conclusions are seen as adding weight and solemnity (and thus legitimacy) to the exercise that may serve several functions. These include raising public awareness and a call for accountability for conduct apparently (or clearly) violating fundamental rights.

Peoples' tribunals take on a variety of cases that may be grouped into the following, sometimes overlapping, categories:[20]

- Violations by a state of the rights of citizens or residents of that state, including violations of the rights of peoples within that state[21]
- The use of force by a state against another state or people in another state – these tend to involve both examination of *jus ad bellum* (legality of the use of force) issues as well as *jus in bello* (international humanitarian law) issues[22]
- Claims of the denial of the right to self-determination[23]
- 'Historical' or thematic issues[24]
- The treatment by regions or groups of states of particular groups of peoples[25]

[20] For a different categorisation based on the work of the PPT, see Luís Moita, 'Opinion Tribunals and the Permanent People's Tribunal' (2015) 6(1) *JANUS.NET e-journal of International Relations*, http://observare.ual.pt/janus.net/en/previous-issues/98-english-en/vol-6,-n-%C2%BA1-may-october-2015/articles/305-opinion-tribunals-and-the-permanent-people-s-tribunal.

[21] See, e.g., Wieringa, Chapter 5 in this volume.

[22] See Byrnes and Simm, above n. 1.

[23] See, e.g., Permanent Peoples' Tribunal, *Session on Western Sahara*, Brussels, 10–11 November 1979; Permanent Peoples' Tribunal, *Session on East Timor*, Lisbon, 19–21 June 1981; Permanent Peoples' Tribunal, *Session on Tibet*, Verdict, 20 November 1992 (revised version, 14 December 1992). See François Rigaux, 'L'autodeterminazione nelle sentenze del Tribunal Permanente dei Popoli' ['Self-determination in the Verdicts of the Permanent Peoples' Tribunal'] in Gianni Tognoni (ed.), *Tribunale Permanente dei Popoli: Le Sentenze 1979–98 [Permanent Peoples' Tribunal: Judgments 1979–1998]* (Casa Editrice Stefanoni, 1998) 747.

[24] Permanent Peoples' Tribunal, *Session on The Conquest of America and International Law*, Padua-Venice, 5–9 October 1992; Permanent Peoples' Tribunal, *Session on International Law and the New Wars*, Rome, 14–16 December 2002; Permanent Peoples' Tribunal, *Session on the Right of Asylum in Europe*, Berlin, 8–12 December 1994. See also François Rigaux, 'La conquête de l'Amérique et le droit international' ['The conquest of America and International Law'] (1992) 4 *African Journal of International and Comparative Law* 486 (based on presentation to the PPT).

[25] See, e.g., Permanent Peoples' Tribunal, *Session on the Right to Asylum in Europe*, Berlin, 8–12 December 1994; Tribunal 12: see Dehm, Chapter 7 in this volume.

- The interaction between state law and the violations of the rights of persons by 'private' individuals (including corporations) and the responsibility of business, especially transnational corporations, in the violation of human rights[26]
- The role of international organisations, especially international financial institutions, in the regulation of the international and national economic and social systems[27]
- Challenges to the fairness or justness of particular bodies of established international law (in particular those relating to protection of intellectual property)[28]

Generally, peoples' tribunals arraign individual states, international organisations, individual corporations or a combination of these. It is less common for peoples' tribunals to 'put on trial' named individuals, although this has been done in several cases (including, in the case of the Tokyo Women's Tribunal, people who were long dead).

Peoples' tribunals are normally composed of persons from different countries and expert in (international) law or other fields, who have been selected for the particular tribunal by the organisers or drawn from a standing list. Some peoples' tribunals hew closely to a traditional court model, with legally trained members as judges and formal legal presentations and findings focusing on the positive law.[29] Others adopt different, less legalistic formats in relation to the composition of the tribunal, the terminology used to describe the various actors, the conduct of the proceedings and the nature and scope of their findings and recommendations. Peoples' tribunals generally differ from other courts or tribunals by including a majority of non-lawyers as judges and jury. For example, the original Russell Tribunal included writers, poets, lawyers, politicians

[26] See, e.g., Permanent Peoples' Tribunal, *The European Union and Transnational Corporations in Latin America: Policies, Instruments and Actors Complicit in Violations of the Peoples' Rights, Deliberating Session*, Madrid, 14–17 May 2010; *Session on Canadian Mining Transnational Corporations*, Montreal, 29 May–1 June 2014; and *Session on Transnational Corporations in Southern Africa*, Manzini, Swaziland, 16–17 August 2016.

[27] See, e.g., Independent Peoples' Tribunal on the World Bank in India (2007); Permanent Peoples' Tribunal, *Session on the Policies of the International Monetary Fund and the World Bank*, West Berlin, 26–29 September 1988, and *Session on the Policies of the International Monetary Fund and the World Bank II*, Madrid, 1–3 October 1994. See Simm and Byrnes, above n. 1, 11–14.

[28] See, e.g., Permanent Peoples' Tribunal, *Session on Agrochemical Transnational Corporations*, Bangalore, 3–6 December 2011.

[29] See, e.g., the Tokyo International Women's Tribunal, discussed by Dolgopol in Chapter 4 in this volume.

and mathematicians, as well as a playwright, physicist and trade unionist.[30] Günther Anders, a member of the First Russell Tribunal, wrote to the organisers requesting clarification regarding his role: Was he invited to participate in the capacity of judge, jury or expert on current events?[31] These issues arise in contemporary peoples' tribunals, where non-lawyers sit as members of a jury of conscience in a merger of the roles of judge and jury. Moreover, some peoples' tribunals have acknowledged the complainants as activists demanding redress for injustice in an attempt to remedy the indignity and passivity that accompanies designation as a victim.

1.3 The Dignity of Victim-Witnesses Claiming Justice

Many peoples' tribunals see themselves as following a procedure that broadly corresponds to that of an international or domestic court, at least so far as providing an opportunity for the consideration of evidence and presentation by 'both sides' of their cases. However, such tribunals do not adhere strictly to evidentiary and procedural rules. Of course, there is a considerable variety of procedural models that are used in formal courts, and some of these are quite similar to the approaches adopted by many peoples' tribunals. In some cases the use of more flexible procedures and rules in peoples' tribunals reflects the perception that the type of issues and evidence to be considered may not be particularly amenable to examination through a formalistic legal prism. Legal procedures may marginalise or render invisible the nature of the violation that has been suffered by those seeking acknowledgement of a wrong. Equally, close replication of such procedures may make difficult the application of standards beyond positive law, whether a peoples' law or moral and ethical standards not embodied in the relevant law.

The PPT on Global Corporations and Human Wrongs noted the power of 'dominant law' to 'inflict a second violation on communities of suffering':

> The first [violation] is the original violence which imposed upon them the condition of being the violated. The second, through a judgement of denial, results in the apparent negation of their experiential suffering from the violation that instead is the consequence of mere misfortune. Law has

[30] John Duffett (ed.), *Against the Crime of Silence, Proceedings of the International War Crimes Tribunal* (Simon & Schuster, 1970) 17.

[31] Klinghoffer and Klinghoffer, above n. 2, 117.

> the power and authority, it seems, to 'categorise' suffering, its determination and 'judgement', inscribing upon the social memory the thin, but crucial, line between 'violation' and 'misfortune'.[32]

The Tribunal noted that, before formal tribunals, often 'the truths of suffering fail to satisfy the strict evidentiary and causational tests imposed by law in order to transform the assumption of misfortune into the naming of violation', rendering 'the truths of suffering of the victimised officially invalid within the law-constructed public memory'.[33] It saw its role as seeking 'to reinvigorate the struggle to reclaim the right of the violated peoples to demand judgement'.[34]

In peoples' tribunals, an effort is made to recognise the active role of victims in seeking justice, referring to them as 'collective victims', 'victim-peoples' and 'victim-complainants'[35] as well as 'the protagonists of the demand for justice'.[36] The focus on victims as a group risks losing a specific focus on the wrongs committed against individuals in a search for collective justice. At the same time, it potentially reduces the feelings of social isolation that individual victims might otherwise feel. Dignity is an important value that peoples' tribunals see themselves restoring to those who demand justice before them. For example, the PPT session on European Union and Transnational Corporations in Latin America formulated the injuries it was examining primarily as a loss of dignity. It articulated its ability to provide a remedy, referring to

> the calm confidence and persistence with which the victim-witnesses bring their cases before the judges of an ideal and non-institutional justice, knowing that, at this moment, its intention and the reparation at play are of a moral nature: the kind that can be granted by ethical bodies, such as this Permanent Peoples' Tribunal. . . . This is the reason for the impressive seriousness that distinguishes complainants' presence in these symbolic proceedings, which are, therefore, much more than a parody of those who are scandalously absent in official courts. This is because the victims . . . are seeking, by reasonably discussing the injustice suffered, to make that injustice visible and to be publicly vindicated,

[32] Permanent Peoples' Tribunal, *Session on Global Corporations and Human Wrongs*, University of Warwick, Coventry, UK, 22–25 March 2000, 'Findings and Recommended Action', section 3.2.

[33] Ibid., n. 5. [34] Ibid., section 3.2.

[35] Permanent Peoples' Tribunal, *The European Union and Transnational Corporations in Latin America: Policies, Instruments and Actors Complicit in Violations of the Peoples' Rights, Deliberating Session, Madrid, 14–17 May 2010: The Judgement* (2010), 14.

[36] Ibid., 15.

> entirely and solely as a means of restoring their dignity and self-esteem which have been so violently shattered.[37]

The Tokyo Women's Tribunal in 2000 also saw itself as restoring dignity to victims in place of the shame, fear and regret that they continued to suffer as a result of having been forced into sexual slavery by the Japanese Army during World War II.[38] The Tokyo Women's Tribunal was at the more formal and legal end of the spectrum of international peoples' tribunals, grounding itself on the legal fiction that it was a continuation of the International Military Tribunal for the Far East and using the same international legal standards.[39] The incommensurability of this legal structure with the experience of the victim/survivors was evident.

> The victims were there primarily as the 'witness.' They were fashioned into a legal subject. But now and again one could sense the existence of something that cannot be captured within the somewhat dry, rational legal discourse and its procedures.[40]

1.4 The (Non-)Appearance Of Defendants

While most peoples' tribunals make a point of inviting the states, international organisations or corporations that are the subject of the tribunal's proceedings to participate, such 'defendants' rarely respond and almost never appear. The gesture of invitation is normally an attempt to formally offer the conditions of a fair (that is, adversarial) procedure that will permit the defendant to put its side of the story and to challenge the evidence or interpretation of the prosecutors/plaintiffs, a classic attribute of fair trial. In many cases the defendants simply ignore the tribunal's invitation and activities.[41] A defendant's refusal to respond or appear makes it easier for critics to argue against the legitimacy of the tribunal,

[37] Ibid. See Rosalba Icaza, 'Global Europe, guilty! Contesting EU neoliberal governance for Latin America and the Caribbean' (2010) 31(1) *Third World Quarterly* 123.

[38] Ustinia Dolgopol, 'The judgement of the Tokyo Women's Tribunal' (2003) 28(5) *Alternative Law Journal* 242, 247. See further Dolgopol, above n. 29.

[39] See the Women's International War Crimes Tribunal for the Trial of Japan's Military Sexual Slavery, *Judgement on the Common Indictment and the Application for Restitution and Reparation* (2001), and Karen Knop, 'The Tokyo Women's Tribunal and the Turn to Fiction' in Fleur Johns, Sundhya Pahuja and Richard Joyce (eds.), *Events: The Force of International Law* (Taylor & Francis, 2011) 145–64.

[40] Rumi Sakamoto, 'The Women's International War Crimes Tribunal on Japan's Military Sexual Slavery: A legal and feminist approach to the "comfort women' issue"' (2001) 3(1) *New Zealand Journal of Asian Studies* 49, 58.

[41] For example, Permanent Peoples' Tribunal, *Session on Agrochemical Corporations*, Bangalore, 3–6 December 2011.

notwithstanding the fact that the opportunity to appear was provided. The tribunals' lack of legitimacy in this respect is frequently relied on by the states or institutions targeted to justify the rejection of the proceedings and findings. This in turn adds to perceptions of their illegitimacy.

Tribunals have sought to pre-empt criticism that they have failed to accord due process. This has sometimes involved the appointment of an amicus curiae (or sometimes 'defence counsel'[42]) to put the case of the absent defendant. In other cases, the tribunal has sought to consider the known position of the defendant to the extent that can be derived from public statements in different fora.[43] The appointment of amici curiae or lawyers to present the defendant's case is only a partial answer to the concerns about due process when these tribunals are seen in orthodox terms. At the same time, even before international tribunals, a state's refusal to appear in proceedings does not generally prevent the tribunal from proceeding to hear the case and reach a judgment or decision; the waiver of the right to appear undermines any claim that due process has been denied.

Other tribunals have been less concerned that an impugned respondent is not actually present. They argue that the alleged violations reflect asymmetrical power relationships where the views of powerful defendants are well known and heard in many fora, unlike the views of those bringing a case. Arundhati Roy expressed this view in her opening address to the World Tribunal on Iraq:

> Before the testimonies begin, I would like to briefly address as straightforwardly as I can a few questions that have been raised about this tribunal.
>
> The first is that this tribunal is a Kangaroo Court. That it represents only one point of view. That it is a prosecution without a defense. That the verdict is a foregone conclusion.
>
> Now this view seems to suggest a touching concern that in this harsh world, the views of the U.S. government and the so-called Coalition of the Willing headed by President George Bush and Prime Minister Tony Blair have somehow gone unrepresented. That the World Tribunal on Iraq isn't aware of the arguments in support of the war and is unwilling to consider the point of view of the invaders. If in the era of the multinational

42 Permanent Peoples' Tribunal, *Session on Tibet*, Verdict, 20 November 1992 (revised version, 14 December 1992), 12–13.

43 For example, the 'Judgment of the Permanent Peoples' Tribunal on the Armenian Genocide (1984)' in Gérard Libaridian (ed.), *A Crime of Silence, The Armenian Genocide: Permanent Peoples' Tribunal* (Zed Books, 1985).

> corporate media and embedded journalism anybody can seriously hold this view, then we truly do live in the Age of Irony, in an age when satire has become meaningless because real life is more satirical than satire can ever be.[44]

Despite the regular failure of defendants to attend or to respond, there are occasional examples of states or companies involved that do respond to the allegations made before a tribunal or to the course of proceedings.[45] This suggests that allowing allegations to go unanswered before such tribunals, even though they have no formal status, can still do reputational damage to the defendant. Seeking to put one's case demonstrates a good faith commitment to engaging on the issue, and presenting the defendant's case may influence the factual findings and legal conclusions of the tribunal.

Several recent tribunal hearings have created sufficient pressure on named corporate defendants that they have responded to the allegations raised against them. For example, in the London session of the Russell Tribunal on Palestine, there were a couple of responses from corporate 'defendants'. Some were simply dismissive. Veolia Environnement responded to claims that the involvement of its subsidiary, Veolia Transport, in building the Jerusalem Light Railway involved breaches of international law, noting that it had originally invested in the project at the time of the Oslo Accords 'when there was a prospect of a peaceful settlement of the Israeli-Palestinian conflict'.[46] It noted that it had always 'sought to obey international law' and that 'if it were ruled by a properly constituted judicial court that we were in breach of International Law, then we would withdraw'.[47]

[44] Arundhati Roy, 'Opening Speech of the Spokesperson of the Jury of Conscience' in Müge Gürsöy Sökmen (ed.), *World Tribunal on Iraq: Making the Case against War* (Olive Branch Press, 2008), 2.

[45] For example, the Consulate-General of the People's Republic of China in Milan provided a collection of documentary material to the PPT session on Tibet, although it did not otherwise take part in the proceedings: Permanent Peoples' Tribunal, *Session on Tibet*, Verdict, 20 November 1992 (revised version, 14 December 1992), 7 and 12.

[46] Letter of 8 October 2010 from Veolia to Russell Tribunal on Palestine: 'Corporates' and the EU's Responses', Russell Tribunal on Palestine, London Session, www.russelltribunal onpalestine.com/en/sessions/london-session/corporates-responses.

[47] On 30 May 2011 a French court dismissed a claim brought by the France Palestine Solidarity Association against Veolia, and the Versailles Court of Appeal rejected an appeal on 22 March 2013. *Association France-Palestine Solidarité and Palestine Liberation Organization v. Société Alstom transport SA and ors*, Appeal judgment, 11/05331, ILDC 2036 (FR 2013). The Russell Tribunal found Veolia guilty of a number of violations. The security company G4S also responded, stating that it did not consider that the hearings of the RToP would help the peace process: Email from Michael Clarke, Public Affairs

The pension fund Zorg en Welzijn (PFZW)also wrote to the Tribunal to explain its responsible investment policies and procedures, particularly as they related to the Occupied Territories, noting its concern 'about ongoing violations of international law in that context and about possible complicity in such violations by companies that are active in Israel and the occupied territories'. It further stated that it was 'determined to attempt within its policy framework to use its influence as a shareholder in those companies' to address those concerns, and that 'due to a recent change in one of the benchmarks that is tracked for the pension fund's listed equity investments, PFZW is no longer invested in any of the Israeli companies mentioned [in the letter sent by the RToP to PFZW].'[48] Whether driven by a sense of social responsibility and commitment to address an agreed problem or by concerns about bad publicity if they did not (or both), the engagement of these corporations with the Tribunal shows the possibilities that they might generate.

1.5 Standards Applied by Peoples' Tribunals

Peoples' tribunals draw on international law, national law, and 'peoples' law', as well as moral and ethical standards. As Blaser commented in 1992:

> Legal standards applied by tribunals include some conventional standards applied conventionally, some conventional standards applied unconventionally, and some unconventional standards.[49]

How peoples' tribunals use international law and the extent to which they contribute to its development are key questions for international lawyers. First, admitting peoples' tribunals to a discussion of international law is only possible on the basis of a legal pluralist approach to international law that admits of law made by entities other than states.[50] For example, the 1993 Hawaiian International People's Tribunal used international law, US constitutional law and indigenous Hawaiian

Director, G4S, to the Russell Commission [sic], 18 November 2010, 'Corporates' and the EU's Responses', above n. 46.

[48] Statement by PFZW to the Russell Tribunal on Palestine, attached to Letter from PFZW to the Russell Tribunal on Palestine, 12 November 2010, p. 6, 'Corporates' and the EU's Responses', ibid.

[49] Arthur W. Blaser, 'How to advance human rights without really trying: An analysis of nongovernmental tribunals' (1992) 14 *Human Rights Quarterly* 339, 357.

[50] Sally Engle Merry, 'Legal Vernacularization and Ka Ho'okolokolonui Kanaka Maoli, The People's International Tribunal, Hawai'i 1993' (1996) 19 *PoLAR* 67, 76, 79.

Kanaka Maoli law to reach its decision that the annexation of Hawaii in 1898 by the United States was illegal.[51] International peoples' tribunals take issue with formal constraints of international law that exclude non-state applicants, such as peoples, and non-state respondents, such as corporations. In this way, panellists of peoples' tribunals have articulated their function as providing justice to those who are excluded by formal legal processes and preventing the impunity of those who escape legal scrutiny by virtue of their lack of international legal personality.

Second, proponents of international peoples' tribunals have used the metaphor of law as a language to highlight the political impact of excluding certain groups from international law on the basis of their status as a non-state. The responses to the questions that peoples' tribunals pose about international law have implications for the question often fielded by international lawyers from domestic lawyers, namely, whether international law is really law, and in defining the boundary between law and non-law.

A foundational premise of international peoples' tribunals is that states do not have an exclusive monopoly on the creation, interpretation and application of international law. While non-state actors are increasingly accorded formal roles in monitoring and applying international law, they participate very much as 'second-class citizens'. As Saguier writes, quoting Rajagopal:

> Mainstream accounts of . . . international law . . . 'predetermine the actors for whom international law exists – i.e. state officials, economic actors, such as corporations, and cultural actors, such as the atomised individual who is the subject of rights. They do not ask the elemental question of *for whom* international law exists.[52]

Nevertheless, peoples' tribunals select their sources of law not according to the formal criterion of its creator, but according to its content. The emphasis on content over form is evident in cases before international peoples' tribunals. Activists involved in the World Tribunal on Iraq declared:

[51] Ward Churchill, Sharon Helen Venne and Lilikalā Kame'eleihiwa, *Islands in Captivity: The Record of the International Tribunal on the Rights of Indigenous Hawaiians* (South End Press, 2004); *Interim Report, Kanaka Maoli Nation, Plaintiff v. United States of America Defendant, Ka Ho'okolokolonui Kanaka Maoli, The People's International Tribunal, Hawai'i 1993*, 20 August 1993.

[52] Balakrishnan Rajagopal, *International Law from Below* (Cambridge University Press, 2003), quoted and adapted by Marcelo Saguier, 'The Potential of Peoples' Tribunals in Latin America to Pressure TNCs into Adopting Human Rights Responsibilities', *Documento de Trabajo No. 41, Area de Relaciones Internacionales FLACSO/Argentina*, March 2010, 11 (117 vol. 3) (emphasis in original).

> [I]nternational law is not in essence a series of procedures and forms. It is the content. We should adopt a flexible form and at the same time rigorously seek to apply international law. We should also keep in mind that many bodies that in procedure and form claim to stick to international law are in effect condoning its violation.[53]

Seeing law as 'a dynamic social-political field, which is open for development', including by peoples,[54] frees up the space for participation by collectives, such as the network that organised the series of tribunals making up the World Tribunal on Iraq.

People's law is unique to peoples' tribunals. Perhaps most striking is the Universal Declaration of the Rights of Peoples (or Charter of Algiers), a civil society instrument adopted in 1976 and used by the Permanent Peoples' Tribunal as a primary source of law.[55] The Algiers Declaration takes as its starting point articles 1, 55 and 56 of the Charter of the United Nations on the rights of peoples to self-determination, and articulates what other rights peoples possess.[56] The purpose of the Algiers Declaration was to move the rights of peoples out of the preamble and into the text of the articles. While in many of its earlier decisions the PPT referred to the Algiers Declaration and does so sometimes still as a formal gesture, the focus has become very much the positive law of nations, though the right to reject or amend law that is at odds with the interests of peoples is still maintained. The enduring impact of the Algiers Declaration and the thinking that underpins it can be seen in analysis of the adverse impacts of globalisation on people and assertions of the illegitimacy of the positive international law that permits or promotes such outcomes. The existence and content of the Algiers Declaration demonstrate the ways in which proponents of peoples' tribunals have supplemented the formal sources of international law, deemed lacking in their application to peoples:

[53] Sökmen above n. 44, 470. [54] Hülya Üçpınar, in Sökmen, above n. 44, 477.

[55] See François Rigaux, 'The Algiers Declaration of the Rights of Peoples' in Antonio Cassese (ed.), *UN Law, Fundamental Rights: Two Topics in International Law* (Sijthoff & Noordhoff, 1979) 211; Richard Falk, 'The Algiers Declaration of the Rights of Peoples and the Struggle for Human Rights' in Antonio Cassese (ed.), *UN Law, Fundamental Rights: Two Topics in International Law* (Sijthoff & Noordhoff International Publishers, 1979) 225; François Rigaux (ed.), *La Carta di Algeri: La Dichiarazione Universale dei Diritti dei Popoli [The Charter of Algiers: the Universal Declaration of the Rights of Peoples]* (Edizioni Cultura della Pace, 1988).

[56] Charter of the United Nations, 24 October 1945, 1 UNTS XVI, arts. 1, 55 and 56.

> Naturally, to the extent that law and morality in world affairs are a reflection of the state system, the Algiers Declaration will be dismissed with scorn. Governments did not participate in the norm-shaping process, either directly or indirectly. The fundamental claim of the Algiers Declaration, in contrast, is that the peoples of the world possess the ultimate law-making authority, and that the validity of governmental law-making capacity rests on a prior delegation of competence by the people.[57]

Richard Falk, an international lawyer who has participated in multiple peoples' tribunals, argues that 'we must struggle to make international law work on behalf of the victims of state politics and oppressive structures in the world. And it's partly to liberate international law that this [Hawaiian] tribunal is so important.'[58] This reverses the usual understanding of the relationship of international law to peoples' tribunals – that it is not peoples but international law that is in need of liberation.

The idea of international law as a language is useful in highlighting its political implications. Within a legal pluralist framework, Sally Engle Merry's idea of vernacular law allows us to understand how international law, and law in general, is a dynamic and developing language that changes with its speakers. In the context of the questions who owns law and to whom international law belongs, vernacular law may be spoken not just by the representatives of states but also by indigenous peoples whose political community and claims to autonomy are not recognised to fit into a state:

> Members of small, isolated communities increasingly speak in the global arena, whether they are Penang tribesmen or Kiapo from the Amazon.
>
> And what they speak is law. Human rights is obviously a Western liberal legalist construction, but in the post-colonial world, it is no longer owned by the West. As indigenous groups seek to define a space for themselves in the modern world, they seize and redefine law as the basis for their claims to justice. The law they mobilize is not simply the law of the state or the United Nations but an appropriated notion of law that joins indigenous concepts with state and global law. Thus, although they talk rights, reparations, and claims – the language of law – they construct a new law out of the pieces of the old. Like the English spoken in Africa, the colonial law imposed by the West is developing its own cadences and vocabulary. It is becoming a vernacular law rather than transnational imperial law.[59]

[57] Falk, above n. 15, 817.
[58] Falk, cited in Interim Report, above n. 51, 7.
[59] Merry, above n. 50.

Law is also conceived as a language in contrast to the language or grammar of politics. In relation to the World Tribunal on Iraq, Ayça Çubukçu refers to the tendency of lawyers to correct 'the grammar of the non-lawyer who wished to express "politics" in the tongue of law'. Nonetheless, a political perspective 'recognized the need to act in multiple languages and grammars, including the poetic, the artistic and the political, as well as the legal'.[60]

1.6 Liability and Responsibility before Peoples' Tribunals

Peoples' tribunals are fluid in the type of liability that they ascribe to the defendants in the cases they hear. Under current international law the forms of liability differ as between states, individuals and corporations. States can only be held to account under a theory of *delictual* (or civil) liability, as elaborated in the international law of state responsibility. States do not bear criminal liability under international law, although whether they should was a contested issue until 2000 when the International Law Commission decided to omit any form of criminal responsibility of states from its draft articles on the law of state responsibility.[61] Until that time there had been a number of proposals to elaborate a concept of state crime and these were current for the first three decades or so of the post-Russell Tribunal era of peoples' tribunals. Accordingly, those proceedings included findings that states had committed international crimes, as well as conclusions that other states had been complicit in the commission of those crimes.[62]

Notwithstanding the disappearance of the concept of the criminal responsibility of states under international law from the law of state responsibility, references to states committing criminal acts still appear regularly in the charges and findings of peoples' tribunals. For the present at least, the notion of an international penal law that applies to states has little purchase in current international law, although criminologists

[60] Çubukçu, above n. 18, 437.

[61] See Alain Pellet, 'Can a state commit a crime? Yes, definitely!' (1999) 10 *European Journal of International Law* 425; James Crawford, *The International Law Commission's Articles on State Responsibility: Introduction, Text and Commentaries* (Cambridge University Press, 2002) 16–20, 35–38.

[62] See, e.g., Permanent Peoples' Tribunal, *Session on Guatemala*, Madrid, 21–31 January 1983, Verdict, V (Guatemala and the United States held to have committed international crimes; other countries found complicit in the commission of those crimes).

have developed the concept of state crime.[63] It is not clear whether these references are made in an effort to keep that issue alive or simply to express the seriousness of the violations alleged (many of which would amount to violations of fundamental rules of international law or jus cogens).

The imposition of criminal liability on individuals under international law is, of course, well established. The catalogue of international crimes includes the crimes in the Statute of the International Criminal Court – war crimes, genocide, crimes against humanity and aggression – but extends beyond those. Many tribunals have 'indicted' named individuals, generally high-level political or military leaders, and charged them with crimes against humanity, war crimes and the crime of aggression.[64] In adjudicating upon those cases, tribunals have drawn on the extensive body of international criminal law developed in the national and international criminal tribunals established over the last 100 years or so, particularly those set up since the 1990s. The extent to which tribunal proceedings involve the presentation of evidence and its detailed assessment in a final judgment or verdict varies from case to case, with some tribunals being quite fastidious and legalistic, while others are more broad-brush in their approach.

Unlike nearly all formal international tribunals, peoples' tribunals are not restricted to arraigning only states or only individuals. Formal tribunals are thus limited to adjudicating only on questions of delictual liability or on issues of individual criminal responsibility in any one proceeding. Those peoples' tribunals that arraign individuals also frequently address issues of state responsibility as well, underlining the perspective that it is important to demand accountability both of states but also of the individuals through whom a state acts.

Another dimension of peoples' tribunals is their engagement with the responsibility and liability of corporations, in particular transnational corporations, for human rights violations. Even though corporations enjoy some rights under specific regimes, such as trade and investment agreements[65] and in some cases under human rights law,[66] in general they are not treated as subjects of international law bound to observe

[63] See, e.g., Penny Green and Tony Ward, *State Crimes: Governments, Violence and Corruption* (Pluto Press, 2004).

[64] Permanent Peoples' Tribunal, *Session on Guatemala*, above n. 62, Verdict, V.

[65] See Peter T. Muchlinski, 'Corporations in International Law (June 2014)', *Max Planck Encyclopedia of International Law* (online), paras. 26–29.

[66] Ibid., paras. 37–41.

human rights.[67] International law does not impose criminal or civil liability directly on corporations, despite efforts over many years to move in that direction.[68] Nevertheless, international criminal liability may be imposed on the officers and employees of a corporation if their acts as part of their duties amount to crimes under international law. Otherwise international law largely leaves it to states to regulate the activities of corporations and, indeed, in some cases requires states to ensure that corporations do not infringe on the human rights of others. Corporations may be held liable under national laws imposing criminal or civil liability in relation to actions that would amount to international crimes or other violations of human rights.[69] There are few formal international fora where corporations can be held to account for alleged violations of human rights. Peoples' tribunals have examined the actions of transnational corporations in various contexts and contribute to discussions about the international law that applies to corporations, invoking doctrines of national and international complicity.[70]

1.7 Critiques of Peoples' Tribunals

Peoples' tribunals are usually controversial, sometimes intensely so. As a result, it is unsurprising that they are the subject of critiques from both progressive and conservative standpoints. Critiques of peoples' tribunals may be articulated by the 'defendants' whose actions a particular tribunal scrutinises or by their supporters. Critics find such tribunals wanting in terms of their legitimacy and authority, allege that they are biased and question whether they are truly representative of those in whose name they speak. Peoples' tribunals will always find it difficult to escape the criticisms of those whose principal criterion for the acceptability of such proceedings is whether they conform to the ideal of a domestic adversarial court proceeding and whose only source of legitimacy is the state. Compliance or not with the formalistic requirement of court proceedings

[67] Ibid., paras. 30–36.

[68] Ibid., paras. 30–36, 42–46. See also Kevin Jon Heller, *The Nuremberg Military Tribunals and the Origins of International Criminal Law* (Oxford University Press, 2012) 253–54 (rejecting suggestions that the Nuremberg trials provide support for the international criminal responsibility of corporations under international law).

[69] See, e.g., the invocation of domestic and international law relating to corporate complicity in Asa Winstanley and Frank Barat (eds.), *Corporate Complicity in Israel's Occupation: Evidence from the London Session of the Russell Tribunal on Palestine* (Pluto Press, 2011).

[70] See, e.g., the findings of the Russell Tribunal on Palestine: Winstanley and Barat, ibid.

fails to appreciate the other functions that such tribunals can perform even if they can never point to the state as a source of authority because they are not established by states.[71]

1.7.1 Legitimacy and Authority

A question commonly raised in relation to peoples' tribunals is their legitimacy and authority. The legitimacy of any institution may derive from a range of factors. These include its institutional origins, membership, normative framework, procedures, the nature and weight of the evidence it considers, the cogency of its analysis, its functions, expectations among the constituencies to which its activity is relevant and its impact.[72]

State challenges to the legitimacy and authority of the original Russell Tribunal provide a clear exposition of the issues at stake. When Bertrand Russell and his colleagues sought to organise the First Russell Tribunal in London, the British government refused to grant visas to witnesses from North and South Vietnam, thus preventing the tribunal from taking place in the United Kingdom.[73] The French government also refused to grant visas to some participants, thereby stymying the organisers' efforts to shift the hearings to Paris. The reasons were set out in letters to the organisers, and the exchanges between the various parties are a vivid illustration of the conceptual and political issues to which such events

[71] See, e.g., Marcel Merle, 'Les mécanismes par lesquels l'opinion publique exerce une influence sur le droit international' ['The Influence of Public Opinion on International Law'] in *Le droit international et l'opinion publique [International Law and Public Opinion], Collected Courses of the Hague Academy of International Law*, Vol. 138 (Martinus Nijhoff, 1973) 399. For a response by a prominent member of the Permanent Peoples' Tribunal, see François Rigaux, Allocution du Professeur Fr. Rigaux, vice-président du Tribunal, Séance inaugurale du 11 janvier 1975, *Tribunal Russell II sur la répression au Brésil, au Chili et en Amérique Latine*, 5 (criticising Merle's comments) (on file with authors).

[72] For example, Borowiak identifies four aspects of the legitimacy of an institution of this sort: 'authorization, rationale, credibility, and recognition': Craig Borowiak, 'The World Tribunal on Iraq: Citizens' tribunals and the struggle for accountability' (2008) 30 *New Political Science* 161, 181. See also Daniel Bodansky, 'Legitimacy in International Law and International Relations' in Jeffrey L. Dunoff and Mark A. Pollack (eds.), *Interdisciplinary Perspectives on International Law and International Relations: The State of the Art* (Cambridge University Press, 2012) 321.

[73] See the correspondence between Bertrand Russell and the then Prime Minister and the Home Secretary, in Duffett, above n. 30, 20–25.

can give rise.[74] The French President, Charles de Gaulle, wrote to Jean-Paul Sartre, President of the Tribunal, as follows:

> I have no need to tell you that justice of any sort, in principle as in execution, emanates from the state. . . . This is why the government has decided to oppose the Tribunal's meeting in our country since, through its very form, the Tribunal would be acting against that very thing which it is seeking to uphold.[75]

In his open letter in response, Sartre argued:

> [R]eal justice must derive its strength equally from the State and from the masses. We are not proposing to set ourselves up in place of any pre-existing system of justice, as De Gaulle pretends to believe. . . . We are attempting to do something else. To begin with, we wear no robes, not even symbolic ones. Jurors – and De Gaulle should know this – don't wear them. We are simply going to hold hearings in a case which should in the ordinary way come before an international tribunal which does not exist.[76]

The purpose of establishing the original Russell Tribunal was thus to fill the 'gap' following the completion of its work by the International Military Tribunal at Nuremberg.[77]

Charles de Gaulle's argument that 'justice emanates from the state' assumes that peoples' tribunals lack legitimacy as they have not been authorised by states. However, the emanation of a tribunal from the font of state authority is neither a necessary nor sufficient criterion of legitimacy. International courts and tribunals created by states also face crises of legitimacy, such as where respondents in the International Court of Justice do not appear or ignore unfavourable decisions or where states refuse to hand over fugitives indicted by the International Criminal Court.[78] While peoples' tribunals confront similar concerns about their

[74] See the correspondence and other public statements in ibid., 17–36.

[75] De Gaulle in Duffet, above n. 30, 28. The French version of the letter is available at 'Le Tribunal Russell et le "procès" du 11 septembre', bernat, 10 June 2008, www.acipa-ndl.fr/signez-les-petitions/itemlist/tag/TPP.

[76] Jean-Paul Sartre, 'Answer and Commentary to De Gaulle's Letter Banning the Tribunal from France' in Duffett, above n. 30, 29, at 32.

[77] For an example of this justification, see Permanent Peoples' Tribunal, *Session on the Filipino People and the Bangsa Moro People*, Antwerp, 30 October–1 November 1980 ("I General Introduction").

[78] The United States did not participate in the merits phase after it lost the initial phase: *Military and Paramilitary Activities in and Against Nicaragua (Nicaragua v. USA) (Jurisdiction and Admissibility)* [1984] ICJ Rep 392.

legitimacy, their legitimacy derives from sources other than state power and arises in large measure from their claims and capacity to represent peoples, the nature of their investigations, the quality of evidence before them, their procedures and their reasoning.[79]

The original Russell Tribunal claimed legitimacy on the basis of providing justice to the masses. As Russell argued in his opening address:

> The International War Crimes Tribunal is a revolutionary tribunal. We have no armies and no gallows. We lack power, even the power of mass communication. It is overdue that those without power sit in judgment over those who have it.[80]

Indeed, Sartre saw the tribunal's lack of legal standing as an advantage as, in his view, it meant that the tribunal could not be influenced by any state.[81] Given the problems that the Russell Tribunal faced in finding a state willing to allow the proceedings to take place on its territory, it might be expected that it would be wary of directly offending its host state. However, tribunals held since then have been forthright in their condemnation of states that host them. An example is the final session of the World Tribunal on Iraq held in Istanbul which was critical of Turkey's role as a key ally of the 'Coalition of the Willing' that invaded Iraq in 2003.[82]

> Who appointed Bertrand Russell or Lelio Basso? . . . The claim of representation rests ultimately on the popular acceptance of the Algiers Declaration's understanding of exploitation and oppression as a by-product of an imperial world order that needs to be dismantled to allow the peoples of the world to experience lives of dignity and satisfaction. . . . The Basso group, therefore, has no special competence aside from the persuasiveness of its critique and its positive vision.[83]

If the authority of peoples' tribunals comes from peoples,[84] who are the peoples on whose behalf peoples' tribunals claim to act?[85] While this

[79] 'The force of our Tribunal lies in the impeccability of its procedures and the thoroughness of its investigations': 'Opening Statement to the First Tribunal Session by Bertrand Russell (Stockholm)' in Duffett, above n. 30, 50.

[80] Ibid., 51. [81] 'Jean-Paul Sartre's Inaugural Statement to the Tribunal', in ibid., 40, 43.

[82] See Çubukçu, above n. 18, 426, for a list of the sessions of the World Tribunal on Iraq.

[83] Falk, above n. 15, 818.

[84] Yayori Matsui, "Women's International War Crimes Tribunal on Japan's Military Sexual Slavery: Memory, identity and society" (2001) 19 *East Asia* 119, 133.

[85] Herbert (Philippines), cited in 'The WTI as an Alternative: and Experimental Assertion', in Sökmen, above n. 44, 470.

might have been self-evident (at least in their public admissions) to the key personnel involved in the original Russell Tribunal, the network structure of the World Tribunal on Iraq (avoiding the statist language of 'international' tribunal)[86] has been transparent in its consideration of these questions. Richard Falk considers that the legitimacy of the World Tribunal on Iraq rested on 'an ethos of concern and responsibility for fundamental law and morality . . . expressive of the impulse to feel, think and act as a global citizen in an increasingly globalizing world'.[87] Jan, an activist involved in the World Tribunal on Iraq, referred to the UN Charter: 'The UN Charter starts "We the peoples" not "we, the states" or "we, the governments" but it sets out saying "we, the peoples."'[88] Eman, another activist, responded to the question of legitimacy: 'I think we get our legitimacy from what we do, what we achieve.'[89] Clearly, how legitimacy is measured and what is achieved is a subjective standard that is not defined solely by reference to the source of authority claimed by a tribunal or other process.

Participation and the attributes of the participants measure legitimacy:

> Precisely the fact that 'the people' – in Iraq and globally – harboured political differences complicated any claim to 'representing' or alternatively 'being on behalf' of them.. . . 'When we say legitimacy, does legitimacy mean talking on behalf of others? I do not think so . . . we get legitimacy from the fact that we – I – participated in the protests, all of us participated.'[90]

According to Tina Dolgopol, one of the prosecutors at the Tokyo Women's tribunal, it was 'one of the few times a group of non-western, regionally based non-government organisations predominantly headed by women were able to gain the attention of the international community and the world's media on an issue of importance to them.'[91]

1.7.2 The Question of Bias

A major critique levelled at peoples' tribunals is that they are biased. Governments, international organisations and corporations against which

[86] Borowiak, above n. 72, 177.

[87] Richard A. Falk, 'World Tribunal on Iraq: Truth, Law and Justice', chapter 13 in Richard A. Falk, *The Costs of War, International Law, the UN, and the World Order After Iraq* (Routledge, 2008), 180.

[88] Jan, in Sökmen, above n. 44, 476.

[89] Eman, in Sökmen, above n. 44, 473.

[90] Çubukçu, above n. 18, 436.

[91] Dolgopol, above n. 38, 242.

peoples' tribunals have made adverse findings argue that the outcome of the tribunal is pre-determined, given the composition of its panel of judges/jury. Peoples' tribunals are contrasted with official courts and tribunals, whose judges are assumed to be independent and neutral.[92] The First Russell Tribunal attracted such criticism:

> The mock trials being conducted in various parts of the world under the auspices of the Bertrand Russell Peace Foundation . . . cannot be considered a serious judicial proceeding. In large part, the Tribunal is composed of persons with no judicial training who are leading critics of the United States. No evidence of any war crimes by North Vietnamese was considered and no defense to any of the charges has been presented.[93]

In similar vein, Richard Goldstone, former South African judge and chief prosecutor of the International Criminal Tribunals for the former Yugoslavia (ICTY)/ International Criminal Tribunals for Rwanda (ICTR) commented in relation to the Russell Tribunal on Palestine (RToP) hearing on the question of whether Israel was practising apartheid:

> It is not a 'tribunal.' The 'evidence' is going to be one-sided and the members of the 'jury' are critics whose harsh views of Israel are well known.[94]

Most peoples' tribunals are the result of an initiative organised by an advocacy group or affected group or held in response to a request from

[92] For a discussion of the criticism made of formal international tribunals on grounds of partiality or bias, see Simm and Byrnes, above n. 1, 43.

[93] Benjamin Ferencz, 'War Crimes Law and the Vietnam War' (1968) 17(3) *American University Law Review* 423, n 91. Braunig suggests that notwithstanding his dismissal of the Russell Tribunal, Ferencz nonetheless engages with (though rejects) the principal findings of the Tribunal and is in agreement with the Tribunal's call for a permanent international criminal tribunal. Marian Braunig, 'Von Nürnberg nach Vietnam: Das "Russell Tribunal" von 1967 in Historischen Perspektive' ['From Nuremberg to Vietnam: The "Russell Tribunal" in Historical Perspective'] in Manfred Berg and Philipp Gassert (eds.), *Deutschland und die USA in der internationalen Geschichte des 20. Jahrhunderts: Festschrift für Detlev Junker* [*Germany and the USA in the International History of the 20th Century: Essays in Honour of Detlev Junker*] (Franz Steiner Verlag, 2004) 492. She notes that other commentators, such as international law professor Antony D'Amato considered that the procedures were at least as stringent as those adopted at some of the war crimes trials that followed World War II, 500–501, citing Anthony A. D'Amato, Harvey L. Gould, and Larry D. Woods, 'War Crimes and Vietnam: The Nuremberg defense and the military service resister' (1969) 57 *California Law Review* 1055, 1074. Those authors make extensive use of the evidence produced to the Russell Tribunal: see 1076–97, especially at 1076–81 and 1094–97.

[94] Richard Goldstone, 'Israel and the Apartheid Slander', *New York Times*, 31 October 2011, www.nytimes.com/2011/11/01/opinion/israel-and-the-apartheid-slander.html.

such a group. This has implications for their perceived bias. The organisers of a tribunal will usually choose both judges/jury, prosecutors and, if applicable, the defence or amicus. Expertise and community standing are criteria generally employed by tribunal organisers. In most cases tribunal members will be seen to have a perspective on the issues that accords with, or is at least sympathetic to, that of the organisers. Nonetheless, some organisers appoint those who may be seen as 'independent' and 'impartial', particularly lawyers or (former) judges. At the more legalistic end of the tribunal spectrum, the membership of a tribunal will comprise lawyers or judges exclusively.[95]

There are isolated cases in which a tribunal has not found in favour of the 'prosecution' on all the complaints or charges put before it.[96] In one notable case in the Kuala Lumpur War Crimes Tribunal hearing, the defence representative successfully challenged a judge for bias resulting from her earlier close involvement in activities relating to the specific issues to be determined.[97] Similar charges to those before the Kuala Lumpur Tribunal had been considered against former US president George W Bush.[98] But such cases are unusual and seen only in those tribunals that seek to replicate closely the procedures of a state-based court. Peoples' tribunals tend to find the charges or complaints before them made out. This makes the transparency and cogency of their analysis and the strength of the evidence relied on critical to their claims to be taken seriously.

A critique frequently made of peoples' tribunals is that, when dealing with a situation involving conflict between two sides, they generally

[95] Tokyo Women's Tribunal; Kuala Lumpur War Crimes Tribunal. See Richard Falk, 'Toward a jurisprudence of conscience', *Foreign Policy Journal*, 28 November 2011, www.foreignpolicyjournal.com/2011/11/28/toward-a-jurisprudence-of-conscience/.

[96] For example, in its hearings on the Brazilian Amazon and Tibet, the Permanent Peoples' Tribunal found that the commission of crimes against humanity had been established, but it was unable to conclude that genocide had taken place in either case: Permanent Peoples' Tribunal, *Session on the Brazilian Amazon*, Paris, 12–16 October 1990, Judgement, 23, and Permanent Peoples' Tribunal, *Session on Tibet*, Verdict, 20 November 1992 (revised version, 14 December 1992). See Michael Kirby, 'Decision of the Permanent Tribunal of Peoples in its Session on Tibet, Strasbourg, France, November 1992' (1994) 68 *Australian Law Journal* 135.

[97] The Defence challenged Judge Niloufer Bhagwat's participation in the Kuala Lumpur War Crimes Tribunal hearing on the ground that she had served as prosecutor in the World Tribunal on Iraq and as a judge on the Tokyo International Tribunal for War Crimes in Afghanistan, www.informationclearinghouse.info/article5855.htm.

[98] See Notes of Proceedings of the Kuala Lumpur War Crimes Tribunal, Case No. 1-CP-2011, 19 November 2011, 15–35.

inquire into the violations by only one side to a conflict or dispute. This is indeed often the case. However, in many cases it will involve an examination of issues that may not have received much prominence and be the perspective of a less powerful or marginalised party, while the position and influence of the other party may have ensured that its stance is well-known. For example, the First Russell Tribunal argued that by collecting and publicising evidence of violations of the laws of war by the United States in Vietnam, it provided Western audiences with information that was otherwise largely unavailable to them, while there was no shortage of material documenting alleged violations by the Vietcong forces. When challenged on this issue, Sartre responded:

> I refuse to place in the same category the actions of an organization of poor peasants, hunted, obliged to maintain an iron discipline in their ranks, and those of an immense army backed up by a highly industrialized country of 200 million inhabitants.[99]

The Permanent Peoples' Tribunal on Sri Lanka held in Dublin in 2010 argued that it was reasonable for the Tribunal not to examine alleged violations by the Liberation Tigers of Tamil Ealam (LTTE) because 'humanitarian law was created to protect citizens from the State' and '[a]ny crime committed by individuals or groups can be judged and punished by the State.' Crimes committed by the state were often accompanied by impunity; further, international human rights law applied only to the state.[100] However, while the state is the addressee of international human rights law, the law of armed conflict applies equally to non-state actors as it does to the state. Nevertheless, organisers who wish to highlight the wrongs committed by one party to a conflict are unlikely to examine those alleged to have been committed by the party with which they are aligned. This is even more the case when the purpose of a tribunal is to highlight the experiences of the less powerful party to the conflict.

The financing of such tribunals is also an issue. While the judges, jurors and advocates generally provide their time on a pro bono basis, travel and accommodation expenses for participants and witnesses and

[99] 'Imperialist morality: Interview with Jean-Paul Sartre on the War Crimes Tribunal', *New Left Review I/41*, January–February 1967, 3, 7, quoted in Mark Boyle and Audrey Kobayashi, 'In the face of epistemic injustices?: On the meaning of people-led war crimes tribunals' (2015) 33(4) *Environment and Planning D: Society and Space* 697, 705.

[100] Permanent Peoples' Tribunal, *Report on the Session on Sri Lanka*, Dublin, 14–16 January 2010, 10.

venue hire may all have to be covered. Much of the funding must come from or be raised by the organisers or supporters of the tribunal, thus leaving tribunals open to the critique that it is a case of 'he who pays the piper calls the tune.' There is relatively little that tribunals can do to avoid such criticism, though crowdsourcing may be one way in which the expenses of future tribunals might be partially covered.[101] The Permanent Peoples' Tribunal's session on Sri Lanka sought to address this issue directly, noting in the report of its 2010 Dublin session:

> The PPT certifies that the resources which have covered the organizational and financial needs of the sessions correspond mainly to the voluntary work of the members of the NGOs supporting the initiative, and that no economic contribution has been derived from sources directly or indirectly related to Tamil organizations, nor to states involved in the events considered in this session.[102]

1.7.3 The Composition and Representativeness of Peoples' Tribunals

Peoples' tribunals consistently claim to represent and vindicate the interests of various constituencies, whether peoples, oppressed political communities or marginalised groups.[103] The role that these tribunals play and their legitimacy depends in part on the extent to which their practice lives up to this claim of representativeness or providing a context in which peoples who cannot find a legal or other state-based forum to present their claims.

Like official tribunals, peoples' tribunals are vulnerable to the critique that they are the creation of elites, dominated by Europeans and Westerners and that therefore they cannot respond comprehensively to the concerns of peoples in developing countries.[104] This was certainly true of

[101] The International Monsanto Tribunal held 14–16 October 2016 in The Hague financed its proceedings through the use of crowdfunding, www.monsanto-tribunal.org/home/crowdfunding/.

[102] PPT, Dublin Tribunal, above n. 100, 8.

[103] See, e.g., Tognoni, Tognoni and Fraudatario, Chapters 2 and 6 in this volume.

[104] As David Torell puts it:

> [W]ithin the 'mock-trial' phenomena there hide questions and facets of protest rarely articulated with such distinction in other forms of nonviolent protest. Well-organized and expensive, it does not come from below, but from the sidelines of a civil society elite. Clearly it is not an option for just anyone to initiate, it requires money and resources and the 'celebrity' of public intellectuals.

many peoples' tribunals in the 1970s and 1980s – many of which were organised by bodies in the Global North and concerned violations in the Global South. Nonetheless, many of those were held in response to requests from organisations and peoples located in the Global South and involved the participation not only of victims-survivors as witness but also of jurors or judges who came from the regions in question. Furthermore, many of these tribunals have explored the responsibility of the states of the Global North and the international normative and institutional regimes that represent their interests in contributing to and providing support for violative practices and policies.

Nevertheless, there is validity in the general critique. Among other matter, it is reflected in the languages used by, and the panellists who comprise, the judge/jury of, international peoples' tribunals. Illustrative are the opening words of the testimony of Nermin Al-Mufti, a witness at the World Tribunal on Iraq final session in Istanbul, who spoke in Arabic: 'First, I would like to tell you that I am not going to give my testimony in English, because it is the language of the occupiers.'[105] Janine Odink has pointed to a need to translate the decisions of the PPT into languages other than Italian and Spanish and highlighted the need for more panel members from Asia and Africa.[106] The Western, particularly European, dominance of peoples' tribunals is partly the result of historical facts, in particular the Russell Foundation being based in the United Kingdom and the Permanent Peoples' Tribunal established in Rome. It is also the result of the world economic system, with more funds available in the West to support such initiatives than in the developing world. Yet international peoples' tribunals need to make greater efforts to be more inclusive in their choice of panellists and working languages. There is also the possibility that national peoples' tribunals in the developing world draw on or critique international law, but due to language limitations on both sides, their findings are not well known.

Such issues speak to current debates in international law about the extent to which it is able to escape its past as an instrument to justify colonialism, which Third World Approaches to International Law (TWAIL) critics see as continuing. Unwittingly or despite their

David Torell, 'Remember the Russell Tribunal?' in Anna Reading and Tamar Katriel (eds.), *Cultural Memories of Nonviolent Struggles: Powerful Times* (Palgrave Macmillan, 2015) 123–24.

105 Nermin al Mufti, in Sökmen, above n. 44, 302, cited in Çubukçu, above n. 18, 427.

106 Odink, above n. 17, 231.

best efforts, international peoples' tribunals often replicate the hierarchical structures of international law with organisers and judges overwhelmingly from the rich world. Yet further critiques can be made of peoples' tribunals that overlap with important critiques of international law more generally. For example, some proponents of peoples' tribunals tend to make a naïve distinction between the form and content of international law.[107] Scholars of the TWAIL movement remind us that not only are the origins of international law closely intertwined with European colonialism but also international law continues to have imperial effects in the world today.[108] However, most peoples' tribunals take an eclectic and critical approach to international law, both drawing both on its emancipatory promises and recognising its historical origins and reinforcement of old and new power hierarchies.

Another important dimension of representativeness is gender balance. Just as uneven gender representation is a feature of nearly all official international courts and tribunals,[109] so too in international peoples' tribunals, the majority of panel members have been male. Quite apart from the desirability of gender balance and representation as a general principle, 'mainstream' international peoples' tribunals frequently consider the gendered impact of the laws, policies and practices that are the subject of complaint. For example, the PPT hearing on Mexico included the issue of impunity for femicides in the context of the drug war.[110] The Asian garment workers' tribunals considered how pay and working conditions of predominantly female workers affected their reproductive health and their ability to meet cultural expectations of women's role in the home.[111] There is a substantial body of feminist literature on the impact that the gender of decision-makers has on the process and

[107] See, for example, 'international law is not in essence a series of procedures and forms. It is the content.' Activist cited in Sökmen above n. 44, 470.

[108] See Part II 'Postcolonialism', in Prabhakar Sing and Benoit Mayer (eds.), *Critical International Law: Postrealism, Postcolonialism, and Transnationalism* (Oxford University Press, 2014), and Luis Eslava, Michael Fakhri and Vasuki Nesiah (eds.), *Bandung, Global History and International Law* (Cambridge University Press, 2017).

[109] Hilary Charlesworth, 'Transforming the United Men's Club: Feminist futures for the United Nations' (1994) 4 *Transnational Law and Contemporary Problems* 421, 425–26.

[110] For example, witnesses gave evidence about femicides and gender violence in the May 2012 session. See further Icaza, Chapter 8 in this volume.

[111] Simm and Byrnes, above n. 1, 7.

outcomes of cases.[112] The Tokyo Women's Tribunal is one of only a few peoples' tribunals where female judges outnumbered their male counterparts and was designed to have judicial representation from all continents.[113] It is unclear to what extent international peoples' tribunals make particular efforts to ensure gender balance in their jurors, advocates, witnesses and victims/complainants, though it does appear that recent years have seen more women serving on such tribunals.

Nevertheless, there is a stream of women's courts in which feminist activists have adopted the format of peoples' tribunals as most suited to their goals. At the International Tribunal on Crimes against Women, held in Brussels from 4 to 8 March 1976, there was no panel of judges; this was based on the rationale that '[w]e were all our own judges.'[114] While the 1976 Brussels Tribunal was dominated by representatives from European countries, since then there has been a series of women's tribunals predominantly in Asia and Africa, organised by the Asian Women's Human Rights Council and the non-government organisation El Taller.[115] World Courts of Women have been held on all continents but primarily in countries in Asia and Africa.[116]

1.8 Conclusion

The review undertaken in this chapter of the history and current practice of peoples' tribunals shows that this form of social and legal activism

[112] Nienke Grossman, 'Sex on the bench: Do women judges matter to the legitimacy of international courts?' (2011) 12 *Chicago Journal of International Law* 648. See further, the feminist judgments projects in Canada: 'Women's Court of Canada' (2006) 18 (1) *Canadian Journal of Women and the Law*, the United Kingdom: Rosemary Hunter, Clare McGynn and Erika Rackley (eds.) *Feminist Judgments* (Hart Publishing, 2010), Australia: Heather Douglas, Francesca Bartlett, Trish Luker and Rosemary Hunter (eds.) *Australian Feminist Judgments* (Hart Publishing, 2015), United States: Kathryn M. Stanchi, Linda L. Berger and Bridget J. Crawford (eds.), *Feminist Judgments: Rewritten Opinions of the US Supreme Court* (Cambridge University Press, 2016) Ireland: Mairéad Enright, Julie McCandles and Aoife O'Donoghue (eds.), *Northern/Irish Feminist Judgments: Judges' Troubles and the Gendered Politics of Identity* (Hart, 2017).

[113] The designated Indian male judge was unable to attend due to illness; hence there were three female judges and one male judge.

[114] Diana E. H. Russell, 'Introduction' in Diana E. H. Russell and Nicole Van de Ven (eds.), *Crimes against Women: Proceedings of the International Tribunal* (Les Femmes, 1976) xv.

[115] See further Dianne Otto, 'Beyond legal justice: Some personal reflections on people's tribunals, listening and responsibility' (forthcoming) *London Review of International Law*, doi.org/10.1093/lril/lrx007, and Simm, Chapter 3 in this volume.

[116] See list in Borowiak, above n. 72, 45. See further Simm, Chapter 3 in this volume.

continues to be viewed as a valuable form of activism by those seeking the recognition of and redress for serious violations of human rights. While there is considerable variety in the way such tribunals have been organised over the last few decades, they share a number of features. The first is that they all represent a 'formal' response to the (perceived) failures or inability of state-sponsored national and international institutions to prevent or redress systematic violations of human rights. Secondly, they manifest a belief in the emancipatory and protective power of international law, and those involved claim the right as the beneficiaries of that law to own it, interpret it and call states to account for violating it. Thirdly, they challenge the state monopoly on the creation of law, maintaining that it is for peoples and people to formulate a law that promotes the realisation of their rights.

While the primary concern of some tribunals is to promote the implementation of existing positive law, many tribunals are not uncritical users of international law. Rather, they critique those international legal concepts and structures that bolster and are invoked in support of injustice and seek to challenge the oppressive dimensions of international law. As a result, they regularly seek to push existing international law to develop in a direction that will provide enhanced protection to oppressed peoples and marginalised groups.

The criticisms levelled at peoples' tribunals and the practice of individual tribunals frequently reflect states' desires to reassert their monopoly on authoritative lawmaking and the interpretation and application of international law. Critics also castigate peoples' tribunals for their failure to comply with a formalist and limited model of adversarial litigation and fail to understand the nature of the social activity in which peoples' tribunals are engaged. Peoples' tribunals perform multiple roles that official institutions and procedures still fail to adequately perform. This is why peoples' tribunals have been growing in popularity and have become a common form of resistance for social movements.

2

The History of the Permanent Peoples' Tribunal

GIANNI TOGNONI

2.1 When, How and Why the PPT Came into Being

The Permanent Peoples' Tribunal (PPT) was formally established about forty years ago, in Bologna, on 24 June 1979. Its first president was François Rigaux, a Belgian lawyer who had worked closely with Lelio Basso, the creator and founder of the PPT, who died in December 1978. Rigaux shared with Basso a militant and, at the same time, conceptual and utopian vision of international law; one so bound to the lives of individuals and peoples as to make it an instrument of liberation and a life lived in dignity.

The immediate origins of the PPT are easily identifiable. They were the two Russell Tribunals, addressing, respectively, the US aggression against Vietnam (1966–67) (First Russell Tribunal) and the Latin American dictatorships (Second Russell Tribunal), a tragedy of repression which started in Brazil (1969) and spread to practically the entire region, with Chile (1973) and Argentina (1976) being two of the most well-known, harsh and long-lasting examples.

Lelio Basso was the final speaker at the first tribunal[1] and presided at the second, which ended with all the representatives of the resistance-liberation movements making a plea for a permanent tribunal to give visibility and a voice to peoples.[2]

One fundamental step for the translation of this hope into a contextualised operational project for the history of those times, and even more so for what lay ahead, was the formulation and promulgation in Algiers

[1] Lelio Basso, 'Summing-up of the Second Session' in Peter Limqueco and Peter Weiss (eds.), *Prevent the Crime of Silence: Reports from the Sessions of the International War Crimes Tribunal founded by Bertrand Russell* (Allen Lane, 1971) 324,.

[2] See Bertrand Russell Peace Foundation (ed.), *The Betrand Russell Tribunal on Brazil and Repression in Latin America* (Bertrand Russell Peace Foundation, 1973); Pedro Muñoz (ed.), *La violación de los derechos humanos en latinoamérica, documentos del Tribunal Russell II* [*The Violation of Human Rights in Latin America: Documents from the Second Russell Tribunal*] (Editorial Euros, 1976). For further primary and secondary materials related to the Second Russell Tribunal, see the Bibliography in this volume.

of the Universal Declaration of the Rights of Peoples, a few months after the conclusion of the last session of the Second Russell Tribunal.[3] This document consists of thirty short articles written against a backdrop of 'great hope and great unrest', in the 'conviction that effective respect for human rights also includes respect for the rights of peoples'.[4]

Even at that early stage, there was the worrying perception that the last decades of the century would see a reversal in the hierarchy of values and categories, ushering in a new phase in global history. Against the undisputed role of the priority and obligatoriness of international human rights law in the thirty years after the Universal Declaration of Human Rights, actors, powers, strategies and economic ideologies began to assert themselves and give themselves legitimacy, forming a fully autonomous sphere that presented itself as source, measure, and guarantor of global governance models. The response of jurisprudence and the instruments of international law to these rapid, profound and pervasive changes was totally inadequate in terms of reaction time and content.

The PPT arose, therefore, not as a separate entity or initiative but as an instrument for the development of a complex ongoing project, in which the lead role was to be played by actors and jurisdictions ('peoples' being the main 'experts' in the field of self-determination), all well-defined but at the same time unpredictable due to the great variety of characteristics, issues to be resolved, answers required, content and prospects.[5]

3 Universal Declaration of the Rights of the Peoples, Algiers, 4 July 1976, www.algerie-tpp.org/tpp/en/declaration_algiers.htm; Fondazione Lelio e Lisli Basso, *La Dichiarazione di Algeri* [*The Declaration of Algiers*] (Nottetempo, 2016). See generally François Rigaux, 'The Algiers Declaration of the Rights of Peoples' in Antonio Cassese (ed.), *UN Law, Fundamental Rights: Two Topics in International Law* (Sijthoff & Noordhoff International Publishers, 1979) 211; Richard Falk, 'The Algiers Declaration of the Rights of Peoples and the struggle for human rights' in Cassese, 225; François Rigaux (ed.), *La Carta di Algeri: La Dichiarazione Universale dei Diritti dei Popoli* [*The Charter of Algiers: The Universal Declaration of the Rights of Peoples*] (Edizioni Cultura della Pace, 1988); Antonio Cassese and Edmond Jouve, *Pour un droit des peuples: essais sur la Déclaration d'Alger* [*For a Law of Peoples: Essays on the Declaration of Algiers*] (Berger Levrault, 1978).

4 Preamble of the Universal Declaration of the Rights of Peoples.

5 See generally Gianni Tognoni, 'La storia del Tribunale Permanente dei Popoli' ['The History of the Permanent Peoples' Tribunal'] in Linda Bimbi and Gianni Tognoni (eds.), *Speranze e inquietudini di ieri e di oggi. I trent'anni della Dichiarazione Universale del Diritto dei Popoli* [*Hopes and Concerns of Yesterday and Today: Thirty Years of the Universal Declaration of Peoples' Law*] (EdUP, 2008) 95; Gianni Tognoni, 'Alle radici del Progetto TPP' ['The roots of the PPT Project'] in Gianni Tognoni (ed.), *Tribunale Permanente dei Popoli: Le Sentenze 1979–1998* [*Permanent Peoples' Tribunal: The Judgments 1979–1998*] (Casa Editrice Stefanoni, 1998) i.

The concrete history of what the PPT is, and above all what it has done, in terms of cases heard, judgments passed, conceptualisations formulated and technical points elaborated during the very articulate course of these years, may be found in the bibliography that appears at the end of this volume, which, while not being able to detail the rich array of meetings, materials and life stories, can still provide an outline of the paths followed and the overall direction taken.

What we propose to do here, in a world that has changed profoundly since the PPT was first set up, is to re-evaluate whether the 'instrument' that was formulated then can fulfil its function of providing a 'comprehensive service' for the changeable and living history of the self-determination of peoples, who, in turn, have redefined/reconceived themselves as regards not only their reciprocal relations but also and even more so their structural identity and their political, economic and legal history.

This assessment will cover five points, each of which underlies a basic characteristic of the PPT. Reference will be made to cases heard in different sessions so as to provide clearer and more instructive examples to illustrate not so much what has been done but what can/should be considered desirable/feasible for the future.[6]

2.2 The Basic [Hypo]-Thesis

Confirming and making explicit the rationale, role, legitimacy and specificity of the opinion courts from which it originated, the [hypo]-thesis adopted by the PPT, as its identity and working methodology, is that law can, and therefore should, be used as a 'research tool'. In the years immediately following World War II, when the regulatory framework of fundamental and constitutional rights crystallised, the process for the transferability of these principles to the lives of real people has not followed a linear path – far from it. The radical novelty of a period which sees the proclamation of rights is inevitably followed by a time of interpretative regression-resistance.

[6] A list of the sessions of the PPT appears in the Bibliography in this volume. All the final verdicts or judgments of the PPT's sessions may be found on the website of the Tribunal (listed in reverse chronological order): http://permanentpeoplestribunal.org/category/jurisprudence/?lang=en. Not all the verdicts are available in English on the PPT website. The titles of all sessions are given here in English.

First of all, the category of 'peoples' (with all the implications, imprecisions, ambiguities and perceptions of a term that forms the basis of the preamble of the Universal Declaration of Human Rights) is very provocative in terms of law, even in its most open forms, and even more so in terms of politics and power. The Algiers Declaration should be read as a sort of 'research protocol', just like Article 3 of the Italian Constitution.[7] 'Declarations' are, by definition, starting points. Peoples must emerge from the confines of prologues or 'founding' articles and, in all their diversity as human groups with concrete needs-desires-dreams-dramas, become the 'controllers' of states that claim to be the only representatives and authentic interpreters of the 'law', its practicality and its obligatoriness. 'Control' is not exercised by verifying a more or less faithful adherence to given rules but by adapting creatively and quickly to scenarios which are necessarily subject to profound changes.

It is important for the role and meaning of the PPT to reflect that research is an essential part of the PPT's identity and critical to its role as an instrument-service for the development of an all-embracing project. This does not mean reiterating principles. The great variability of cases (which dramatically document and make explicit the lives of real persons-people in different places and at different times for whom there is a distance between 'due and achievable rights' and 'accessible and enjoyed rights') makes it vital not to look to assertions but to research. This research must be carried out not so much by external experts as by researchers, who, in the participatory dialectic of a 'process', together find, qualify, exclude, assess, judge evidence and look at possible solutions to see whether or not they exist, or are feasible, so they may be made explicit or formulated from first principles. The first case presented to the PPT and recognised as admissible, relevant and perfectly symbolic of the PPT's research methodology in the interpretation of the rights of

[7] Article 3 of the Constitution of the Italian Republic provides:

> All citizens have equal social dignity and are equal before the law, without distinction of sex, race, language, religion, political opinion, personal and social conditions. It is the duty of the Republic to remove those obstacles of an economic or social nature which constrain the freedom and equality of citizens, thereby impeding the full development of the human person and the effective participation of all workers in the political, economic and social organisation of the country.

www.senato.it/documenti/repository/istituzione/costituzione_inglese.pdf.

peoples involved the Saharawi people.[8] Still today they are witnesses, a provocation, 'judges' of an international community that is indefinitely deferring the translation of basic principles as regards the recognition of the existence of a people (a classic case of decolonisation), whose representativeness and legitimacy no one disputes but who, in effect, have no right to exist as an autonomous subject with inviolable rights.

Among the subsequent cases heard by the PPT, which can be placed at the opposite extreme of this research scenario, are the indigenous peoples of the Brazilian Amazon[9] or the thousands of deaths in Bhopal, India,[10] or the victims of Chernobyl.[11] These peoples are all easily identifiable, found even within states with advanced constitutions, 'subjects' of countries that have signed binding treaties. They are, however, concretely and symbolically 'orphans' with no rights, who are prepared to seek ways to translate 'fundamental' principles (first into concepts so they may then be put into practice) not only to give an identity to the 'victims' but also to allow them to become subjects of 'renewed rights', regardless of the absence of adequate legislation.

2.3 The Methodological Specificity of an Epithet

The term 'permanent' in the title of the PPT is not primarily intended to have a temporal connotation or one of duration. It is closely connected to the [hypo]-thesis formulated in the previous section. The PPT project does not consist of just hearing one case after another, to examine and detail specific violations of fundamental rights of 'peoples' resulting from commission or omission, or the 'lack' of formal competence of existing institutions. It is clear that each case requires specific attention, which is given as quickly as possible. The PPT's mission is to be an 'instrument and service', to give *those* peoples, in their quest for respect, self-determination and dignity of life, a chance to speak out, to fight and to

8 Permanent Peoples' Tribunal, *Session on Western Sahara*, Brussels, 10–11 November 1979.

9 Permanent Peoples' Tribunal, *Session on the Brazilian Amazon*, Paris, 12–16 October 1990.

10 Permanent Peoples' Tribunal, *Hearing on Industrial Hazards and Human Rights (Bhopal I)*, Bhopal, India, 19–23 October 1992; Permanent Peoples' Tribunal, *Session on Industrial Hazards and Human Rights (Bhopal II)*, London, 28 November–4 December 1994.

11 Permanent Peoples' Tribunal, *Session on Chernobyl: Environment, health and Human Rights*, Vienna, 12–15 April 1996.

gain visibility. All the peoples who have turned to the PPT (in various ways, according to different needs and contexts) have been witnesses and beneficiaries of this methodology of attention, which starts with the 'preparatory phase' of the case and ends with a ruling – a process that lasts at least a year.[12] The 'permanence' of an organisation that can quickly get down to work and which provides consolidated know-how and targeted competence despite the permanent scarcity of economic resources has been, and still is, one of the most specific and original characteristics of the PPT.

However, at an even deeper level, 'permanence' means continuity of work on the original research project. If we wish to contribute to the endeavour of helping international law regain its role of promoter of space and substantial autonomy (not merely 'declared' or one that is 'compatible' with the imbalances of power) for real peoples facing often dramatic developments in their lives, we must be lucidly and candidly aware of the need for long-term work. This work is not the sum of individual cases but the research-construction of a culture of rights that is not resigned to the inevitability of changing power relationships, countered by the re-proposition of rules that are no longer relevant or efficient.

If there was a need for this in the seventies, when history seemed a mix of hopes and threats, it has become even more urgent in recent decades, during which the goal of a 'universal' project has entered into crisis, gradually replaced by jurisprudence that theorises, favours or imposes an inevitable and unpunishable inequality as regards the chances of these 'peoples' (or however we wish to describe groups of human beings) of getting access to their rights. In the individual 'cases' it deals with, the PPT's primary, concrete and, therefore, *also* symbolic function is to offer a reminder and reaffirmation that history has meaning only as a permanent research project on the conditions of 'universality' of fundamental rights. The 'permanent' search for a single basic project, through the ever-changing variability of cases, is indispensable if we are to avoid the dispersal and fragmentation of objectives and problems that appear so diverse and distant from each other in terms of content and location in space and time that the formation of a shared consciousness among the many 'peoples' – be they minorities or majorities, ethnic groups or countries, people within the same state or dispersed in the most

[12] For the procedure of the Tribunal, see *Statute of the Permanent Peoples' Tribunal* (1979), http://tribunalepermanentedeipopoli.fondazionebasso.it/wp-content/uploads/2016/06/statute.pdf.

disparate regions of the globe – is prevented. A rereading of PPT 'cases' in this light is all the more important in a world that is set on imposing the interpretative key of 'globalisation' as the only legitimate and politically realistic way of considering these many differences. This orientation creates a 'centre' that declares itself to be the legitimate interpreter of rules, effectively marginalising many 'peoples' and their specific rights.

The idea of 'permanence' in the PPT's work methodology also means reaffirming, case after case, that the lead role in history is still played by 'peoples' and their specific search for existence and dignity. Their rights are rooted in the concrete reality of the lives of individuals and groups and not in generic endless promises of a 'globally' better future in the hands of privileged minorities who express and manage powers, assigning themselves the role and mandate of providing security as a surrogate and condition of democracy. The permanent methodology of the PPT is to propose a right that endures, develops and changes in a participatory exercise of awareness-raising, providing a voice that neither passively accepts nor is coerced into 'solutions', that obey laws or models that claim to be the condition and instrument of a right measured according to economic development indicators.

2.4 The Right/Duty of Visibility and Memory

The PPT is a research project pursued by a marginalised minority, on the confines between the concreteness of reality and meticulously documented facts and the ineffectiveness of pronounced judgments, which always seem to have a 'symbolic' value. Does all this make any sense? Is it worthwhile? Is it possible to give an answer to these kinds of issues? And who should provide the answers? The PPT provides answers to questions posed by concrete 'peoples' (whatever the definition we wish to give to this term), who believe it is important for *their* history, which often does not coincide with the direction, priorities and assessments of global history. The PPT is a forum, an instrument at the service of memory and visibility, giving voice to minority peoples. History seen through PPT judgments is that seen through the eyes of 'rights researchers'. It draws a map where it is possible to recognise many (though certainly not all) of the most representative issues of the most recent history. The following includes only a few of these issues:

- *Desaparecidos* (the disappeared): This surreal term, programmatically elaborated and proposed by the Argentine dictators as a certification of non-existence for which there was no legal accountability, is to be found in the PPT judgment of 1980.[13] It could now be considered a global term to define any people which does not exist for the international law of states: any people that had no homeland and every homeland, present in all times and in all 'dictatorships' (military, economic, political, national and international), from Guatemala to Mexico to Colombia and the universe of Africans immigrating to a Europe which has abdicated its own memory and identity as the home of rights.

- *Genocides*:[14] from 'post-colonial' East Timor (Lisbon, 1981)[15] and the one perpetrated for centuries in Guatemala (Madrid, 1983),[16] to the well-known but forgotten and denied extermination in Armenia (Paris, 1984)[17] which remains a thorny issue of our times, the one in Tibet (Strasbourg, 1992),[18] the tragedy that unfolded in former Yugoslavia (Berne-Barcelona, 1995),[19] and the recent ones involving the Tamil people (2010–13) and the Rohingyas of Myanmar (2017).[20]
- *Impunity* (Bogota, 1991):[21] a hallmark of current international law, applied across the board, from the 'classic' crimes against humanity

[13] Permanent Peoples' Tribunal, *Session on Argentina*, Geneva, 3–4 May 1980.

[14] See generally Simona Fraudatario and Gianni Tognoni, 'La definición jurídica y substancial del genocidio a la prueba del encuentro entre el Tribunal Permanente de los Pueblos y las víctimas' ['The Juridical and Substantive Definition of Genocide on Trial in the Encounter between the Permanent Peoples Tribunal and Victims'], paper presented at the Conferencia Bianual de La International Association of Genocide Scholars, Buenos Aires, 19–22 July 2011, www.genocidescholars.org/sites/default/files/document%09%5Bcurrent-page%3A1%5D/documents/IAGS%202011%20Simona%20Fraudatario.pdf.

[15] Permanent Peoples' Tribunal, *Session on East Timor*, Lisbon, 19–21 June 1981.

[16] Permanent Peoples' Tribunal, *Session on Guatemala*, Madrid, 21–31 January 1983.

[17] Permanent Peoples' Tribunal, *Session on the Armenian Genocide*, Paris, 13–16 April 1984. An English version of the verdict available in Gérard Libaridian (ed.), *A Crime of Silence, The Armenian Genocide. Permanent Peoples' Tribunal* (Zed Books, 1985),

[18] Permanent Peoples' Tribunal, *Session on Tibet, Verdict,* 20 November 1992 (revised version, 14 December 1992). See François Rigaux, 'L'autodeterminazione nelle sentenze del Tribunal Permanente dei Popoli' ['Self-determination in the verdicts of the Permanent Peoples' Tribunal'] in Tognoni (ed.) (1998), above n. 5, 747.

[19] Permanent Peoples' Tribunal, *Crimes against Humanity in the Former Yugoslavia*, Berne, Switzerland, 17–20 February 1995; *Crimes against Humanity in the Former Yugoslavia, Second Session*, Barcelona, Spain, 7–11 December 1995.

[20] Permanent Peoples' Tribunal, *Session on Sri Lanka and the Tamil People*, Dublin, 14–16 January 2010; *Session on Sri Lanka and the Tamil People*, Bremen, 7–10 December 2013; and Session on State Crimes Allegedly Committed in Myanmar against the Rohingyas, Kachins and Other Groups, Kuala Lumpur, 18–22 September 2017.

[21] Permanent Peoples' Tribunal, *Proceedings on Impunity for Crimes against Humanity in Latin America, Final Hearing*, Bogotá, 25 April 1991.

perpetrated by dictatorships that go unpunished, to the economic crimes that are unpunishable because of the omission or absence of a formal category including these crimes in international law and jurisdiction.

For each of these issues, the record of official history gives us almost rulelike labels-designations justifying them or making them the subject of jurisprudential discussions, political bargaining or indefinite postponements. The PPT's 'point of view' – namely that of the peoples who have been given a voice through this instrument of research-memory – is to affirm that there is no doctrine or ideology or global order that can abolish the age-old, universal, simple and full right of habeas corpus, of individuals and their collective lives as peoples.

2.5 When the Obviousness of Research Areas Becomes 'Provocative'

In its goal of providing a forum-instrument for independent research at the service of fundamental rights, the PPT has taken up three particularly significant issues that should be specifically underlined, because they still constitute, and probably will for some time to come, a critical research agenda for a culture, and, therefore, the concrete practices, of the rights of 'peoples' and the individuals-groups that constitute them.

2.5.1 The Field of Economic Crimes and Its Autonomy from the Categories of International Law

The sessions devoted to the activities and roles played by the World Bank and the International Monetary Fund (IMF) (Berlin, 1988; Madrid, 1994)[22] exemplify the importance of this chapter. Economic crimes underlie all the latest scenarios of violation of fundamental rights, but at the same time they lie outside the jurisdiction of the International Criminal Court, which from the adoption of its statute[23] in 1998 and the

[22] Permanent Peoples' Tribunal, *Session on the Policies of the International Monetary Fund and the World Bank*, West Berlin, 26–29 September 1988; Permanent Peoples' Tribunal, *Second Session on the Policies of the International Monetary Fund and the World Bank*, Madrid, 1–3 October 1994. See Antoni Pigrau Solé, 'Las políticas del FMI y del Banco Mundial y los Derechos de los Pueblos' ['The politics of the IMF and the World Bank and the law of peoples'] (1995) 29–30 *Revista CIDOB Afers Internacionals* 139.

[23] Rome Statute of the International Criminal Court, Rome, 17 July 1998, 2187 UNTS 90, in force 1 July 2002.

commencement of its work in 2002, should have replaced, with its authority, the role of courts of opinion. The main issue addressed in these sessions was in fact, beyond the clear responsibilities of the World Bank and of the IMF, to make explicit something obvious in concrete terms, but provocative in its implications, namely the extension of economic development models and how their mechanisms relegate the role of fundamental individual and collective rights to that of 'dependent variables'.

The literature that 'describes' these facts, to denounce or defend them, is endless and need not be cited here. The provocation issued by the PPT is to dispute that what happens is the expression of a project that is compatible with the fundamental framework of universal rights (because it produces side effects such as massive violations of rights) and to declare-judge it as fundamentally incompatible with an order that claims to be at least oriented towards basic rights, while it substantially belies the entire 'rule of law culture' in which we live.

Economic crimes 'affect' people, the environment, future generations and the culture of democracy in a way which is not 'collateral'. The importance of this area has become central to PPT activities over the last few years, with a series of cases that have specifically concerned Colombia (2005–8),[24] European transnational corporations in Latin America with the complicity of the European Union (2006–10),[25] Mexico (2011–14)[26] and 'living wages' for garment workers as a human right (2009–15).[27]

The material produced in these cases of the PPT (each divided into several sessions in which hundreds of witnesses and thousands of citizens actively participated) cannot be summarised here. Even if we leave out all the factual documentation, it surely represents, in terms of jurisprudence, a unique body of work that documents and makes explicit what could and should be the implications of an approach which recognises as the principal and legitimate juridical subjects those who are considered by formal courts of law to be 'victims' who are called to give evidence so that the systematic violations that have erased their lives and dignity can be made 'justiciable'.

24 Permanent Peoples' Tribunal, *Transnational Corporations and Peoples' Rights in Colombia (2006–8): final hearing*, Bogotá, 21–23 July 2008.

25 Permanent Peoples' Tribunal, *The European Union and Transnational Corporations in Latin America: Policies, Instruments and Actors Complicit in Violations of the Peoples' Rights, Deliberating Session*, Madrid, 14–17 May 2010.

26 Permanent Peoples' Tribunal, *Free Trade, Violence, Impunity and Peoples' Rights in Mexico (2011–14): final hearing*, Mexico City, 12–15 November 2014.

27 Permanent Peoples' Tribunal, *Living Wage for Garment Workers in Asia: Final Session*, Colombo, 17–20 December 2015.

2.5.2 *The Roots of International Law*

The session dedicated to a rereading of the 'conquest' of America, five centuries after its 'discovery' (Padua, Venice, 1992),[28] is central to the understanding of the logic behind the PPT's research and its role. The ruling (the result of highly interdisciplinary academic research, as well as intense interaction with international movements mobilised for such a symbolic anniversary) provides very up-to-date arguments for a profound rethinking of the nature and role of international law. This rethinking should also include the speech made by Eduardo Galeano[29] (together with the one made by the author, a member of the PPT jury, at the close of the Berlin session four years earlier). International law was established in the early 1500s to justify the legitimacy of a conquest disguised as a discovery of civilisation – retrospectively, of course, starting in the places and according to the interests of the conquerors, and in the name of a 'doctrine' of evangelisation, which in a way anticipates and reproduces the ideology of globalisation. International law arises as a service to a policy that sets out the rules of the game based on models of civilisation and economy that are declared to be the exclusive, legitimate, binding terms of reference. The mentors, therefore, cannot be punished for any 'collateral damage' inflicted in the 'periphery', no matter how genocidal, because those effects had not been expressly intended and declared beforehand.

The 1992 session on the 'conquest' of the Americas took place during a time in history when a new interpretation of international law was developing, one which imposed itself or tried to impose itself. After the first Gulf War (1991), on the eve of the 'humanitarian' war in former Yugoslavia and the push towards the doctrine of security and its developments in Afghanistan and Iraq, war was seen and adopted as a legitimate, even inevitable, part of politics. The PPT session on the New Wars (2002),[30] ten years after that on the Conquest of the Americas and on

[28] Permanent Peoples' Tribunal, *The Conquest of America and International Law*, Padua-Venice, 5–9 October 1992. See also François Rigaux, 'La conquête de l'Amérique et le droit international' ['The conquest of America and international law'] (1992) 4 *African Journal of International and Comparative Law* 486 (based on presentation to the PPT).

[29] Eduardo Galeano, 'Five Hundred Years of Solitude' in Permanent Peoples' Tribunal, *The Conquest of the Americas and International Law: Decision*, 5–8 October 1992, 5–7.

[30] Permanent Peoples' Tribunal, *International Law and the New Wars*, Rome, 14–16 December 2002.

the eve of the 2003 Iraq War, reads like an updated and 'prospective memory' of what had happened five centuries earlier.

On the other hand, in terms of jurisprudence and to stress once again the need for an ever-greater and timely contextualisation of international law as a *sine qua non* to make it relevant in practical terms to emerging problems, it seems appropriate to mention, as an original contribution on the competences of international law, a case that points in the opposite direction to the general/global scenarios just mentioned: the ruling on 'Fundamental rights, participation of local communities and infrastructure projects – from the Turin-Lyons high-speed rail to global reality (Turin-Almese, 2015)'.[31] The case concerned lack of community consultation in the construction of a high-speed rail link between Italy and France, where part of the territory subject to the project is under military control. This project is representative of several other European megaprojects involving construction of railways, motorways and mining. International legal issues raised by the case include application of the Aarhus Convention,[32] to which both Italy and France are parties, and European Union directives on civil society and public access to environmental information.[33]

The case makes explicit one of the most open and least explored frontiers of current international law, when its jurisdiction extends to scenarios in which the violation of fundamental human rights does not find 'a judge in Berlin'.[34] It is the case of a local community in the

[31] Permanent Peoples' Tribunal, *Fundamental Rights, Participation of Local Communities and Infrastructure Projects – from the Lyon-Turin High-speed Rail to the Global Reality*, Turin-Almese, 5–8 November 2015.

[32] Convention on access to information, public participation in decision-making and access to justice in environmental matters, 25 June 1998, in force 30 October 2001, 2161 UNTS 447 (Aarhus Convention).

[33] Directive 2003/4/EC of 28 January 2003 on public access to environmental information, OJ 2002 No. L41/26 and Directive 2003/35/EC of 26 May 2003 providing for public participation in respect of the drawing up of certain plans and programmes relating to the environment, OJ 2003 No. L156/17; cited in Judgment, above n. 31, 18.

[34] [Eds.] 'To find a judge in Berlin' means to have access to a judicial or other independent forum that will provide protection based in law against the exercise of arbitrary power by the state. The phrase is derived from a story told in a poem by François Andrieux (1759–1833) of an encounter between Frederick the Great of Prussia and a miller in Potsdam who refused to sell Frederick his mill, the clatter of which was disturbing Frederick in his summer palace at Sans Souci. When Frederick stated that he could take the mill without payment, the miller responded "Yes, if there were no judges in Berlin." Frederick relented in the face of this response: Andrieux, 'Le meunier de Sans Souci', *Wikisource*, https://fr.wikisource.org/wiki/Le_Meunier_Sans-Souci.

historical, economic, cultural heart of a country like Italy, whose constitution is the guarantor of fundamental rights, under a now stable democracy in a Europe that continues to present itself, at least for its citizens, as a guarantor of inviolable rights-liberties. The right infringed is that of the concrete participation of a community in decisions affecting its territory, health and development model, in the name of an economic project declared 'strategic' at national and international levels. The 'inversion' of the hierarchies of values of the rights in question (fundamental rights and political-economic ones) has shifted from the global to the local scenario. The situation is not uncommon and illustrates the gravity of the changes underway. The conflict may explode or remain unresolved, which may lead to state repression-militarisation in the heart of democracy, with only mystifying, delaying, repressive answers being found for years.

The ruling, which was also brought to the attention of the European Parliament,[35] is interesting in terms of the 'continuity' it suggests of the violation of fundamental rights in contexts that are considered/declared to be central and democratic, with what happens in 'peripheral and unstable' scenarios (with all the consequences of the lack of enforcement of international law previously discussed).

2.5.3 *The Peoples Who Do Not Belong*

In its years of activity, the PPT has often had to address, in a variety of ways, the (paradoxical?) problem of defining the term 'peoples' which coincides with its identity.[36] Beyond the work previously carried out in which this issue was addressed in its historical, legal and doctrinal aspects,[37] the true challenge was the concrete history that was being lived.

It was and still is inevitable that something that is not defined by international law – dependent as it is on the jurisdiction-culture-practice of states and their functions, powers and responsibilities – would lead, at least in appearance, to very heterogeneous interpretations and qualifications of the situations in which peoples find themselves in the absence of

[35] 'Delivery of the Judgment to the European Institutions', *Permanent Peoples' Tribunal*, 26 October 2016, http://permanentpeoplestribunal.org/strasburgo-26-ottobre-2016-la-sentenza-su-grandi-opere-e-diritti-fondamentali-al-parlamento-europeo/.

[36] See the sources cited above n. 3.

[37] See also, e.g., François Rigaux (ed.), *Le concept de peuple* [*The Concept of People*] (Story-Scientia, 1988).

clearly defined categories of judgment. The choice made by the PPT is entirely consistent with what was said previously about its role as a 'permanent research tool': an explicit acceptance of the risk of dealing with real urgent demands, without censoring a priori what is not completely 'defined', with an activity focused on first acquiring empirical data so as to be able to address, as flexibly as possible, issues brought to our attention by groups of human beings who presented themselves as 'peoples' who needed help and protection, precisely because they did not belong and did not correspond to any entities that had previously been defined or adopted by official juridical categories.

We insist on this point, at the end of the PPT process of memory-for-the-future, because it is perhaps one of the most original novelties, although less formally developed in terms of jurisprudence. When they come as the 'object' of an intervention that denies them any rights, first and foremost the right to have a primordial and inviolable identity, that of existence, the peoples who do not belong are, in fact, the most sensitive indicators of the challenge faced today. The world aims to standardise rules and procedures rigidly to ensure complete freedom of trade in goods, while making personal and collective rights a flexible and precarious 'dependent variable' to be included, perhaps, as a 'safeguard clause' when the absolute right of market, trade and finance appears to coincide with the violation of the fundamental rights of concrete people-communities. Here we only have space to mention some of the most relevant judgments to support the previous statements.

The session on the right of asylum in times of economic globalisation and restrictions on the fundamental right to 'migrate' (Berlin, December 1994)[38] anticipated what is happening to an ever greater extent in the Mediterranean, or in the deserts of Mexico or the seas between Asia and Australia, to the people who do not belong and who are denied their identity as human beings because they cannot show a valid state identity card.

The important judgment on minors (Trento, Macerata, Napoli, April 1995)[39] was followed by the analysis of slave labour in the name of consumption and leisure time (Brussels, 1998).[40] The two judgments

[38] Permanent Peoples' Tribunal, *Right of Asylum in Europe*, Berlin, 8–12 December 1994.

[39] Permanent Peoples' Tribunal, *Violations of the Fundamental Rights of Children and Minors*, Trento, 27–29 March 1995; Macerata, 30 March 1995; Naples, 1–4 April 1995.

[40] Permanent Peoples' Tribunal, *The Rights of Workers and Consumers in the Garment Industry*, Brussels, 30 April–5 May 1998.

concerning the 'people of Bhopal' (Bhopal, 1992; London, 1994)[41] and the many similar ones, cross-cutting and involving all countries and communities hit by environmental disasters, are cases that are extremely well-documented in worrying reports, though the subjects involved have basically been left the orphans of judgments capable of binding those private and state actors responsible (Bangalore, 2011).[42] The 'people' of Chernobyl (Vienna, 1996)[43] are known to all but are hidden and invisible to national and international bodies only because they had the misfortune of 'existing-as-victims' just before the disappearance of the state to which they belonged with the fall of the Berlin Wall.

The peoples of the former Yugoslavia, in the sessions held in Berne (February 1995) and Barcelona (December 1995),[44] were judged in their precise historical context. This was well before the international community began to investigate (by setting up an ad hoc tribunal but washing their hands of any direct and profound responsibility) single and carefully chosen individuals from the many and well-known protagonists of that event, which in the meantime was also included in the PPT session on the 'humanitarian' wars.

2.6 Conclusion

Today, the PPT continues its mission, forty years after the rules and horizons were set out in the Declaration of Algiers, with an agenda that is unfortunately still full. The question has often been asked, also as part of a more general history of courts of opinion, if there is still a need and a place for them in a world of politics, law and culture that has changed so much. In recent times, there has been a renewed intensity in requests to be given a voice in this forum, so that it is difficult to provide a formal response from within ongoing work. The mission of the PPT is first to listen and set out to identify and implement the instruments that can give back rights to their rightful owners – working with them, not just for them. Those most competent to judge this work are the peoples, however they may be defined, that come for help, following up proceedings, urging us forward, each time with a different commitment to 'research', analyse, qualify and judge. What is clear is the disproportion that exists

[41] Above n. 10.

[42] Permanent Peoples' Tribunal, *Session on Agrochemical Transnational Corporations*, Bengaluru, 3–6 December 2011.

[43] Above n. 11. [44] Above n. 19.

between the urgency-drama of the issues and the answers that need to be implemented so they can enter the lives – hopes? resistance? consciousness? liberation? – of the peoples. It is often hard to live with the everyday reality of scarcity of resources and lack of time to explore, create more extensive and permanent networks and give more visibility to what should/could and can/must be done, complying fully with the duty to leave no violations unpunished.

It is always a new experience – to the extent that one cannot allow tiredness to set in – to meet those who continue to ask, also through the forum of the PPT, whether it is still possible to give to the 'hope in fundamental right(s)' one chance more than the opportunities so easily provided for their violation.

PART II

The Politics of Bearing Witness and Listening

3

Peoples' Tribunals, Women's Courts and International Crimes of Sexual Violence

GABRIELLE SIMM*

3.1 Introduction

Since the early 1990s, international criminal law has been the focus of much feminist activism and contestation.[1] The substantive law, rules of evidence and victim-centred procedures are often compared favourably with domestic laws on sexual violence. International criminal courts and tribunals have a higher representation of female judges than all other international courts and tribunals (with the exception of the European Court of Human Rights),[2] and there is evidence that a critical mass of judges who come from nontraditional backgrounds can influence shifts in decision-making.[3] As a result of the success of feminist advocates in shaping these international institutions, Janet Halley argues that the jurisprudence of the International Criminal Tribunals for the former Yugoslavia and for Rwanda (ICTY and ICTR) shows that 'feminism rules'.[4]

At the same time, unofficial or peoples' tribunals – civil society initiatives – dealing with international crimes of sexual violence against

* Thanks to Christine Chinkin and Dianne Otto for their comments at the 'Peoples' Tribunals and International Law' seminar held at Melbourne Law School on 13 September 2013, to Olivera Simić and to members of the Feminist Legal Research Group at University of Technology Sydney Faculty of Law for very useful comments and to Monique Dam for excellent research assistance.

1 Janet Halley, 'Rape at Rome: Feminist interventions in the criminalization of sex-related violence in positive international criminal law' (2009) 30 *Michigan Journal of International Law* 1.

2 Nienke Grossman, 'Sex on the bench' (2012) 12 *Chicago Journal of International Law* 648.

3 Patricia M. Wald, 'Women on international courts: Some lessons Learned' (2011) *International Criminal Law Review* 401, 403. In the UK context, see Erika Rackley, *Women, Judging and the Judiciary: From Difference to Diversity* (Routledge, 2012).

4 Janet Halley, *Split Decisions: How and Why to Take a Break from Feminism* (Princeton University Press, 2006) 22.

women continue to proliferate. These peoples' tribunals sometimes explicitly address official international criminal courts and tribunals and seek to influence the development of international criminal law. At other times, they aim to provide a different sort of justice and the acknowledgment, support and memorialisation of gendered harms that victims-survivors feel is lacking in official courts. The most famous example dealing with sexual violence crimes is the Tokyo Women's Tribunal, which convened in 2000 as the 'continuation' of the International Military Tribunal for the Far East (the Tokyo Tribunal) to investigate the Japanese military 'comfort women' system.[5] However, the Tokyo Women's Tribunal was not the first, nor the last, of its kind. More recently, three women's hearings were held in Phnom Penh, Cambodia, in 2011, 2012 and 2013, to address sexual violence in conflict.[6] Since 1994, a series of women's tribunals have addressed a range of gendered harms, most recently in 2015 with a Women's Court organised by women in the countries of the former Yugoslavia. This selection of examples, among many others, indicates that feminist activists have not been content with the official fora for addressing crimes against women but have continued to organise their own tribunals and courts outside formal structures.

What constitutes an international crime of sexual violence?[7] The benchmark definition is found in the Rome Statute which established the International Criminal Court. It includes 'rape, sexual slavery, enforced prostitution, forced pregnancy, enforced sterilisation and any other form of sexual violence of a comparable gravity'.[8] A broader term often used is sexual and gender-based violence (SGBV) that appears to encompass human rights violations that do not amount to international

[5] See Dolgopol, Chapter 4 in this volume.

[6] See Dianne Otto, 'Impunity in a Different Register: People's Tribunals and Questions of Judgment, Law, and Responsibility' in Karen Engle, Zinaida Miller and DM Davis (eds) *Anti-Impunity and the Human Rights Agenda* (Cambridge University Press, 2016), 291; Beini Ye, 'Transitional justice through the Cambodian women's hearings' (2014) 2 *Cambodian Law and Policy Journal* 23. See also Andrea Durbach and Lucy Geddes, '"To Shape our own lives and our own world": exploring women's hearings as reparative mechanisms for victims of sexual violence post-conflict' (2017) *International Journal of Human Rights* http://dx.doi.org/10.1080/13642987.2017.1360019.

[7] See generally Anne-Marie De Brouwer, Charlotte Ku, Renée Römkens and Larissa van den Herik, *Sexual Violence as an International Crime: Interdisciplinary Approaches* (Intersentia, 2013).

[8] Rome Statute of the International Criminal Court, Rome, 17 July 1998, 2187 UNTS 90, in force 1 July 2002, article 7(1)(g).

crimes. Sexual violence is usually understood to mean rape, but the definition of rape itself is contested. Indeed, the ICTY and ICTR were lauded for expanding the definition of rape beyond a mechanical description of physical acts and for finding that coercive circumstances such as war might vitiate consent without necessitating further proof.[9] These tribunals also found that rape could constitute genocide[10] and crimes against humanity,[11] in addition to being a war crime.[12]

Yet the emphasis by many feminist scholars on international sexual violence crimes has been critiqued by other feminists as a 'fixation'[13] that creates a hierarchy of harms. It risks devaluing non-sexual harms suffered in conflict or other extraordinary circumstances and 'ordinary' sexual violence crimes.[14] To the extent that they privilege sexual violence in certain contexts above 'ordinary' sexual violence, or devalue non-sexual harms, women's courts and tribunals are vulnerable to the same critiques made of official state and international criminal courts. The implications for feminists of 'using international law's violence as a site to address violence against women' particularly given its 'disproportionately coercive impact on certain regions of the globe' are under-theorised.[15] Conflating sexual violence with female victims marginalises the male victims of sexual violence, although women continue to suffer sexual violence crimes to a greater extent than men.[16] Further, the assumption that women's courts and tribunals deal primarily (only?) with sexual

9 *Prosecutor v. Kunarac (Foča case)*, ICTY, Appeals Chamber, IT-96-23 and 23/1 12 June 2002 [130], adopted in *Gacumbitsi v. The Prosecutor*, ICTR, Appeals Chamber, 2001-64-A [152]-[157].

10 *Prosecutor v. Jean-Paul Akayesu*, ICTR, Case No ICTR-96-4-T, Trial Judgment, 2 September 1998.

11 *Kunarac*, above n. 9.

12 Rome Statute, articles 8(2)(b)(xxii) and 8(2)(e)(vi) in international and non-international armed conflicts.

13 Nicola Henry, 'The fixation of wartime rape: Feminist critique and international criminal law' (2014) 23 *Social and Legal Studies* 93.

14 Kiran Grewal, 'Rape in conflict, rape in peace: Questioning the revolutionary potential of international criminal justice for women's human rights' (2010) 33 *Australian Feminist Law Journal* 57; Hilary Charlesworth and Christine Chinkin, 'An alien's review of women and armed conflict' in Dale Stevens and Paul Babie (eds.), *Imagining Law: Essays in Conversation with Judith Gardam* (Adelaide University Press, 2016) 171.

15 Doris Buss, 'Performing legal order: Some feminist thoughts on international criminal law' (2011) 11 *International Criminal Law Review* 409, 423.

16 See Sandesh Sivakumuran, 'Lost in translation: UN responses to sexual violence against men and boys in situations of armed conflict' (2010) 92 *International Review of the Red Cross* 259.

violence leads to awkward questions about how to name the type of justice they dispense: Gender justice? Feminist justice? And what is the difference?[17]

This chapter examines the treatment of international crimes of sexual violence by peoples' tribunals through a focus on the former Yugoslavia. Through analysis of the documents produced by these tribunals and accounts by those who were present, it examines the broader significance of such tribunals beyond their meaning for the participants by exploring two key questions. First, what do peoples' tribunals offer to victim-survivors of international crimes of sexual violence that is lacking in official courts? Second, to what extent do 'mainstream' peoples' tribunals suffer from the same defects as official courts in marginalising international sexual violence crimes, thereby rendering 'women's tribunals' necessary to deal with these issues? In responding to these questions, this chapter provides an overview of peoples' tribunals and women's courts and tribunals and the ways in which they are similar to, and differ from, official courts and tribunals. Next, it analyses the Berne and Barcelona Hearings of the Permanent Peoples' Tribunal (PPT) and the Women's Court in Sarajevo against the backdrop of the ICTY. It concludes by reflecting on the approaches taken by peoples' tribunals and women's courts to law and justice.

3.2 Peoples' Tribunals

The first peoples' tribunals modelled themselves explicitly on criminal trials.[18] Organisers of the original Russell Tribunal in 1967 invoked the precedent, and borrowed the name, of the International Military Tribunal held at Nuremberg to try Nazi leaders after World War II. The Tribunal's president, French philosopher Jean-Paul Sartre, spoke of the Russell Tribunal standing in for a permanent court which in 1967 did not yet exist.[19] Despite agreement in Rome in 1998 to establish a permanent

[17] On gender justice, see Louise Chappell, *The Politics of Gender Justice at the International Criminal Court* (Cambridge University Press, 2016).

[18] Gabrielle Simm and Andrew Byrnes, 'International Peoples' Tribunals in Asia: Political theatre, juridical farce or meaningful intervention?' (2014) 4 *Asian Journal of International Law* 103; Arthur Jay Klinghoffer and Judith Apter Klinghoffer, *International Citizens' Tribunals: Mobilizing Public Opinion to Advance Human Rights* (Palgrave MacMillan, 2002).

[19] Jean-Paul Sartre, 'Answer and Commentary to De Gaulle's Letter Banning the Tribunal from France' in John Duffett (ed.), *Against the Crime of Silence: Proceedings of the*

international criminal court, peoples' tribunals continue to be held. So what do peoples' tribunals offer that state courts and tribunals lack?

One way in which peoples' tribunals differ from criminal trials and more closely resemble the human rights jurisdiction is their focus on state crime and collective responsibility. State responsibility for crimes was included in the International Law Commission Draft Articles on State Responsibility until 2000 so that state crime could well have been adopted as part of international law from 1967 to 2000, a period when many peoples' tribunals were active.[20] However, since Nuremberg and Tokyo, international criminal law has focused on *individual* criminal responsibility.[21] This may go some way to satisfying demands for accountability, but in many cases, activists who organise peoples' tribunals call for systemic change. This is particularly the case with feminist theory and activism, which in the legal context has drawn attention to the implicit valorisation of masculinity in apparently neutral international law.[22] Human rights treaty bodies offer communications mechanisms that may be available to individuals and groups, provided the state against whom the complaint is made is party to the relevant instruments.[23] International courts and tribunals, such as the International Court of Justice (ICJ), are the appropriate forum for deciding issues of state responsibility in disputes between states. However, legal barriers, such as difficulties in establishing jurisdiction and the lack of standing of peoples, individuals, and other non-state actors to appear before the

International War Crimes Tribunal (Clarion/Simon & Schuster, 1970) 28; Peter Limqueco and Peter Weiss (eds.), *Prevent the Crime of Silence: Reports from the Sessions of the International War Crimes Tribunal Founded by Bertrand Russell* (Allen Lane, 1971) 29, 32–33.

20 On 'the ghost' of former draft article 19, see James Crawford, Jacqueline Peel and Simon Olleson, 'The ILC's Articles on Responsibility of States for Internationally Wrongful Acts: Completion of the Second Reading' (2001) 12 *European Journal of International Law* 963, 977.

21 Gerry Simpson, *Law, War & Crime: War Crimes, Trials and the Reinvention of International Criminal Law* (Polity Press, 2007).

22 Hilary Charlesworth, Christine Chinkin and Shelley Wright, 'Feminist approaches to international law' (1991) 85 *American Journal of International Law* 613; Hilary Charlesworth and Christine Chinkin, *The Boundaries of International Law: A Feminist Analysis* (Manchester University Press, 2000); Doris Buss and Ambreena Manji (eds.), *International Law: Modern Feminist Approaches* (Hart Publishing, 2005).

23 For example, provided the state subject to the complaint is party to both the head Convention and its Optional Protocol, complaints can be made under the Optional Protocol to the Convention on the Elimination of All Forms of Discrimination against Women, New York, 10 December 1999, 2131 UNTS 83, in force 20 December 2000.

Court, combined with political pressures, mean that the Court is not necessarily available to hold states responsible.[24]

The similarities between official courts and peoples' tribunals have been unsettling for states, concerned that observers might mistake peoples' tribunals for 'the real thing'. In particular, the source of legitimacy of state courts comes into question when non-state actors take on this role. In order to introduce a level of gravitas into proceedings, official courts have rituals and costumes, such as the robes and wigs or caps (depending on whether it is the civil or common law system) worn by judges. Having civil society actors 'play-acting' the role of judges draws unwelcome attention to the ritual, ceremony and performative aspects of official courts.[25] In international law, parties often play a part in selecting who will judge the case. For example, at the ICJ there is provision for parties to nominate an ad hoc judge where none of the judges has the nationality of the state party to the dispute.[26] In arbitration each party typically selects one arbitrator, with the chair selected by either the arbitrators or a neutral third party.[27] Peoples' tribunals attract criticism for selecting judges known for their sympathy to the cause at issue. Nevertheless, the panels of peoples' tribunals, who are typically chosen by a much broader group of people, are maligned as biased and having prejudged the outcome. Hence peoples' tribunals are sometimes regarded as threatening because, by taking on the role of a court, they highlight the fragility of the legitimacy and authority of official courts and tribunals.

While peoples' tribunals adopt a juridical format and, like official courts and tribunals, pass judgment on the evidence presented, their approach to law is somewhat different. Dianne Otto identifies three functions of peoples' tribunals.[28] First, they seek to enforce existing law.

[24] See Byrnes and Simm, Chapter 1 in this volume.

[25] Christine Chinkin, comments made at 'International Law and Peoples' Tribunals' seminar, Melbourne Law School, 13 September 2013; on ritualism in the UN human rights system, see Hilary Charlesworth and Emma Larking (eds.), *Human Rights and the Universal Periodic Review: Rituals and Ritualism* (Cambridge University Press, 2015).

[26] Statute of the International Court of Justice, San Francisco, 26 June 1945, TS 993, in force 24 October 1945, article 31.

[27] Parties to disputes arbitrated under the auspices of the Permanent Court of Arbitration are entitled to 'judges of their own choice': Convention for the Pacific Settlement of International Disputes, The Hague, 18 October 1907, UKTS 6 (1971) Cmnd 4575, in force 26 January 1910, articles 37 and 45; at the International Court of Justice (ICJ) parties are entitled to appoint an ad hoc judge if there is no judge of their nationality sitting on the court: ICJ Statute, article 31(2) and (3).

[28] Otto, above n. 6.

Where official courts fail to enforce existing law due to legal or political factors that protect those in power, peoples' tribunals call attention to the injustice of this bias. Most peoples' tribunals do not claim to enforce law in the sense of policing their 'verdicts'; but as tribunals of opinion or ethical tribunals, their public statements assist in creating political pressure for official bodies to carry out their duties. Second, peoples' tribunals seek to create new law – that is, to create an opening or new way of looking at the world. In this way, peoples' tribunals challenge lawyers to be creative and imaginative in their interpretation of law. Third, peoples' tribunals are deeply critical of law and look beyond law to a type of justice that cannot be rendered in official courts and tribunals.

A key aspect of justice beyond the law is that peoples' tribunals provide an opportunity for victim-activist witnesses to testify and receive acknowledgement of the injustice they have suffered. In peoples' tribunals, the emphasis is on a panel, whose members are sometimes referred to as judges, sometimes as a jury, that listens to those testifying.[29] Less attention is given to the accused's defence: in peoples' tribunals, defendants are usually absent as they typically decline the invitation to send a representative or provide evidence. Peoples' tribunals invite reflection on the extent to which all of us, including panel members and organisers, are implicated in the wrongs suffered by the victims and which are the subject of trial.[30] Peoples' tribunals also invite the listeners to take action to challenge the injustice.

While there are clear features that differentiate peoples' tribunals from state courts, peoples' tribunals also differ from each other in important ways. Peoples' tribunals range from the extremely formal and legalistic to more informal and poetic conceptions of justice. Some peoples' tribunals are held as part of a protest or rally to publicise an issue and attract world media attention. One such example was the Global Tribunal on Violations of Women's Human Rights, also known as the Vienna Tribunal, held in Vienna in 1993 at the United Nations World Conference on Human Rights.[31] It aimed to publicise the widespread neglect of violations of women's rights. Similarly, the Nobel Women's Initiative held an

29 Ibid.

30 See, e.g., Dehm, Chapter 7 in this volume: 'We are accusing not just the EU, or European governments, or specific officers. But we are accusing everyone, on all levels, because it's a very complex problem. . . . We're accusing ourselves and all citizens of Europe.'

31 Charlotte Bunch and Niamh Reilly, *Demanding Accountability: The Global Campaign and Vienna Tribunal for Women's Human Rights* (Center for Women's Global Leadership and United Nations Development Programme, 1994).

International Tribunal on Crimes against Women of Burma in New York in 2010.[32] The testimony – organised as accounts of sexual violence, violations of political and civil and economic, social and cultural rights – aimed to maintain international pressure on the government in an election year. Other tribunals draw attention to the performative aspects of a trial. Tribunal 12 on Migration and Asylum in Europe was held in Stockholm in 2011.[33] The audience purchased tickets to view actors playing asylum-seekers providing testimony on their experiences. Had asylum-seekers given evidence in person, they would have risked being arrested and removed from Europe. In addition to the audience of around 1,500 in Stockholm, the performance was digitally streamed live to approximately 6,000 people throughout Europe.[34]

To what extent do peoples' tribunals suffer from the same defects as formal courts in excluding from consideration harms suffered by women? Or are peoples' tribunals a juridical form and a site for activism which can be adopted by feminists? The plethora of women's courts and tribunals appears to indicate that they are well suited for such purposes. Such tribunals have the potential to act as safe spaces in which women whose rights have been violated have the opportunity to tell their stories on their own terms, rather than having their testimony truncated into questions and answers to conform to the rules of evidence. This is particularly important in relation to sexual violence where testifiers sometimes experience giving evidence in court as re-traumatisation rather than an opportunity for catharsis.

Peoples' tribunals constantly confront scepticism about their legitimacy, and this risk is particularly acute in peoples' tribunals dealing with 'women's issues'. Like international criminal trials, they have been derided as show trials. While peoples' tribunals provide access to a form of civil society justice as an alternative to official justice, they thereby risk further marginalising and 'ghettoising' violations suffered by women as unworthy of official consideration. Like track II peace negotiations conducted outside official government channels, women's tribunals enable the 'main game' to proceed in parallel in official courts and tribunals that remain oblivious to 'side issues' raised by feminist activists.[35]

[32] Nobel Women's Initiative, 'International Tribunal on Crimes Against Women of Burma', www.nobelwomensinitiative.org/category/international-tribunal-on-crimes-against-women-of-burma/.

[33] Tribunal 12 archive, www.web.archive.org/web/20130318105617/http://tribunal12.org/.

[34] Dehm, above n. 30. [35] Chinkin, above n. 25.

Yet there is also a risk that women's tribunals unrealistically raise the expectations of victim-survivors, who may not understand the difference between official courts and peoples' tribunals.[36] These women may be disappointed at the dismissive response or, worse, silence of states and other entities whom they regard as responsible for the injuries they have suffered, despite the verdict of a women's tribunal. Yet risks and challenges, such as an official court or tribunal deciding to find an accused not guilty or states refusing to enforce a judgement by handing over a fugitive, are equally present in international criminal justice.

3.3 Women's Courts and Tribunals

One of the first peoples' tribunals to address 'women's issues' was the International Court on Crimes against Women held in Brussels in 1976 (the Brussels Tribunal).[37] It modelled itself on the Russell Tribunal held ten years earlier. Simone de Beauvoir, who was also a panel member at the Russell Tribunal, sent a message of support as she was unable to attend: 'The Tribunal is in itself a feat. It heralds more to come. I salute this Tribunal as being the start of a radical decolonisation of women.'[38] European participants provided the bulk of the evidence, although testifiers from all parts of the world participated. Most testimony was devoted to violence against women, which included prostitution and pornography. Testimony was also provided on sexual and reproductive freedom, crimes perpetrated by the medical profession, persecution of lesbians, crimes within the family, economic crimes, third world women, immigrant women and religious minority women. The Tribunal organisers' decision to exclude male reporters from the proceedings generated much controversy both within and outside the tribunal.[39] The publication of proceedings included a 'herstory', outlining the developments that led to the tribunal, and a critique of the tribunal, analysing its impact, consequences and image in the media.[40]

Starting in 1994, there has been a series of World Courts of Women. Civil society organisations, El Taller and the Asian Women's Human Rights Council, have held women's courts primarily in Africa and Asia.

[36] Dogolpol, above n. 5.

[37] Diana E. H. Russell and Nicole Van de Ven (eds.), *Crimes Against Women: Proceedings of the International Tribunal* (Les Femmes, 1976), www.dianarussell.com/f/Crimes_Against_Women_Tribunal.pdf.

[38] Ibid., 5. [39] Ibid., 164. [40] Ibid., Part III and IV.

The first session, the Asian Court of Women on Violence against Women, was held in Lahore, Pakistan, in 1993.[41] Several World Courts of Women have been held as counter-conferences to international meetings and summits. For example, the International Court of Women on Reproductive Technologies was a counter-summit to the UN Conference on Population and Development held in 1994 in Cairo, while the World Court of Women against Racism was held at the NGO Forum of the World Conference against Racism, in Durban in 2001.[42] One of the first World Courts of Women was the Asian Court on Trafficking and War Crimes against Women in Tokyo.[43] Organised in conjunction with sixty-four women's groups in Japan, it was the precursor to the better known Tokyo Women's Tribunal held in 2000. The court condemned war crimes, including organised and systemic rape, torture, detention, forced displacement and abduction that constituted acts of military sexual slavery, and demanded that Japan prosecute and punish the criminals and compensate the families and survivors.[44]

The aims and methodology of the World Courts of Women are articulated in terms of providing an alternative justice, one that is less rational and more poetic than that provided in official courts, or in many other peoples' tribunals. Corinne Kumar, the Secretary-General of El Taller International, writes that the World Courts of Women seek 'a new political imaginary' which 'speaks to an ethic of care':[45]

> Women's Courts are radically feminist in nature because they underline that women are the most vulnerable subjects of the state, and that their personal experience of violence, rape, torture or discrimination is a political issue. The specific feminist methodology of Women's Courts insists on an intersection between political and personal, which is given affective and aesthetic expression (women sing, weep, laugh and yell during the trials) representing thereby both their survival and resistance. Their testimonies, the space they occupy and the affectivity they are allowed to express, help to create different kinds of judicial system and juridical practices. Women's Courts therefore aim at evolving new concepts of justice itself.[46]

[41] Since then hearings have taken place in Bangalore, Cairo, Vimochana, Kathmandu, Beirut, Beijing, Nairobi, Casablanca, Auckland, Havana, Sydney, Dhaka, Mumbai, Lusaka, Bamako, Caracas, Karachi, Bali and Puerto Alegre: Corinne Kumar, 'Towards a New Political Imaginary' in Müge Gürsoy Sökmen (ed.), *The World Tribunal on Iraq: Making the Case against War* (Interlink Publishing Group, 2008) 448, 462.

[42] Ibid., 462–64. [43] Ibid., 462.

[44] Asian Women's Human Rights Council, *In the Court of Women II: Asia Tribunal on Women's Human Rights in Tokyo* (Asian Women's Human Rights Council, 1994).

[45] Kumar, above n. 41, 452. [46] Ibid.

Unlike the Brussels Tribunal, the World Courts of Women are not women-only spaces; however, they are organised by women and the majority of witnesses, experts and panellists are usually women. Other peoples' tribunals usually include women in a range of roles, but they are more similar to the majority of official courts and tribunals where male participants are represented in higher numbers. A distinctive feature of the World Courts of Women as articulated by Kumar is their commitment to 'different kinds of judicial system and judicial practices'. The reference to 'an ethics of care' recalls psychologist Carol Gilligan's 1982 work, *In a Different Voice*, arguing that women are different from men because women have an increased empathy with the sufferings of others, whereas Gilligan claims that men are more abstract and interested in logic and reason.[47] In the context of peoples' tribunals dealing with international sexual violence crimes, there is a risk that associating women and feminist methodology with the affective and aesthetic will further marginalise feminist approaches to such crimes.

Aside from the World Courts of Women, there have been other women's tribunals organised independently as ad hoc events as well as women's tribunals organised by the Center for Women's Global Leadership at Rutgers University in the United States. In addition to the women's tribunals already mentioned, which have tended to focus on violence against women, the Women's Tribunal on Sexual Violence on (sic) Women during Conflict, held in Kathmandu, 8 December 2014, is particularly relevant here. It is important to acknowledge that women's tribunals have also been held to highlight the gendered aspects of trade and climate change, for example, rather than focusing solely on violence against women.[48]

Organisations with experience in holding women's tribunals have published guides to assist others. In 2005 the Center for Women's Global Leadership published 'Women Testify', which is based on the center's experiences of organising women's tribunals.[49] In 2016 the Asia Pacific

[47] Carol Gilligan, *In a Different Voice* (Harvard University Press, 1982, 1993).

[48] See, e.g., Asia Pacific Women's Tribunal on the World Trade Organization, Hong Kong, 14–15 December 2005: Don't globalise hunger!, 'WTO Guilty as Charged', www.dontglobalisehunger.org/wto_guiltyascharged.php; Tribunals on Gender and Climate Justice have been held in India, Pakistan, Nepal and Bangladesh: White Band, 'Tribunals on Gender and Climate Justice', www.whiteband.org/en/book/export/html/13601.

[49] Niamh Reilly and Linda Posluszny, *Women Testify: A Planning Guide for Popular Tribunals and Hearings* (Center for Women's Global Leadership, Rutgers University, 2005).

Forum for Women, Law and Development, an umbrella organisation, published 'Speak and Be Heard' written by Grace Harbour, who works with the UN Mechanism for International Criminal Tribunals.[50] The guide is based on interviews with organisers of some of the best known women's tribunals as well as documentary research. Guides cover issues such as the possibilities and limits of women's tribunals, witness safety and dignity, strategic decisions (about timing, selection of judges and witness for instance), logistics, media, the preparation of witnesses to testify and conduct media interviews and continuing momentum after a tribunal has concluded. 'Women Testify' provides sample statements by witnesses and judges while 'Speak and Be heard' includes a list of women's tribunals, a pro forma for legal frameworks to be used by judges, a sample verdict template and sample witness consent form.

3.4 The International Criminal Tribunal for the Former Yugoslavia

The conflict in the former Yugoslavia has been subject to extensive international judicial scrutiny.[51] Established in 1993 pursuant to UN Security Council resolution 827, the ICTY began its first trial in mid-1996.[52] Ongoing cases are being finalised by the UN Mechanism for International Criminal Tribunals. In 1995, two sessions of the PPT considered the extent to which the conduct of the conflict in the former Yugoslavia was consistent with international humanitarian law. Twenty years later, in 2015, the Women's Court: Feminist Approach to Justice convened in Sarajevo to address ongoing injustices arising from the conflict.[53] In light of the attention given to crimes of sexual violence committed in the wars in the former Yugoslavia, particularly at the ICTY where over a third of cases included prosecutions for sexual violence crimes, this section compares the PPT hearings in 1995 and the Women's Court held in 2015.

[50] Asia Pacific Forum on Women, Law and Development, 'Speak and Be Heard: APWLD Guide to Women's Tribunals' (2016), http://apwld.org/apwld-launches-speak-and-be-heard-apwld-guide-to-womens-tribunals/.

[51] *Application of the Convention on the Prevention and Punishment of the Crime of Genocide* (Bosnia and Herzegovina v Yugoslavia) [1996] ICJ Rep 595; *Application of the Convention on the Prevention and Punishment of the Crime of Genocide* (Bosnia and Herzegovina *v* Serbia and Montenegro) [2007] ICJ Rep 43.

[52] UN SC Resolution 827 (1993) concerning Yugoslavia, 25 May 1993, UN Doc S/RES/827.

[53] Women's Court - Feminist Approach to Justice, www.zenskisud.org/en/index.html.

The ICTY is the longest running and probably best resourced international criminal tribunal to date. Its jurisprudence includes some of the most progressive and innovative judgments on international sexual violence crimes. When the ICTY made some of its earlier decisions, feminists were struggling to achieve recognition of women's rights as human rights and of harms suffered to a greater extent by women as war crimes, crimes against humanity and genocide. As part of the ICTY's legacy project, in 2016 prosecutors from the ICTY published an analysis of its sexual crimes jurisprudence that aims to assist prosecutors at national levels.[54]

While the jurisprudence of the ICTY has often been celebrated as embodying the desired outcome of feminist advocacy, some feminists have appraised it from a more critical perspective.[55] Many of these critiques apply to the field of international criminal law more generally.[56] Examples include the ICTY's foregrounding of sexual crimes, which risks backgrounding no less serious economic, social and political harms. The treatment of victims as witnesses in a criminal trial, divorced from their identities pre- and post-conflict, is a disempowering experience that amplifies the impact of the crime.[57] Further 'many victims of sexual violence who have testified before the ICTY have found their experiences as witnesses humiliating and disrespectful.'[58]

The ICTY had a prosecutorial policy of indicting perpetrators of all nationalities of sexual violence against victim-survivors of all nationalities. Cases involving sexual violence documented crimes committed in

[54] Baron Serge Brammertz and Michelle Jarvis (eds.), *Prosecuting Conflict-related Sexual Violence at the ICTY* (Oxford University Press, 2016).

[55] Kirsten Campbell, 'The gender of transitional justice: Law, sexual violence and the International Criminal Tribunal for the former Yugoslavia' (2007) 1 *International Journal of Transitional Justice* 411; Kirsten Campbell, 'The trauma of justice: Sexual violence, crimes against humanity and the International Criminal Tribunal for the former Yugoslavia' (2004) 13 *Social & Legal Studies* 329.

[56] Frédéric Mégret, 'International Criminal Justice: A Critical Research Agenda' in Christine Schwöbel (ed.), *Critical Approaches to International Criminal Law: an Introduction* (Routledge, 2014) 17, 37; Doris Buss, 'Is international criminal law feminist?' (2011) 11 *International Criminal Law Review* 409; Leila Nadya Sadat, 'Avoiding the creation of a gender ghetto in international criminal law' (2011) 11 *International Criminal Law Review* 655.

[57] Doris Buss, 'Knowing women: Translating patriarchy in international criminal law' (2014) 23 *Social & Legal Studies* 73.

[58] Katherine M. Franke, 'Gendered subjects of transitional justice' (2006) 15 *Columbia Journal of Gender and Law* 813, 818.

Bosnia and Herzegovina, Croatia and Kosovo, perpetrated by Bosnian Serbs and Serbians, Bosnian Croats and Croatians, Bosnian Muslims, Kosovo Albanians and foreign fighters.[59] The prosecutorial policy of the ICTY to charge defendants of all ethnicities with sexual crimes against victims of all ethnicities has challenged, but not dismantled, a hierarchy of wrongs.[60] Feminists have challenged the focus on rapes of Bosnian women by Serbs as detracting from the seriousness of rapes perpetrated by, and against, individuals of other ethnicities.[61] Further, the ICTY's acceptance of 'ethnic rape' as genocide potentially contributes to the ongoing social ostracism of victim-survivors and children born of rape.[62]

3.5 The Permanent Peoples' Tribunal Berne and Barcelona Hearings

While the ICTY was preparing for trials, the PPT held two hearings on the conflict in the former Yugoslavia in Berne, Switzerland, in February 1995[63] and in Barcelona, Spain, in December 1995.[64] These hearings had a broader scope than the ICTY processes, as they included consideration of the responsibility of states and international agencies. They also directed attention to the role of the media in 'creating a climate of fear and xenophobia and ... instigating racial hate'.[65] The PPT suggested a broader range of individuals who could be charged than did the ICTY at the time, including Slobodan Milošević (who was indicted by the ICTY in 1999) and Franjo Tudjman, the presidents of the Federal Republic

[59] Saeeda Verrall, 'The picture of sexual violence in the former Yugoslavia conflicts as reflected in the ICTY judgments' in Brammertz and Jarvis, above n. 54, 302.

[60] Olivera Simić, 'Rape, Silence and Denial' in Martina Fisher and Olivera Simić (eds.), *Transitional Justice and Reconciliation: Lessons from the Balkans* (Routledge 2016) 102. See also Olivera Simić, *Silenced Victims of Wartime Rape* (Routledge, forthcoming).

[61] On ethnic rape in Rwanda, see Doris Buss, 'Rethinking "rape as a weapon of war"' (2009) 17 *Feminist Legal Studies* 145.

[62] Karen Engle, 'Feminism and its (dis)contents: Criminalizing wartime rape in Bosnia and Herzegovina' (2005) 99 *American Journal of International Law* 778.

[63] Permanent Peoples' Tribunal, *Crimes against Humanity in the Former Yugoslavia I*, Berne, Switzerland, 17–20 February 1995, English version on file with author, Italian version available on the PPT website (hereafter Berne).

[64] The Permanent Peoples' *Crimes against Humanity in the Former Yugoslavia II*, Barcelona, Spain, 7–11 December 1995, English version on file with author, Italian version available on the PPT website (hereafter Barcelona).

[65] Ibid, 13–14. See further Dubravka Žarkov, *The Body of War: Media, Ethnicity, and Gender in the Break-up of Yugoslavia* (Duke University Press, 2007).

of Yugoslavia and Croatia respectively. The PPT also made findings about crimes, such as genocide, that were not then under investigation by the ICTY.[66]

The Barcelona Tribunal noted that it took place 'in parallel' with the ICTY, which

> could render meaningless any parallel activity of the PPT, the role of which, as an instance of opinion, is to draw attention and to fill a major gap in the international law. . . . It is not so. On the contrary, the PPT feels that the development of a procedure in parallel to that of the UN tribunal, far from weakening the UN initiative, reinforces and enhances it.[67]

The Barcelona Tribunal continued that its jurisdiction, 'owing precisely to its being an opinion tribunal – includes the political responsibilities and the causes at the root of crimes against humanity, which nonetheless lie beyond the field investigated by criminal courts'.[68] A legal advisor to the ICTY, Payam Akhavan, attended the Barcelona Tribunal and gave a presentation on the ICTY's work.[69] Further, he proposed a collaboration between the Barcelona Tribunal and the UN Tribunal 'so that the latter could make use of the conclusion of the former and comply more effectively with its mandate'.[70]

The PPT in Berne heard oral evidence from around thirty-five witnesses, including on sexual violence, especially against Muslim women.[71] The jury recommended inquiries be undertaken into systemic violations of human rights, 'especially those committed against women and children such as sexual abuse, mutilation, and other offences perpetrated against male individuals'.[72]

> The Tribunal identifies clear traits of crimes against humanity and of genocide in the criminal practice, documented in detail, of the massive and systemic sexual violence exerted by the Serbian troops on Muslim women as a form of war and as an element of the policy of 'ethnic purge.' In fact, this violence constitutes a Crime against Humanity inasmuch as it is both a sexual violence damaging the women's freedom and dignity, and a violence aimed at forcing them to become pregnant – ie. of determining

66 See further Andrew Byrnes and Gabrielle Simm, 'Peoples' Tribunals, international law and the use of force' (2013) 36 *UNSW Law Review* 711, 734–35.

67 Barcelona, above n. 64, 9.

68 Ibid.

69 Payam Akhavan was Chief Prosecutor at the Iran People's Tribunal held in The Hague in 2012 which also dealt with crimes of sexual violence: Payam Akhavan, 'Is grassroots justice a viable alternative to impunity?: The case of the Iran People's Tribunal' (2017) 31 *Human Rights Quarterly* 73.

70 Barcelona, above n. 64, 15.

71 Berne, above n. 63, 10.

72 Ibid., 11.

> the birth of Serbian children and Muslim women and therefore violating not only these women's sexual freedom, but also their right to the self-determination of motherhood. Hence, women are twice reduced to objects: through sexual violence and by the imposition of unwanted motherhood.[73]

The Barcelona session of the PPT applied the accepted international definition as set out in the Genocide Convention to the rapes of Muslim women by Serbs. It paid particular attention to genocidal intent and concluded that the perpetrators, their military commanders and political leaders were responsible 'for crimes against humanity and for the crime of genocide including in the latter category, ethnic rapes'.[74] It then

> recommended that the Hague Tribunal [the ICTY] qualify as a crime against humanity the acts of ethnic rape, according to article 5 of its statute, and also as genocidal deeds following the ascertainment of the corresponding intentions, interpreting the provisions of article 4 of the Statute in these terms.[75]

While the Barcelona Tribunal referred to other instances of war crimes committed by Croats and Bosniaks against Serbs, it did not mention rape committed by other nationalities against Serbian women.

The PPT hearings in Berne and Barcelona were 'ahead of their time', best viewed as predecessors to the jurisprudence, if not the actual establishment, of the ICTY. Held in two sessions over several days in 1995, they were part of a range of civil society campaigns aiming to influence the ICTY to recognise sexual violence as international crimes.

3.6 The Women's Court: Feminist Approach to Justice – Sarajevo

Even in cases where the ICTY convicted perpetrators of international sexual violence crimes, the women who survived found the legal process wanting. Writing in 2015, Janine Natalya Clark provides the example of three women whom she interviewed whose assailants were sentenced to terms of between nine and eighteen years by the ICTY. In a context where many perpetrators were not charged or were found not guilty, these women who were able to testify before the ICTY might be regarded as having received the best that international criminal justice could offer. Yet twenty years later, all three women continued to suffer the ongoing effects of their rapes in the form of physical and mental health problems,

[73] Barcelona, above n. 64, 19. [74] Ibid., 34. [75] Ibid., 40.

relationship breakdown, the need to relocate and severe economic hardship. One woman received threats from her rapist after he was released; in another case, one of the assailants was still free.[76]

In 2015, a Women's Court was held in Sarajevo, Bosnia. Žarana Papić proposed the idea of a women's court in 2000 and the idea was revived in 2006.[77] Preparations began in earnest in 2010 by feminist networks in the seven countries of the former Yugoslavia, led by Women in Black, 'a world-wide network of women committed to peace with justice' whose members conduct silent vigils while dressed in black.[78] Titled the Women's Court: Feminist Approach to Justice, the court aimed to provide a space for the testimonies of women about the violence they suffered during and following the wars of the 1990s in both public and private spheres. The Women's Court was designed to remedy what organisers considered to be the defects of the ICTY. In addition, the Special Court for War Crimes in Serbia had by this time lost credibility among organisers and victim-witnesses due to the accused being released pending trial and a decrease in the numbers of trials.[79]

While Belgrade had been considered as a potential venue as a way of bringing the court to the 'the belly of the beast', it did not feel safe there for victim-witnesses following the return to power of some perpetrators and their accomplices in the 2012 elections and attacks on organisers of the Women's Court in 2014. Sarajevo was selected as '"the most Yugoslav city", a multi-ethnic city, the geographical centre of the former Yugoslavia' and important both symbolically and in real terms for the amount of suffering that had occurred there.[80]

As with most peoples' tribunals, the defendants were absent, so the focus of the Women's Court was on the victim-survivors who testified. At sessions held in the Bosnian Cultural Centre, Sarajevo, from 7 to 10 May 2015, thirty-five women gave evidence before a supportive audience of around 400 human rights activists, survivors, researchers and journalists.[81]

[76] Janine Natalya Clark, 'Transitional justice as recognition: An analysis of the Women's Court in Sarajevo' (2016) 10 *International Journal of Transitional Justice* 67, 70–71.

[77] Staša Zajović, 'The Women's Court: A Feminist Approach to Justice – Review of the Process of Organizing the Women's Court' in Staša Zajović, *Women's Court: About the Process* (Women in Black, 2015) 2 www.helsinki.org.rs/doc/stasa%20zajovic%20tekst%20eng.doc. See also Sara de Vido, 'Il Tribunale delle donne in Sarajevo' [The Women's Tribunal in Sarajevo] in Silvia Camilotti and Susanne Regazzoni (eds.), *Venti anni di pace freddo in Bosnia Erzegovina* [*Twenty Years of Cold Peace in Bosnia Herzegovina*] (Edizioni Ca' Foscari, 2016) 47.

[78] Women in Black, www.womeninblack.org

[79] Zajović, above n. 77, 12.

[80] Ibid., 16.

[81] Clark, above n. 76, 78.

Women testified about losing their homes, their husbands being killed, the conscription of their sons, women's resistance to warmongering and their experiences of sexual violence.[82] The testimony 'highlighted the continuity of violence against women in both war and peace'.[83] 'The core of the process is *listening* to women . . . The women whose voices are heard at these public hearings have suffered grave injustice'.[84] The seven judges, referred to as Judicial Council members, comprised academics and activists, several of whom engage in both research and activism, working in disciplines such as law, sociology and history from countries of the former Yugoslavia, the United Kingdom, the United States and Australia.[85] Organisers of the Women's Court saw it not as a substitute for, but rather as a supplement to, official mechanisms.[86] The designation 'court' or 'tribunal' was intended metaphorically.[87] Its aim was not to find individuals guilty and pass sentence on them, so its focus was not on the rights of the accused but on 'naming . . . the social, political, economic forces which have offered structural support to, and thus led to, injustice'.[88] It addressed not only the perpetrators but also the relevant national and international institutions and decision-making bodies.[89] According to its website, the Women's Court 'does not deliver judgments, but does deliver public condemnations. . . . WC can initiate appropriate measures against a perpetrator of a crime, including collecting evidence for legal action.'[90] Nevertheless, the Women's Court did issue Preliminary Decisions and Recommendations. Women in Black also plan to publish a collection of testimonies and related materials.[91] In the absence of an official judgment, my analysis of the Women's Court here relies on the preliminary decisions and reflections by the organisers and journalists who attended.

[82] Ibid., 79–80. [83] Ibid.

[84] Daša Gordana Duhaček, 'The Women's Court: A feminist approach to in/justice' (2015) 22 *European Journal of Women's Studies* 159, 161.

[85] Professor Vesna Rakić-Vodilenić (Belgrade, Serbia) President; Charlotte Bunch (Center for Women's Global Leadership, Rutgers University, USA); Dr Kirsten Campell (Goldsmiths College, London, UK), Gorana Mlinarević (activist and feminist researcher, Sarajevo, Bosnia and Herzegovina); Professor Dianne Otto (Melbourne Law School, Australia); Dr Latinka Perović (Institute for the History of Serbia, Belgrade, Serbia); Vesna Teršelič (Dokumenta-Centre for Dealing with the Past, Zagreb, Croatia): Coalition for RECOM, 'Women's Court: Preliminary Decisions and Recommendations' (2015), www.recom.link/womens-court-preliminary-decisions-and-recommendations.

[86] Duhaček, above n. 84, 160. [87] Ibid., 161. [88] Ibid. [89] Ibid., 162.

[90] Women's Court - Feminist Approach to Justice, 'Methodology of Work', www.zenskisud.org/en/Metodologija.html.

[91] Thanks to Olivera Simić for drawing my attention to the Preliminary Decisions and planned publication.

Following two days of testimony, the Judicial Council read the Preliminary Decisions and Recommendations, addressing the witnesses and acknowledging them as 'an authentic part of history'. The Judicial Council drew attention to the differences between official courts and women's courts, stating that '[i]n formal legal proceedings you are treated as victims or as providing legal evidence but in the Women's Court you decided to speak loudly and under your own names, and in your own way.' It organised the issues raised by the witnesses as 'five thematic crimes', namely, the crime of war against the civilian population, the crime of using women's bodies as a battlefield, the crime of militaristic violence, the crime of persecution of those who are different in war and peace and the crime of economic and social violence. The statement of Preliminary Decisions then denounced war as systemic criminality and listed those responsible, namely all states in the Balkan region, citizens, religious leadership, communities and corporations and individuals who profiteered. As with most peoples' tribunals, the Women's Court found states, corporations and groups responsible rather than named individuals. Finally, the Judicial Council made recommendations as follows: record the history presented through the Women's Court; end militarism; uphold the economic and social rights of women and reverse privatisation; provide social and health services to women; provide reparations and redress and an end to impunity; end the 'patriarchal and militaristic attitudes that perpetuate and feed all forms of violence and discrimination against women'; and finally condemn intolerance and violence on the basis of differences.[92]

What was the feminist approach to justice that the organisers claimed characterised the Women's Court? After two years of preparation, organisers identified the need to create a safe space for women to testify. They started feminist discussion circles in which women were able to discuss readings, learn from each other and critically reflect. These processes later 'became part of support to potential witnesses'.[93] A feminist 'ethics of care' for women witnesses was a key aspect of what organisers identified as feminist about the women's court.[94] Another motivation for the Women's Court was to make visible women's contributions to the processes of transitional justice, from which they are marginalised.[95] 'Autonomy' and 'appreciation of different rhythms of work' were also listed as feminist principles by which the Women's Court operated.[96]

92 Preliminary Decisions, above n. 85. 93 Zajović, above n. 77, 10. 94 Ibid., 7.
95 Ibid., 5. 96 Ibid., 4.

The focus of the court was broader than many peoples' tribunals that focus primarily on international crimes of sexual violence. The Women's Court considered 'ethnically-based violence, militaristic violence, the continuity of gender-based violence and economic violence (including privatisation)'. For example, one of the participants in the organising process for the court expressed the aim of the women's court as follows:

> To show at the WC the continuum, the unbroken thread of violence when a woman's body becomes the battlefield, and how after the war it becomes a redundant, worthless piece of goods on the market within the process of privatization, through economic politics.[97]

Failure to accept responsibility, for example, by attempting to transfer it to 'another nation' or denying or minimising violence committed 'in our name' was cited as a key issue to be addressed.[98]

The Women's Court provides the opportunity to assess why the women who organised it found it necessary despite the legal scrutiny, both official and unofficial, already levelled at that particular conflict and its impact on women. The first factor appears to be that the women's court aimed to examine not only the conflict but also the continuity of violence against women, before, during and after the conflict. Organiser Staša Zajović considers that a feminist methodology is not just about gender violence but also about structural violence. The second factor is the attention given to other aspects of violence, apart from sexual violence. Holding a women's court may be an attempt to remedy the decontextualisation of crimes from women's lived experiences, noted by testifiers and feminist academics as a problematic feature of criminal trials.[99] A third important feature of the women's court is that the organisers conceived it as a process, not just an event. The Women's Court for the Former Yugoslavia involved thousands of women in seven countries in a range of activities over years, thereby reaching a greater audience than those who attended the four days of hearings in Sarajevo in May 2015. At the same time, events such as peoples' tribunals have the advantage of focusing media attention and thereby publicising under-reported issues. These three reasons go some way to explain

97 Ibid., 15.

98 Women's Court – Feminist Approach to Justice, 'About the Women's Court', www.zenskisud.org/en/o-zenskom-sudu.html.

99 Cf the focus on contextualising sexual violence in chapters 6 and 7 of Brammertz and Jarvis, above n. 54.

why a peoples' tribunal was considered necessary, despite the ICTY, but do not demonstrate why specifically a *women*'s court was considered essential.

The Women's Court did not refer to the PPT sessions in Berne and Barcelona; its reference point was the ICTY. As discussed previously, the PPT foreshadowed findings that the ICTY would later make, analysing 'ethnic rape' as a war crime, as a crime against humanity and as genocide. The jurisprudence of the ICTY, binding as it is, appears to have fulfilled the need, if it existed in the countries of the former Yugoslavia, for a clear official legal statement of the nature of the wrongs.

3.7 Conclusion: Peoples' and Feminist Approaches to Law and Justice

In comparing peoples' tribunals and the Women's Court in the former Yugoslavia, each addresses itself to the official body, the ICTY, rather than to other unofficial mechanisms of law and justice. When the PPT held its hearings in 1995, there was no other international peoples' tribunal on this topic. In 2015, the organisers of the Women's Court did not refer to the PPT hearings. Neither tribunal claimed to supplant the official court, rather each aimed to complement it. The methodologies of the PPT and Women's Court were similar, focusing on process rather than outcome. In the twenty years since the Berne and Barcelona hearings, the PPT's methodology has become more like that of the Women's Court, i.e., involving a series of preparatory hearings in different locations leading to a summit.[100] Perhaps the main difference between the two was the Women's Court's explicit focus on women.

Memorialisation and rewriting the historical record are aims shared by peoples' tribunals and women's courts. A key feature of the Women's Court in 2015 is looking back twenty years to assess and acknowledge the continuing effects of sexual violence crimes on women's lives post-conflict. In 2000 the Tokyo Women's Tribunal looked back seventy years and produced a record focused squarely on the violations suffered by 'comfort women' whose experiences had been marginalised in the Tokyo

[100] See, e.g., Permanent Peoples' Tribunal, *Transnational Corporations and Peoples' Rights in Colombia*.

trial. In 2013 the Cambodian Women's Hearing with the Young Generation aimed to educate young people – many of whose parents were forced to marry under the Khmer Rouge regime – and to make connections with ongoing sexual violence more than thirty years after the conflict had ended.[101] There are other examples of peoples' tribunals seeking to assess the legacy of historic wrongs by writing counter-histories that include the stories of the subalterns.[102] Nevertheless, the desire to include aspects of women's experiences in the official record is informed by feminist methodologies that aim to avoid splitting theory from practice.

In light of the discussion, I return to the two questions posed, namely, what do peoples' tribunals offer to victim-survivors of international crimes of sexual violence that is lacking in official courts? Second, to what extent do 'mainstream' peoples' tribunals suffer from the same defects as official courts in marginalising international sexual violence crimes, thereby rendering 'women's tribunals' necessary to deal with these issues?

Peoples' tribunals and women's courts raise the question: What does law look like and to whom?[103] This question had greater significance for the Tokyo Women's Tribunal and the Cambodian Women's Hearings than for the Women's Court for the former Yugoslavia. Since the British and French governments refused to grant visas to the organisers of the First Russell Tribunal, the authority of non-state mechanisms to interpret, pronounce and apply international law has been and continues to be a source of controversy. One way of understanding peoples' tribunals and women's courts would be to see them as an example of legal pluralism. Legal pluralism acknowledges a range of law co-existing in the same space, rather than a sharp distinction between law, created and administered by the state, and non-law, comprising religious, customary, indigenous and civil society codes and practices. It is difficult to find an example of a peoples' tribunal that claims to supplant state mechanisms.

[101] Cambodian Defenders Project, 'Women's Hearing with the Young Generation on Gender-based Violence during the Khmer Rouge Regime Report on the Proceedings' (2013), http://gbvkr.org/wp-content/uploads/2014/05/WomenHearingEng.pdf.

[102] See the Permanent Peoples' Tribunal, *Session on the Armenian Genocide*, Paris, 13–16 April 1984, English version available in Gérard Libaridian (ed.), *A Crime of Silence, The Armenian Genocide: Permanent Peoples' Tribunal* (Zed Books, 1985); and Permanent Peoples' Tribunal, Session, *The Conquest of Latin America and International Law*, Padua-Venice, 5–8 October 1992.

[103] Thanks to Karen O'Connell for this point.

Rather, most peoples' tribunals and women's courts argue that they have different objectives and that their authority derives from elsewhere.

Peoples' tribunals and women's courts might also be seen as a gift back from civil society or women that remedies the defects in state-based law by making it more complete and just. States and their judicial institutions might resist this interpretation, as it is grounded in a view of official law as incomplete and imperfect in ensuring justice. Proponents of women's courts might also resist such a view as falling into the familiar trope of women as a supplement to the masculine norm. Both peoples' tribunals and women's courts appear to envisage law and justice as overlapping but distinct, such that where they do not overlap, there is a gap.[104] Hence, unofficial tribunals appear to regard law as capable of doing both justice and injustice and see themselves as stepping into the breach to provide justice where official courts have failed to do so.

It is difficult to find examples of where both women's courts and 'mainstream' peoples' tribunals have dealt with same issue.[105] This alone suggests that mainstream tribunals do not address 'women's issues' with the same attention and detail as women's courts do. The PPT hearings in 1995 are a rare example of a tribunal that attempted to address sexual violence in conflict substantively as part of a consideration of violations of international humanitarian law in the former Yugoslavia. Yet the PPT and the Women's Court addressed the issue in different ways. The PPT produced a written judgment that in many ways pre-empted the more detailed decisions of the ICTY. The Women's Court eschewed a written judgment in favour of a long preparatory process and oral pronouncement, suggesting that the perceived gap between law and justice renders such attention to law unnecessary.[106]

[104] Lia Kent, 'Interrogating the "gap" between law and justice: East Timor's serious crimes process' (2012) 34 *Human Rights Quarterly* 1021, 1023.

[105] For a useful list of peoples' tribunals until 1992, see Arthur W. Blaser, 'How to advance human rights without really trying: An analysis of nongovernmental tribunals' (1992) 14 *Human Rights Quarterly* 339, 366; and until 2006, Craig Borowiak, 'The World Tribunal on Iraq: Citizens' tribunals and the struggle for accountability' (2008) 30 *New Political Science* 161, 171–73.

[106] The 350-page judgment of the Tokyo Women's Tribunal is an obvious contrast here: *The Prosecutors and the Peoples of the Asia-Pacific Region v. Hirohito et al and the Government of Japan* (PT 2000-1-T) (corrected 31 January 2001), https://web.archive.org/web/20051113024358/http://www1.jca.apc.org/vaww-net-japan/english/womenstribunal2000/judgement.html.

4

The Tokyo Women's Tribunal

Transboundary Activists and the Use of Law's Power

USTINIA DOLGOPOL

4.1 Introduction

Peoples' tribunals tend to be an outgrowth of civil society's perceptions about the shortcomings of the state system and a desire to influence how the international community understands state violence.[1] Despite the creation of the various ad hoc international and hybrid criminal tribunals and the International Criminal Court, individuals and organisations remain frustrated at the lack of response to mass human rights violations.[2] Although the need to hold individuals responsible for the commission of atrocities, especially those who were in positions of power, remains unquestioned by the majority of victims and civil society organisations[3], there is also an increasing realisation that trials will be limited

[1] Cenap Çakmak, 'Civil society actors in international law and world politics: Definition, conceptual framework, problems' (2008) 6 *International Journal of Civil Society Law* 7, 9; see also Gabrielle Simm and Andrew Byrnes, 'International Peoples' Tribunals in Asia' (2014) 4 *Asian Journal of International Law* 103.

[2] In the following pages, the terms 'mass violations of human rights' and 'mass atrocities' will be used interchangeably.

[3] The rights and interests of victims were subjects of discussion at the Kampala Review Conference. See Review Conference of the Rome Statute of the International Criminal Court, Kampala, 31 May–11 June 2010, Official Records RC/11, https://asp.icc-cpi.int/iccdocs/asp_docs/ASP9/OR/RC-11-ENG.pdf, 4, and Annex V(a) 'Stocktaking of international criminal justice, The impact of the Rome Statute system on victims and affected communities', https://asp.icc-cpi.int/iccdocs/asp_docs/RC2010/RC-11-Annex.V.a-ENG.pdf. An overview of the issues discussed at the conference can be gleaned from the following documents: REDRESS, 'The impact of the ICC on victims and affected communities: A report of the victims' rights working group' (2010), www.redress.org/Stocktakingreport2010.pdf; Eric Stover, Camille Crittenden, Alexa Koenig, Victor Peskin and Tracey Gurd, 'The impact of the Rome Statute system on victims and affected communities', discussion paper (April 2010), www.law.berkeley.edu/wp-content/uploads/2016/03/Stover-Crittenden-Koenig-Peskin-Gurd_-The-Impact-of-the-Rome-Statute-System-on-Victims-and-Affected-Communities-2010-04.pdf. See also the website of REDRESS:

in number, thus leaving many survivors with a sense that the harms they have suffered have gone and will continue to go unrecognised and unpunished.[4] In addition, survivors and activists have questioned how particular situations come to the attention of international authorities, that is, the extent to which the international political context is the key determinant for international condemnation and action such as the establishment of an ad hoc tribunal or truth commission.[5]

'Comfort women' is a term utilised by the Japanese military, but co-opted by the women due to its recognition amongst the public and the press as a signifier of their horrific experience. Although the crimes were committed during World War II, the motivations that culminated in the creation of the Women's International War Crimes Tribunal for the Trial of Japan's Military Sexual Slavery (Tokyo Women's Tribunal) were an outgrowth of a sense of injustice that no one had been made responsible for the atrocities that they had had to endure. Another motivation was that the international community lacked an understanding of the societal factors that enabled the military to put in place a system that could treat thousands of women in such a horrifying manner. Despite an international campaign that had resulted in several United Nations bodies and agencies calling on the government of Japan to acknowledge the nature of the wrongs that were committed in its name and to undertake acts of restitution including the payment of reparations,[6] the government of Japan made only a minimal effort to acknowledge the historical accuracy of the events surrounding the creation of the comfort women system and refused to pay reparations directly to the women.[7]

www.redress.org/. Reports produced by the ICC Outreach unit can be accessed at www.icc-cpi.int/en_menus/icc/structure%20of%20the%20court/outreach/Pages/outreach.aspx.

4 Gerry J. Simpson, 'War Crimes: A Critical Introduction' in Timothy L. H. McCormack and Gerry J. Simpson (eds.) *The Law of War Crimes: National and International Approaches* (Kluwer Law International, 1997) 1; Tina Dolgopol, 'Gender, ethics and the discretion not to prosecute in the "interests of justice" under the Rome Statute for the International Criminal Court' in Francesca Bartlett, Reid Mortensen and Kieran Tranter (eds.), *Alternative Perspectives on Lawyers and Legal Ethics, Reimagining the Profession* (Routledge, 2011) 169.

5 Simm and Byrnes, above n. 1, 107–9, 111–12 and 121–22.

6 A list as well as the text of the various resolutions and recommendations from the UN treaty bodies, the Human Rights Council, the former Subcommission on the Prevention of Discrimination and Protection of Minorities, Special Rapporteurs of the former UN Commission on Human Rights and the International Labour Organisation are available at Women's Active Museum on War and Peace, http://wam-peace.org/en/resources/.

7 The creation of the Asian Women's Fund and the problems faced in obtaining a full and frank apology from the government of Japan is contained in Etsuro Totsuka,

This refusal to make a compensatory payment has led to dissatisfaction within South Korea about the agreement that was reached between the governments of South Korea and Japan on 28 December 2015.[8] The purpose of the agreement was to resolve the comfort women issue 'finally and irreversibly'.[9] Although Japan has made the payment of 1 billion yen to South Korea as set out in the agreement, this money has been given to the Foundation for Reconciliation and Healing established by the Korean government.[10] It is this foundation that will disburse the monies given by Japan. Individuals and organisations within Korea view this as a consolatory payment rather than direct compensation. They also question the sincerity of the apology offered by Japan.[11] This relates in part to the continual protests being made about memorials that have been erected in cities around South Korea. In 2017 Japan recalled its ambassador to Korea and the Consul-General in Busan.[12]

I have argued elsewhere that the holding of the Tokyo Women's Tribunal should be considered a form of justice.[13] This chapter, whilst underpinned by that point of view, will not revisit those arguments but rather will explore the basis on which individuals create, structure and publicise one type of peoples' tribunal and how their desire to bring about what they perceive to be a laudable goal relates to the desires and needs of those who have been affected by atrocities. Although there was an emotional 'high' at the end of the proceedings in Tokyo in 2000[14] and

'Commentary on a victory for "comfort women": Japan's judicial recognition of military sexual slavery' (1999) 8 *Pacific Rim Law & Policy Journal* 47.

8 The full text of the statements made by the Foreign Ministers of Japan and South Korea was published in the *Wall Street Journal*: WSJ Staff, 'Full text: Japan-South Korea statement on 'comfort women', 28 December 2015, http://blogs.wsj.com/japanrealtime/2015/12/28/full-text-japan-south-korea-statement-on-comfort-women/.

9 Ankit Panda, 'The "final and irreversible" 2015 Japan-South Korea comfort women deal unravels', *The Diplomat*, 9 January 2017, http://thediplomat.com/2017/01/the-final-and-irreversible-2015-japan-south-korea-comfort-women-deal-unravels/; Benjamin Lee, 'South Korea-Japan Comfort Women Agreement: Where do we go from here?', *The Diplomat*, 6 September 2016, http://thediplomat.com/2016/09/south-korea-japan-comfort-women-agreement-where-do-we-go-from-here/.

10 Lee, above n. 9.

11 Ibid.; Panda, above n 9.

12 Arirang, 'Japan's envoy to Korea back home amid protest against "comfort women" statue', 10 January 2017, www.arirang.com/News/News_View.asp?nseq=199723.

13 Ustinia Dolgopol, 'Redressing partial justice: A possible role for civil society' in Ustinia Dolgopol and Judith Gardam (eds.), *The Challenge of Conflict: International Law Responds* (Martinus Nijhoff, 2006), 475.

14 The *Summary of Findings and Preliminary Judgment* (hereinafter *Preliminary Judgment*) were delivered on 12 December 2000, https://web.archive.org/web/20051113024358/http://www1.jca.apc.org/vaww-net-japan/english/womenstribunal2000/judgement.html;

to some extent at the time the final judgment was delivered in The Hague in December 2001,[15] for many of the women there is still a sense that justice has not been achieved, as there has not been a reckoning with the government of Japan.[16] In 2013 the South Korean English-language television station produced a documentary that features several comfort women, some of whom participated in the Tokyo Women's Tribunal.[17] The women interviewed continue to call on the government of Japan to take responsibility for what was done to them. As noted this view has influenced the reaction in South Korea to the agreement the government reached with Japan.

This creates a tension for those involved in peoples' tribunals. Whilst organisers of such tribunals may have qualms about state power and wish to challenge that power, the victims and survivors of state atrocity continue to want an admission by the state (whether the originator of such actions or the successor state) of its responsibility for the harm they have suffered. Although they understand that the holding of events such as a peoples' tribunal is an acknowledgement by the global community of the harms they endured and they are fully cognisant of the support such tribunals represent, victims and survivors continue to want a more formal level of accountability. In the case of the comfort women, state accountability is the ultimate goal.[18] How do we as activists acknowledge these differences in perceptions and how do we work honestly with those

Christine Chinkin, 'Editorial comments: Women's International Tribunal on Japanese military sexual slavery' (2001) 95 *American Journal of International Law* 335.

15 *The Prosecutors and the Peoples of the Asia-Pacific Region v. Hirohito et al and the Government of Japan* (PT 2000-1-T) (corrected 31 January 2001) (hereinafter *Final Judgment*), https://web.archive.org/web/20051113024358/http://www1.jca.apc.org/vaww-net-japan/english/womenstribunal2000/judgement.html.

16 Shogo Suzuki, 'Overcoming past wrongs committed by states: Can non-state actors facilitate reconciliation?' (2012) 21 (2) *Social & Legal Studies* 201, 203.

17 Arirang, '"Comfort women", one last cry', 2013, www.youtube.com/watch?v=5yHHfYOGumI.

18 In 2016 the Malaya Lolas, the women forced to become sexual slaves in Mapanique, Candaba, the Philippines whose situation was considered by the Tokyo Women's Tribunal, filed a complaint with the Special Rapporteur on Violence Against Women, its Causes and Consequences, and the Special Rapporteur on Contemporary Forms of Slavery, including its Causes and Consequences, to pressure the governments of Japan and the Philippines to negotiate an agreement that would include an admission of the responsibility by the government of Japan for the violence the women suffered and that would provide for adequate compensation. The Complaint, drafted by the Center for International Law, Manila, and the European Center for Constitutional and Human Rights contains numerous references to the Judgment of the Tokyo Women's Tribunal: Malaya Lolas, 'Individual Complaint for Consideration and Action to United Nations

whose suffering is the means by which we continue to challenge the authority of states?[19] To what extent have we sufficiently explained the limits of state accountability, and the difference between the long-term 'democratisation' of the international system[20] versus their personal need for justice?

There is little doubt that peoples' tribunals have had an impact on the international community,[21] and no system can truly alleviate the pain and suffering experienced by those victimised by violence. However, this does not lessen the need for further reflection on our methods of work. Later in this chapter I examine the positive and negative aspects of utilising a law-bound procedure such as that which governed the Tokyo Women's Tribunal. Prior to considering those issues, however, I trace the background to the creation of the Tribunal and the goals of the transboundary activists involved in its organisation.

4.2 The Tokyo Women's Tribunal

Before embarking on a discussion describing the planning that preceded the holding of the Tribunal, including the process that culminated in the decision to conduct the proceedings in a manner that mirrors those of a formal hearing, a brief overview of the 'comfort women system' will assist the reader's understanding of the issues put to the Tribunal and the process by which evidence was chosen and placed before the judges of the Tribunal.

Research continues to be undertaken about the creation of the euphemistically named comfort stations; the evidence now in the public domain indicates that the first comfort stations established at the behest of the military were built in Shanghai during 1932.[22] As Japan's war in China

Special Rapporteurs', 2 November 2016, www.ecchr.eu/en/international-crimes-and-accountability/sexual-violence/philippines.html.

19 David Kennedy, *The Dark Sides of Virtue: Reassessing International Humanitarianism* (Princeton University Press, 2004), preface and chapter 1.

20 See Çakmak, above n. 1, 10, for a discussion outlining the perceived successes of non-government organisations in bringing about a greater level of democratic responses to global issues.

21 Fleming Terrell, 'Unofficial accountability: A proposal for the Permanent Women's Tribunal on Sexual Violence in Armed Conflict' (2005) 15 *Texas Journal of Women & Law* 107, 118–20; see also Arthur W. Blaser, 'How to advance human rights without really trying: An analysis of nongovernmental tribunals' (1992) 14 *Human Rights Quarterly* 339.

22 Asian Women's Fund, 'Who were the comfort women? The establishment of comfort stations', www.awf.or.jp/e1/facts-01.html.

progressed, the number of comfort stations increased and at some point between 1936 and 1937 the number of military brothels expanded exponentially.[23] It appears that one of the factors influencing the decision of the military to pursue this policy was the international outcry that followed Japan's takeover of the cities of Shanghai and Nanjing (then referred to as Nanking).[24] Various government and military officials became concerned about the international condemnation of Japan's behaviour as well as the Chinese reprisals against Japanese soldiers.[25] As the Japanese moved into Southeast Asia, Burma and the Pacific, comfort stations were established in each of the areas they occupied.[26] The precise number of women and girls placed into the comfort stations is unknown, but based on the records available it appears the number is between 150,000 and 200,000.

Various acts of sexual violence were committed whilst the women were forcibly held in the comfort stations. In addition the women were subjected to acts of torture such as having lit cigarettes placed on their bodies and implements inserted into them. Forced abortions took place at a number of the comfort stations. There was little or no freedom of movement.[27] As the war drew to a close, the majority of the women were abandoned by the Japanese military; of those who survived, some were repatriated by the Allied forces while others had to find their own way home. Some chose not to return to their families because of the shame they felt at what had happened to them. The majority of women who

23 Ustinia Dolgopol and Snehal Paranjape, *Comfort Women, an Unfinished Ordeal* (International Commission of Jurists, 1994), www.icj.org/wp-content/uploads/1994/01/Japan-comfort-women-fact-finding-report-1994-eng.pdf.

24 Extract from written notification of Warnings by Naosaburo Okabe, Chief of Staff of the North China Area Army sent on 27 June 1938, while acting as Chief of Staff of the North China Area Army; Asian Women's Fund, 'Who were the comfort women? Observations and directions in the military', www.awf.or.jp/e1/facts-03.html.

25 Documents detailing the military's involvement are referred to in the *Final Judgment* of the Tokyo Women's Tribunal, above n. 15, paras. 92–98.

26 A brief overview of the Allied documents describing the extensive nature of the comfort women system is set out in Ustinia Dolgopol, 'Knowledge and responsibility: The Ongoing Consequences of Failing to give Sufficient Attention to the Crimes against the Comfort Women in the Tokyo Trial' in Yuki Tanaka, Tim McCormack and Gerry Simpson (eds.), *Beyond Victor's Justice? The Tokyo War Crimes Trial Revisited* (Martinus Nijhoff, 2011) 252–54; see also *Final Judgment*, above n. 15, paras. 99–108, and Dolgopol and Paranjape, above n. 23, 29–41.

27 See 'Statements of Victims' in Dolgopol and Paranjape, above n. 23, 55–119; extracts of the testimonies of former comfort are interspersed throughout *Final Judgment*, above n. 15.

have come forward indicated that they were not able to discuss their suffering with those close to them, and many of the Korean survivors have described lives of utter isolation.[28] There have been ongoing consequences for the women's psychological and physical health.[29]

Following a 1988 seminar in South Korea, the issue of the comfort women began to be discussed more openly within that country and also within Japan. The willingness of one of the Korean survivors, Kim Hak Soon,[30] to speak publicly about her ordeal encouraged women's organisations in the Philippines to urge women in their country who had endured the same treatment to come forward.[31] Civil society organisations in a number of countries began to collaborate on projects designed to unearth documents and materials that would provide the public with more complete evidence about the comfort women system. As a result research was undertaken in Japan, South Korea, the Philippines, the United Kingdom and Australia.

This research revealed the existence of diaries penned by military officials, Japanese military records and materials created by the police forces operating at the time Japan occupied the Korean peninsula and Taiwan. The evidence collected by activists and scholars included the reports compiled by the Allied Nations about the operation of the comfort women system, as well as descriptions of the acts of individual soldiers that amounted to war crimes.[32] The war-related documents found in Japan contained details about the military's involvement in the creation and operation of the Comfort Stations.[33] Public meetings, symposia and other events were held in South Korea, the Philippines and Japan which highlighted the results of the research being undertaken and provided a space for the women to speak publicly about their ordeal.

Despite increasing levels of public support within Japan for Japanese accountability and repeated calls by the international community[34] for

[28] *Final Judgment,* above n. 15. [29] Ibid., paras. 312–42.

[30] Yayori Matsui, 'Women's International War Crimes Tribunal on Japan's Military Sexual Slavery: Memory, identity, and society' (2001) 19(4) *East Asia* 119, 121.

[31] Dolgopol and Paranjape, above n. 23, 16.

[32] Yoshiaki Yoshimi, *'Comfort Women': Sexual Slavery in the Japanese Military during World War II* (translated by Suzanne O'Brien) (Columbia University Press, 2000); Ustinia Dolgopol, 'Rape in War – Mythology and History' in Indai Lourdes Sajor (ed.), *Common Grounds – Violence Against Women in War and Armed Conflict* (ASCENT, 1998) 122; Dolgopol, above n. 26.

[33] Yoshimi, above n. 32.

[34] The report of the International Commission of Jurists (Dolgopol and Paranjape, above n. 23) received a significant amount of media attention and was referred to extensively in

Japan to apologise and to take other affirmative steps towards making restitution, civil society organisations both within Japan and regionally came to the conclusion that the government would not offer a meaningful apology. Nor would the Japanese government undertake the steps necessary for full restitution including the payment of compensation and the creation of written and artistic materials acknowledging the suffering of the women. There also was a concern that the government would not publicly acknowledge the extent of the system or assist in bringing to light the 'truth' about what had taken place.[35] This combination of factors culminated in the decision to establish the Tokyo Women's Tribunal.[36]

By the mid-1990s it had become evident that efforts to create an international criminal court that would have jurisdiction over the most serious crimes committed in times of armed conflict had a strong likelihood of success. Some of the individuals involved in the comfort women issue had links to organisations interested in the creation of such a body. Several women who had worked with the women in their home countries or who had been active in the international efforts to obtain redress for the comfort women were present during the negotiations for the Rome Statute of the International Criminal Court as members of the Women's Caucus for Gender Justice (Women's Caucus).[37] These individuals held seminars about the comfort women system in an effort to demonstrate the importance of elucidating the full range of gender crimes that occur

the reports to the then UN Commission on Human Rights (UNCHR, *Report of the Special Rapporteur on Violence against Women, Its Causes and Consequences: Mission to the Democratic People's Republic of Korea, the Republic of Korea and Japan on the Issue of Military Sexual Slavery in Wartime*, 5 February 1996, E/CN.4/1996/53/Add.1.) and its then Subcommission on Prevention of Discrimination and Protection of Minorities ('Appendix: An analysis of the legal liability of the Government of Japan for "comfort women stations" established during the Second World War', *Report of the Special Rapporteur on Systematic Rape, Sexual Slavery and Slavery-like Practices during Armed Conflict*, 22 June 1998, E/CN.4/Sub.2/1998/13, appendix).

35 Despite the efforts of Professor Yoshimi (above n. 32), there were concerns that more documents existed and that the government was not putting them into the public domain. See Totsuka, above n. 7 and Yasuaki Onuma, 'Japanese war guilt and post-war responsibilities of Japan' (2002) 20 *Berkeley Journal of International Law* 600.

36 I was present in Rome as part of the Women's Caucus for Gender Justice during the negotiations that culminated in the creation of the International Criminal Court. The decision to organise a tribunal was taken at this time. The material in this section is based on the author's participation in the organising committee and her observations of the process that culminated in the holding of the Tokyo Women's Tribunal.

37 Yayori Matsui, Indai Sajor, Rhonda Copelon and Ustinia Dolgopol.

in the context of conflict.[38] During the internal discussions held by Women's Caucus members, the issue of Japanese accountability was raised and the idea of holding a civil society tribunal was put forward. Over the next few days the idea gained traction and concerned individuals agreed to work on the structure of such a tribunal. Women from the Philippines and South Korea agreed to speak with their national organisations to discuss the idea and to canvass the views of the women on holding such a tribunal. These discussions resulted in the decision to hold a tribunal that was more formal in its procedures and conduct than some of the previous women's tribunals.[39]

Steps were taken to contact organisations in other countries where women had come forward, such as Indonesia and China, and to work with individuals who had undertaken research on the issue in Malaysia (where women had spoken privately about the trauma they had endured, but were not willing to speak publicly). As the work of the Tribunal went forward and began to receive publicity, women's groups from East Timor approached the organising committee to indicate that some of the women in Timor who had lived through the Japanese occupation of their country were willing to testify about their experiences. Although Dutch women in Indonesia had been subjected to the horrors of comfort stations, most were not willing to speak openly about the atrocities they had endured; therefore, their experiences were brought before the Tribunal through an Indonesian-born Dutch woman who had migrated to Australia.[40]

Having made the decision to be as inclusive as possible despite the courtlike structure settled upon for the Tribunal, individuals and groups worked tirelessly in their home countries to offer suggestions about the Tribunal's operating procedures, to gather documentary and oral evidence and to discuss the handling of the evidence before the Tribunal.

[38] Yayori Matsui, a Japanese journalist and renowned feminist, was at the forefront of the efforts to create the Tribunal. The organisations principally responsible for the organisation of the Tribunal were the Korean Council for Women Drafted into Military Sexual Slavery (a South Korean-based organisation now called the Korean Council for the Women Drafted for Military Sexual Slavery by Japan); www.womenandwar.net; ASCENT (a women's human rights organisation based in the Philippines); and VAW-Net Japan (now the Violence Against Women in War Research Action Center [VAWWRAC]), http://vawwrac.org/.

[39] See Terrell, above n. 21, 118–32.

[40] Jan Ruff O'Hearne remains the only person of European descent to speak publicly in detail about her experiences during World War II: see Jan Ruff O'Hearne, *50 Years of Silence* (Tom Thompson/Harper Collins, 1994).

Meetings were held in Shanghai, Manila and Taipei to ensure that groups from all of the individual countries were in agreement about the range of issues to be covered before the Tribunal. This process included the drafting of 'indictments' that named particular officers from the Japanese military. None of those named had faced charges at the various war crimes trials held in the Asia–Pacific region at the close of World War II.[41] The decision to 'indict' the wartime Emperor, Hirohito, was a result of the desire of the women and organisations in a number of countries to ensure that the Tribunal addressed the then government's responsibility and that its conclusions did not foster a view that the comfort women system resulted from the 'rogue' actions of certain military officers. In addition to the criminal law component of the Tribunal, it was decided that a portion of the hearings would be devoted to the responsibility of the government of Japan for conduct that amounted to an international wrong.[42] The Application for Restitution and Reparations filed by the prosecutors claimed reparations for the harm that had been inflicted on the women due to the criminal acts of the accused as well as reparations for the ongoing failure of the government to prosecute the perpetrators and to provide adequate reparations.[43]

Almost from the start of the process, those working on the Tribunal were conscious of the need to create a repository of information that would be available to the international community. The effort to locate wartime diaries, search government archives and undertake research in the archives of the United Kingdom, the United States and Australia was a manifestation of the view that the material before the Tribunal had to match the quality of material that might come before a state-created body and should be of significance to individuals who were interested in researching this field.

For many of those working on the issue, the use of the language of the law was seen as a way of presenting their efforts as 'neutral', that is, this was not to be viewed as a political effort in the sense that there was a political ideology behind the Tribunal. Rather the focus was on providing a forum that would acknowledge what had occurred and would assess the facts against recognised objective international law standards concerning criminal liability and the obligation to make restitution. Some of those involved also hoped that holding the Tribunal might create sufficient pressure on the government to change its attitude towards

[41] *Final Judgment*, above n. 15, paras. 13 and 16–20.
[42] Ibid., paras. 14, 15 and 21.
[43] Ibid., para. 21.

reparations, in particular, the payment of compensation and the inclusion of materials about these events in the history books utilised in Japanese schools.[44]

Before interrogating this use of legal language and ritual, it is important to consider the role of transboundary activists in the international arena. Whilst not offering an in-depth analysis of transboundary activists, the following section canvasses some of the issues associated with the potential power they can wield due to their creation of networks and their ability to determine their methods of work in a manner which is not hampered by the constraints of diplomacy or institutional bureaucracy.

4.3 The Role of Transboundary Activists

Burgerman has described the transnational activities of civil society activists as follows:

> Networks of activists operate across borders, within political systems irrespective of their nationality, occupying a political space that ignores the boundaries between states: they infiltrate government and intergovernmental bureaucracies; they attempt, with varying degrees of success to engage in the arena of international politics, formerly considered the sole preserve of states; they are simultaneously insiders and outsiders.[45]

This description fits those involved in the comfort women issue. Some of the individuals and organisations had success lobbying their national governments in terms of creating special classes of benefits for women in their jurisdiction[46] and mobilising public opinion in a manner that put pressure on their governments to seek a meaningful apology from the government of Japan.[47] Within Japan, individuals lobbied members of

[44] See Onuma, above n. 35, and Hirofumi Hayashi, 'Disputes in Japan over the Japanese Military "Comfort Women" System and its perception in history' (2008) 617(1) *Annals of the American Academy of Political and Social Science* 123.

[45] Susan D. Burgerman, 'Mobilizing principles: The role of transnational activists in promoting human rights principles' (1998) 20(4) *Human Rights Quarterly* 905, 923, quoted in Çakmak, above n. 1, 11.

[46] South Korea has put in place special health and social security benefits.

[47] The governments of South Korea and China have been particularly active. See, e.g., 'Asia, South Korea warns Japan over comfort women review', *BBC News*, 1 March 2014, www.bbc.com/news/world-asia-26394850; 'China, S Korea criticize Hashimoto over comfort women comments', *Japan Today*, 15 May 2013, www.japantoday.com/category/politics/view/china-s-korea-criticize-hashimoto-over-comfort-women-comments.

the Diet and were able to work with minority parties to draft bills that would have given meaningful restitution.[48] In this sense they became insiders. As noted previously,[49] groups and individuals succeeded in obtaining international attention for the issue with a range of United Nations bodies adopting reports, resolutions and statements on the issue; thus, they became significant actors on the international stage.

Perhaps the ongoing scrutiny of statements made by Japanese politicians such as those attributed to the mayor of Osaka[50] in mid-2013 and the statements made by Katsuto Momii, chairperson of NHK, Japan's national public broadcaster, and chief cabinet secretary Yoshihide Suga in early 2014[51] were a result of the efforts of the comfort women activists. The Tribunal, as well as the continuing efforts of groups in South Korea and Japan, have put the issue firmly into the minds of journalists and a range of international non-government organisations. This level of analysis makes it more likely that statements and actions that might once have received domestic comment alone are now subject to scrutiny internationally.

[48] A list of the bills introduced in the Diet is contained in the materials available on the website of the Digital Museum: Asian Women's Fund, 'Attempts at legislation in the Japanese Diet', www.awf.or.jp/e4/legislation.htm. Ibid.

[49] See above n. 6.

[50] Yoshiaki Kasuga, 'UN Secretary-General criticizes Hashimoto's "comfort women" remark', *Asahi Shimbun*, 3 June 2013, http://archive.fo/4Z6Ni; Mark Willacy, 'Japanese politician defends use of sex slaves', ABC News, 14 May 2013, www.abc.net.au/news/2013-05-14/japanese-politician-defends-wartime-use-of-sex-slaves/4687332; see also 'Japanese politician says "comfort women" were wartime necessity' interview with present author, *ABC Radio Australia*, 14 May 2013, www.radioaustralia.net.au/international/radio/program/connect-asia/japanese-politician-says-comfort-women-were-wartime-necessity/1130652; Ida Torres, 'S Korean President Park criticizes Japan during visit with US Defense secretary', *Japan Daily Press*, 1 October 2013, http://japandailypress.com/s-korean-president-park-criticizes-japan-during-visit-with-us-defense-secretary-0136890/; Ida Torres, 'Former US diplomat Armitage says Hashimoto's remarks "harmful" to Japan', *Japan Daily Press*, 31 May 2013, http://japandailypress.com/former-us-diplomat-armitage-says-hashimotos-remarks-harmful-to-japan-3129811/.

[51] Mari Yamaguchi, 'Japan NHK boss under fire for comfort women remark', *Washington Times*, 27 January 2014, www.washingtontimes.com/news/2014/jan/27/japan-nhk-boss-under-fire-for-comfort-women-remark/#ixzz2wShYOtf1; Seana Magee, 'Japan comes under fire at U.N. Security Council over history issues', *Kyodo News/Philippines Today*, 30 January 2014, www.philippinestoday.net/archives/13220; Asahi Shimbun (with contribution from Akihiko Kaise), 'Insight: Abe administration maintains delicate balancing act over Kono Statement', 15 March 2014, http://archive.is/MhExS; 'Seoul welcomes Tokyo's announcement to stand by sex slavery apology', *The Korea Times*, 15 March 2014, www.koreatimes.co.kr/www/news/nation/2016/12/116_153419.html.

Transboundary activists can be effective because they are often engaged in the collection of information about mass violations of human rights and can relay victim accounts of their experiences. Although they may come from elite groups within society,[52] the fact that such activists have taken the time to listen to the stories of victims and have chosen to empathise with victims and survivors enables them to speak with a conviction that is missing from the dialogue of diplomats. They move between the outsider's world of the victim, the person who has been marginalised by a human rights violation, to the insider's world of negotiation, bargaining and influencing state and government action internationally and domestically.[53]

The idealism of transboundary activists may have an impact that is sometimes underrated. Whilst the world of *Realpolitik* suggests that only those with power can influence events, the appeal to a moral good may in fact touch a need of other international actors to feel that the work they undertake is worthwhile. The aspirations that motivated many of those who assisted in the creation of the United Nations to make the world safer and more just[54] have not been totally overshadowed by the demands of power politics.

In reflecting on the idealism involved in the organisation of the Tribunal, one of the motivations of many of those from Japan was their hope that the Tribunal would change attitudes within the government and society.[55] Because the comfort women issue had received a significant amount of support from the general public, it was hoped that the government's intransigence could be overcome by generating further publicity and garnering additional public support. The measures

[52] Kennedy, above n. 19.

[53] See Çakmak, above n. 1, 123–28, for a discussion of how non-government organisations influenced international treaties and declarations. This was my experience while working for the International Commission of Jurists at the United Nations.

[54] Mary Ann Glendon, 'Propter Honoris Respectum: Knowing the Universal Declaration of Human Rights' (1998) 73 *Notre Dame Law Review* 1153.

[55] Foucault observes that most societies have their major narratives and that these may have a connection to their 'cultural system': Michel Foucault, *The Archaeology of Knowledge and the Discourse on Language* (Pantheon Books, 1972) 320. The bombings of Hiroshima and Nagasaki form a narrative for modern Japan that can obscure the behaviour of Japan in the Asian region during the war. This should not be taken to suggest that the bombings were in any way justified. Rather, the observation relates to the particular narrative that people chose to repeat as it does not force them to confront other more difficult narratives. For a discussion about how this narrative has affected Japanese society in relation to the comfort women issue, see Onuma, above n. 35.

of restitution being advocated included not only compensation and an apology but also a change in the narrative included in history textbooks in use in secondary schools. Those focusing on this issue believed it was connected to the need for a better understanding of the militarism that had permeated Japanese society prior to the outbreak of World War II and, in addition, the need to connect that history to issues associated with political patronage that were perceived as undermining Japanese democracy.[56] The depth of feeling about this should not be underestimated and demonstrates the diverse goals of those engaged in the process – wanting both to assist victims and to further societal transformation.

Again, these aims were influenced by the notion that a process and decision that mirrored those of a court would have a greater effect on society at large than other types of public events. However, as is the case in the legal system, a criminal or civil trial is not a venue for an exploration of the myriad ways in which cultural, political and historical matters converge so as to produce mass violations of human rights. Without such an examination, it is not clear that the public or those in positions of power develop a full understanding of the factors that contributed to such an outbreak of violence, or appreciate the consequences of such violence for the victims and for the society inflicting these types of harms.[57] It is not obvious that the need for such an exploration was sufficiently conveyed to either the Tribunal itself or the general public. This is an important issue to consider in the context of people's tribunals: Whom precisely are we (organisers) seeking to influence and how do we measure our impact? Is media attention alone sufficient, or are we able to find mechanisms for gauging changes in attitude over time?

Transboundary activists often form loose coalitions and operate in the knowledge that change is a slow process and requires sustained effort on the part of significant numbers of groups and individuals. These coalitions can be maintained over long periods or may be transient in nature. A small number of the participants in the Tokyo Women's Tribunal have continued to maintain contact with one another. Some individuals assist from time to time, while others continue to work on the issue regularly. These contacts occur across national boundaries.

[56] Although the issues are not precisely the same, the connection activists may make between history and social attitudes has its parallel with indigenous issues in Australia.

[57] See generally Martha Minow, *Between Vengeance and Forgiveness, Facing History after Genocide and Mass Violence* (Beacon Press, 1998), and Mark Osiel, *Mass Atrocities, Collective Memory and the Law* (Transaction Press, 1997).

The judges of the tribunal recognised that an 'interim' judgment would have to be issued within a few days of the completion of the Tribunal given the effort of the survivors to come to Tokyo. They determined that findings could be made with respect to the complicity of Emperor Hirohito and the general nature of Japan's state responsibility. From early in the process they had emphasised that a 'final' judgment containing thorough findings of fact and a detailed legal analysis would have to be produced in the months following the Tribunal. The final judgment was delivered in The Hague on 4 December 2001.[58] The original intention of the organisers was to produce a simplified version of the final judgment and to create a complete set of records from the Tribunal (transcripts of the testimony and documentation introduced at the Tribunal). It was hoped that a 'plain language' version of the judgment would be more accessible to the survivors and the community groups working with them and would help them understand the nature of the analysis that had been undertaken by the judges. In addition, a shorter, more accessible version of the final judgment could be translated into local languages more easily. This would allow organisations working with the women to use the ideas contained in the judgment in their public education campaigns and lobbying efforts that they might engage in domestically or internationally.

Despite working towards a common goal and maintaining their focus on the interests of the comfort women, the delegates from the participating country teams could not overcome differences of outlook and culture to produce a document that would have created a bridge between the world of the professional and the world of the women.[59] This is not a problem unique to the participants at the Tribunal. The issues that prevented the participants from coming to an agreement were not about ideological issues such as a tribunal being a political versus a legal mechanism as described by Ayça Çubukçu in her discussion of the World Tribunal on Iraq.[60] Nonetheless, perceptions about who had suffered to the greatest extent, who would benefit from the production of a document and where such work might be undertaken influenced the final decision not to pursue the creation of a plain language text of the

[58] *Final Judgment*, above n. 15.

[59] See also, Dianne Otto, 'Beyond legal justice: Some personal reflections on people's tribunals, listening and responsibility' (forthcoming) *London Review of International Law*, doi.org/10.1093/lril/lrx007.

[60] Ayça Çubukçu, 'On cosmopolitan occupations' (2011) 13(3) *Interventions: International Journal of Postcolonial Studies* 422, 434–38.

judgment or to have the documents that were submitted to the Tribunal digitised. Groups in each country were left to produce their own summaries in the manner they believed best suited the situation of the survivors and their own needs with respect to lobbying efforts.

By failing to reach an agreement about how a uniform plain language version of the judgment could be produced, the organisers and the participants at the post-Tribunal meetings did not come to grips with the problems that community organisations would face in explaining the work of the Tribunal. Legal language can exclude those affected by violations of their rights from understanding the reasons why the acts committed against them are considered to be violations of international law (whether criminal law or human rights law) and give rise to state accountability under the law of state responsibility. If one purpose of such a process is to empower those whose rights have been violated, then creating materials that improve their knowledge and understanding of the law and its limits should be an integral part of the holding of people's tribunals.[61] Despite my continuing belief in the utility of the tribunal process, I believe this is an important issue for all those involved in people's tribunals. What efforts do we undertake to make our expertise accessible to those whose interests we claim to represent? How much time is put into the dissemination of knowledge in comparison to lobbying those with power and influence?

These questions are connected to the issues raised in the following section about the power of law's language. We have the ability to utilise that language for an end we identify, but how does our ability to exercise the power associated with the law affect those who are excluded from or marginalised by that power?

4.4 The Language and Power of the Law

In this section, I address the use of the trial-like mechanism and the reliance on the formalities and structure of law, along with the role of people, like me, who are lawyers or academics and can utilise law's language. Foucault speaks about the will to truth and the need to understand the power dynamics involved in any form of discourse that focuses on this will to truth.[62] Among his observations are the exclusionary powers of institutions and disciplines such as the law.[63] The language and discipline

[61] On the Iran Tribunal held in 2013, see www.irantribunal.com/index.php/en/.

[62] Foucault, above n. 55, 318.

[63] Ibid., 318–19, 324–25.

of the law creates structures for what is acceptable discourse (one need only think about rules of evidence). It also creates rituals about the manner in which that discourse may take place.[64] Therefore, adopting a legal framework inevitably means that certain types of observations and information will be acceptable whilst other types of knowledge will be excluded.[65] In addition the language itself has an exclusionary force. Only those who understand and are capable of utilising the power of that language can participate actively in the ritual.

However, one also could argue that the use of the law in this manner subverts the state-based system of law. Margaret Davies argues that law can be viewed as having vertical and horizontal dimensions.[66] The vertical is associated with state-based law and the 'exclusionary tactics of the nation state', whereas 'the horizontal is based on relationships of actual proximity or contiguity.'[67] She discusses the Tokyo Tribunal, and whilst acknowledging some of the issues traversed in this paper, notes:

> On the other hand, however, I would see such an activist intervention in the formal law as an attempt to relocate and redefine it beyond the state and government and beyond the spaces and institutions formally constituted by vertical law. Given that the survivors were at least partly in control of the process, the flattened law of the tribunal is more participatory and inclusive than vertically defined law. . . . The spaces of law were extended by the enactment of law in an alternative setting; . . . in addition the tribunal was motivated by a need for law to emanate from grassroots movements, thus equalising the sources, the subjects and the content of the law.[68]

Her description of the horizontal could be related to the notion of trans-boundary activists as having a democratising effect on the state system.[69]

64 Ibid., 324–25.

65 Nicola Henry, 'Memory of an injustice: The 'comfort women' and the legacy of the Tokyo Trial' (2013) 37(3) *Asian Studies Review* 362, 365.

66 Margaret Davies, 'Feminism and the Flat Law Theory' (2008) 16 *Feminist Legal Studies* 281.

67 Ibid., 282. One of the other issues Davies raised is the way exclusions are created by 'the gendered values read into [laws] so called "neutral" doctrines', at 284. This relates to some of the critiques of the international legal system and its failure to address crimes committed against women. It is not just that the law may not encompass the full range of harms experienced by women, but that those who make the decisions about what will and will not be prosecuted do not always fully understand their own prejudices or the impact of their decisions on marginalised groups such as women. See Dolgopol, above n. 4, 176–78, 181–83.

68 Davies, above n. 66, 297 (footnotes omitted).

69 See Çakmak, above n. 1, 11.

Having identified the mystique associated with the law, it is important to think about why the women wanted the language and structure of the law to be used, and the way in which that also made them outsiders to the process. The organisers and country groups wanted the tribunal to reflect the desires of the women. The fact that as a group of people with some, although in most cases limited, formal education, they chose a legal framework speaks to the power of such a framework. Some thought the injustices they suffered would be better recognised and better understood by the global community if they were put in the context of a war crimes tribunal. Reports by those intimately involved in the discussions that led to the creation of the Tribunal and who were working closely with the various country groups indicate that the women wanted those responsible for their enslavement and the acts of sexual violence they endured to be judged and labelled as criminals.[70]

It is hard to say how organic this process might have been as I was not privy to the nationally based discussions. Although the original idea was to have a tribunal, the exact format and the manner in which it would be conducted was not determined at the initial stage. It arose after the national consultations. Many of the women were aware of the proceedings taking place with respect to the former Yugoslavia. They may not have been aware of the exact nature of the International Criminal Tribunal for the former Yugoslavia, but they knew such a body existed and that some of the matters it was hearing related to crimes against women. During the discussions they would have been informed of the establishment of the International Criminal Court. Therefore it may be the case that there was a mutuality of interest in moving to a more formal structure – the women's belief that justice was a product of what courts do, and the desire of those who had been working with them to have an outcome that would mirror what could be achieved in a judicial setting.

However, once the decision had been made to structure the Tribunal in this fashion, it meant that the women could not participate in future negotiations about the exact operation of the Tribunal. Not knowing the language of the law, they were not in a position to debate the intricacies of what constituted crimes against humanity or war crimes. Nor were they in a position to discuss the complexities of the law of state responsibility, in particular the nature and extent of the liability of Japan for its

[70] Rumiko Nishino, 'Le tribunal d'opinion de Tôkyô pour les "femmes de réconfort"' ['The Tokyo opinion tribunal for "comfort women"'] (2009) 58 *Droit et cultures* 75, https://droitcultures.revues.org/2079.

violations of international law during the 1930s and 1940s that might have been imposed at the end of World War II, as well as that resulting from its continuing failure to provide reparations for those wrongs. Some of the non-lawyer delegates to the preparatory meetings struggled with a number of the legal concepts and the manner in which lawyers debate ideas.

Although everyone working on the Tribunal was conscious that the women were the reason it was taking place,[71] once a legal framework was chosen, the women were outsiders to the language in which the Tribunal was conducted and had little influence over the precise procedures adopted for the Tribunal. However, the ongoing discussions taking place at the national level probably minimised the extent to which the women felt as if they were 'cogs in a wheel' – which is sometimes the reaction of victims and witnesses to the trial process. The overwhelmingly positive reaction to the closing statements of the Tribunal and the delivery of the initial judgment indicates that the women were very much aware of what had taken place and what was being said by those with the ability to use the language of the law to reach conclusions about the atrocities they had suffered.[72]

Having said this, there is no escaping the fact that the organisers did not discuss explicitly the question of whether or not the legal framework with its connection to existing power structures and all of its past failures with respect to the rights of women was the best framework to be used in this context. No one questioned the fact that a judicial process cannot explore the nature of power, the political machinations and the societal structures that feed into the violation of rights. Judgments are always limited in their scope,[73] and although we may strive to improve both the content and the application of the law, we cannot move away from the fact that law always serves the dual function of empowering and disempowering.[74]

[71] See Dolgopol, above n. 13, 493–94, for a discussion of the aspects of the tribunal that allowed the women to express their artistic and cultural 'selves' as well as allowing them to build relations with one another.

[72] See Matsui, above n. 30; Nishino, above n. 70, para. 16.

[73] Minow, above n. 57.

[74] Victor Southwell, 'The case of the invisible woman: Essentialism, intersectionality and marginalisation in feminist discourse' (1994) 27 *Comparative & International Law Journal of South Africa* 357; Sherene Razack, 'Beyond universal women: Reflections on theorizing differences among women' (1996) 45 *University of New Brunswick Law Journal* 209.

Those of us who have engaged with international law know that it 'still hesitates between the sovereignty of states and the protection of human beings'.[75] What obligation arises from this knowledge to ensure that those at the grassroots truly understand the purpose of the exercise they are about to undertake? As in other proceedings, witnesses are asked to come forward and relive their trauma so that society at large may better understand the pain and suffering they endured. We are asking them to serve the larger purpose of 'healing' society:

> Richard Goldstone, the Chief Prosecutor of the Yugoslav War Crimes Tribunal, said that 'people don't relate to statistics, to generalizations. People can only relate and feel when they hear somebody that they can identify with telling what happened to them.[76]

Despite the good intentions we organisers espouse, there is an element of objectification of witnesses. They are there because we believe they serve a larger good. Many of them may understand this purpose, and some may wish to take on the role of educating both their own and the international community. For some witnesses, their decision to come forward may be related to the hope that their willingness to share their pain will have a positive effect on the legal and moral order that governs the actions of states. Should we discuss in a more forthright manner what can and cannot be accomplished by our efforts? I am not seeking to underestimate the commitment to social change on the part of those who have been affected by mass violence, nor do I question their ability to make choices about their lives. Rather, I wonder if we do not assume the immediate gratification of telling their story in a public forum with the support that is available at that moment in time will somehow translate into a deeper restoration of dignity and a sense of vindication than may in fact occur. Perhaps the long-term outcomes are so difficult to define and delineate that it is not possible to explore the potential consequences. I raise the question because it troubles me. What is my responsibility to others in pursuing my cause, my need to feel that I am making a contribution to the development of international law? In seeking to make others accountable, what level of accountability applies to me?

75 Pierre-Marie Dupuy, 'Between the Individual and the State: International Law at a Crossroads?' in Laurence Boisson de Chazournes and Philippe Sands (eds.), *International Law, the International Court of Justice and Nuclear Weapons* (Cambridge University Press, 1999) 449, 461.

76 Michael Scharf, 'The case for a Permanent International Truth Commission' (1997) 7 *Duke Journal of Comparative & International Law* 375, 387–88.

However, in contrast to this dilemma about the objectification of witnesses and survivors, it also is true that those peoples' tribunals that focus on the horrors of war represent the political will for change referred to by Koskenniemi in his discussion of the *Nuclear Weapons* case.[77] He asserts that nuclear weapons should be banned, not because they breach the rules of international humanitarian law but because the '(massive) killing of the innocent' is against our moral judgment.[78] Another legal scholar, Richard Falk, has observed that initiatives such as the World Tribunal on Iraq '[rest] on an ethos of concern and responsibility for fundamental law and morality . . . expressive of the impulse to feel, think and act as global citizens in an increasingly globalizing world'.[79] These scholars are representative of individuals and groups in society who believe the continual highlighting of the brutality of war will reduce both the incidence as well as the casualties of war. Davies observes that '[f]or legal subjects . . . their empowerment and disempowerment . . . [is] determined in part by their relationship to the matrix of the law/state/culture.'[80] Law may provide marginalised groups with a means of challenging their position in society, it may act as a barrier to gaining increased recognition or it may foster continued exclusion.

A broader view of what was accomplished by the activism related to the comfort women issue would suggest that overall those efforts were empowering. Prior to the Tokyo Women's Tribunal, the efforts being made to gain publicity for the issue had affected the attitude of the women's governments and societies. In China, South Korea and the Philippines, the publicity surrounding the issue gave the women a space to speak openly about their experiences rather than maintain a secrecy caused by shame. Their communities were generally supportive. Their governments, initially reluctant to become involved in the issue, did eventually raise the topic in bilateral discussions and supported the efforts of the women to gain international recognition of their right to restitution. Special measures relating to health and social security were put in place in South Korea.

[77] International Court of Justice, *Legality of the Threat or Use of Nuclear Weapons (Advisory Opinion)* [1996] ICJ Rep 226.

[78] Martti Koskenniemi, *The Politics of International Law* (Hart, 2011) 198, 211.

[79] Richard Falk, *The Costs of War: International Law, the UN and the World Order after Iraq* (Taylor and Francis, 2008), quoted in Çubukçu, above n. 60, 427.

[80] Davies, above n. 66, 285.

Following the Tokyo Women's Tribunal, the international media gave increasing amounts of attention to Japan's failure to offer meaningful redress. The resolutions adopted by various national and regional parliaments, as well as by numerous city councils both internationally and in Japan, were debated and adopted in the period following the Tribunal.[81] The careful research and analysis of the issue undertaken by the prosecutors and judges would have made the case for restitution more obvious. Despite the passage of time, the women involved in the Tribunal continue to receive invitations to speak at international gatherings. The Director of the Women's Active Museum on War and Peace was asked to speak about the Tribunal at the International Criminal Court in 2012.[82]

4.5 Conclusion

I remain in a quandary about whether to focus on the exclusionary nature of what we as organisers undertook or to focus on the desire of the women to participate in a courtlike structure. The exclusionary power of the law cannot be overlooked, and our motivation for adopting a structure so inextricably connected to state power should be analysed more carefully. However, even as an activist who is well aware of the limits of the law, I continue to believe that there is some utility to the 'rule of law' – that is, that some order is better than the exercise of power based on the will of individuals. Even accepting that the structure of the law serves the interests of a particular system, the law's ability to constrain the worst abuses of autocratic power is better than having no available constraints.

Some commentators would argue that the deep-seated inequalities perpetuated by the law (given its state-centric origins) can only be unmasked if we do not try to tame the law and work within the system.[83]

[81] A list of these resolutions is available on the website of the Women's Active Museum on War and Peace: http://wam-peace.org/en/. The museum is based in Tokyo and houses the papers of Yayori Matsui, one of the main organisers of the Tokyo Women's Tribunal. It was funded in large part by a bequest from her estate. The museum's collection and its work are described on its website.

[82] Mina Wantanabe, 'The People's Tribunal on Comfort Women', Guest Lecture, Office of the Prosecutor, International Criminal Court, 15 May 2013, www.icc-cpi.int/about/otp/Pages/guestLecture.aspx?name=Mina-Watanabe.

[83] Pierre Bourdieu, 'The force of law: Towards sociology of the juridical field' (1986–87) 38 *Hastings Law Journal* 805, 814; Louis Althusser, 'Ideology and Ideological State Apparatuses (Notes towards an Investigation)' in Slavoj Žižek (ed.), *Mapping Ideology* (Verso, 1994) 127.

Accepting the bounds of the discipline may have hobbled our ability to imagine a different structure or more egalitarian legal order. However, for those of us who feel compelled to respond to the crimes and behaviours that we believe pose a challenge to our common humanity, taking some form of action in the here and now appears necessary. Peoples' tribunals may fall within the realm of legal pragmatism,[84] but each offers a unique insight into a particular aspect of the power imbalances that affect our lives. Their cumulative effect, given their connection to the creation of new global networks of individuals who seek to challenge the existing state structure, may assist in shifting the focus of international law from the protection of the state to the protection of human beings.

[84] Thomas C. Grey, 'Freestanding legal pragmatism' (1996) 18 *Cardozo Law Review* 21, 29–30.

5

The International People's Tribunal on 1965 Crimes against Humanity in Indonesia

An Anthropological Perspective

SASKIA E. WIERINGA*

5.1 Introduction

The crimes against humanity committed in Indonesia after 1 October 1965 count as one of the least known genocides in modern history.[1] The surviving victims are haunted by stigma, and the perpetrators live with impunity. The government of Indonesia has never taken any judicial steps to deal with this period and it does not seem likely it will do so in the near future, in spite of promises made by the current president, Joko Widodo. In the absence of a formal juridical process, what role can human rights activists, researchers and legal experts play?

In this chapter, I first reflect on the rationale of the organisers for establishing a People's Tribunal, its structure and the mandate of the Panel of Judges, and provide an overview of the proceedings. This is followed by a concise historical introduction to the events it considered and a summary of the major legal conclusions reached by the Panel of Judges. The chapter describes my own role as chair of the Foundation International People's Tribunal and the coordinator of the research team and assesses the significance of the Tribunal both within and outside of

* Chair Foundation IPT 1965. I thank Nursyahbani Katjasungkana for her inspiration and insightful comments.

[1] The application of the term 'genocide' in relation to the mass killings in Indonesia is contested. However, as will be discussed, the Panel of Judges of the IPT 1965 concluded that the term 'genocide' was applicable, and I therefore use the term throughout this chapter, in addition to the terms that are most widely used, 'massacres' and 'mass killings'. See IPT 1965, *Final Report of the IPT 1965: Findings and Documents of the International People's Tribunal on Crimes against Humanity Indonesia 1965* (hereafter *Final Report*) (20 July 2016), http://tribunal1965.org/pdf/IPT_report_of_judges.pdf. Ultimus Publishers in Bandung has published the *Final Report* in English and Indonesian (March 2017).

Indonesia. I also deal with some major ethical and practical concerns and conclude with some reflections on this People's Tribunal in the light of other tribunals.

The Foundation IPT on the 1965 Crimes against Humanity in Indonesia (Foundation IPT 1965 or IPT 1965) was formally established in March 2014. The hearings of the Tribunal established by the Foundation IPT 1965, the International People's Tribunal on 1965 Crimes against Humanity in Indonesia (hereafter the Tribunal), were held in November 2015. The *Final Report* of the Panel of Judges was presented in July 2016 and published in both English and Indonesian in 2017.

As Simm and Byrnes argue, there is a gap in the official structure of accountability for grave human rights violations, as the international human rights structures built to ensure peace and security often fail to do so, particularly if states refuse to accept their responsibilities.[2] As I will argue, people's tribunals, such as the one established by IPT 1965, both expose the inadequacy of international legal standards and, in their very recourse to international human rights law, attempt to strengthen the legitimacy of the United Nations (UN) system. For both victims and activists have a 'desire for law'[3] and demand accountability of the state for their suffering. If that state, in this case Indonesia, is unwilling to provide justice and truth, at least a people's tribunal can validate their experiences of suffering and humiliation and confirm the hope that justice is still possible via international recognition.

5.2 Setting Up the Tribunal

The 1965 killings in Indonesia can be classified as one of the worst mass murders of the twentieth century. However, this genocide is hardly known internationally. For more than three decades, Soeharto's 'New Order' government ruled the country with authoritarian power, silencing all voices which campaigned for human rights. Instead, the pattern of violence was repeated in the annexation by Indonesia of East Timor between 1975 and 1999[4] and in West Papua.[5]

2 Gabrielle Simm and Andrew Byrnes, 'International Peoples' Tribunals in Asia: Political theatre, juridical farce or meaningful intervention?' (2014) 4(1) *Asian Journal of International Law* 103.

3 Andrew Byrnes and Gabrielle Simm, 'Peoples' tribunals, international law and the use of force' (2013) 36 (2) *University of New South Wales Law Journal* 711, 743.

4 Peter Kasenda, *Soeharto; bagaimana ia bisa melanggengkan kekuasaan selama 32 tahun?* [*How Could Soeharto Perpetuate his Power for 32 Years?*] (Kompas, 2002).

5 See Edwards on the Biak Massacre People's Tribunal, Chapter 9 in this volume.

After the fall of the dictator President Soeharto in 1998 hopes were raised that the impunity of the perpetrators of the crimes after 1965 would be lifted. The National Human Rights Commission (KomnasHAM) produced a report in 2012 which concluded that the atrocities committed during those years must be seen as crimes against humanity.[6] This landmark report, of which only an executive summary is publicly available, is based on the results of an investigation conducted in six regions between 2008 and 2012 (Flores (Maumere), Bali, Maluku (Buru), North and South Sumatera and South Sulawesi) and the testimonies of 349 witnesses and survivors. Although the report does not attempt to extrapolate the numbers of victims nationwide, overwhelming evidence is given of 'widespread and systematic' killings, exterminations, enslavement and forced labour, forced eviction and banishments, arbitrary deprivation of freedom, torture, rape and other forms of sexual violence and enforced disappearances. These activities were violations of international criminal law (and national law) at the time they were committed. Such offences are codified as crimes against humanity in the Rome Statute of the International Criminal Court to which Indonesia is not yet a party, although the Statute could not be applied retrospectively in any event. The offences also constituted crimes at a national level according to Law No 26/2000 on Human Rights Courts, which closely follows the wording of the Rome Statute. It is this law to which the *KomnasHAM Report* refers.

KomnasHAM acknowledged that the victims were targeted for their alleged ties with the Partai Komunis Indonesia (PKI or Indonesian Communist Party). It recognised the Indonesian State as the mastermind of the crimes, underlining that 'these events were the result of state policy to exterminate members and sympathizers of the PKI which was deemed to have conducted resistance against the state'.[7] Its report was submitted to the Office of the Attorney General which returned it on procedural grounds. To this day the Attorney General has taken no action. Only when the film *The Act of Killing* by Joshua Oppenheimer was launched in 2012 and screenings took place in several countries were the eyes of the international community opened to these atrocities.[8] In Indonesia, *The Act of Killing* could only be screened secretly. A comprehensive report on the mass killings in *Tempo* magazine in September 2012 helped raise new awareness in the country about this massacre. Oppenheimer's

[6] Komnas HAM, *Ringkasan Eksekutif; laporan penyelidikan pelanggaran HAM berat peristiwa 1965–66* [*Executive Summary, Report on the Research into Grave Human Rights Violations 1965–66*] (hereafter *KomnasHAM Report*) (KomnasHAM RI, 2015).

[7] Ibid., 3.

[8] *The Act of Killing* film, www.theactofkilling.com.

second film, *The Look of Silence* (2014),[9] which was screened more widely in the country despite a rather belated official ban, also increased public awareness.

The primary responsibility for ending the impunity of the perpetrators and providing justice for the victims lies with the state of Indonesia. However, it has failed over the last fifty years to investigate these crimes, to prosecute perpetrators, to officially and fully apologise and to provide reparations and other meaningful remedies to the victims and their families. This failure and unwillingness to act has persisted in spite of repeated demands made by victims, human rights activists and scholars, especially since the end of the Soeharto regime in 1998, which saw the beginning of the so-called reformasi era. Meanwhile, discriminatory policies and violence by hardline Muslim and anti-communist groups against the surviving victims of 1965–66 and their families continue and have gone unpunished. Meetings are regularly disrupted by such militia, and former prisoners receive visits from security personnel, particularly in the rural areas.[10] Hopes were again raised in 2014 that the Indonesian government would undertake action against the perpetrators of the post-1965 crimes against humanity when a new president took office. Mr Joko Widodo had promised in his campaign to address serious human rights violations including the post-1965 massacres, but he has disappointed his supporters on this issue.

In March 2013 a group of exiles, human rights activists, journalists and researchers decided to organise a people's tribunal. These activists were convinced that the failures of the Indonesian state to deal with the crimes against humanity committed after October 1965 must not be allowed to silence the voices of victims and their families or to permit the government of Indonesia to escape accountability for these crimes. Our concept note stated that the purpose of the Tribunal was to redress the tendency to trivialise, excuse, marginalise and obfuscate this genocide and the other crimes against humanity, particularly the rapes and other forms of sexual violence and torture of women prisoners. It was also established out of the belief, expressed repeatedly by the victims as well as their families, that acknowledging and assigning responsibility for the crimes

9 *The Look of Silence* film, www.thelookofsilence.com/.

10 Personal communication from former prisoners during meetings of the Forum 1965, an alliance of various organisations of victims, set up by members and supporters of the Indonesian IPT 1965 team. I attended meetings of this Forum during the first half of 2016.

would help ensure that they lived out their remaining years in greater dignity, peace and security.

We opted for a small horizontal management structure, consisting of a general coordinator, the well-known women's and human rights lawyer Nursyahbani Katjasungkana, and two secretariats, in Jakarta and in The Hague. The latter was tasked with organising the hearings for the preparation of which several teams were set up headed by members of the Organizing Committee (OC).[11] Nursyahbani Katjasungkana, who headed the team in Jakarta, tried to get political support there, organised seminars and workshops with human rights activists and the victims' organisations, maintained contact with the Indonesian prosecutors and issued invitations to the judges to participate. She also regularly spent time in The Hague to oversee our work there. In the Netherlands we held regular meetings with exiles.

The jurisdiction of the Tribunal was defined in the Charter of the Tribunal.[12] This Charter was approved by the judges and gave the Tribunal jurisdiction over genocide and crimes against humanity under customary international law as well as under Indonesian human rights law. The Charter declared that the Tribunal had an obligation to state clearly, based on the evidence presented, whether or not all charges were supported by sufficient evidence and to pronounce a judgment on the basis of the evidence presented.

The prestige of the seven judges invited to participate contributed to the weight of the Tribunal internationally.[13] Some judges had an eminent legal background (Zak Yacoob and Geoffrey Nice), and others had a distinguished career in other international courts (Helen Jarvis and Mireille Fanon Mendès-France), were leading international rights experts (Cees Flinterman), had expertise in human rights (Shadi Sadr) or were highly respected scholars (John Gittings). The team of prosecutors was likewise impressive. The chief prosecutor was Indonesia's leading human rights lawyer T. Mulya Lubis. The other Indonesian prosecutors were all respected human rights lawyers: Antarini Arna, Uli Parulian

[11] On the organisation of the Tribunal and the names of those involved on the Organising Committee and in other roles, see generally *Final Report*, above n. 1, 10–15.

[12] See Nursyahbani Katjasungkana and Saskia E Wieringa, 'Narrative Report of the IPT 1965' (hereafter IPT Narrative Report), www.tribunal1965.org/narrative-report-hearings-of-the-international-peoples-tribunal-on-the-1965-crimes-against-humanity-in-indonesia/.

[13] IPT 1965, '1965 Tribunal Hearings: The Judges' (October 2015), www.tribunal1965.org/1965-tribunal-hearings-the-judges/. For a fuller description of the background of the judges of the Tribunal, see IPT Narrative Report, above n. 12.

Sihombing, Rinto Tri Hapsoro and Bahrain Van Halen. The prosecutorial team was completed by Silke Studzinsky, an international expert on sexual violence. These experts from all over the world lent credibility to the Tribunal.

5.3 Historical Background

In the early morning of 1 October 1965 a group of middle-ranking Indonesian national army officers, led by Colonels Untung and Latief and calling themselves the September 30th Movement (G30S Movement), abducted and murdered six top army generals and a lieutenant. This group was chaired by the shady figure of Sjam, the head of the Special Bureau of the PKI, a secret department, directly under the command of party leader Aidit. Apart from the PKI chair, very few other PKI leaders seem to have known, let alone approved, of the plans of the G30S group. The conspirators were strong supporters of President Soekarno and claimed to have taken the President under their protection to prevent a military coup against him.[14]

General Soeharto, who was informed of the impending action but took no measures to inform or protect his superior officers, took control of the army and quickly aborted this attempted purge of the top echelon of the army.[15] There were some scattered attempts at revolt in a few other cities. All in all, only a small number of army units, as well as some PKI youth department volunteers who had been called up for guard duty at the last moment, were involved. This episode is hereafter referred to as the 'events of 1965'. To this day there are aspects of these 'events' that remain unclear, in particular the role of General Soeharto. The stated intention of the G30S group was to bring the generals before President Soekarno.[16] Why some of them were shot when they resisted arrest and the others

[14] There is a broad consensus in the literature about these aspects of the G30S affair. The most extensive review of this literature can be found in John Roosa, *Pretext for Mass Murder: The September 30th Movement and Soeharto's Coup d'État in Indonesia* (University of Wisconsin Press, 2006).

[15] Colonel Latief, one of the plotters, visited General Soeharto, a good friend of his, just before the planned action, and possibly earlier as well. Colonel Untung may also have visited him. See Kasenda, above n. 4, and H. Soebandrio, *'Yang saya alami': peristiwa G30S* [*What I Experienced: The G30s Affair*] (Bumi Intitama Sejahtera, 2006). Roosa, above n. 14, also mentions Latief's visit to Soeharto.

[16] Harold Crouch, *The Army and Politics in Indonesia* (Cornell University Press, 1978); Roosa, above n. 14; Ulf Sundhaussen, *The Road to Power: Indonesian Military Politics, 1945–1967* (Oxford University Press, 1982).

were murdered on a training field for nationalist volunteers remains unclear. The lieutenant in charge of the abductions (Dul Arif) went missing and his statement was never recorded. PKI chair Aidit went on the run, was captured a few weeks later and killed extra-judicially, so his statement was not recorded either.[17]

A recent analysis of the trial of Colonel Untung suggests that the order to kill the generals came from 'trusted sources', i.e., from officers higher in rank than the two colonels who headed the military operations of the G30S group.[18] During his trial Colonel Latief revealed that he had informed General Soeharto of the impending actions himself.[19] Soeharto swung into action after he learnt that the country's top generals had been killed (apart from General Nasution, who managed to escape) and that President Soekarno did not support the G30S group. His handling of the situation was so uncannily effective that some observers suspect he may not have been improvising.[20] It is indeed very likely that several scenarios had been prepared by various groups, as the political situation at the time was highly volatile, partly caused by rumours of the president being ill and by the accelerating economic crisis. Foreign powers such as the United States were also meddling in Indonesia's internal affairs.[21]

On 1 October 1965 General Soeharto immediately claimed that a coup had been attempted and vowed to annihilate those involved in the G30S Movement. On 6 October 1965 the PKI was specifically mentioned as being the *dalang* (puppeteer) of this group. In the meantime in Aceh, a province in a state of high military alert as a result of Soekarno's policy of Confrontation with Malaysia, the killing of PKI members had already started.[22] This occurred although it was evident that the party was totally

[17] It is also unclear why he was brought to Halim, the headquarters of the rebel officers.

[18] Coen Holzappel, 'Professional blindness and missing the mark – the thirtieth September movement as seen by the perpetrators: between registered facts and authoritative opinions – part one' (2014), *Rozenberg Quarterly*, www.rozenbergquarterly.com/professional-blindness-and-missing-the-mark-the-thirtieth-september-movement-as-seen-by-the-perpetrators-between-registered-facts-and-authoritative-opinions.

[19] Abdul Latief, *Pledoi Kol. A. Latief: Soeharto terlibat G30S* [*The Defence of Colonel A. Latief: Soeharto's Involvement in G30S*] (Institut Studi Arus Informasi, 2000).

[20] Kasenda, above n. 4; Roosa, above n. 14; Suar Suroso, *Bung Karno: korban perang dingin* [*Bung Karno: Victim of the Cold War*] (Hasta Mitra, 2008).

[21] Peter Scott, 'The United States and the overthrow of Soekarno, 1965–67' (1985) 58(2) *Pacific Affairs* 239–64; Bradley Simpson, *Economists with Guns: Authoritarian Development and U.S.-Indonesian Relations, 1960–1968* (Stanford University Press, 2008); and Suroso, above n. 20.

[22] Jess Melvin's work on the extermination of the PKI in Aceh after 1 October 1965 demonstrates clearly the leading role of the army in orchestrating the mass killings and

unprepared for this attack and the majority of its leaders were in no way involved, let alone the millions of members and sympathisers. On 10 October 1965 General Soeharto established the Command for Restoration of Security and Order (KOPKAMTIB), an extra-constitutional security and intelligence agency in charge of political prosecution and control with extra-legal powers: to destroy the PKI and hunt down and arrest its members and sympathizers.

A mass campaign of sexual slander against members of the progressive women's organisation Gerwani (Gerakan Wanita Indonesia, Indonesian Women's Movement) was organised. Members of Gerwani were accused of having castrated and tortured the generals.[23] This was the start of an extremely successful propaganda campaign, the effects of which persist fifty years later. The PKI was painted as having betrayed the nation and as being against religion (read Islam) and against the national ideology, the Pancasila (five pillars).[24] This was accompanied by a campaign of terror against suspected communists and alleged associates including socialist women, left-wing activists, intellectuals, members of peasant groups and labour unions and sympathisers of President Soekarno in general, as well as against members of the Chinese community. In addition, artists and groups associated with popular culture and those who belonged to indigenous religions were harassed; many of them were imprisoned, tortured and/or killed or disappeared.[25]

In 1966 Soeharto managed to oust President Soekarno from power and the following year he was inaugurated as president. The political, military

the very prompt reactions of Soeharto and allied officers. Jess Melvin, 'Mechanics of Mass Murder: How the Indonesian Military Initiated and Implemented the Indonesian Genocide: The Case of Aceh', PhD thesis, University of Melbourne (2014), http://hdl.handle.net/11343/42278.

23 Saskia Wieringa, *Sexual Politics in Indonesia* (Palgrave/McMillan, 2002).

24 The Pancasila are the five pillars of society, conceived by the nation's founding fathers, Sukarno and Hatta. It comprises five principles held to be inseparable and interrelated: (1) Belief in the one and only God, *Ketuhanan Yang Maha Esa*; (2) Just and civilized humanity, *Kemanusiaan Yang Adil dan Beradab*; (3) The unity of Indonesia, *Persatuan Indonesia*; (4) Democracy guided by the inner wisdom in the unanimity arising out of deliberations amongst representatives, *Kerakyatan Yang Dipimpin oleh Hikmat Kebijaksanaan, Dalam Permusyawaratan dan Perwakilan*; (5) Social justice for all of the people of Indonesia, *Keadilan Sosial bagi seluruh Rakyat Indonesia.* They are referred to in the Preamble of the Constitution and are to be found all over the country, in school books and on pillars along the road.

25 Prior to the G30S Affair the cultural association linked to the PKI, LEKRA (Lembaga Kebudayaan Rakyat, People's Cultural Association) had been very active in promoting 'people's art'.

and economic machinery he established remained intact after his enforced resignation. This partly explains why the ghost of Communism can still be conjured up when elite groups deem it necessary, and why the stigma of being associated with the PKI still remains strong.[26]

From late October 1965 onwards the army trained and armed militia units and recruited religious groups, student organisations and right-wing trade unions to help implement the massacres. Hundreds of thousands of innocent people were murdered, imprisoned, tortured and raped and many of them disappeared. Between October 1965 and March 1966, it is reliably estimated that between 500,000 and 1 million people were killed and more than 1.7 million people were imprisoned without trial.[27] The campaign of terror did not stop then, though it slowed down. Moreover, the so-called New Order of President Soeharto revoked the passports of hundreds of students and PKI sympathisers who happened to be abroad and who refused to support this government. For years many of them were effectively stateless and suffered from uncertainty about their status before they were eventually granted asylum by the Netherlands and other European countries.

5.4 The Indictment and the Conclusions of the Panel of Judges

The prosecution submitted that the inhumane acts committed in Indonesia after the 'events of 1965' were crimes against humanity in international law. It also argued that derogation was not permitted under any circumstances, as the prohibition of crimes against humanity is a jus cogens norm under international customary law.[28] Crimes against humanity in customary international law are fundamentally inhumane acts committed as part of a widespread or systematic attack against

[26] See, for instance, Ariel Heryanto, *State Terrorism and Political Identity in Indonesia: Fatally Belonging* (Routledge, 2006), and Baskara T. Wardaya et al. (eds.), *Menelusuri akar otoritarianisme di Indonesia* [*Unravelling the Roots of Authoritarianism in Indonesia*] (ELSAM, 2007).

[27] Robert Cribb (ed.), *The Indonesian Killings of 1965–6: Studies from Java and Bali* (Monash University Centre of Southeast Asian Studies, 1990); Robert Cribb, 'Unresolved problems in the Indonesian killings 1965–66' (2002) 42 (4) *Asian Survey* 550–63; Douglas Kammen and Katharine McGregor, *The Contours of Mass Violence in Indonesia, 1965–68* (NUS Press, 2012).

[28] M. Cherif Bassiouni, *Crimes against Humanity: Historical Evolution and Contemporary Application* (Cambridge University Press, 2011) 263.

civilians; they involve acts that are crimes in most national criminal law systems.[29] Written material submitted to the Tribunal was supplemented by four days of hearings in November 2015 in The Hague at which witness testimony and further arguments were presented to the judges.

After some months of deliberation the Panel of Judges presented its final conclusions in a report on 21 July 2016, accompanied by a video in which Presiding Judge Zak Yacoob read out the major conclusions and recommendations.[30] In summary, the Panel of Judges concluded that the state of Indonesia was 'responsible for and guilty of crimes against humanity consequent upon the commission and perpetration, particularly by the military of that state through its chain of command, of the inhumane acts' alleged by the prosecutors. The Judges further ruled:

> [A]ll these acts were an integral part of a broad and widespread systematic attack against the Communist Party of Indonesia (Partai Komunis Indonesia, PKI), its affiliate organisations, its leaders, members and supporters and their families (as well as those alleged to have been sympathetic to its aims), and more broadly against many people having no connection at all with the PKI, in what became a widespread purge, which included many supporters of President Sukarno and progressive members of the Nationalist Party of Indonesia, PNI.

They stressed that 'each inhumane act was . . . a crime in Indonesia and in most civilized countries of the world.'[31]

The judges further stated that 'the State of Indonesia failed to prevent the perpetration of these inhumane acts or to punish those responsible for their commission. To the extent that some crimes were committed independently of the authorities, by so-called "spontaneous" local action, this did not absolve the State from the obligation to prevent their occurrence and to punish those responsible.'[32]

Thus the Panel of Judges concluded that the Indonesian state must be held responsible for mass killings, imprisonment, enslavement, torture, enforced disappearance and sexual violence. These conclusions are in conformity with the charges in the indictment submitted by the prosecution. They are also consistent with the analysis of the 2012 *KomnasHAM*

[29] Law No. 26, Year 2000, Establishing the Ad Hoc Human Rights Court, Article 9; Rome Statute of the International Criminal Court, Rome, 17 July 1998, 2187 UNTS 90, in force 1 July 2002, Article 7; UN SC Resolution 827 (1993) concerning Yugoslavia, 25 May 1993, S/RES/827, para. 5; UN SC Resolution 955 (1994) concerning Rwanda, 8 November 1994, S/RES/955, para. 3.

[30] *Final Report*, above n. 1, 79. [31] Ibid. [32] Ibid.

Report. In their reasons, the judges refer both to domestic and to international legal standards. Four issues dealt within the *Final Report* deserve particular attention. First, the judges found that a number of the exiles had been deprived of their full and unconditional rights of citizenship. They argued that 'the policy of involuntary or forcible exile, apart from being inhumane conduct, formed part of a widespread systematic state attack against a substantial and significant targeted sector of the civilian population, and may well be a crime against humanity in the form of persecution.'[33] This ruling will hopefully spark debate, as involuntary or forced exile is not explicitly listed as a crime against humanity in the Rome Statute, nor is it mentioned in the 2012 *KomnasHAM Report.*

The second issue was the question of propaganda as incitement to murder, which had been highlighted in the research report. The judges concluded:

> [T]he official version of what happened to the prisoners at Lubang Buaya was totally false. The true facts were known to the military leadership under General Suharto ... [t]he sustained propaganda campaign against those accused of being linked to the PKI helped to justify the extra-legal persecution, detention and killing of alleged suspects, and to legitimize sexual violence and all the inhumane conduct already described. Unchallenged for more than three decades, this propaganda contributed not only to the denial of civil rights of survivors but also to their continued persecution. Spreading false propaganda for the purpose of preparing the ground for violence is integral to the commission of that violence. The act of preparing for the crime cannot be said to be separate from the crime itself. This preparation paved the way and was the beginning and part of the overall, broad attack.[34]

Thirdly, the prosecution had also laid charges of complicity against other states, notably the United States, United Kingdom and Australia. All three countries had been invited to defend themselves at the hearings, as had Indonesia,[35] but none of them had accepted this invitation. The judges concluded that the United States, the United Kingdom and Australia were all complicit to different degrees in the commission of these crimes against humanity and that they were all aware of what was taking

[33] Ibid., 81.

[34] Ibid., 81. Lubang Buaya is the name of the field where the generals were murdered and buried in a deserted well. It was a training ground for socialist volunteers, in relation to the anti-Malaysia campaign of President Soekarno. See Wieringa, above n. 23.

[35] We had asked lawyers from Leiden University to prepare an amicus curiae submission stating the position of the government of Indonesia, but they were unable to do so.

place in Indonesia.[36] The United States 'gave sufficient support to the Indonesian military, knowing well that they were embarked on a programme of mass killings and other criminal conduct for the charge of complicity in crimes against humanity to be justified.'[37]

Finally, the Tribunal addressed the question of whether genocide had been committed. The prosecution had not included the count of genocide in its indictment,[38] though the research report had presented arguments in support of such a charge. There were two main reasons for not including the charge. Some argued that they did not support the application of the term 'genocide' to groups other than those specifically mentioned in the 1948 Genocide Convention, namely, those belonging to a 'national, ethnical, racial or religious group'.[39] The other reason was that, as prosecutors for this highly sensitive Tribunal, they were already under heavy attack. If they had included genocide in the indictment, their situation would have become even more difficult.

Two genocide scholars submitted an amicus curiae (friend of the court) brief in which they urged the judges 'to analyse [the] evidence to determine that the events of the case at issue constitute genocide as the partial destruction of the Indonesian national group'.[40] The judges eventually decided to consider the arguments on this question of genocide based on the material presented in the research report and the amicus brief.[41] They concluded that the evidence put before the Tribunal by the prosecution included acts that fall within the prohibition in the Genocide Convention. These acts had been committed against a significant and substantial section of the Indonesian nation or 'Indonesian national group', a protected group under the Genocide Convention, and were committed with the specific intent to annihilate or destroy that subgroup in whole or in part. The same analysis arguably also applies to crimes committed against the Chinese ethnic minority group, on which material had also been presented in the research report. The judges insisted that, although Indonesia had neither signed nor ratified the 1948 Genocide Convention at the relevant time (and as of mid-2017 had still not

[36] *Final Report*, above n. 1, 71–72, 81–82. [37] Ibid., 81.

[38] IPT 1965, 'Indictment' (2015), www.tribunal1965.org/indictment-1965-tribunal/.

[39] Convention on the Prevention and Punishment of the Crime of Genocide, Paris, 9 December 1948, 78 UNTS 277, in force 12 January 1951, Article II.

[40] Brief submitted to the Tribunal on 11 November 2015 by Dr Daniel Feierstein and Mrs Irene Victoria Massimino of the Universidad Nacional de Tres de Febrero, Buenos Aires, Argentina.

[41] IPT Research Report, Part 1, 50, 53.

done so), the prohibition against genocide contained in the Convention was a rule of customary international law that had been binding on Indonesia by 1965.[42]

5.5 An Anthropologist's Perspective

Since the early 1980s I have been studying the Indonesian women's movement. I became intrigued by the sudden disappearance of the third largest women's organisation in the world at the time, Gerwani. When some ex-prisoners, former members of this organisation, asked for my help to document their history and particularly the circumstances of its demise, I agreed. They still had to report to the police regularly, could not travel around the country freely and were prevented from visiting their former friends and colleagues. I had more freedom of movement but my interviews with former Gerwani members also had to be carried out with great circumspection, and I could only access leaders at the national and higher regional levels, mostly in public or other safe spaces (for instance, religious institutions or non-government organisations [NGOs]). They were particularly troubled by the false accusation that the young women of their group had performed a naked dance at the site where the generals were murdered and had tortured and castrated the generals in an orgy. While in prison they had heard the stories of those young girls who were brought in, terribly tortured and forced to sign false statements (as 'proof' some of them were photographed naked within the prison walls).

In 1986 I wrote my first paper on the history of the women's movement in Indonesia and the influence of the events of 1965 on the movement as a whole and Gerwani in particular for a conference at Leiden University. It created an enormous controversy both in Indonesia and in Leiden. My paper was banned from the conference proceedings and I myself was blacklisted from Indonesia for thirteen years.[43] This period was the height of the oppression of the military regime, and those involved from the University of Leiden preferred their good relations with the Soeharto regime over academic freedom.

During that time I finished my PhD but could not defend it, as it first had to be checked with my informants. We had agreed I would be responsible for the analysis, but they would have the last say on issues

[42] *Final Report*, above n. 1, 78, 82.

[43] Sita van Bemmelen, Madelon Djajadiningrat-Nieuwenhuis, Elsbeth Locher-Scholten and Elly Touwen-Boomsma (eds.), *Women and Mediation in Indonesia* (KITLV Press, 1992).

of security. After an underground visit to Indonesia in 1994 I was finally able to graduate in 1995. The thesis was quickly translated and became widely used by activists in Indonesia.[44]

I was naive enough to believe that once I had written it all down, Gerwani would somehow be rehabilitated and the slander would not be believed any more. After a few years I realised that this was not the case.[45] Gerwani members continued to face the stigma attributed to them. I then decided to write a novel on my experiences researching this period in the Indonesian women's movement. I produced a political thriller entitled *The Crocodile Hole* (named after the field where the generals were dumped in a well).[46] This book was also immediately translated, and though Gerwani members and women activists appreciated it very much and it soon sold out, the stigma continued, and the lies about Gerwani continued to be believed.[47] Next I collaborated with a Swedish film-maker Maj Wechselmann in a documentary film on Gerwani and the campaign against them. In contrast to many Western scholars who ignore the strong impact of sexual slander on a conservative and deeply religious nation, she immediately grasped the impact of this campaign.[48] The resulting film, *The Women and the Generals* (2012), was shown on Swedish television and circulates in activist circles but has not had a wide impact.[49]

[44] Saskia E. Wieringa, 'The Politicization of Gender Relations in Indonesia', PhD thesis, University of Amsterdam, published as *Penghancuran Gerakan Perempuan di Indonesia* [*The Destruction of the Women's Movement in Indonesia*] (Garba Budaya, 1999) (translated by Hersri Setiawan). These two versions have been screened for the security of my informants. The unabridged version was published in English in 2002: Wieringa, above n. 23.

[45] Though Ibu Sulami, one of Gerwani's leaders, with whom I collaborated closely during my research, wrote me a moving letter after she had read the first draft of my thesis, telling me that she could now die in peace, that this was a golden thread of hope in the last days of her life, as she now knew that the history of her organisation had been honestly documented.

[46] Saskia Wieringa, *Het Krokodillengat* [*The Crocodile Hole*] (LaVita, 2007), translated into English as *The Crocodile Hole* (Yayasan Jurnal Perempuan, 2015).

[47] During the Ubud Writers' Festival in 2015 we were prohibited from launching the book formally and instead organised a book 'lunch' which was disturbed three times by members of the security forces. Saskia Wieringa, '*The crocodile hole* in Ubud: How a feminist lunch evades a book ban' (2016) 19(1) *Tijdschrift voor Genderstudies* 107.

[48] See Saskia Wieringa, 'Sexual Slander and the 1965–6 Mass Killings in Indonesia: Political and Methodological Considerations' (2011) 41 *Journal of Contemporary Asia* 544–66, for an analysis of these politics of ignorance by male-stream scholars.

[49] The film can be viewed at https://vimeo.com/119472614 or at www.wechselmann.se/en/2013/03/26/the-women-and-the-generals/.

After the launch of *The Act of Killing* by Joshua Oppenheimer in the Netherlands in 2013, a group of some thirty-five exiles sat together in my house with the director and Stanley Prasetyo, a former commissioner of the National Human Rights Commission who had been involved in the research on 1965, and some other human rights activists to discuss what steps we could take to end the impunity of the perpetrators of the post-October 1965 crimes against humanity. Nursyahbani Katjasungkana, a prominent human and women's rights lawyer in Indonesia, shared her experiences as the chief prosecutor for Indonesia of the Tokyo Women's International War Crimes Tribunal on Japan's military sexual slavery.[50] Those present at the meeting decided a people's tribunal might end the silence at national and international level, help restore the dignity of the victims and hopefully set in motion a process that would ensure non-recurrence. Nursyahbani Katjasungkana received the mandate from the exiles to organise this tribunal.

In March 2014 the Foundation IPT was formally established. I am the chair and the other board members are Sungkono and Sri Tunruang (treasurer). My major duties were trying to obtain funding, liaising with the Dutch government, assisting Nursyahbani in setting up secretariats in Jakarta and in the Netherlands, and coordinating the team that was preparing the research report. We managed with very great difficulty to get just enough funds for the material expenses related to the hearings. Many funding agencies were hesitant to touch this issue, knowing that the Indonesian government would not take it lightly. The Dutch government was not happy the hearings would be held in The Hague and suggested we hold them in Jakarta. We explained that we would prefer that as well but that it would be much too dangerous to hold the hearings in Jakarta, and that The Hague, with its image as the City of International Justice, would be best qualified.

Initially I had hoped we could use the *KomnasHAM Report*. However, as this report was still under embargo, we had to start from scratch in preparing a research report for the prosecution on which it could base the indictment. In the end, forty researchers and activists responded to requests for assistance, sending in whole chapters, summaries of their research work or sometimes databases. More than half of the researchers were Indonesian, and most of those submitted their work in Indonesian. We prepared a report of some thousand pages,

50 See further Dolgopol, Chapter 4 in this volume.

less than half of which was in Indonesian, which most of the prosecutors but not the judges could read.

As coordinator I myself filled in various gaps, providing an overview of the scholarly arguments of who masterminded the actions of the G30S group, an analysis of the propaganda campaign against the PKI and arguments on whether the mass killings could be classified as a genocide, as well as material about the campaign of sexual slander on which I had already written. I also wrote a chapter on the complicity of Dutch and Indonesian psychologists who developed tests which were supposed to measure the level of 'communistness'.[51] In the absence of any kind of legal process for the vast majority of detainees, these tests replaced a juridical trial.[52] With a small group of co-editors (Sri Wahyuningrum, the late Wijaya Herlambang, Ratna Saptari, Annie Pohlman and Jess Melvin), we collected various kinds of data for thirteen regions all over Indonesia.

During the hearings I was anxious to find out whether the judges considered the materials brought before them sufficient. After all we had worked on a totally voluntary basis, for a short period of time, while paid staff had taken several years to compile the reports of both KomnasHAM and Komnas Perempuan (National Commission on Violence against Women[53]). Fortunately, Mariana Amaruddin from Komnas Perempuan had received official permission to attend the hearings. She confirmed the materials on sexual violence that had been compiled by our researchers, which I had presented as an expert witness. Sadly, KomnasHAM did not agree to having a commissioner attend our hearings; yet the responsible commissioner for the 1965 case, Dianto Bachriadi, came of his own accord. He too testified that the material brought before the judges was totally consistent with the report of the Commission which he had helped

[51] A classification system was used to determine who should be tried. Category A were those who were involved in the actual abductions and murders of the generals and the other actions of the G30S group. Category B were those who were not supposed to be released soon, and members of category C spent only a few years in prison.

[52] These arguments will be published in 2018 in a monograph provisionally titled *Imagined Evil* (Routledge).

[53] The Komisi Nasional anti Kekerasan terhadap Perempuan (Komnas Perempuan) (National Commission against Violence against Women) was set up in 1998 after the so-called May riots of that year in which many ethnic Chinese women were raped. It is an independent state institution. Its legal basis is Presidential Decree 181/1998, which was renewed by the Presidential Regulations 65 and 66/2005.

prepare. These two testimonies significantly supported the case the prosecutors brought before the judges.

5.6 Practical Matters

Organising the Tribunal was a major challenge. Two factors enabled us to implement it. First was the political momentum. This was initially created by the finalisation of the report on the 1965 crimes against humanity of KomnasHam in 2012,[54] which had been preceded by a 2007 report on sexual violence by Komnas Perempuan that had received far less attention.[55] Both reports contain excellent analyses of the types of violence and violations committed by the state after the 'events of 1965'. The momentum was increased by the wide attention received by the brilliant films of Joshua Oppenheimer. The presidential campaign and the subsequent election of the candidate most likely to address grave human rights violations also gave hope that this was the time to attract international attention to the massacres. Finally, we could use the slogan 'breaking 50 years of silence', as 2015, the year in which we held the hearings, was the fiftieth anniversary of the 'events of 1965' which led to the massacres and the destruction of the PKI as well as the toppling of the president. At the national level, the progressive magazine *Tempo* published two issues on the 'events of 1965': one on perpetrators and one on the PKI-affiliated cultural association LEKRA.[56] These publications sparked great interest.

The second contributing factor was the willingness of so many specialists, victims and students to contribute their expertise, experiences and time to help organise the Tribunal. Researchers undertook research, film-makers documented the process and prepared the live streaming, media specialists ran the social and other media and set up the website, security experts devised a security plan, the prosecutors and the registrar gave legal advice and their time prior to and during the hearings, the

[54] Although the full report is not yet officially released, the executive summary is lengthy and gives an excellent and detailed overview of the results of the research.

[55] Komnas Perempuan, *Laporan Pemantauan Ham Perempuan: Kejahatan Terhadap Kemanusiaan Berbasis Jender – Mendengarkan Suara Perempuan Korban Peristiwa 1965* [*Gender-Based Crimes against Humanity: Listening to the Voices of Women Survivors of 1965*] (Komnas Perempuan, 2007).

[56] In October 1965 the special issue 'Pengakuan Algojo 1965' ['The Confession of a 1965 Butcher'] was published. In September 2013 the special issue was called 'LEKRA dan geger 1965' ['LEKRA and the 1965 tumult'].

translating team worked as hard as they could to translate Indonesian material into English for the judges and the many student volunteers made themselves helpful in numerous ways. And, of critical importance, our judges devoted their time and expertise prior to, during and after the hearings, finalising the report which was released in July 2016. During the hearings about a hundred volunteers were working towards the success of the Tribunal.

We faced multiple challenges. First, due to the sensitivity of the issue, it was extremely hard to get any funding. Our major donor to this day does not want to be publicly acknowledged. We first received a modest grant from a small Dutch-based charity which helped us develop our website. By the end of 2014 we finally had the green light from our major donor. Closer to the hearings crowd-funding became more effective and that helped us pay for the last expenses and the presentation of the Final Report.

Most of our funding went into the hearings themselves. We decided we needed an impressive venue, not an inconspicuous university lecture hall. We first approached the Peace Palace, which had hosted the Iran Tribunal, but they refused on the basis that they are a politically neutral institution.[57] In the end we found the beautiful location of the New Church in The Hague. It could be well secured, which was important as we had received indications that disturbance might occur.[58] The rest of the money went into other material costs such as travel expenses and lodging of our judges, prosecutors and witnesses. A small amount went to the secretariats and to meetings with victims in Indonesia.

5.7 Ethical Concerns

Victim-survivors and their families continue to suffer discriminatory policies and violence perpetrated by Muslim hardliners and other

[57] The Iran Tribunal rented space 'in the building of The Hague Academy of International Law, immediately adjacent to the historic Peace Palace, which houses the International Court of Justice': Payam Akhavan, 'Is grassroots justice a viable alternative to impunity?: The case of the Iran People's Tribunal' (2017) 39(1) *Human Rights Quarterly* 73, 87. The Director of the Peace Palace explained to us that he had felt unhappy about this when he came to know of it.

[58] In the Netherlands the only intimidation we experienced was the threat from the Indonesian government that any Indonesian students with an Indonesian scholarship might lose that if they participated in the Tribunal. In the end, Indonesian students from all over Europe travelled to The Hague to assist.

anti-communist groups in Indonesia today. The spectre of a communist revival can be conjured up at any moment by particular military or political groups, who control the militias of thugs who carry out raids or other forms of violence. When we started organising the Tribunal, our major concern was to guarantee the safety of the victims. We needed to hold consultations with them, but we were aware that those meetings would attract the attention of such militias. Several planned meetings had to be cancelled. For instance, on 27 October 2013 the Forum Anti Komunis Indonesia (FAKI, Anti-Communist Forum) attacked and broke up a meeting organised by victims and survivors in Jogjakarta. Similarly the meeting organised in Bukit Tinggi on 22 March 2015 was forcibly disbanded by thugs. In Salatiga, the following day, militia supported by the police dissolved the meetings organised by the victims' support organisation LPH YAPHI (Lembaga Pengabdian Hukum Yayasan Pengabdian Hukum Indonesia, Rights Service Institution Foundation for the Service of Rights in Indonesia) in collaboration with the victims' organisation YPKP 1965 (Yayasan Penelitian Korban Pembunuhan 1965, Foundation for Research on the Victims of the Killings of 1965) and to which Komnas Perempuan, KomnasHAM and LPSK had been invited. The purpose of this meeting had been to discuss a new regulation on health allowances for victims of past human rights violations. These attacks were reported to President Joko Widodo, the Chief of Police Headquarters and the Chief Military Commander in Jakarta, but there was no response.

In the second half of 2015, tensions increased. The major issues triggering these strains were the fiftieth anniversary of the 'events of 1965' and the impending hearings of the Tribunal. For example, on 2 July 2015, members of the mass organisation Ansor (the youth wing of the Muslim mass organisation Nahdlatul Ulama), and leaders of other religious groups, attacked people whom they identified as making up a 'new style' Communist movement. These latter groups were identified as various human rights organisations that had been supporting victims of the crimes against humanity after 1 October 1965. They burned so-called PKI flags (which they must have made themselves) in the centre of Blitar.[59] The yearly presidential address to the nation on 17 August 2015 (Independence Day) was also very tense. Victims of the 1965 crimes against humanity hoped the president would apologise, while right-wing groups protested fiercely. In the end the president did not apologise.

[59] Redaski, 'Ormas Di Blitar Aksi Perangi PKI Gaya Baru', *Adakita News*, 2 July 2015, www.adakitanews.com/ormas-di-blitar-aksi-perangi-pki-gaya-baru.

Ultimately, a series of successful meetings was held in Solo, Jombang Cirebon, Jepara, Kupang, Aceh, Semarang, Surabaya and Medan in 2014 and the beginning of 2015. The members of the various victims' organisations welcomed the idea of the Tribunal, though we warned them that the Tribunal would not be able to ensure that any perpetrator would be brought to justice or that they would get compensation. They were pleased that international attention would be paid to their plight and hoped it would minimally reduce the stigma they still experienced.

Out of concern for the security of the witnesses and the prosecutors, an extensive security plan was drawn up. The Jakarta Secretariat lobbied the National Human Rights Commission, the National Commission on Violence against Woman, the Witness and the Victims' Protection Institute (LPSK) and the Advisory Council to the President to prepare a Standard Operational Procedure for the Security of the Witnesses and Victims. On 13 October 2015, a training workshop on this security plan was conducted by the IPT 1965 Jakarta Secretariat in collaboration with human rights defenders.

Human rights lawyers accompanied the witnesses to and from the Tribunal. During the sessions themselves, extra security officials were employed and the police were on standby. For each charge or crime, we invited and prepared at least one direct and one expert witness. Ultimately, seven factual/eye witnesses appeared before the Tribunal at its hearings from 10 to13 November 2015. Due to the quickly deteriorating security situation prior to the hearings, a number of witnesses were forced to use a pseudonym or to testify behind a screen. Fortunately, no incidents occurred during the sessions, and all witnesses and prosecutors were able to leave the Netherlands safely.

As was expected the Indonesian government reacted negatively to the Tribunal. The organisers were labelled 'enemies of the state' by various functionaries, including the Minister of Defence. When the delegation arrived back in Jakarta on 15 November 2015, the Aliansi Anti-Komunis Indonesia (Indonesian Anti-Communist Alliance) greeted them at the airport with large banners stating 'Selamat Datang Pengkhianat Bangsa' (Welcome Home, Traitors of the Nation) and 'Pengkhianat Jangan Kembali ke Indonesia' (Traitors don't come home to Indonesia).[60]

[60] Febriana Firdaus, 'Aliansi Anti-Komunis Indonesia "jemput" tim IPT 1965 di bandara', *The Rappler*, 15 November 2015, www.rappler.com/indonesia/112911-aliansi-anti-komunis-indonesia-tim-ipt-1965.

A group of police picked up the delegation and took them to the police station near the airport.[61] Lawyers from the Jakarta Legal Aid Institute (Lembaga Bantuan Hukum, LBH), a Commissioner of the National Commission on Human Rights and a human rights advocate from Kontras, as well as members of other human rights groups, also came to the airport to make sure that the delegation came back home safely. Members from the state institution LPSK accompanied the delegation to their homes.

In December 2015 the militia Pemuda Pancasila, which featured prominently in *The Act of Killing* as the perpetrators of most of the 1965 killings in Medan, sent a letter demanding that chief prosecutor T. Mulya Lubis, Nursyahbani Katjasungkana and prosecutor Uli Parulian Sihombing apologise to the Indonesian public for organising the IPT 1965. The letter informed the recipients that if they did not comply with this order, the Pemuda Pancasila could not be held responsible for any unrest that might result.

There were other ethical concerns about potentially endangering witnesses. In Palu (Central Sulawesi), for instance, a careful process of reconciliation has been underway for some years, with the mayor apologising for the crimes committed in 1965 in which he had participated. The activists involved were reluctant to join the Tribunal process, as they feared it might antagonise the authorities. Another concern was voiced by those activists who feared that a narrow form of nationalism might be stimulated by organising the Tribunal abroad, and particularly in the Netherlands, the former colonial ruler. Such sentiments were indeed voiced in the press by conservative generals such as Kivlan Zen and by the Minister of Defence. But more moderate and progressive media realized that this Tribunal simply could not have been held in Indonesia itself.[62]

After the hearings, the judges, particularly Helen Jarvis and John Gittings who were mandated to draft the report, worked for a number of months on the Final Report. As the situation in Indonesia was still

[61] Interestingly, the police used the word *mengamankan* (to put into safety) when they met the delegation at the gate. Everyone panicked, for that was the euphemism used during the 1965–66 mass murders to arrest people after which nothing more was heard of them. But this time the word was used in a respectful sense and the delegation was led away via a back gate and guided to their transport.

[62] See the list of press coverage of the Tribunal in Indonesia up until the end of 2015 in the IPT Narrative Report, above n. 13. The generally progressive media such as Rappler, BBC.com and the *Jakarta Post*, among others, reported positively. The conservative media such as the Muslim newspaper *Republika* were opposed.

very volatile, with anti-human rights generals and politicians regularly lashing out at anything they considered a revival of the PKI, it was not possible to present the Final Report of the panel of judges in Jakarta, as we had hoped. Instead, Nursyahbani Katjasungkana and our major film-maker went to South Africa, where Presiding Judge Zak Yacoob read extracts from the Final Report. The video made of this reading was presented simultaneously in five cities: Jakarta, Melbourne, Phnom Penh, Amsterdam and Stockholm. We had kept the venue of the presentation in Jakarta secret until right before the event, so media, which we had kept informed, attended in large numbers, but the right-wing militia fortunately did not.

5.8 Impact of the Tribunal

The significance of the Tribunal cannot be estimated according to the number of convictions. Its impact must be judged in different ways. As a people's tribunal, it derives its power from the voices of victims, and of national and international civil societies. Though the Tribunal had the format of a formal court, it was not a criminal court.

But was the Tribunal then a juridical farce or a political theatre, as Simm and Byrnes provocatively ask?[63] From the beginning all involved were very aware that the Tribunal would not lead to any formal judicial process and that no actual perpetrators would be prosecuted. As a people's tribunal, we realised that the power of the Tribunal lies in its capacity to examine evidence, develop an accurate historical record of the genocide and other crimes committed and apply principles of international law to the facts as found. This Tribunal stepped into the lacuna left by the state of Indonesia, but it did not purport to replace the role of the state of Indonesia in the legal process. Other international peoples' tribunals have contributed to creating a climate of respect for human rights and to the healing process of the victims and their families. In that sense, the IPT 1965 was a meaningful intervention as it has tangible results, some of which I will mention.

But we, the organisers, were very aware of the potential theatrical impact. We deliberately selected a monumental former church with an impressive interior to give cachet to the Tribunal.[64] The sessions were

[63] Simm and Byrnes, above n. 2.

[64] The building has a secular function now: it has been turned into a congress and cultural centre.

live streamed and accessible all over the world. In Indonesia, collective screenings were held in several places, with moderators from various human rights organisations. Tens of thousands of people watched the sessions, which are still accessible via YouTube.[65]

The pronouncement of the Panel of Judges on the applicability of the term 'genocide' for the mass killings in Indonesia after 1 October 1965 is significant. This is the first occasion on which a legal institution has come to this conclusion for Indonesia. But it will still be a long process until a more formal human rights body issues a similar statement or resolution on the topic. The process of bringing about such a pronouncement is underway. The Foundation IPT 1965 submitted a report to the UN Human Rights Council as part of the third cycle of the Council's Universal Periodic Review, in which Indonesia's progress on human rights was discussed in May 2017.

If we consider the major objectives of the Tribunal, to fight impunity, to break the silence and to restore the dignity of the victims, a preliminary assessment of the outcome of the Tribunal can be made. Impunity involves 'a failure by states to meet their obligations to investigate violations; to take appropriate measures in respect of the perpetrators, particularly in the area of justice, by ensuring that those suspected of criminal responsibility are prosecuted, tried and duly punished; to provide victims with effective remedies and to ensure that they receive reparation for the injuries suffered; to ensure the inalienable right to know the truth about violations; and to take other necessary steps to prevent a recurrence of violations'.[66] Key concepts thus are the right to truth, to justice and to rehabilitation and the guarantee of non-recurrence. Even in the more liberal Reformasi era (after 1998), the Indonesian state has done virtually nothing to guarantee these rights.

In a formal sense, impunity still continues. Nobody has faced criminal charges. But the Tribunal did contribute to creating an archive of truth, and the researchers and activists involved will continue to extend that archive. Through publications, social media and our website, we will contribute to the rewriting of Indonesian history which so far has been

[65] The tag IPT1965 lists a number of testimonies, documentaries and other products, many of which were prepared by our media team, with English subtitles where necessary. Narrowing down to live stream gives access to the hearings, including the testimonies in Indonesian.

[66] Diane Orentlicher, *Report of the Independent Expert to Update the Set of Principles to Combat Impunity*, UN Doc E/CN.4/2005/102/ Add. 1, 7.

dominated by New Order historians, who wrote a version of 'history of the winners'.[67] This public 'archive of the oppressors' must be replaced or at least complemented by an 'archive of the oppressed'.[68] The massacres and mass incarcerations took place over such an enormous region and over such a long time that only the Indonesian state will ever be able to account for their magnitude. So far it has not cared to do so, so that even now there is no certainty about how many people were murdered or imprisoned. Very few of their graves are known. Many bodies were dumped in rivers or caves with underground rivers, so they were carried to the sea. Others were dumped in unmarked mass graves.[69] Every effort by a victims' organisation or other NGOs to identify the killing sites must be seen as an act of resistance to forgetting, to the silencing of the largest mass murder in Indonesia's history.

The Tribunal has had most success in breaking the silence around the genocide and other crimes against humanity. Hundreds of articles have been written, particularly in online media but also in mainstream print media in Indonesia.[70] Some major international papers also reported on the Tribunal. Approximately 300 participants attended the Tribunal each day, including about 30 media representatives, both from Indonesia and from the international media. Many thousands of people all over the world watched the hearings via live streaming.[71] In Indonesia, *nobar* (watching together) and discussions were organised in several cities. In Jogjakarta, the *nobar* was banned by a fundamentalist group and people from the intelligence services. Film-makers and photographers

[67] Katharine McGregor, *History in Uniform; Military Ideology and the Construction of Indonesia's Past* (NUS Press, 2007).

[68] Louis Joinet, 'Le rôle des archives dans la lutte contre l'impunité' (2003) 72 *Matériaux pour l'Histoire de Notre Temps* 50, cited in Gabrielle Simm, 'The Paris Peoples' Tribunal and the Istanbul Trials: Archives of the Armenian Genocide' (2016) 29 *Leiden Journal of International Law* 245, 250–51.

[69] Very close to our house in East Java a mass grave of possibly 800 bodies was located. We only found this out recently. The grave is not marked, and it is so far not known who was buried there. The same guide who pointed this mass grave out to us took us to four other smaller sites on a nearby plantation where bodies were dumped. Saskia E. Wieringa, 'Kuburan Massal di Kebun Raya Purwodadi' ['Mass grave in the Botanical Garden in Purwodadi'], *Yayasan Bhinneka Nusantara*, 31 March 2016, www.web.archive.org/web/20160331012717/http://bhinnekanusantara.org/kuburan-massal-di-purwodadi/.

[70] From August to November 2015, there were 84,494 visitors to our website, which was attacked continuously – most frequently the writings on Gerwani by Saskia Wieringa, which received 4,966 attacks. For details, see IPT Narrative Report, above n. 13.

[71] Media statistics released at the end of November 2015: IPT 1965 on YouTube received 773 visitors, while the live stream IPT 1965 was accessed 19,802 times.

were invited to document the work of the Tribunal and its background. This material will serve archival, educational and advocacy purposes.

The surge in narrow nationalist feelings after the November 2015 hearings had an unexpected positive result. Coordinating Minister of Politics, Law and Security, Luhut B. Panjaitan, organised a national seminar on the topic in April 2016. It generated enormous media exposure. Both victims and supporters of the New Order participated. Through online media, TV shows and news reports, hundreds of thousands of Indonesians were able to listen to the gripping stories of some survivors. Angry that the national seminar generated sympathy for the victims, conservative retired generals such as Kivlan Zen organised a counter-seminar on 1–2 June 2016, in which only military and other supporters of the New Order participated. Many concluded on social media that 'the djinn [genie] is out of the bottle', meaning that the silence behind which New Order strongmen could hide the crimes committed by the army and militias trained by them after 1 October 1965 had definitively been broken.

Two other developments must be mentioned here. The first is that a group of young activists involved in the IPT, journalists themselves and active on social media, have set up an online platform for members of the third generation – those whose grandparents were directly involved, either as victims or as perpetrators. They are encouraged to ask the questions that they were never allowed to ask, about a missing grandparent, about the loss of status and property that families of prisoners typically experienced, about the origin of shame and humiliation or about why certain families always had to be shunned. On the platform they can share these stories. The platform is called Ingat 65 (Remembering 65).

Secondly, the divisive tactics of the regime, infighting and discouragement, resulted in some disagreements between the various organisations of victims. Due to the discussions prior to and directly after the Tribunal, to which members of all victims' organisations were routinely invited, they have set up a Forum 1965, which meets regularly and discusses issues of general interest to the victims at the national level. Many IPT members have also joined this forum.

The work of the IPT 1965 is not yet over. There are many challenges ahead. The results of the Tribunal must be made more widely known both within Indonesia and internationally. Lobbying at the national level in Indonesia and internationally will have to be intensified. This may stimulate a process of reconciliation in the country. Educational materials for various target groups, such as students, on the 'events of 1965' and their aftermath must be prepared, as knowledge of this period is still dominated by army propaganda. IPT 1965 will stimulate efforts to build an integrated documentation and archive system and assist where possible with various national and local efforts at memorialisation.

5.9 Conclusion

Although the Tribunal was not a formal juridical institution, its pronouncements carry weight and will be recognised in international and national fora in times to come. The Final Report of the Panel of Judges of the IPT 1965 contains some interesting arguments that will spark further debate. These concern the role of propaganda in relation to incitement to hatred and mass murder and to the position of the exiles who lost their citizenship. And of course its arguments as to why the Indonesian mass murders qualify as genocide under the 1948 Genocide Convention will continue to be discussed. All this points to a conclusion that this Tribunal is a meaningful intervention in a world in which impunity for the perpetrators of the genocide and other crimes against humanity in Indonesia still continues, and in which the victims still experience shame, stigma and humiliation.

The lack of enforceability of the carefully argued judgement of our Panel of Judges is of course deeply regrettable, but the Final Report will continue to shame Indonesia internationally. How the Indonesian state will react ultimately is unknown. At the time of writing, narrow nationalist forces call for the uniqueness of Indonesian human rights as opposed to the alleged foreignness of international human rights standards.[72] The lawmakers who advance these arguments are apparently unaware that the present Indonesian human rights law is based on the Rome Statute. Whether Indonesia will ever resort to the international or domestic adjudication of its past human rights abuses is doubtful, but the Final Report of the Judges of the IPT 1965 strengthens the demands of both national human rights commissions to deal with these past abuses. It has already boosted the morale of victims and will help ensure that the world will not forget these crimes.

[72] Margareth S. Aritonang, 'Lawmakers want 'nationalist' figures for Komnas HAM', *Jakarta Post*, 23 December 2016, www.thejakartapost.com/news/2016/12/23/lawmakers-want-nationalist-figures-for-komnas-ham.html.

6

The Participation of Peoples and the Development of International Law

The Laboratory of the Permanent Peoples' Tribunal

SIMONA FRAUDATARIO AND GIANNI TOGNONI

6.1 Introduction

A striking feature of the opinion tribunals and peoples' tribunals that have been held in recent decades in various parts of the world, above all in Asia and Latin America, is the participation of heterogeneous social actors and networks of peoples who identify with the victims of violations of human rights, conceived both collectively and individually.

Increasing attention has been paid in recent years to these experiences, mostly in the social and legal disciplines, by academics, intellectuals and independent researchers, as well as by those affected. Each experience has been appreciated as both an opportunity and an instrument for making visible situations that are unknown or rather not addressed by the international and national authorities responsible for the implementation and protection of human rights. There has been an emphasis on designating and documenting the violations and their effects, leaving to one side the role that the victims play in the process of clarifying the facts, the charges and the reconstruction and affirmation of the 'truth'

The descriptive terms 'peoples' tribunals' and 'opinion tribunals' are normally considered equivalent. They both describe initiatives taken with the aim of addressing problems that existing international law is unwilling or unable to confront – failures that highlight the inequality of states and the fact that the institutions and categories of international law do not consider these matters to be their responsibility. In fact, the terms 'opinion tribunal' and 'peoples tribunal' represent aims and objectives that can be complementary, even though they involve inevitable differences in emphasis and perspective. The term 'opinion tribunal' suggests a morally justified and necessary action to fill a gap in international law.

At the same time it evokes and presents itself as a lower-ranking, substitute institution seeking to change public opinion as an alternative to invoking a law that is effectively unavailable. The decisions that are adopted by the judges of such tribunals describe them as non-binding and not enforceable due to the lack of recognition by the community of states of these pronouncements as 'legally' valid tools.

The term 'peoples' tribunal' formally introduces the centrality of subjects-actors ('peoples') as distinct from states, the latter seeing themselves as the exclusive holders of the power to interpret and guarantee the principles, values and rules of international law including the Universal Declaration of Human Rights 1948. The 'peoples', already recognised in the preamble of the Universal Declaration,[1] put themselves forward as rights holders and responsible for the interpretation and implementation of the principles that are necessary to make international law a living and evolving tool. The challenges that stand in the way of ensuring respect for human rights require an innovative perspective, not just adherence to the accepted juridical categories established at a precise historical moment and to an 'order' that sees peoples merely as beneficiaries of laws, even when these laws demonstrate their impotence through the grave breaches of them that occur and go unremedied.

Opinion tribunals and peoples' tribunals clearly coincide in documenting and judging a gap in international law, which is the centrality of peoples as active subjects capable of thinking of themselves as promoters of large-scale programs that test methodologies and analytical criteria to judge, culturally, doctrinally and politically, the delays, the absences and the ambiguity of international law by systematically entering the fight for truth and justice as essential element for the progress of law.

A reflection of this type seems particularly relevant at a time when, as during the last decades, there has been a profound change in the role of states. Economic, and to a greater extent, financial globalisation has created actors and power relations that have erased and replaced

[1] Preambular paragraph 5 of the Universal Declaration provides: 'Whereas the peoples of the United Nations have in the Charter reaffirmed their faith in fundamental human rights, in the dignity and worth of the human person and in the equal rights of men and women and have determined to promote social progress and better standards of life in larger freedom'. UN GA Resolution 217A (III) (1948) preamble to the Universal Declaration of Human Rights, 10 December 1948, UN Doc A/RES/3/217A. The Preamble of the United Nations Charter opens with the words 'We the Peoples of the United nations determined to save succeeding generations from the scourge of war . . . have resolved to combine our efforts to achieve [the goals set out in the Preamble].'

categories that seemed well-established on the basis of the universality of individual and collective human rights. International law's ability to guarantee rights has been marginalised and questioned, even more so its capacity to promote universal access to fundamental rights whether at an international or state level. In this global scenario, real peoples find themselves in a subaltern position without effective representation of their rights.

The history and experience of the Permanent Peoples' Tribunal (PPT) is presented in this chapter as an example of an experimental laboratory of possible paths that are increasingly necessary when aiming for a law *for* and *by* peoples.[2] The range of cases dealt with by the PPT for nearly forty years of activity has allowed the Tribunal to confront many of the concrete situations that can be considered as a memory of the resistance and of the struggles of people for justice. The Tribunal formulates a framework of rules that see peoples as subjects and holders of rights, and not just as victims of breaches unpunished by an international law that has abdicated its role as an effective instrument for the promotion and the protection of self-determination and the dignity of peoples.

It is necessary to highlight that the laboratory of the PPT has not been the only or the most important among the many movements and initiatives that have arisen over the last decades. However, the initial insight of its founder, Lelio Basso, was that establishing a 'permanent' tool of exploration and experimentation in the form of the PPT might well provide a more systematic overview of abuses of power, of the inevitable partiality, of solutions proposed, of the necessity for long-haul efforts and of the possibilities for change.

This reflection on the history of the PPT has selected 'participation' as a connecting thread and key concept to summarise and highlight the specificity of its methodology. This concept not only describes the processes provided for in the Statute of the PPT for accepting petitions from peoples, holding public hearings and formulating judgments but also includes identifying the central nucleus of the 'PPT project': to experiment and restore forms of democracy and justice through the practice of

[2] This chapter builds on the description of the mission of the Permanent Peoples' Tribunal and the analysis of its work by Tognoni in Chapter 2 in this volume. See also Tognoni, 'La storia del Tribunale Permanente dei Popoli' ['The History of the Permanent Peoples' Tribunal'] in Linda Bimbi and Gianni Tognoni (eds.), *Speranze e inquietudini di ieri e di oggi. I trent'anni della Dichiarazione Universale del Diritto dei Popoli Popoli* [*Hopes and Concerns of Yesterday and Today: Thirty Years of the Universal Declaration of Peoples' Law*] (Edup, 2008) 95.

an active participation of peoples and an active listening for the translation of their claims and requests in juridical and political perspective for their present and future.[3]

6.2 Participation as the Historical, Political and Methodological Root of Opinion/Peoples' Tribunals

The origin of the Permanent Peoples' Tribunal is well known. The Russell Tribunals – the first on Vietnam (1966–67) and the second on dictatorships in Latin America (1974–76) – serve to contextualise the issue under discussion. The Russell Tribunals were conceived as instruments of investigation and denunciation. The First Russell Tribunal focused on crimes of aggression and war crimes committed by the United States against Vietnam; the second on the expansion of dictatorships in Latin America. Although they might appear as two similar experiences, they presented different objects for investigation and, as a consequence, adopted different methodologies.[4]

The First Russell Tribunal, promoted by the English philosopher Bertrand Russell, occurred in a context of protest against war and a global discourse about peace and non-violence. Through the participation of intellectuals, scientists, Nobel Laureates and others, it aimed to point out the types of crimes committed by the United States, thereby legitimating a protest that already existed. The Second Russell Tribunal, established on the initiative of Lelio Basso, had to 'break the silence' about complex facts and events that were still unfolding and whose gravity was possible to understand only from a critical and multidisciplinary perspective.

This Second Russell Tribunal started to take shape in 1971, when a group of Brazilian exiles proposed that Lelio Basso establish a tribunal to draw the attention of the international community to the generalised and systematic nature of the violations that were being committed in Brazil. It did not take long to understand that what had happened in Brazil was

[3] See *Statute of the Permanent Peoples' Tribunal* (1979), http://permanentpeoplestribunal.org/wp-content/uploads/2016/06/statute.pdf.

[4] François Rigaux, 'Lelio Basso e i tribunali di opinione' ['Lelio Basso and Opinion Tribunals'] in *Lelio Basso e le culture dei diritti* [*Lelio Basso and the Cultures of Law*], Fondazione Internazionale Lelio Basso (Carocci editore, 2000) 21–31. Rigaux's essay recounts the engagement of Lelio Basso in the evolution of international law, comparing the First Russell Tribunal with the Second and these experiences with the Nuremberg and Tokyo Tribunals.

not an isolated event and that it required a regional and international perspective in order to understand the causes of and mechanisms for the continuing and violent political, social and economic reconfiguration underway in Latin America.[5]

The coup d'état in Chile in 1973 raised the awareness of European civil society, which was especially capable of sharing the fear of injustice and terror as the result of past or present experiences under devastating dictatorial regimes. This empathy quickly transformed itself into expressions of solidarity that formed the basis of popular support for the Second Russell Tribunal. Lelio Basso saw that it would be politically relevant to convert the numerous forms of solidarity into an active participation articulated into focused activities and the constitution of working groups with different roles and responsibilities for the three sessions that were held.[6] The Italian jurist and politician knew from the start that broad popular participation could achieve justice and democracy through a concerted effort, a conscious use of law and a political view of the participation of people. Basso understood that the presence and active role of peoples and the involvement of renowned persons could legitimate the 'truth' that was being investigated.

The significant level of popular participation seen in the sessions of the Second Russell Tribunal was a clear expression of the need to fill the gap between violations of human rights and the promises of international

[5] Simona Fraudatario, 'Le reti di solidarietà per il Tribunale Russell II negli archivi della Fondazione Lelio e Lisli Basso' ['Solidarity Networks of the Second Russell Tribunal in the Archives of the Lelio and Lisli Basso Foundation'] in Giancarlo Monina (ed.), *Memorie di repressione, resistenza e solidarietà in Brasile e in America Latina* [*Memories of Repression, Resistance and Solidarity in Brazil and Latin America*], with a preface by Gianni Tognoni (Ediesse, 2013) 315. See also Leticia da Costa Paes, 'O Legado do Tribunal Russell II para o Brasil e para História contemporânia dos Direitos Humanos' ['The legacy of the Second Russell Tribunal for Brazil and the contemporary history of human rights'], in *Justiça de Transição, Direitos Humanos e Contracultura* (2014) 8 *Re-Vista*,; Alberto Filippi, 'O legado de Lelio Basso na América do Sul e seus arquivos de Roma: as particularidades históricas das transições democráticas e a constitucionalização dos novos direitos' ['The legacy of Lelio Basso in South America and his archives in Rome: the historical particularities of democratic transitions and the constitutionalisation of new rights'], *Revista Anistia Política e Justiça de Transição nº 08*, Ministério da Justiça, 2º semestre 2012, 94, www.justica.gov.br/central-de-conteudo/anistia/anexos/2013revistaanistia08.pdf; Fundacão Lelio Basso – ISSOCO, 'A digitalização dos fundos do Tribunal Russel II' ['The digitisation of the documents of the Second Russell Tribunal'], *Revista Anistia Política e Justiça de Transição nº 08*, Ministério da Justiça, 2º semestre 2012, 438, www.justica.gov.br/central-de-conteudo/anistia/anexos/2013revistaanistia08.pdf.

[6] The three sessions of the Second Russell Tribunal took place in Rome (20 March–5 April 1974), Brussels (11–18 January 1975) and Rome (10–18 January 1976).

law, by demanding a concrete relation between the life of peoples and their suffering and those principles 'proclaimed and abandoned without protection'.[7] It is precisely in the space left by this rupture that the Russell Tribunal and peoples' tribunals more generally insert themselves. The metaphor of the bridge used by the Argentinean writer Julio Cortázar – who was a judge of the Second Russell Tribunal – on the occasion of the founding of the PPT in Bologna in 1979 perfectly describes the primary mission of the PPT and is, at the same time, the key to interpreting the concept of participation with which we are concerned.[8] Cortázar knew how to perceive and synthesise the active role that peoples have played in claims that there be a match between real life and human rights, and the use of law as a tool for democratisation of societies and institutions.

The role of peoples in promoting effective human rights is clearly affirmed in the Universal Declaration of the Rights of Peoples (also known as the Declaration of Algiers),[9] proclaimed in Algiers in 1976 as a result of the intensive work of the Second Russell Tribunal. Faced with the impossibility of attributing significance to the plural concept of peoples[10] which varies over time and space, the Declaration concentrates, rather, on the roles that are attributed to them. According to the Declaration, peoples are not beneficiaries of rights recognised from above, but actors in formulating and affirming rights. Peoples do not simply

[7] Lelio Basso, 'Discorso introduttivo alla prima Sessione' ['Introductory Address to the First Session'] in Linda Bimbi (ed.), *Tribunale Russell II. Brasile, violazione dei diritti dell'uomo* [*The Second Russell Tribunal – Brazil: violations of human rights*] (Feltrinelli, 1975) 12.

[8] Julio Cortázar, 'Ponti e cammini' ['Bridges and Paths'] in Gianni Tognoni (ed.), *Tribunale Permanente Dei Popoli, le sentenze: 1979–1991* [*The Permanent Peoples' Tribunal: Judgments 1979–1991*] (Nuova Cultura editrice, 1992), 27.

[9] *Universal Declaration of the Rights of Peoples*, Algiers, 4 July 1976, http://permanentpeoplestribunal.org/wp-content/uploads/2016/06/Carta-di-algeri-EN-2.pdf.

[10] See François Rigaux, *I diritti dei popoli e la Carta di Algeri* [*The Rights of Peoples and the Charter of Algiers*] (Edizioni gruppo Abele, 2012), 31. See further Antonio Cassese and Edmond Jouve, *Pour un droit des peuples: essais sur la Déclaration d'Alger* [*For a Law of Peoples: Essays on the Declaration of Algiers*] (Berger-Levrault, 1978); Fondazione Lelio Basso (ed.), *Droits de l'homme et droits de peuple* [*Human Rights and Peoples' Rights*] (Arti Grafiche della Bada, 1983); François Rigaux, *Le concept de peuple* [*The Concept of 'People'*] (Story-Scientia,1988); Fondazione Internazionale Lelio Basso (ed.), *Popoli, minoranze, Stato nazione: Giornate biennali in onore di Lelio Basso* [*Peoples, Minorities, Nation State: Seminars in honour of Lelio Basso*] (1991); Fondazione Internazionale Lelio Basso (ed.), *Il Diritto di autodeterminazione alle soglie del 2000: Genesi, evoluzione, attualità* [*The Right to Self Determination at the Turn of the Millennium: Origins, Evolution, Current Developments*] (Anterem Roma, 1999); Bimbi and Tognoni, above n. 2, 95.

exist but also have the imprescriptible and inalienable right of self-determination, which includes rights to decision, election, action and liberation through international law.[11]

The creation of the PPT as a permanent institution of denunciation arose from the need to make breaches of international law visible. This corresponds to the most immediate mandate of the Tribunal. In addition, the PPT's most important mission consists in a continual search for instruments of observation and interpretation of the real from a comparative and critical perspective, drawing on the capacity of law to prevent violations, to protect victims and those aggrieved and to guarantee the existence of peoples.

6.3 Participation as an Incentive and Opportunity to Develop Innovative Categories and Perspectives of International Law

A review of the various sessions of the PPT permits one to identify the features of a methodology of participation by peoples and victims in cases that arose as a reaction against impunity and failures to acknowledge wrongs. While each of the more than forty sessions that have taken place to date has had its own specific reason for making visible and denouncing violations, each one is part of a common practice of emancipation.

The active presence of peoples in the sessions of the PPT is manifested specifically at the different stages of the proceedings. The two main stages are (a) the request for a hearing that affected social groups address to the Tribunal, and (b) the investigation and documentation of the cases presented. Both stages share a critical approach to international law that permits a primary identification and reconstruction of the mechanisms of normative and structural impunity and their consequences in society, institutions and the law itself. In fact, the request for a hearing sent to the Tribunal and the charges presented in the sessions are already an explicit form of practice questioning the essence, limits and application of international law.

In almost all the judgments of the PPT there is recognition of the victims and affected people and of their role. Beyond the affirmation of

[11] Article 1 of the *Universal Declaration of the Rights of Peoples* affirms that '[e]very people has the right to exist.' This article is part of the section dedicated to the right to existence. Other articles of the Declaration refer to the right to political self-determination, the economic rights of peoples, the right to culture and the rights of minorities: above n. 9.

their dignity, the Tribunal usually highlights the force of the claim not only emphasising emotional dimensions but also making conscious use of the language of human rights and the law, giving them a concrete meaning and perspective. The critical role of the peoples involved has been described in one of the recent works of the PPT in terms of their being 'protagonists' of the claim.[12] This reference comes, not by chance, from the session about European Transnational Corporations in Latin America, which concluded in 2010 in Madrid. These proceedings were the culmination of a long process that began in the 1990s in which the PPT explored the relationship between economics and law. In the judgment, the PPT devoted a paragraph to the victims, describing them as 'the main actors' in the 'transformation of the legal framework' that makes possible the existence and systematic repetition of the abuses that they suffer at the hands of transnational corporations. The agency of peoples is understood in terms of a 'relevant subjectivity',[13] surpassing, in fact, the procedural meaning attributed to victims, traditionally conceived as simple objects of unjust and violent actions.

The Tribunal makes possible the rapprochement between peoples and international law by resetting the role of institutions as guarantors of the well-being of individuals conceived as members of a collectivity.[14] It simultaneously enriches the concept of peoples and renews that of law. In fact, in the sessions, a process of emancipation of peoples occurs, which connects their reality to the processes of justice. At the same time, it is possible to recover the original role attributed to international law, so that far from being an instrument of control, it can be an instrument of liberation from every form of domination, exclusion and negation. The 'judges' of the PPT leave behind the traditional role of adjudicators, transcending the criminal and punitive dimension of international law

[12] Permanent Peoples' Tribunal, *The European Union and Transnational Corporations in Latin America: Policies, Instruments and Actors Complicit in Violations of the Peoples' Rights, Deliberating Session*, Madrid, 14–17 May 2010, Judgment, 15.

[13] Ibid., 14.

[14] Lelio Basso was also a member of the Italian Constituent Assembly and collaborated in editing article 3 of the Italian Constitution, which affirms: 'All citizens have equal social dignity and are equal before the law, without distinction of sex, race, language, religion, political opinion, personal and social conditions. It is the duty of the Republic to remove those obstacles of an economic or social nature which constrain the freedom and equality of citizens, thereby impeding the full development of the human person and the effective participation of all workers in the political, economic and social organisation of the country'. See Constitution of the Italian Republic, 22 December 1947, www.senato.it/documenti/repository/istituzione/costituzione_inglese.pdf.

in order to transform themselves into guides whose role is to direct the interpretation of the facts through the reconstruction of the truth in a way that legitimates the denunciation of wrongs and the resistance of peoples. It is in this sense that participation becomes a way of returning to peoples the role of participant observers and promoters of justice, and, to the judges of the PPT, the task of guaranteeing the 'liberation' of the same law from incomplete categories and ineffective formulae.

In this view of justice, neither utopian nor idealistic, people and judges join in a collective effort to use law as a point of departure for a reflection about ways to improve the societies in which we live. The proceedings of the PPT contemplate neither the inapplicability of the law nor the automatic classification of claims and their proponents according to existing international law. Rather, they contemplate an ongoing analysis of the significant features of each society with the aim of orienting necessity and hopes in viable ways to make a better future. Participation is therefore a method of generating transformation in society (and law) and for identifying legal instruments that realise the democratisation of institutions and societies desired by the Tribunal.

6.4 Scenarios and Experiences of an International Law from Peoples' Point of View

The complexity of the cases heard by the Tribunal does not permit an exhaustive examination of them. The judgments, which are public documents, have achieved a narrative faithful to the diversity of voices that the Tribunal has heard and to the analysis presented to it. The judgments comprise a body of literature through which the path of peoples, even humanity, may be traced towards the awareness of its own role in regard to international law and the formulation of a common language of rights.

In order to appreciate the extensive variety of peoples which have participated in the PPT's sessions, it is enough to scan the titles of the sessions that represent the voices and lives of numerous groups.[15] In the Tribunal's activities it is possible to recognise 'generations' of cases, a simplification that does not negate the specificity of each case. The generations inspired an essay by François Rigaux, who illustrates the

[15] Judgments of the PPT are available at www.permanentpeoplestribunal.org. They are also listed in the Bibliography that appears in this volume, together with links to English versions available online where an English version is not available on the PPT website.

developments through an examination of the historical and legal evolution of the principle of self-determination in the PPT.[16]

A first generation of cases involved the participation of peoples whose requests refer to the violation of their right of self-determination. This covers the first decade of the PPT's activities, when it gave voice to situations involving calls for liberation from colonial rule and afforded recognition to invisible peoples, not recognised by international law, such as ethnic groups, minorities, social actors, collectives and 'national groups' with social, political and economic aspirations. In 1979, the PPT dedicated its first session to the Saharawi people, which is an emblematic case of justification and legitimation of disappearance and extinction of a people.[17] The session concluded with a fundamental affirmation of their existence and their right to be an active presence in international law. This was also the main claim of the following sessions on the cases of the Philippines (1980),[18] El Salvador (1981),[19] Guatemala (1983),[20] Zaire (1982),[21] Nicaragua (1984),[22] Afghanistan (1981, 1982)[23] and Puerto Rico (1989),[24] which examined complex and more subtle forms of colonial occupation and economic domination.

At this first stage, the dialectic of negation and affirmation of the right of peoples to exist and their right to self-determination, and who face internal and external aggression against their sovereignty, has produced significant advances in international law. This could be due to the capacity to translate petitions, charges and insights into the formulation or revision of the prevailing formal principles and categories of international law that failed to reflect adequately the lives of specific peoples and their need for justice. The Tribunal has rejected the abstract but

[16] François Rigaux, 'L'autodeterminazione nelle sentenze del Tribunal Permanente dei Popoli' ['Self-determination in the Verdicts of the Permanent Peoples' Tribunal'] in Gianni Tognoni (ed.), *Tribunale Permanente dei Popoli: Le Sentenze 1979–98* [hereafter *PPT Verdicts 1979–98*] (Fondazione Lelio Basso, Casa Editrice Stefanoni, 1998) 747.

[17] Permanent Peoples' Tribunal, *Session on Western Sahara*, Brussels, 10–11 November 1979.

[18] Permanent Peoples' Tribunal, *Session on the Filipino People and the Bangsa Moro People*, Antwerp, 30 October–1 November 1980.

[19] Permanent Peoples' Tribunal, *Session on El Salvador*, Mexico, 9–12 February 1981.

[20] Permanent Peoples' Tribunal, *Session on Guatemala*, Madrid, 21–31 January 1983.

[21] Permanent Peoples' Tribunal, *Session on Zaire*, Rotterdam, 18–20 September 1982.

[22] Permanent Peoples' Tribunal, *Session on the Interventions of the United States in Nicaragua*, Brussels, 5–8 October 1984.

[23] Permanent Peoples' Tribunal, *First Session on Afghanistan*, Stockholm 1–3 May 1981; *Second Session on Afghanistan*, Paris, 16–20 December 1982.

[24] Permanent Peoples' Tribunal, *Session on Puerto Rico*, Barcelona, 27–29 January 1989.

fallacious doctrine that peoples can be represented only by states. Additionally, it has also promoted a new interpretation of crimes against humanity and genocide, advancing a view of the former as an independent category not linked to war crimes, and referred to crimes such as forced disappearance and forced displacement, at a formative period of formal international law making on those subjects and well before these crimes were codified in the Rome Statute of the International Criminal Court.[25]

Peoples whose experiences were never considered as genocide in official histories have advanced such claims before the Tribunal, with the objective of having them recognised as such.[26] These include the cases of Armenian genocide (1984),[27] Argentina (1980),[28] Timor,[29] the Brazilian Amazon (1990),[30] the former Yugoslavia (1995)[31] and the other examples already mentioned (the Philippines, El Salvador and Guatemala). The session on the Armenian people was a significative exercise of historical memory to return dignity to the victims faced with impunity and denialism.[32] The judgment is juridically relevant even today, if we consider the opposition of the Turkish government to the recognition of their responsibility in the extermination of the Armenian peoples and its description as genocide. The additional value of this session was also the recognition of the moral and ethical duty in the politics of any state

[25] Rome Statute of the International Criminal Court, Rome, 17 July 1998, 2187 UNTS 90, in force 1 July 2002.

[26] See Simona Fraudatario and Gianni Tognoni, 'La definición jurídica y substancial del genocidio a la prueba del encuentro entre el Tribunal Permanente de los Pueblos y las víctimas' ['The Juridical and Substantive Definition of Genocide on Trial in the Encounter between the Permanent Peoples Tribunal and Victims'], paper presented at the 9th Biennial Conference of the International Association of Genocide Scholars, Buenos Aires, 19–22 July 2011, www.genocidescholars.org/sites/default/files/document%09%5Bcurrent-page%3A1%5D/documents/IAGS%202011%20Simona%20Fraudatario.pdf.

[27] Permanent Peoples' Tribunal, *Session on the Armenian Genocide*, Paris, 13–16 April 1984. An English version of the verdict is available in Gérard Libaridian (ed.), *A Crime of Silence, The Armenian Genocide: Permanent Peoples' Tribunal* (Zed Books, 1985),.

[28] Permanent Peoples' Tribunal, *Session on Argentina*, Geneva, 3–4 May 1980.

[29] Permanent Peoples' Tribunal, *Session on East Timor*, Lisbon, 19–21 June 1981.

[30] Permanent Peoples' Tribunal, *Session on the Brazilian Amazon*, Paris, 12–16 October 1990.

[31] Permanent Peoples' Tribunal, *Crimes against Humanity in the Former Yugoslavia*, Berne, Switzerland, 17–20 February 1995; *Crimes against Humanity in the Former Yugoslavia, Second Session*, Barcelona, Spain, 7–11 December 1995.

[32] See also Gabrielle Simm, 'The Paris Peoples' Tribunal and the Istanbul Trials: Archives of the Armenian Genocide' (2016) 29 *Leiden Journal of International Law* 245.

to respond to genocide, given that genocide is not simply a domestic issue but of interest to, and a responsibility of, the international community.

In the other cases involving charges of genocide, the PPT has employed the category of genocide in a provocative manner to encourage a more flexible use of that term, one that admits of variation and plural forms.[33] In this sense, in the history of the Tribunal, genocide is considered as expression of the institutional intention to destroy peoples' life and future. This innovative analysis adopted by the PPT has required an updating of the legal categories, by taking into account social, cultural, political and economic factors as cause of the action of destruction. This perspective is certainly more faithful to the original proposal by Raphael Lemkin[34] – which was rejected by states in the drafting of the Genocide Convention[35] in 1948[36] – and, by the way, to the real forms of violence against peoples developed since that time, after the Holocaust.[37] As the PPT declared in its judgment on the Armenian genocide delivered in 1984, the attention paid to the specific cases of genocides is the result of the belief that this crime represents the gravest violation of the rights of peoples.[38] And, we can add, the more 'mutable' if we consider its dissemination and affirmation of genocide as strategic and current practice of the power. The persistence of this form of collective destruction is also

33 The centrality of the question of genocide in the history of the PPT was the subject of the international seminar organized by the International Lelio Basso Foundation in 1993: 'The concept of genocide today and in the Convention of 9 December 1948'. The results of this work, of great contemporary relevance, were published as *Genocide/genocides* (Associazione Nuova Cultural, 1995). More recently, the Argentinian Centre on Genocide Studies and the International Association on Genocide Scholars have held several conferences in Buenos Aires on this issue, providing visibility and sparking debate on the PPT investigation on genocide.

34 Rafael Lemkin, *Axis Rule in Occupied Europe: Laws of Occupation – Analysis of Government – Proposals for Redress* (Carnegie Endowment for International Peace, 1944), chapter 9.

35 Convention on the Prevention and Punishment of the Crime of Genocide 1948, Paris, 9 December 1948, 78 UNTS 277, in force 12 January 1951.

36 Steven R. Ratner, Jason S. Abrams and James L. Bischoff, *Accountability for Human Rights Atrocities in International Law: Beyond the Nuremberg Legacy* (Oxford University Press, 3rd edn., 2009) chapter 2 ('Genocide and the Imperfections of Codification'); William A. Schabas, *Genocide in International Law: The Crimes of Crimes* (Cambridge University Press, 2nd edn., 2009).

37 See also Daniel Feierstein, *Genocide as Social Practice: Reorganizing Society under Nazism and Argentina's Military Juntas* (Rutgers University Press, 2014).

38 Permanent Peoples' Tribunal, *Genocide of the Armenians, Judgment*, Paris, 13–16 April 1984, http://permanentpeoplestribunal.org/wp-content/uploads/1984/04/Armenia_TPP_it.pdf.

confirmed by the recurring demand of attention and investigation which the PPT has recently received, such as the cases of the Tamil people (Dublin 2010; Bremen, 2012) and of the Rohingyas, Kachin and other minorities in Myanmar (London, 2017; Kuala Lumpur, 2017).

A second generation of sessions focused on the analysis of violations not just of political self-determination but also of economic social and cultural self-determination. The two sessions devoted to the policies of the International Monetary Fund and the World Bank (1988, 1995) inaugurated the line of inquiry still open today on the structures and institutions of economic and financial power that have become global agents and not only influence human and peoples' rights but also tend to replace international law with a new paradigm and reference point. The testimony of numerous, global peoples has demonstrated their understanding of the impact of the imposition of an economic model on their lives and has highlighted the incongruities, the illegitimacy and the arbitrariness of the interests of the 'extraterritorial' economic powers that are imposed as a framework and are inconsistent with the fundamental principles of the international law. It corresponds to how the Uruguayan writer Eduardo Galeano, who participated as a judge in the 1988 session,[39] used the image of 'monetary religion' in his incisive text, 'The bitter paradox of Mr Money', which was included in the session. The proselytisers of this religion

> don't get their hands dirty. They don't kill anybody, they just applaud the spectacle. Their impositions are called recommendations. Their threats are called letters of intent. When they say stabilise they mean defeat. They call hunger, austerity and the help that the noose offers to the neck, cooperation.[40]

In the following passage Galeano captured perfectly the submission of states and politics to economic and financial power, the conscious and deliberate impotence of states faced with the inevitable serious consequences:

> International finance is a monopoly of power, a dictatorship of the north over the south. However, its instrumental character in the service of a bigger system does not imply innocence. The technocracy usually vindicates the privilege of irresponsibility. . . . Due to this, notwithstanding that

[39] Permanent Peoples' Tribunal, *Session on the Policies of the International Monetary Fund and the World Bank*, West Berlin, 26–29 September 1988.

[40] Eduardo Galeano, 'Il paradosso amaro di Don Dinero' ['The bitter paradox of Mr Money'] in *PPT Verdicts 1979–98*, above n. 16, 310 (author's translation).

> in the letters of intent, the concentration of risk does not appear explicitly, nor the dismantling of national sovereignty, all this is implicit. And although it is true that those tortured and disappeared are not mentioned in the adjustment programs, it is also true that they are its natural consequence.[41]

The third theme, that of impunity, was investigated in connection with the 'young' democracies in Latin America, in the session on the impunity for the crimes against humanity in Latin America, a travelling investigation held over two years that concluded in Bogotá in 1991.[42] Denouncing impunity as a mechanism of neutralising the role that peoples play in guaranteeing the functioning of their own democracy, the Tribunal and peoples involved identified the close relationship between impunity and the imposition of free market policies. These had led to and explain the reformulation of internal and external sovereignty of states, profoundly limiting the free determination of peoples in their access to economic, social and cultural rights. This 'limitation' is a reflection of forms of growing inequality and is manifested in massive, persistent and generalised cascades of violations of fundamental human rights in many social sectors across the globe.

In the face of the inaction and persistent powerlessness of law, the PPT has considered it necessary to inquire into the structural causes of violations. To call international law to account in court provided the opportunity to reflect, in order to clarify its roots and alliances, to understand its ambiguity and collusion and to explore its identity and presumed legitimacy. The session on the Conquest of the Americas and international law (1992)[43] documented in that historical context how international law was conceived: an instrument to justify a posteriori the logic of domination in the name of the conversion to the religion of the free market.

6.5 The Changing Scenario of the New Millennium

Contrary to what some might have expected, the establishment of the International Criminal Court (ICC) (1998–2002) did not initiate or

[41] Ibid., 311.

[42] Permanent Peoples' Tribunal, *Session on Impunity for Crimes against Humanity in Latin America*, Bogotá, 22–25 April 1991.

[43] Permanent Peoples' Tribunal, *The Conquest of America and International Law*, Padua-Venice, 5–9 October 1992.

herald a new trend towards more effective binding rules and mechanisms for the prevention of violations and promotion of humans' and peoples' rights. Apart from the intrinsic limitations of the jurisdiction conferred on the ICC by its Statute (which does not include economic and environmental crimes), the last decade of the millennium had already seen an expanding gap between the binding role of international law in the field of human rights and its concrete, timely, universally effective application. The increasingly dominant role of transnational corporate powers and of interstate free trade treaties led to a situation characterised by much broader and a priori accepted areas of impunity, as well as to the emergence of peoples without states and transversal to states and much more exposed to the violation of their fundamental rights. The exclusion of the right to a living wage from the fundamental rights institutions is possibly one of the most explicit and model examples of a 'new' situation.

The perception of the dramatic seriousness of the scenarios characterising the era of globalisation of the market coincides with the nullification of the universal rights of human beings. The diversified participation of peoples in the affirmation of the permanent inviolability of their rights is documented by the intensity and quality of the requests which reach the PPT.

Several groups of peoples organised in global networks that cross state borders have requested the Tribunal to hold sessions in order to give visibility to the abuses of power by business, to recognise their responsibility which has been disguised with the adoption of voluntary codes by transnational corporations. These requests have resulted in a first group of sessions such as those on workers and consumers in the garment industry (1998), on Elf Aquitaine (1999)[44] in the African continent and on Global Corporations and Human Wrongs (2000),[45] which grew out of the need for reflection by activists, academics and lawyers. The next set of sessions reflects more substantially the need for participation of people and communities directly involved in the documentation and analysis of the consequence of the activities of the transnational corporations (TNCs) in their daily life. For example, the session on Agrochemical Corporations (2011)[46] was made possible thanks to the long-running work

[44] Permanent Peoples' Tribunal, *Session on Elf-Aquitaine*, Paris, 19–21 May 1999.

[45] Permanent Peoples' Tribunal, *Session on Global Corporations and Human Wrongs*, University of Warwick, Coventry, UK, 22–25 March 2000.

[46] Permanent Peoples' Tribunal, *Agrochemical Transnational Corporations*, Bangalore, 3–6 December 2011.

of those affected who had come together in solidarity in a worldwide network known as the Pesticide Action Network. The already mentioned session on European Transnational Corporations in Latin America played an essential role in the construction of new alliances between aggrieved people in Europe and Latin America through a bi-regional network Enlazando Alternativas (Enhancing Alternatives). These sessions were particularly relevant for the presentation of evidence on the continuous generation of social costs by TNCs and for demanding the recognition of the categories of corporate and environmental crimes and the definition of the responsibility of both states and transnational corporations for the abuses committed against individuals and people.

In this rapid sketch of the cross-border victims of neoliberal economic policies, it is necessary to mention, because they are representative, the victims of environmental disasters (represented significantly by petitioners in the two sessions on Bhopal, 1992–94[47], and the session on Chernobyl, 1996);[48] the peoples forced into exile and refused asylum or refuge (Berlin, 1994);[49] the women victims of labour exploitation, united in the recognition of the right to a dignified wage in the session on living wage as a fundamental right held in Asia from 2011 to 2014;[50] and finally, the children of the session on the fundamental rights of the child and young people that took place in 1995 in the Italian cities of Trento, Macerata and Naples.[51] Migrants, exiles, mothers and children constitute an anonymous and horizontal group affected by the structural economic repression and the indicators of the crisis in the legal system.

47 Permanent Peoples' Tribunal, *Hearing on Industrial Hazards and Human Rights (Bhopal I)*, Bhopal, India, 19–23 October 1992; Permanent Peoples' Tribunal, *Session on Industrial Hazards and Human Rights (Bhopal II)*, London, 28 November–4 December 1994.

48 Permanent Peoples' Tribunal, *Session on Chernobyl: Environment, Health and Human Rights*, Vienna, 12–15 April 1996.

49 Permanent Peoples' Tribunal, *Session on the Right of Asylum in Europe*, Berlin, 8–12 December 1994.

50 The process was promoted by the Asia Floor Wage Alliance (AFWA), a network of social movements on the rights of women working in the garment industry. In collaboration with the Permanent Peoples' Tribunal from 2009 to 2015, the AFWA organised four National Peoples' Tribunals in Sri Lanka, India, Cambodia and Indonesia and a final session in Sri Lanka for recognition of the living wage as fundamental human right. See Permanent Peoples' Tribunal, *Living Wage for Garment Workers in Asia*, www.permanentpeoplestribunal.org/42-living-wage-for-garment-workers-in-asia-2009–2015/?lang=en.

51 Permanent Peoples' Tribunal, *Violations of the Fundamental Rights of Children and Minors*, Trento, 27–29 March 1995; Macerata, 30 March 1995; Naples, 1–4 April 1995.

The sessions on Colombia (2006–2008)[52] and Mexico (2011–14)[53] are as emblematic of the Tribunal's work in conceptualising the relevant issues as they are of its approach to inclusive participation.[54] The former were essentially devoted to the investigation and categorisation of the impact of the actions of numerous TNCs, primarily North American and European, on the rights of peoples in that country. The Colombian session was articulated in seven pre-hearings devoted to sectors of business production. The session aimed to document the impacts on peoples, communities and territories, to reconstruct the modus operandi of TNCs and to analyse the state's submission to their demands and needs and the mechanisms through which they benefitted from the Colombian conflict.

The session on Mexico used the same methodology as the Colombian session, articulated in ten thematic pre-hearings on affected peoples' rights. The Mexican chapter of the PPT considered the results of the previous Colombian process as a point of departure to demonstrate and underline the illegitimacy of free trade agreements, such as the North American Free Trade Agreement (NAFTA) and its institutions, whose impact has led to a distorted reconfiguration of the state, its institutions, society and the environment. As the social actors participating in the

[52] Permanent Peoples' Tribunal, *Transnational Corporations and Peoples' Rights in Colombia (Colombia, 2006–2008)*, final session, Bogotá, 21–23 July 2008, Judgment. Details and findings of the six thematic hearings leading up to the final session are available in Spanish on the PPT website. /

[53] Permanent Peoples' Tribunal, *Sessions on Free Trade, Violence, Impunity and Peoples' Rights in Mexico (2011–2014)*, final hearing, Mexico City, 12–15 November 2014, Final ruling. Details and findings of the ten thematic hearings leading up to the final session are available in Spanish on the PPT website. See also Andrés Barreda (ed.), *Juicio al Estado mexicano por la violencia estructural causada por el libre comercio: Audiencia final del capítulo México del Tribunal Permanente de los pueblos. Sentencias, fiscalías, y relatorías* [*Judgment on the Mexican State for the Structural Violence Caused by Free Trade: Final Hearing of the Mexican Chapter of the Permanent Peoples' Tribunal: Verdicts, Prosecutions And Reports*] (Itaca, 2016), http://editorialitaca.com.mx/wp-content/uploads/2017/02/JUICIO_AL_ESTADO_MEXICANO_LA_AUDIENCIA_FINAL-TPP.pdf.

[54] The Session on Transnational Corporations and the rights of peoples in Colombia (2006–2008), above n. 52, which was articulated in a long process involving preliminary thematic hearings on the different extractive industries and their impact on the life of Colombian peoples. The lengthy work of accusation, resistance and documentation was the subject of a study, the results of which are published in Antoni Pigrau Solé and Simona Fraudatario (eds.), *Colombia entre violencia y derechos: Implicaciones de una sentencia del Tribunal Permanente de los Pueblos* [*Colombia between Violence and Rights: Implications of a Judgment of the Permanent Peoples' Tribunal*] (Ediciones Desde Abajo, 2012).

session alleged, the Mexican state has had usurped[55] its role of guaranteeing the well-being of groups and its citizens. Rather, impunity and violence are at the service of a simulated legitimacy displayed for the international community.

The term *desvío de poder* (deviation of power) was central to the petition and charges directed at the Mexican state by the peoples participating in the session. The concept referred to the implementation of public policies of free trade and the crimes committed in terms of 'devastation' of the national economy and the 'dismantling' of the rights included in the 1917 Constitution. The term was symbolically adopted by the groups affected to express the implication of every single abuse committed by state and private actors.

The organisation of both processes in a series of thematic stages of investigation and participation was required by the complexity of the questions considered and the diversity of the petitions. This was also to guarantee, on the one hand, that the relevant questions were explored in the necessary depth and, on the other, a common path of rendering visible social actors and violations, and learning and raising awareness of the groups participating. The groups included associations of lawyers, women and migrants with their associations, environmental defenders, freedom of speech activists, peace activists and advocates for a just development, communities and peasant organisations, indigenous people, workers and unions, groups of students, professors and academics and investigators from different documentation centres or human rights monitors. Far from being divided by borders, these social actors promoting the sessions on Mexico and Colombia are emblematic as they

[55] The Inter-American Commission on Human Rights used the variant *desviación de poder* in Case 11.430, *Gallardo Rodríguez v. Mexico*, 15 October 1996, Inter-American Commission on Human Rights, Report No 43/96, www.cidh.org/annualrep/96eng/Mexico11430.htm. It is used to describe 'as a serious crime committed in a direct manner by the Mexican state by the implementation of public policies of free trade, in a manner not only using law to benefit certain special interest groups, but also to devastate the national economy and dismantle the institutional order that had been constructed based on the 1917 Constitution which has resulted in the breakdown in the social fabric and the disappearance of a whole set of references whose absence triggered quantitatively and qualitatively generalized violence, and whose synthesis translates into the violation with impunity of the rights of peoples'. (Text of the General Indictment [*Acusación General*] presented in the Introductory Hearing of the Permanent Peoples' Tribunal, *Session on Free Trade, Violence, Impunity and the Rights of peoples in Mexico*, Ciudad Juárez, 27–29 May 2012, PPT Archive.

represent the people affected by the global economy, the activities of transnational corporation, states and financial institutions.

The features of 'transversality'[56] they share are also visible in the process of solidarity with people all over the world. This form of solidarity corresponds to the transfer of experience, strategies, methods applied and knowledge acquired. Three petitions that recently reached the Presidency of the Tribunal came from this form of transmission of the practice of resistance. The first one refers to the session held in Montreal in 2014 on the extensive power of Canadian mining corporations in the world and on the vulnerability of both environmental resources and communities living in the vicinity of extractive activities.[57] The second was a petition to highlight the human rights claims implicated in the processes of fracking and its consequences on a worldwide scale, which will take place between 2017 and 2018. The last request sought to open a process of investigation and people's participation on transnational corporations in Southern Africa,[58] where the impacts are perhaps less known and less investigated.

6.6 A Memory of a Plural Form of Resistance for the Future

The PPT sessions have provided irrefutable evidence about the extent and the consequences of transformations produced by systems of economic, political, social and cultural domination that enable continual processes of rupture and fragmentation, as well as the networks and popular struggles for indivisible and interrelated rights. The peoples of the PPT – old and new, national or cross-border, minority or majority – each time, in every session held, have recreated the language of human

56 A mathematical term referring to a line crossing two or more lines.

57 Permanent Peoples' Tribunal, *Session on the Canadian Mining Industry (2014–2016)*, Montreal, 29 May–1 June 2014.

58 The Permanent Peoples' Tribunal held its opening session on Transnational Corporations in Southern Africa in Manzini, Swaziland, on 16–17 August 2016. The PPT analysed a sample of cases based in Swaziland, Zimbabwe, South Africa, Zambia and Mozambique, regarding corporate intervention in the critical areas of the extractive industries and land grabbing. In its statement, the PPT recognises that the communities are exposed to the intervention on their lands and life by TNCs, being victims, individually and collectively, of severe and systematic violations of their rights to life and human dignity. The entire process of analysis, documentation and participation of the affected people will be carried out in 2017. See Permanent Peoples' Tribunal, *Session on Transnational Corporations in Southern Africa*, Manzini, 16–17 August 2016, available on the PPT website.

rights and self-determination in a complex narrative that incorporates the concreteness of their everyday suffering, unrelated in the official human rights texts. They have disclosed and denounced situations of massive human rights violations, ignored or kept hidden by the institutional actors which are so often involved and against which no remedies are available. In the charges made by peoples, international law's remoteness from real life has become evident as well as the need for a progressive reconfiguration of it. Their multiple claims of violations – of the rights to life and dignity, to liberty, to work, to health, to food, to the environment, to land and to natural resources – have been articulated in the moments of its *negation* – the right negated – and of the *affirmation* of its original values and meaning. Through the power of 'words with dignity', women, children, migrants, farmers, indigenous peoples, workers and human rights defenders tell individual and global stories interrogating the politics of universality of human rights and transforming the paradigm of human rights into an instrument not related to the contamination of the market-friendly language, as it is 'modernisation', 'development' and 'structural adjustment'.

People have been faced with an international law that is ever more abstract and alien to the language of equity and blind to the growing problems of distribution, protection and life with dignity. They have also diversified the meaning and the interpretation of human rights in contrast with a description of them as a unique, conclusive and neutral body of principles.

In this context, participation raises firstly the problematic of representation of human existence and suffering. Participation is the way for peoples *to exist* and to reaffirm themselves as visible subjects of rights and law and to reject any form of resignation in the face of impunity for abuses of the transnational economic power. Through their participation, peoples oppose the inevitability of human suffering and abuses. Enshrining the memory of past struggles, they imagine the future by creating each time a new agenda for action and networks of solidarity across borders, reaffirming the undeniable priorities of *responsibility, protection* and *prevention,* as the core of peoples' requests for the elimination of all forms of exclusion, inequality and injustice. In this sense we can interpret the concept of people as *agents of claims*, as actors in a profound cultural and political exercise, of awareness and participation, each time expanding the space for the realisation of possible interpretations and applications of the principle of self-determination. The same principle, in its most immediate meaning, implies an *action*, a movement for and towards something. The current constriction of democratic space and the progressive – in many cases violent, exclusion of people from decision-making processes regarding the context and conditions in present day and future – seems to confirm Lelio Basso's prediction at the time of the Second Russell Tribunal, when he warned:

> The paths of development set in motion in the world do not leave any doubt about the fact that, if no alternatives are found to these tendencies, we are heading towards a world in which the power of a few hundred human beings (political, economic and military leaders) Kafkaesquely remote and inaccessible, in many cases completely unknown, will allow the majority of men, the limited possibilities of being slaves, eliminated or excluded.[59]

After decades, this restriction of participation has become the core of one of the most recent examinations by the PPT. The session on fundamental rights, participation of local communities and megaprojects held in Turin, Italy, in November 2014, documented in detail the mechanism of the individual and collective exclusion of people from the deliberations, decision-making and monitoring of the realisation of megaprojects in the territories where they live, accompanied by the commission of violations of fundamental human rights, the criminalisation of social movements and the diffusion of false data regarding the utility and impact of the works. It was on this occasion that the PPT recognised more explicitly participation as the principal tool for reappropriating the public sphere and relocating human rights in the current process of transformation of our society. Referring to the specific cases that were the subject of complaint, the PPT affirmed:

> [P]eople mobilizing against TAV [Lyon Turin high-speed rail]like those against the Notre-Dame-des-Landes airport or other projects, must be considered *sentinels who set off the alarm* in identifying rights violations, . . . to alert the authorities with the view of stopping acts against the interest of all society. Academics, professional, civil servants, farmers, any inhabitants can play this active role of guarantors of democracy and law.[60]

In order to confront the tendency to eliminate or exclude 'the majority' of people, the PPT identifies participation as a defensive and preventive

[59] Permanent Peoples' Tribunal, above n. 12, 6.

[60] Permanent Peoples' Tribunal, *Fundamental Rights, Participation of Local Communities and Infrastructure Projects–from the Lyon-Turin High-Speed Rail to the Global Reality*, Turin-Almese, 5–8 November 2015, Judgment, 20.

means for ensuring the future of democracy and human rights, a motor to activate processes of free and conscious self-determination by peoples and individuals. As we have learnt from the memory of resistance documented by the PPT, not all achievements endure in time and space. Nonetheless, the project of human rights remains, as well as the necessity to interrogate them in a world in transformation, which demands that state and democracy be ethical, the power of the market be held accountable, and international law act as a guarantor of prevention of the violation of rights.

PART III

Legal Pluralism and Popular International Law

7

Accusing 'Europe'

Articulations of Migrant Justice and a Popular International Law

SARA DEHM

> We accuse Europe of continual violations of human rights and the systematic mistreatment of refugees, migrants and asylum seekers![1]

7.1 Introduction

This chapter examines a civil society initiative, Tribunal 12, held in Stockholm in May 2012 as an internationalised articulation of migrant justice. Tribunal 12 sought to put 'Europe' on trial for the systematic violations of the rights and dignity of refugees, asylum seekers and migrants. By adopting a legal and aesthetical framework, the initiative aimed to draw attention to the increased global securitisation of borders, criminalisation of unauthorised migrants and systemic exploitation of undocumented people in Europe. It also intended to generate support for migrant struggles within Europe by highlighting the morally unjust and harmful effects of European border practices. Although the Tribunal differed significantly from earlier international peoples' tribunals in that it did not hear any witness testimonies from migrants themselves, I nonetheless locate Tribunal 12 within a legacy of peoples' tribunals and their entanglement with international law and institutions.

Peoples' tribunals have been generally recognised for their ability to demand or provide a form of accountability for collectively experienced harms committed by state or non-state actors, harms that generally fail to

[1] Tribunal 12. The original Tribunal 12 website (tribunal12.org) is no longer available on the Internet. However, many documents from the original website have been archived at https://web.archive.org/web/20150507160222/http://tribunal12.org:80/. Information about the Tribunal organisers and participants and the final Tribunal 12 Report written by the International Jury (though not the video recordings of the Tribunal sessions) are accessible from this archive.

receive any adequate institutional redress.[2] In this chapter, I examine how Tribunal 12 extended this politics of accountability to address some of the fundamental norms that structure the international domain. My reading of Tribunal 12 emphasises how it named and interrogated not only the harms arising from the contemporary institution and policing of European borders but also the harms from the notion of fixed borders themselves. In doing so, I argue that the Tribunal questioned forms of political community, identity and belonging based on a security–territory–people nexus which continue to be fundamental organising principles for determining modes of inclusion and exclusion in the international legal order.

This chapter explores how Tribunal 12 appealed to international law as a language of popular justice, but also saw it as inextricably limited through its legitimation of state sovereignty, territorial control and borders. The Tribunal's use of international law exemplified an attempt to hold established institutions to account while also seeking to create a different form of justice and political community to that merely envisioned and authorised through international law and institutions.

This chapter proceeds in three parts. First, I explore the marginalised position of migrants within the international legal order through the use of Hannah Arendt's writings on statelessness. Second, I offer a reading of Tribunal 12 that frames the Tribunal's political and ethical claims as a juridical project that constitutes a different basis for international community, belonging and accountability. In particular, I unpack Judith Butler's thinking around the 'performative contradiction' of universals and an ethics of cohabitation to elaborate the productive claims that peoples' tribunals can make in and of the international (legal) order. Finally, I suggest that the importance of peoples' tribunals within international law is their enactment of a popular form of international law that seeks to unsettle and transform the existing norms and institutions

[2] I adopt the terminology of 'peoples' tribunals' rather than that of 'citizens' tribunals' because of Tribunal 12's concern to break down the citizen/migrant distinction (discussed in Section 7.4 of this chapter). I note though that the concept of citizenship can be disaggregated into various components (legal, political, economic, cultural, etc.) and constituted as a performative and relational practice such that migrants can been seen to engage in 'acts of citizenship' when performing certain everyday activities or staging political protests that make greater demand for recognition, equality and inclusion within a political community: see Engin Isin and Greg Nielsen (eds.), *Acts of Citizenship* (Zed Books, 2008). Despite this, Tribunal 12's concern appears to be better encompassed through the notion of constituting a 'people', rather than enacting 'citizenship'.

of international law, rather than simply attempting to democratise or widen the sphere of participation within established structures. In doing so, Tribunal 12 advanced a politics of accountability that challenged the framework and mechanics of international law, rather than merely critiquing its normative content or practical operations.

7.2 Migrant Justice and Technologies of Inclusion in the International Domain

Writing in the aftermath of World War II, political theorist Hannah Arendt was concerned with the production of citizenship – and its antipathy, statelessness – as both legal and political conditions. To become stateless, Arendt remarked, is to be defined as and placed in the position of the 'outlaw'. As an outlaw, a person is not only outside law's protection and must 'transgress' it in order to survive but also their very presence in a territory is criminalised and subject to police action. This means that the stateless lack any form of legal or political protections. The production of statelessness in the twentieth century – as a predicament of the consolidation and universalisation of nation-states – is also the production of a state of rightlessness. As Arendt wrote, the

> calamity of the rightless is not that they are deprived of life, liberty, and the pursuit of happiness, or of equality before the law and freedom of opinion – formulas which were designed to solve problems within given communities – but that they no longer belong to any community whatsoever. Their plight is not that they are not equal before the law, but that no law exists for them.[3]

In this passage, Arendt's key claim is that the condition of statelessness entails not simply a loss of particular rights, but rather a more fundamental exclusion, namely the exclusion from the right to belong to and participate in a political community and the 'loss of a community willing and able to guarantee any rights whatsoever'.[4] This exclusion, for Arendt, starkly demonstrates the fallibility of human rights in their contemporary institutional, political and legal forms. Because of their historical consolidation as *national* rights, human rights are not inalienable and they tend to fail those who need them the most. This meant, for Arendt, that the attainment of human rights is not prior to being included within a

[3] Hannah Arendt, *Origins of Totalitarianism* (World Publishing Company, 1958) 295–96.
[4] Ibid., 297.

political community, which in its modern iteration is expressed as a community of citizens. Rather, it is the right to belong to a political community that is of fundamental importance and is constitutive of, in Arendt's famous pronouncement, 'the right to have rights'.[5] In a world organised around nation-states, the loss of this right, for Arendt, amounts to the 'expulsion from humanity altogether' and well as the loss of a 'place in the world which makes opinions significant and actions effective'.[6]

While Arendt used the language of 'total domination' and absolute political exclusion to describe those people designated as rightless, her analysis can nonetheless help to reveal the difficulties that those deemed excluded from a polis – legally, politically and, in the extreme case, physically – experience when making political claims. Importantly, Arendt's intervention is not a simple collapsing of the rights of Man with the right to citizenship. It is rather a recognition that attaining particular political rights is dependent on the dynamic 'right to exist first as a political subject', that is, to be recognised as a political subject within an instituted community.[7]

The reinvigoration of international law and institutions in the second half of the twentieth century has not diminished the centrality of Arendt's claims. While Arendt urged the creation of a 'law above nations' to counter the production of the condition of rightlessness, the contemporary form of international law where the central subject remains states means that the realisation of human rights are still dependent on a state willing and able to recognise or enforce them. This means that the contemporary world persists, as Arendt had earlier diagnosed, as a 'world organised into nation-states',[8] even if there has been a proliferation of new international norms and regimes and growing recognition afforded to other actors, participants or subjects of international law at the turn of the twenty-first century. Patrick Hayden, in interpreting Arendt's thought for present forms of exclusion and containment, notes that the power of Arendt's contribution is how she highlighted that

> statelessness is not an aberrant or accidental phenomenon occurring despite the best efforts of states to prevent it, but a "normalized" systemic condition produced by an international order predicated upon the power to exclude as the essence of statist politics.[9]

[5] Ibid., 296, 298. [6] Ibid., 297, 296.

[7] Kim Rygiel, *Globalising Citizenship* (University of British Colombia Press, 2010) 96.

[8] Arendt, above n. 3, 280.

[9] Patrick Hayden, 'From exclusion to containment: Arendt, sovereign power and statelessness' (2008) 3 *Societies without Borders* 248, 250.

Similarly, Judith Butler suggests that Arendt's work is powerful for its 'prescience in predicting the recurrence of statelessness and the persistence of territorial violence', for its insistence on the inevitability of statelessness in a world of states.[10] Statelessness then reveals the deep 'structural deficiencies of the international system' and must be seen as a problem of *political* rather than *geographical* space.[11] It is this political configuration of space then that produces people as stateless as an 'anomaly' within the international order and is incapable, Arendt despaired, of guaranteeing the stateless a 'place in the world'.[12]

Statelessness, for Arendt, necessarily refers to both de jure statelessness (those deemed without nationality by a given state) as well as de facto statelessness (those individuals inside a territory threatened by denaturalisation and/or deportation).[13] Worldwide, the Office of the United Nations High Commissioner for Refugees (UNHCR) estimates that approximately 10 million people were affected by statelessness in 2012, of whom 700,000 live in Europe.[14] This number is much higher when Arendt's de facto stateless is considered: a European Commission-funded 'Clandestino' project suggested that there were between 1.9 and 3.8 million undocumented migrants in Europe in 2008, although earlier statistics suggested this number is greater – between 5 and 8 million people.[15] The numerous and dispersed struggles of undocumented people in Europe have been well-recorded by non-governmental organisations as well as articulated by migrants themselves.[16] These struggles

[10] Judith Butler, 'I merely belong to them' (2007) 29(9) *London Review of Books* 26, www.lrb.co.uk/v29/n09/judith-butler/i-merely-belong-to-them.

[11] Hayden, above n. 9, 254, 257, citing Peter Nyers, *Rethinking Refugees: Beyond States of Emergency* (Routledge, 2006).

[12] Arendt, above n. 3, 286, 293–96.

[13] Ibid., 279; Hayden, above n. 11, 255.

[14] UNHCR, 'Global Report 2012 – Addressing Statelessness', 1 June 2013, www.unhcr.org/en-au/publications/fundraising/51b1d61db/unhcr-global-report-2012-addressing-statelessness.html.

[15] Clandestino Project, 'Final Report', 23 November 2009, 109, http://cordis.europa.eu/documents/documentlibrary/126625701EN6.pdf; see also Council of Europe, 'Position on the Rights of Migrants in an Irregular Situation', 24 June 2010, https://wcd.coe.int/ViewDoc.jsp?id=1640817. The term 'undocumented' has been adopted by some migrant struggles (particularly in the United States), and it is generally accepted within much migration studies literature. However, as Brigid Anderson noted at Tribunal 12, the irony is that often so-called undocumented migrants are in fact 'over-documented', but they have the 'wrong' documents. In this sense, the term 'unauthorised' migrants can more accurately reflect their relationship to state power.

[16] For NGO reports, see, e.g., Platform for International Cooperation on Undocumented Migrants, 'PICUM's Main Concerns about the Fundamental Rights of Undocumented People in Europe', October 2010, http://picum.org/picum.org/uploads/publication/Annual%20Concerns%202010%20EN.pdf. For migrant statements, see, e.g., statement

have at times been over access or entitlement to specific state-funded resources such as health, education and housing or about conditions arising from precarious employment and structural exploitation in labour markets. At other times, struggles have involved objecting to the dehumanising, harsh and punitive state measures allegedly in place to deter and police unauthorised migrants.

On a more fundamental level, migrant struggles express demands for political inclusion and issue a challenge to what migration scholar Nicholas De Genova has called the 'production of deportability' for non-citizens. For De Genova, the production of deportability involves official practices that create the 'possibility of deportation', that is the possibility of removing migrants from the space of the nation-state, rather than the act of deportation per se.[17] This ensures that migrants – regardless of their status as documented or undocumented, temporarily legalised or illegalised[18] – live with the constant threat of future police action and removal. Such measures function as a disciplinary technology of social control and exclusion as well as a means of perpetuating the treatment of migrants as a vulnerable and deportable workforce. Rather than absolute exclusion per se, regulatory regimes require and expect migrants to be present within European physical and legal spaces. However, the production of conditions of deportability ensures that migrants are always subjected to forms of 'differential inclusion', functioning as an apparatus for organising global uneven distribution of labour and wealth.[19]

Within international law, migrant struggles for justice have been made and primarily received within a framework of the individual-*as-citizen* of a particular nation-state or the individual-*as-human* as a subject of

issued by the International Migrants Alliance and Migrante Europe, 'IMA Statement on the 5th GFMD', Asia Pacific Mission for Migrants, 3 December 2011, https://web.archive.org/web/20130807223026/www.apmigrants.org/home/item/59-ima-statement-and-critique-of-the-5th-gfmd.

[17] Nicolas De Genova, 'Migrant "illegality" and deportability in everyday life' (2002) 31 *Annual Review of Anthropology* 419, 439; Nicolas De Genova and Nathalie Peutz (eds.), *The Deportation Regime: Sovereignty, Space and the Freedom of Movement* (Duke University Press, 2010).

[18] For an analysis of how law illegalises people, see Catherine Dauvergne, *Making People Illegal: What Globalization Means for Migration and Law* (Cambridge University Press, 2008).

[19] Étienne Balibar, *We, the People of Europe? Reflections on Transnational Citizenship* (translated by James Swenson) (Princeton University Press, 2004) 7.

humanity bearing particular rights and duties. Migrants are able either to appeal to their home states to offer them certain protections owed to them as citizens while living abroad or to look to their state of residence for certain protections based on recognised universal norms or established treaties.[20] In both approaches, migrants remain reliant on states being willing and able to enforce migrant rights claims in order for such rights to be meaningfully recognised. As such, particular states can be accused of not protecting their citizens abroad or of violating the rights of particular groups of migrants within their territory. However, the conditions of possibility for the international order – the fundamental norms of sovereignty that structure the exclusionary political configurations of citizenship and the horizons of deportability – remain beyond accusation within the dominant framework offered by international law.[21]

7.3 Reading Tribunal 12

This section reads Tribunal 12 as a project that puts this international framework on trial. This section explores four elements of Tribunal 12: first, how the Tribunal located its political intervention; secondly, how the Tribunal addressed and constructed 'Europe'; thirdly, how the Tribunal grounded its claim to represent 'people' in the international domain and to generate a different mode of international sociability; and finally, how the Tribunal included the voices and stories of migrants in its sessions. These elements could be broadly thought of as questions of status, authorisation, constitution and procedure, all questions that are linked to a juridical way of thinking.[22] I use this juridical approach to

[20] See, e.g., Brian Opeskin, Richard Perruchoud and Jillyanne Redpath-Cross (eds.), *Foundations of International Migration Law* (Cambridge University Press, 2012). While the fragmentation of international law has seen the proliferation of mechanisms for the articulation, regulation and enforcement of migrants' rights within the different regimes that constitute the international legal order – including, for example, migrants as 'civilians' under international humanitarian law; as 'victims' of human trafficking under international criminal law; as 'workers' subject to international labour standards; as 'service suppliers' under international trade law; or as 'refugees' under international refugee law – these 'status-based' regimes still function largely around an idea of the *individual-as-human*.

[21] Gregor Noll, 'Why human rights fail to protect undocumented migrants' (2010) 12 *European Journal of Migration and Law* 241.

[22] See generally Shaunnaugh Dorsett and Shaun McVeigh, *Jurisdiction* (Routledge, 2012).

read what was essentially a political act performed through a mediated legal form and language.

7.3.1 *Locating Tribunal 12*

As a civil society initiative, Tribunal 12 aimed to 'awaken the conscience of Europe' and to challenge the dominant trajectory of migration politics and policies of European states and supranational institutions. As a one-day event, Tribunal 12 engaged a variety of audiences, both within and beyond Sweden. The Tribunal sessions were held at the Stockholm Kulturhuset, and attended by a small number of people – approximately 300 – throughout the day. By far the greater level of engagement with the Tribunal was mediated through technology: approximately 7,000 people watched the online live streaming of the Tribunal sessions. In addition, more than twenty public screenings were simultaneously held in cities across Europe, ranging from public parks attended by more than 1,000 people to smaller gatherings in local libraries. A recording of the Tribunal sessions was also replayed on Swedish television after the event.

Consequentially, by far the greater level of audience engagement with Tribunal 12 occurred across physical distances. This distance meant that the audience was dispersed and fragmented, making it difficult to generate a sense of a cohesive community or movement. But it also allowed individuals or groups to determine the form and degree of their engagement, providing a resource for community groups to organise their own programs and focus their discussions on local circumstances and national policies in order to complement the broader European-wide focus of the Tribunal sessions.

The Tribunal was a carefully planned staging, consisting of a team of prosecutors who elaborated on the charges against 'Europe', actors presenting witness testimony, academic experts detailing the practices and policies of European states and their effects and a seven-member international jury that issued the final verdict. The day was structured around four thematic sessions: border control, asylum process, undocumented migrants and detention and deportation. In each session, the prosecution first introduced the particular practices of European states, institutions and corporations. After this, evidence was presented by academic 'experts', and testimonies of migrants were read out in order to demonstrate the subjective experiences and effects of exclusionary border practices.

For example, in the border control session, the jury heard about the 16,136 migrant deaths at European borders since 1993.[23] They heard the story of Bahram, a sixteen-year-old Afghani asylum seeker who was smuggled to Bulgaria only to be beaten, starved, interrogated and strip-searched in police custody before being forcibly moved to and detained in a migrant border camp for four months. Here, his application for asylum was rejected, resulting in his presence in Europe becoming illegalised and subject to deportation. The question that was repeatedly asked at the Tribunal was, who was responsible for this violence and these accounts of harm? Was it the product of, or a deviation from, international norms and processes?

The final session consisted of a jury deliberation: here, each jury member provided a personal reflection on the materials they had heard that day. Jury member and Swedish author Henning Mankell, for example, declared that Europe had become 'a monster, a beast'. Somali writer Nuruddin Farah called on Europeans to 'know their own history' as, in his words, 'the life [that] they have is owed to the fact that their people were able to go elsewhere [during periods of war, famine, persecution or hardship] ... sometimes going to countries where [their peace was enabled or secured] through the [dispossession or] massacres of indigenous people.' The jury also formulated a short collective verdict, in which they explicitly 'condemned European governments for violating fundamental norms ... [such as] the equal moral worth of all human beings ... which go beyond existing laws' as well as 'violating existing laws on how governments should handle asylum seekers, detention and irregular migration'.[24] They called for the 'removal of restrictive immigration practices' both within and beyond European territory, condemned the political economy of borders and drew attention to contemporary migrant struggles for justice that present alternative horizons or foundation for community.[25]

Through its constitution and articulated purpose, Tribunal 12 explicitly situated itself within a longer legacy of peoples' tribunals, most notably that of the Bertrand Russell Tribunal in 1967 that had also taken place, in part, in Stockholm.[26] Yet it was also keen to find its own form.

[23] Leanne Weber, 'Death at the Global Frontier', *OpenDemocracy*, 13 June 2012, www.opendemocracy.net/5050/leanne-weber/death-at-global-frontier.

[24] www.icorn.org/article/tribunal-12-verdict. [25] Ibid.

[26] The Tribunal 12 website explicitly states that the project was 'inspired by the International War Crimes Tribunal that was formed by Bertrand Russell and Jean-Paul Sartre in 1967'.

Most notably, unlike earlier tribunals, Tribunal 12 deliberately adopted a 'dramaturgical' mode for organising its sessions and materials. In this sense, its political emphasis was more on a performative staging than on facilitating a forensic trial or providing an avenue of redress for particular victims.[27] This distinguishes it sharply from earlier tribunals and is the product of the particular history and motivation for the Tribunal.

The Tribunal was the culmination of a five-year cultural project, Shahrazad, that brought together non-European exiled and diaspora writers to tell their stories through literary events and collaborations. As an 'offshoot' of the International Cities of Refuge Network, a network that aims to provide a safe haven to persecuted writers, the Shahrazad project was organised primarily around the ideas of freedom of expression and diversity. The project's purpose was to foster spaces for intercultural dialogue based on human rights where European and non-European writers could share their writings and stories of common experiences and aspirations. It also aimed to 'provide Europe with new, more open and sustainable narratives about itself' – narratives that both challenged and affirmed European traditions and ideals. In this sense, the project's purpose can partly be seen as redemptive: attempting to 'revitalise some of [Europe's] capital values: freedom, democracy and solidarity' though bringing stories from outside Europe within.[28]

The Tribunal 12 project developed out of and in connection with the Shahrazad project, with these literary concerns providing a core framework for the Tribunal even though it was organised as an independent project. Thus, rather than arising out of migrant struggles themselves, Tribunal 12 saw itself acting in support of and in solidarity with such struggles. Although migrants and migrant organisations played a key role in devising and planning the Tribunal, for example, through the project's Organising and Reference committees, they were largely absent from the official tribunal proceedings; an element that I will discuss later.

State-centric narratives of the international legal order continue to structure how peoples' or citizens' tribunals have been perceived in relation to international law. While the reception of and publicity around such tribunals have varied according to the time, actors and issue, official, academic or popular representations can generally be divided into two

[27] The Tribunal website emphasises that 'artistic expression [is] an integral part of the tribunal'.

[28] The Shahrazad project also commenced with a small tribunal event, known as the Stavanger or Hospitality Tribunal, held in May 2008.

distinct camps. On the one hand, critics have dismissed peoples' tribunals outright as ideological 'fiascos' or 'kangaroo courts'.[29] In this view, peoples' tribunals have no judicial merit or enforcement powers and merely mimic or mock the legal form.[30] On the other hand, advocates of peoples' tribunals have celebrated them for publicly 'putting wrongs on the scaffold',[31] wrongs that are often state perpetrated or sanctioned and that would otherwise go without recognition or redress. The tribunals are thus narrated as deriving their legitimacy from that fact that they promote a form of 'unofficial accountability',[32] with civil society stepping in to 'fill a gap' in official institutional measures or where state institutions fail to respond. Here, the tribunals are celebrated for their *effects*: in expressing resistance to hegemonic practices, creating an archive or factual documentation or being a public witnessing of moral and legal harms. Christine Chinkin, for example, in her work on the Tokyo Women's Tribunal, puts forward six grounds that legitimate peoples' tribunals, including their use of extensive powerful oral testimony, expert evidence and official reports of recognised civil society bodies to bolster their judgments.[33] As Richard Falk notes in his work on the World Tribunal on Iraq, the motivation for peoples' tribunals 'do[es] not arise from an uncertainty about issues of legality and morality but from a conviction that the official institutions of the state, including the United Nations, have failed to act to protect a vulnerable people'.[34]

Extending this politics of accountability, this chapter highlights how Tribunal 12 put contemporary state and supranational migration governance practices on trial to focus on both breaches of established international norms as well as of more generally conceived moral principles

[29] 'The Russell Tribunal on Palestine: A legal farce and total failure', *NGO Monitor*, 10 November 2011, www.ngo-monitor.org/reports/the_russell_tribunal_on_palestine_a_legal_farce_and_total_failure/.

[30] For a discussion of such critiques, see Christine Chinkin, 'Peoples' tribunals: Legitimate or rough justice' (2006) 24 *Windsor Yearbook on Access to Justice* 201. Attempts have been made though to reclaim such terms with, for example, Arundhati Roy defiantly declaring in her concluding remarks of the World Tribunal on Iraq that 'this court is a kangaroo court': Arundhati Roy, 'Opening Speech of the Spokesperson of the Jury of Conscience' in Müge Gürsöy Sökmen (ed.), *World Tribunal on Iraq: Making the Case against War* (Olive Branch Press, 2008) 2, 3.

[31] Christine Chinkin, 'Editorial comments: Women's International Tribunal on Japanese Military Sexual Slavery' (2001) 95 *American Journal of International Law* 335.

[32] Fleming Terrell, 'Unofficial accountability' (2006) 15 *Texas Journal of Women and the Law* 107.

[33] Chinkin, above n. 30, 335.

[34] Richard Falk, 'World speaks on Iraq' (2005) 62(2) *Guild Practitioner* 91, 92.

such as the 'equal worth' of all humans. This meant that there was a productive slippage between, on the one hand, challenging the denial of particular rights to migrants and, on the other hand, more generally critiquing the morality of institutional attempts to exclude migrants from the normative political community of 'Europe'. In terms of accountability, the Tribunal not only responded to harms arising from the inadequacy of existing norms and international institutions but also articulated a critique of the very structure of the international itself, imagined as a 'community of nations' in which the individual is dominantly incorporated as a 'citizen', even if it is as a citizen of another state. At times, then, the Tribunal recognised the need to unsettle and reconfigure the international domain and its modes of belonging in order to advance the justice-seeking claims of migrants within Europe.

7.3.2 Addressing 'Europe'

Although it adopted a tribunal format, Tribunal 12 represented itself primarily as a political, rather than legal, project.[35] Politically, its task centred on issuing a vocal and public challenge to Europe's treatment of asylum seekers and migrants. In staging this challenge, 'Europe' was framed as neither a natural nor self-evident entity. Rather, its framing constituted a political gesture, oscillating between the general and the particular; between a historically constructed ideal of 'Europe' and its concrete contemporary manifestations; between identifying specific institutional actors and signifying an all-encompassing social collective. This vacillation symbolised a refusal to conclusively define 'Europe' and was the product of and productive for a particular way of thinking about institutional politics, political communities and ethical responsibility. But, as we shall see, it also risked, at times, repeating or prioritising a construction of 'Europe' articulated by states and supranational institutions.[36]

[35] For example, a key Tribunal 12 organiser described the Tribunal as having 'moral' rather than 'judicial value', suggesting that the Tribunal's main contribution was not legal but rather its elaboration of a 'full picture of the problems, and examples of how the systematic violence and practices are used' so that the Tribunal findings and verdicts could be used by activists in pushing for systemic change. Interview with Tribunal 12 organiser (Interview with author, November 2012, on file with author).

[36] On Europe as a historically contested social construct, see Balibar, above n. 19 (narrating Europe's 'hyper-real' qualities) and Roberto Dainotto, *Europe (in Theory)* (Duke University Press, 2010), on how theoretical understandings of the location of 'Europe' have shifted over time. Dainotto seeks to deconstruct the idea of 'Europe' such that it no longer makes sense to speak its name.

A primary function of an address is to name and identify the subject of the address, that is, the subject of responsibility and accountability of an accusation. This means that an address also, in turn, constructs and frames the object of the address.[37] It is a multi-relational act, singling out the accused from a community of other possible addressees as well as in relation to the harmful acts, while simultaneously defining or delimiting the sphere of that responsibility and conduct. In legal proceedings, the subject of responsibility needs to be named with precision, as otherwise its specific conduct cannot be examined or a particular order cannot be enforced. The Tribunal's address to 'Europe' rather negated this demand: while it named 'Europe' as the specific subject of accountability, the precise identity or construction of 'Europe' was left deliberately ambiguous and open. In the accusation, 'Europe' functioned as a sign that at times would refer to the official institutional matrix that regulates legal citizenship, visa enforcement and the asylum process; at other times, 'Europe' designated a community of people, a collective project, both in its material and ideation forms. As one Tribunal organiser put it:

> We wanted 'Europe' not to be defined. It was very deliberate. We are not accusing only the EU, or European governments, or specific officers. But we are accusing everyone, on all levels, because it's a very complex problem, the responsibilities are on different levels and we didn't want that to be explicitly stated [in the accusation], because then we could exclude the others from the responsibilities. In the end, Europe is also talking about ourselves, everyone, that's watching and not watching. . . . We're accusing ourselves and all citizens of Europe.[38]

In framing the accused in this way, the Tribunal created a critical malleability to the identity of the accused that left the precise contours of the accused's identity open for elaboration and repeated interrogation in each session. For example, when discussing the particular failures of law to protect migrants or the stark abuses of legal processes in the asylum process session, 'Europe' as a subject of responsibility included the practices of actors that ranged from national governments and their divergent legislative frameworks to the European Union harmonisation mechanisms such as the Schengen system and Dublin Regulation regime.[39] Actors ranged from intergovernmental organisations such as

[37] On the power of an 'address', see Louis Althusser, *Essays on Ideology* (Verso, 1971) 44–48.

[38] Interview with Tribunal 12 organiser (November 2012, on file with author).

[39] Convention implementing the Schengen Agreement of 14 June 1985 between the governments of the states of the Benelux Economic Union, the Federal Republic of Germany and the French Republic on the gradual abolition of checks at their common borders, OJ

Frontex (the EU border control agency) to private profit-driven corporations such as SERCO that manage immigration detention and deportation within certain European states.[40]

At other times, 'Europe' appeared as a more figural construction, the product of its historical constitution as a political entity in both its material and idealised forms. As one expert witness put it, contemporary 'Europe' and ideas of 'Europeanness' about equality and social welfare could not be cut off from their global histories:

> [the] foundation of European prestige and prosperity, for hundreds of year was precisely colonial empire ... European colonialism as monumental crime against humanity and established a global social and political order of white racial supremacy.[41]

The 'fortification' and expansion of European borders, through practices restricting and policing migration, then becomes a way of creating new global divisions on the basis of race, a twentieth-first century 'redrawing' of W. E. B. Du Bois' 'color line'.[42]

This politics informed why no defence to the European border regime was invited or presented, as the Tribunal did not want to exhaustively name those responsible by inviting a particular defendant (and not others). Such an invitation would have acted to limit the field of responsibility as well as confine the harms to a particular time and place. Rather, in keeping 'Europe' open and deliberately ambiguous, the Tribunal encouraged the jury and audience to reflect on the norms, institutions and people that carry responsibility for the maintenance of exclusionary and violent border practices. Thus, participants were asked to take responsibility for how they understood 'Europe' and framed the accusation.

As the previous quote from a Tribunal organiser explains, the sign of 'Europe' could and should include what he described as 'ourselves'. Here, the accusation encompassed European citizens who are, in a

2000 No. L239/19 (the 'Schengen system'); Council Regulation 343/2003 of 18 February 2003 establishing the criteria and mechanisms for determining the Member State responsible for examining an asylum application lodged in one of the Member States by a third-country national, OJ 2003 No. L50/1 (the 'Dublin Regulation').

[40] See, e.g., Gregory Feldman, *The Migration Apparatus: Security, Labor and Policymaking in the European Union* (Stanford University Press, 2012).

[41] Nicholas De Genova's address to Tribunal 12 (Session 4: Detention and Deportation), available from https://web.archive.org/web/20130318105617/http://tribunal12.org/.

[42] See Nicholas De Genova's address to Tribunal 12 (Session 4: Detention and Deportation) in which he references W. E. B. Du Bois, *The Souls of Black Folk* (AC McClurg, 1903).

certain sense, the 'beneficiaries' of state systems reliant upon established borders and the differential privileges stemming from the institution of citizenship and who are morally culpable for not speaking out about the harm done in the name of a collective Europe. The 'European' part of the audience was called on to take responsibility for the ongoing marginalisation and exclusion of migrants in their proximity and communities. In this way, the 'we' that accused 'Europe' was not entirely absolved of responsibility, its claim to a coherent identity being unsettled and contaminated by traces of both the accuser and the accused. The Tribunal, in this sense, became a project of speaking to and as 'Europe': both critiquing specific institutional practices of exclusion as well as demanding self-reflection by 'Europe's' subjects. Considered in this light, the staging of the Tribunal fed into broader attempts to transform the conversations about 'European' identity, entitlements and belonging.

Yet the Tribunal's construction of 'Europe' risked repeating a certain exclusion of migrants from the recognised political community of Europe. It risked taking established political ideas and legal constructions of Europe and European 'citizenship' as the basis of its construction of Europe, rather than asserting that migrants are already part of the actually existing political and economic communities found within the territorial space of 'Europe'. This is by no means to suggest that migrants should be included within the 'subject of responsibility'. Rather, it attends to how the reiteration and prioritisation of 'Europe's' identity and ideas of political belonging that rest on legal relations sit ambivalently alongside other attempts to broaden what 'Europe' entails or to think European belonging otherwise. After all, as several participants emphasised throughout the proceedings, migrants are 'already Europeans' and participate on a daily basis in the political struggles and forces that make up 'Europe'.

7.3.3 'We Accuse . . .': Performing Communities of Ethical Cohabitation

A third element of the Tribunal's constitution was how it sought to authorise itself through articulating a collective 'we'. The Tribunal deployed a technology of judgment to performatively bring a particular 'we' into being.[43] Rather than grounding itself in a sovereign, bounded

[43] On technologies of law, see Dorsett and McVeigh, above n. 22, 54–80.

'we', the 'we' of the Tribunal was much more decentred, temporary and fleeting: there was no 'we' prior to its articulation at the Tribunal, and there was necessarily no fixed 'we' behind the utterance nor a permanent institution to give it shape.[44] The Tribunal's 'we' is best understood as split between functioning as a descriptive and a performative (that is, a statement that inaugurates or brings a particular state into being).[45] As a descriptive, it described those present at, engaging with or supportive of the Tribunal 12 sessions and verdict. As a performative, it created a paradigmatic 'we', producing and materially enacting a form of community that both negotiates and disavows national units as the primary markers of belonging or the primary mode authorising access to or action within the international domain.

The 'we' behind the Tribunal's accusation of Europe made a claim to and of the international domain that can be described as a jurisdictional practice, that is, a practice that inaugurates legal relations or makes a claim to speak the (or a) law. In this sense, the assertion of a 'we' was also a claim to rightly occupy and people the international domain and, thus, a right to structure and shape the forms of belonging and modes of sociability of the 'international'. But crucially, it was not a right asserted by virtue of legal citizenship, nor was it a simple demand for inclusion within an already textured space. It was rather an attempt to make and think of the international domain in a way that moves beyond an international based on the nation-state system.

Butler's work on the politics of contesting universals enables an understanding of the performative claim that Tribunal 12 made. Butler suggests that universals can be mobilised in such a way as to give rise to a 'performative contradiction'. The performative contradiction arises, for example, when a claim is made to belong to or be covered by an established universal when those making the claim 'are without entitlement' to do so.[46] This collective claiming exposes 'the contradictory character of previous conventional formulations of the universal'. It is not a claim based on 'a priori recourse to a truer criterion of

[44] One tribunal organiser expressed disappointment that there were no follow-up events for the Tribunal, no way of further galvanising the networks created through the project as a way for further solidifying, shaping and mobilising this 'we'.

[45] J. L. Austin, *How to Do Things with Words* (Clarendon Press, 1962); Judith Butler, *Excitable Speech: A Politics of the Performative* (Routledge, 1997).

[46] See generally Butler's remarks in Judith Butler and Gavatri Chakravorty Spivak, *Who Sings the Nation-State?* (Seagull Books, 2007) 58–68.

universality',[47] but rather seeks to rework and fashion the particular content given to the universal anew. Butler uses the example of undocumented people in Los Angeles singing the United States national anthem in Spanish as an act of protest and a way of making a claim to belong to the particular nation.[48] For Butler, this performative act of singing enacted a radical politics of equality and critically articulated an unauthorised plurality to the nation.

Butler argues that such creative interventions require a reworking of dominant languages, institutional forms or power relations: they challenge the modalities of inclusion and belonging offered by 'conventional and exclusionary norms of universality' (such as ideas of the legal 'citizenship' or the 'international community').[49] The claim then inaugurates a distinct gap between the exercise and realisation of a particular norm, such that the gap can be made visible and mobilised. In Butler's words, such claims prompt a 'set of antagonistic speculations on what the proper venue for the claim of universality ought to be. Who may speak [in the name of the universal, here the "international"]? And how ought it be spoken?'[50] And, further, how might or should such claims be received? Framed in this way, Tribunal 12's 'we' drew on pre-existing ideas of an 'international community' and on norms recognised within international law but did so in a way so as to reshape them. In positing and enacting a different form of international sociability, in Butler's words, it 'starts to take what [it] asks for'.[51]

The question of who the 'we' represented and who was included in the 'we' was raised at various moments throughout the Tribunal. One expert participant suggested that the 'we' should be formulated in a way that unsettled the foundational categories offered by law and challenged the citizen/migrant dichotomy as a legitimate basis for political belonging:

> Migrants are already new Europeans, but the question is what Europe is at stake in engaging migrants. . . . We can imagine ourselves as a clean and good conscience of the powers that be, or we can imagine ourselves as

[47] Judith Butler, 'Restaging the Universal: Hegemony and the Limits of Formalism' in Judith Butler, Ernesto Laclau and Slavoj Žižek, *Contingency, Hegemony, Universality: Contemporary Dialogues on the Left* (Verso, 2000) 39.

[48] Butler and Spivak, above n. 45, 58–61.

[49] Butler writes: 'It does suggest, however, that conventional and exclusionary norms of universality can, through perverse reiterations, produce unconventional formulations of universality that expose the limited and exclusionary features of the former one at the same time that they mobilize a new set of demands': Butler, above n. 46, 40.

[50] Ibid., 39. [51] Ibid.

> participating in the struggles with those migrants in the remaking of a new kind of world order in which Europe is a crucial site.[52]

In this perspective, the Tribunal project needed to fit into part of a broader 'remaking' or rearticulation of Europe, giving rise to a new form of international sociability. This form of political community could be paralleled to what Butler has called political communities grounded in an 'ethics of co-habitation'. For Butler, such communities entail negotiating political relations of 'unwilled proximity and unchosen cohabitation', committed to building bonds and institutions for making 'all lives livable and equally so'.[53] They necessitate 'an obligation to live with those who already exist' in all their heterogeneity.[54] This does not mean doing away with foundations or universal claims to a 'we', nor does it mean a refusal to oppose the aggression and hostility of those who occupy or colonise lands, but rather it means recognising that 'we remain obliged to struggle to affirm the ultimate value of that unchosen social world' and to 'find political and economic forms that minimize precarity and establish economic and political equality'.[55]

In the Tribunal's sessions, for example, participants emphasised the need for rights arising from the fact of residence or the fact of mobility as a way of countering the stark policing of the legally constructed categories of 'migrant' and 'citizen'. These rights exceed those rights offered within the framework of international law and thus assert new political demands and claims to justice and inclusion, based on migrants' current activities and physical presence within Europe. Such an articulation of rights resonates with Étienne Balibar's call to move towards grounding 'communities of fate' founded on principles of equality and liberty derived through practices of translation and negotiation, rather than 'communities of destiny' founded on principles of bounded and unified sovereign communities, constituted through practices of inclusion-exclusion.[56] This thus offers us a mode of sociability around contingency, solidarity, cohabitation and openness, rather than a bounded, determined or fixed community. The Tribunal's 'we' then can be seen as grounding a collective that is 'constantly in the making',[57] a *demos* whose foundations and boundaries are always open to contestation and reorganisation.

[52] Nicholas De Genova's address to Tribunal 12 (Session 4: Detention and Deportation).

[53] Judith Butler, 'Precarious life, vulnerability and an ethics of cohabitation' (2012)26 *Journal of Speculative Philosophy* 134, 145.

[54] Ibid., 146. [55] Ibid., 150. [56] Balibar, above n. 19, 131–32.

[57] Butler, above n. 52, 150.

7.3.4 Bearing Witness?

A fourth element of the Tribunal's constitution was how it incorporated the testimony of migrants themselves as those affected by European border practices. Tribunal 12 adopted a 'dramaturgical' framework in order to put forward a structural narrative of the European border regime, rather than providing a forum for people to give testimony in person. This was in stark contrast to earlier peoples' tribunals and demonstrates the varying objectives of peoples' tribunals. This artistic approach was taken partly because of practical difficulties around the Tribunal's location but it was also a broader political statement about the power of states to marginalise people subjected to certain forms of state violence, whether through being held in immigration detention, living with precarious legal status or having been deported from a particular territory.

A key reason for adopting an aesthetic mode for presenting migrant testimony was because some of those people affected by the European border regime would have had difficulties acting as witnesses in Sweden and may have faced serious consequences as a result of their testimony. Many migrants were unable to be present at the Tribunal, particularly if they remained in detention centres or had already been deported from Europe. For undocumented migrants within Sweden, the act of giving testimony would have required them to publicly reveal their status, an act that may have subjected them to a heightened risk of deportation.

Because of the difficulties surrounding the transnational criminalisation of unauthorised migration, Tribunal 12 organisers felt that any migrant testimony presented to the Tribunal would have been unduly restricted through the very state and transnational practices that the Tribunal was putting on trial. That is, it may have been only migrants with a particular legal status, or at a particular stage in the asylum process, who would have been willing and able to provide testimony. In this way, European impositions of sovereignty and border practices might have disproportionately shaped the very voices being heard at the Tribunal as well as dictated those that were excluded. As one tribunal organiser stated, the desire for inclusivity meant that the organisers looked for another medium for including migrant voices:

> [W]e wanted to have testimonies from all over Europe and not only from Sweden. And then we would have had problems because many people can't travel freely. I don't know if that's obvious in the Tribunal. In many

> ways it's also a statement that these people can't be on stage because they're threatened and they are trying to get away from authorities and so on.[58]

Instead, the Tribunal opted to collate testimony prior to the event, speaking to migrants and recording their stories at a less public time and place across a number of European countries. Migrants could also offer their stories through migrant advocacy and activist networks. This meant that the Tribunal was able to capture and present a range of testimony that might otherwise have been excluded. The range of testimony focused both on the emotional effects of European border practices and how migrants put forward their claims and survived and created lives under difficult circumstances. However, this medium meant that testimony was presented in a neat and predetermined form. The audience did not have to negotiate the intimate relations of listeners to difficult stories and the ethical demands that such relations entail. A central question for the organisers was, to what degree would the reading of testimony be seen as a gesture of erasure or perpetuating a symbolic violence of speaking on behalf of migrant?

Ultimately, this question was mediated through another ethical question for the Tribunal: namely, the power and pitfalls of (in)visibility for many unauthorised migrants in Europe. Given that many of the harms on trial were ongoing, adopting an artistic mode for presenting testimony meant that migrants, in particular those without legal authorisation to be in Sweden, would not face any consequences as a result of testifying to the Tribunal. Unlike other migrant activist campaigns that generate their strength from a collective and ongoing public solidarity and create more permanent support networks for dealing with state arrests or deportation attempts,[59] the Tribunal felt that it was unable to provide such support to coincide with the Tribunal event. It could also not guarantee the absence of state presence at the Tribunal, thus mitigating any attempts to create a safe space within which people could testify.[60]

[58] Interview with Tribunal 12 organiser (on file with author).

[59] See, e.g., the recent public campaigns of undocumented people in the United States, including the 'No Borders, No Fear' UndocuBus speaking tour, as well as migrant public sit-ins outside of official institutions.

[60] The use of actors made Tribunal 12 different from two earlier peoples' tribunals dealing with aspects of migration. For example, the focus of the International Migrants Tribunal (Manila, December 2012) was on the harms arising from official labour migration to the global North, and the main charge against countries of the global North was that of human 'slavery'. Here, the tribunal heard testimony from returned migrants, who were

Another reading of the use of the aesthetic form for conveying migrant testimony could be to frame the Tribunal's conduct as a refusal to engage the particular representational mode deployed within state practice. In the area of migration law, law demands that migrants tell their story in a particular way that meets imposed understandings of credibility and plausibleness. As Jennifer Beard and Gregor Noll write, there is a 'deeper sovereign relationship' between authority, truth and law.[61] In addition to defining criteria to be met to satisfy refugee status, international law 'demands that an applicant for refugee status carry the truth or credibility of that status within her as a subject of legal interpretation'.[62] In reading the testimonies, the experiences of migrants were presented as 'fact', rather than as a narrative that needed to be evaluated by or should evoke sympathy from a community of listeners.[63] Responsibility was placed less on the migrants to tell their stories in a mode amenable to legal adjudication, but rather projected onto the community of listeners to listen and act in solidarity with these struggles. Such acts of listening alone cannot undo the structural inequalities arising from, as Arendt writes, a 'world organised into nation-states'. Nevertheless, they can create a heightened sense of awareness of how the institution of citizenship is implicated in the construction of particular political communities, the forms of exclusions it entails and how citizens must act alongside migrants to undo certain systemic harms.

citizens of the Philippines, or migrant activists (from Mexico, Indonesia and Italy, among other places) who had the ability to access legal visas for travelling to the Philippines for the tribunal hearing. No testimony was heard from unauthorised migrants or undocumented people, https://web.archive.org/web/20140414115537/www.apmigrants.org/home/item/83-final-verdict-of-the-international-migrants-tribunal. Similarly, the Permanent Peoples' Tribunal, *Session on the Right of Asylum in Europe* (Berlin, 8–12 December 1994) heard testimony from various witnesses (including nationals from Columbia, Peru and Iran). Interestingly, one of these testimonies was given by a representative instead of in person. A third example is that of the Independent Asylum Commission in the United Kingdom, which produced three reports in 2008 and conducted numerous public hearings and semi-public 'focus groups' across the United Kingdom as a way of gathering testimony as well as invited written and video submissions from asylum seekers. The Commission also encouraged the use of pseudonyms to protect migrant identities, http://independentasylumcommission.org.uk.

61 Jennifer Beard and Gregor Noll, 'Parrhesia and credibility: The sovereign of refugee status determination' (2009) 18 *Social & Legal Studies* 455, 459.

62 Ibid., 460. See also Anthea Vogl, 'Telling stories from start to finish: Exploring the demand for narrative in refugee testimony' (2013) 22 *Griffith Law Review* 63.

63 On law's demand for a particular coherent and plausible narrative in refugee determination cases, see Trish Luker, 'Decision making conditioned by radical uncertainty: Credibility assessment at the Australian Refugee Review Tribunal' (2013) 25 *International Journal of Refugee Law* 502.

7.4 International Civil Society and a Popular International Law

Struggles for migrant justice take many forms, encompassing a diversity of tactics and articulations. Caroline Moulin and Peter Nyers have expressed their dissatisfaction with the idea of a 'global civil society' for its inability to capture the diversity of approaches as well as political subjects that act in internationalised spaces. For Moulin and Nyers, the normative assumption underpinning the concept of a 'global civil society' is that of being comprised of 'groups of citizens' who are linked to established and respected entities such as international NGOs and who celebrate liberal values of 'rational dialogue, consensus, persuasion, individual autonomy, personal responsibility, mutual obligation, and tolerance'.[64] Arguing that such a framework fails to account for the political practices and subjectivities of migrants themselves, Moulin and Nyers extend Partha Chatterjee's influential theorising of 'political society' to the international domain 'as a way of thinking about global political life from the perspective of those who are usually denied the status of political beings'.[65] Chatterjee, writing in the context of democratic politics in postcolonial India, offers a conceptual framework for distinguishing between 'civil society' and 'political society', where the former is 'restricted to a small section of culturally equipped citizens', while the latter makes up the 'majority of the world'.[66]

For Chatterjee, civil society has the language, resources and sense of entitlement to make their voices heard and express their claims to the state as 'rights-bearing citizens'; members of political society, rather, negotiate their relationships with authority through their very presence and the fact that they are governed in particular ways.[67] This means that civil society initiatives tend to affirm the language of the 'nation-state founded on popular sovereignty and granting equal rights to citizens', while political society acts involve mobilising a practical politics around the governmental administration of welfare and services to specific populations.[68] In taking up and extending Chatterjee's concepts to internationalised spaces, Moulin and Nyers do not seek to use these concepts as a 'blueprint' for

[64] Carolina Moulin and Peter Nyers, '"We live in a country of the UNHCR": Refugee protests and global political society' (2007) 1 *International Political Sociology* 356.

[65] Ibid., 358.

[66] Partha Chatterjee, *Politics of the Governed* (Cambridge University Press, 2004) 41.

[67] Ibid., 40. Chatterjee notes that those who make up his 'political society' often need to 'transgress the strict lines of legality in struggling to live and work'.

[68] Ibid., 37.

classifying different acts, but rather as a way of transforming our understanding of the political so as to attend to the multiple transformative acts, demands and effects of what they call 'international political society'.[69]

This schema is useful also in understanding the political claims and possible transformative effects of peoples' tribunals and the social movements within which they are located. Although Tribunal 12's politics of 'respectability' is best understood within a concept of 'international civil society', what is interesting about the initiative is that it attempted to take seriously the need to move beyond an appeal to legal or political citizenship as the basis for articulating its politics of solidarity. The Tribunal illuminated how recourse to the language of formal citizenship or appeals to reform established institutions will be largely inadequate, as the regime of citizenship does not necessarily institute a relationship between those doing the acts of governing and those being governed nor does it guarantee any substantive rights to the governed.

Jury member Saskia Sassen, in her personal verdict, stressed the need to move beyond a migrant/citizen binary, suggesting that the internationalisation of the citizenship regime may be at the heart of the problem generating the uneven relations between the governors and the governed.[70] This aligns with the work of Craig Borowiak, who argues that the material fact of 'being governed' should constitute a moral claim of inclusion within the demos in order to hold the institutions and people to account that govern them. For Borowiak, the 'governed should have opportunities to sanction and demand answers from the powers that govern them'.[71]

7.5 Conclusion

Tribunal 12, through its staging and verdict, suggests a form of law that demands a more just order based on actual presence in political spaces rather than formal legal entitlements. It is a 'popular' form of international law that claims the authority to speak in the name of the 'people', constituting a jurisdiction beyond the international institutional architecture structured around states. Such a 'popular' law uses existing legal principles in order to mobilise such norms rather than how they are intended or usually applied within dominant institutional arrangements. My point in naming the Tribunal and other peoples' tribunals

[69] Moulin and Nyers, above n. 63, 358.

[70] Saskia Sassen's remarks at Tribunal 12 (Session 5: Verdict).

[71] Craig Borowiak, *Accountability and Democracy: The Pitfalls and Promise of Popular Control* (Oxford University Press, 2011) 9.

as a 'popular' form of international law is not to deny or redeem international law from its coercive, technical and institutional registers, or to negate the fact that any claim to act in the name of the 'international' will always be interjected into 'an extant order within which sovereignty is operative' – that is, 'entering into a meeting place where the conditions of sociality are severely constrained'.[72] Rather, perhaps it will allow us to think through the mechanisms and technologies that regulate entry into the international as well as international law's contested orientations, and thus its political possibilities.[73]

Methodologically, this means taking seriously the possibility of thinking ethically about the narratives that we tell of international law.[74] It entails a political commitment to think about the 'critical instability' or 'restlessness' at the heart of international law alongside its normative force[75] in order to attend to the spaces – however fleeting, contradictory and insurrectional – that could shape our understanding of the international domain differently.

While there is certainly nothing inherently progressive or democratic about insurrectional politics, there is something critical about denaturalising boundaries of predefined publics in order to make them, in Craig Borowiak's words, the 'perennial objects of democratic accounting'.[76] This insistent accounting aims to render fragile existing institutional structures 'susceptible to reconfiguration'.[77] While this does not necessarily entail the dissolution of citizenship or ideas of the demos per se, it

[72] Sundhya Pahuja and Shaun McVeigh, 'Rival Jurisdictions: The Promise and Loss of Sovereignty' in Charles Barbour and George Pavlich (eds.), *After Sovereignty: On the Question of Political Beginnings* (Routledge, 2010) 105.

[73] This idea of a 'popular international law' can be contrasted with accounts asserting the 'democratisation of international law' through the inclusion of civil society in international law-making processes. In such narratives, civil society designates a relatively knowable and fixed field of actors that is included within established institutional processes as legal and political citizens. They may shape, interpret or inform the content of international law and the spaces for contestation, but not necessarily have a claim to belonging to or being constitutive of international law per se.

[74] Feminist international lawyers, for example, have long articulated this need. For instance, Anne Orford writes that 'reading and writing about international law involves the reproduction of power relations' such that subverting dominant narratives could 'contribute to the communal project of making it possible to imagine and create other ways of being': Anne Orford, 'Positivism and the power of international law' (2000) 24 *Melbourne Journal of International Law* 502, 528.

[75] Sundhya Pahuja, *Decolonising International Law: Development, Economic Growth and the Politics of Universality* (Cambridge University Press, 2011) 37.

[76] Borowiak, above n. 70, 162.

[77] Ibid., 166. Borowiak rightly notes that 'there is nothing inherently democratic or just about the category of insurgency'.

radically abandons the idea of the demos as a finite, bounded community whose 'authority is final'.[78] For Borowiak, this means recognising that 'citizens alone would [not] have the authority to decide who else should be included and how accountability relations should be comprised.'[79] Instead, the very structures of the international legal order need to be located within the 'field of contestation and answerability'.[80]

Certain elements of the Tribunal project are evidently open to critique. We can question who has access to the sites, language and funding of the initiative. We can problematise its mimicking of the legal institution's split between expert evidence and witness testimony (whereby the Tribunal's structure primarily names the contribution of Western individuals as 'expertise' with the contribution of non-Western migrants relegated to the register of 'experience'). We can question the Tribunal's mode of including migrant voices. Is this an act of speaking for? Is this a denial or capture of individual and grounded experiences in order to make them paradigmatic of a particular 'other'? Does it replicate the reification of state discourses of migrant 'flows'?

While these are all important avenues for critique, in this chapter, I suspend this critical register to hold on to, where possible, the politics of the Tribunal's enunciations and its claim to speak in the name of a cosmopolitan 'we' in its address to 'Europe'. This act offers us a form of 'popular' international law that decentres the nation-state as the dominant vehicle for a jurisdictional claim in the international domain.[81] This permits us to envision 'the international domain' as a site of contestation, whereby its subjects, content and limits are never fully determined, but rather figured out through many processes of constituting the international legal order. In its claim to speak the law, Tribunal 12 highlighted and adjudicated both specific violations of international norms and harms arising from the very structures and constitution of the international domain itself. Like other peoples' tribunals that came before it, this act can be read as a demand for social change that uses the existing norms offered by international law while also serving to imagine and enact the international otherwise.

[78] Ibid., 17. [79] Ibid., 16. [80] Ibid., 17.

[81] Etymologically, the word 'popular', derived from *popularis*, denotes a sense of something 'belonging to the people': a sense of it being the proper domain, possession and quality of the people.

8

The Permanent Peoples' Tribunals and Indigenous Peoples' Struggles in Mexico

Between Coloniality and Epistemic Justice?*

ROSALBA ICAZA

8.1 Introduction

The poet and activist Javier Sicilia has described Mexico as a cemetery full of clandestine graves. According to the National Registry for Missing or Disappeared People (Registro Nacional de Datos de Personas Extraviadas o Desaparecidas, RNPED), there were 27,659 cases of missing or disappeared people between 2007 and 2015. Few of these cases make national or international headlines like the forty-three students from Ayotzinapa in the Mexican state of Guerrero did on 26 September 2014. These young students of the Raúl Isidro Burgos Rural School, some of them minors and indigenous, were kidnapped and, according to the Mexican Attorney General's office, killed and their bodies burned by members of the drug cartel Guerreros Unidos. However, the final report of the Interdisciplinary Group of Experts (Grupo Interdisciplinario de Expertos Independientes, GIEI) of the Inter-American Commission on Human Rights of the Organization of American States stated that the Ayotzinapa case was just one example of forced disappearance committed by local authorities in complicity with drug-trafficking gangs in the country.[1]

* An earlier version of this chapter was published as 'The Permanent Peoples' Tribunals and indigenous people's struggles in Mexico: Between coloniality and epistemic justice' (2015) 1 *Palgrave Communications*, www.palgrave-journals.com/articles/palcomms201520, and appears here in a revised version with permission. I would like to thank Ramón Vera Herrera for his critical observations on the political and ethical relevance of my text given the context of impunity and repression in which the PPT worked in Mexico. I am also grateful to Rolando Vázquez for his extensive comments on the revised version of this chapter and to the editors and the anonymous reviewers for their comments on the earlier version.

[1] The GIEI was created as an independent body to conduct investigations on the Ayotzinapa case. For a complete overview of the GIEI mandate and findings, see http://prensagiei ayotzi.wixsite.com/giei-ayotzinapa.

These forty-three students join the horrifying list of disappearances that include thousands of women and girls abducted, raped and killed every year, the so-called femicides.[2] In such a tragic context, the Final Hearing of the Mexican Chapter of the Permanent Peoples' Tribunal (PPT) held in November 2014 feels so distant, yet the conditions of impunity and violence continue. In such an upsetting context, I have been asked, who benefits from an investigation of the epistemic violence of international human rights law? Answering this question is the difficult task that this chapter aims to undertake.

As such, this chapter is a first attempt to systematise what has been a personal learning process, but one that arises from and in relation with PPT participants on the potential contribution of the tribunals to epistemic justice in Mexico. This approach to learning *with*, instead of *about*, activists and social movements has been termed 'collaborative research', 'committed research' or 'activist research'.[3]

I write this text as a *dialogical process* in the way Mexican anthropologist Xochitl Leyva speaks about such work as a kind of praxis of research as co-labour (collaborative research) in which the written text is a dialogue with the spoken and written word, with visuality, with past and present experiences and with the imagined horizon of autonomy.[4] As a critical supporter and promoter of PPTs in Mexico, but one based in the Global North, I use a question mark in the title to indicate that the

[2] For a recent overview on complex phenomena of femicides in the Americas, see Rosalinda Fregroso and Cynthia Bejarano (eds.), *Terrorizing Women: Feminicide in the Americas* (Duke University Press, 2010).

[3] Xochitl Leyva and Shannon Speed, 'Hacia la investigación descolonizada: nuestra experiencia de co-labor' ['Towards a Decolonised Research: Our Experience of Collaborative Research'] in Xochitl Leyva, Araceli Burguete and Shannon Speed (eds.), *Gobernar (en) la diversidad: experiencias indígenas desde América Latina: Hacia la investigación de co-labor* [*Governing (in) Diversity: Indigenous Experiences from Latin America: Towards a Collaborative Research*] (CIESAS, FLACSO Ecuador y FLACSO Guatemala, 2008) 34; Larissa Barbosa da Costa, Rosalba Icaza and Angélica María Ocampo Talero, 'Knowledge about, Knowledge with: Dilemmas of Researching Lives, Nature and Genders Otherwise' in Wendy Harcourt and Ingrid Nelson (eds.), *Practising Feminist Political Ecologies: Moving Beyond the 'Green Economy'* (Zed Books, 2015) 260; Rosalba Icaza, 'Testimony of a Pilgrimage: (Un)learning and Relearning with the South' in Zuleika Arashiro and Malba Barahona (eds.), *Women in Academia Crossing North/South Borders: Gender, Race and Displacement* (Rowman and Littlefield/Lexington Books, 2015) 1.

[4] Xochitl Leyva Solano, 'Y/osotras ¿Mi/nuestras Luchas Epistémicas Creativas?' ['I/us. My/our creative epistemic struggles?'] in Seminario Virtual Internacional (SVI) *Creación de Prácticas de Conocimiento desde el Género, los Movimientos y las Redes de la RETOS* ['International Virtual Seminar (SVI) Creating Knowledge Practices from Movements, Networks and Gender Concerns in RETOS'], www.encuentroredtoschiapas.jkopkutik.org.

PPT tension between coloniality and epistemic justice contributions is not at all a closed question but a troubled position that is explored from a privileged position in Global North academia with all the limitations that this entails.[5]

This chapter is organised in six sections. The first section introduces a timeline of the PPT's organisation in Mexico. The second briefly contextualises the struggles of indigenous peoples and communities for legal pluralism and autonomy in Mexico, while the third and fourth sections introduce key concepts informing this chapter's analysis. The fifth section presents a glimpse into the epistemic principles driving the methodological decisions taken in the research that inform the ideas advanced in the PPT in Mexico. The final section offers an analysis of the legal conceptualisations underpinning the Mexican Chapter of the PPT and concludes with some reflections on this chapter's argument and epistemic position.

8.2 Permanent Peoples' Tribunals in Mexico

On 21 October 2011 hundreds of Mexican civil society organisations formally submitted a petition to the Lelio e Lisli Basso Foundation in Rome requesting the holding of a Mexican Chapter of the PPT. The General Hearing of the PPT took place from 27 to 29 May 2012 in Ciudad Juárez, in the northern state of Chihuaha under the name 'Dispossession and Predation of Mexico: Free Trade and Power Deviation as Causes of Structural Violence, Impunity and Dirty War against the People of Mexico'.[6]

The PPT Mexican Chapter was organised around seven thematic hearings, including *Femicide and Gender Violence*; *Migration, Refugee and Forced Displacement*; *Environmental Devastation and Peoples' Rights*; *Violence against Workers*; *Misinformation, Censorship and Violence against Communicators*; *Dirty War as Violence, Impunity and Lack of*

[5] Icaza, above n. 3.

[6] All the documents studied for this chapter were produced by the organisers of the PPT in Mexico and were publicly accessible on the TPP Mexico's chapter site (www.tppmexico.org), which unfortunately has been disabled. Final versions of some of the TPP Mexico hearing documents can be found on the PPT website, http://permanentpeoplestribunal.org/38-1-libre-comercio-violecia-impunidad-y-derechos-de-los-pueblos-en-mexico-2011-2012/; others may be found on the Internet Archive, which has saved pages from the tppmexico.org site on a number of occasions: see, e.g., https://web-beta.archive.org/web/20141222074637/http://www.tppmexico.org/ (version of 22 December 2014). Documents which are not available on these sites are on file with the author.

Access of to Justice; and *Violence against Corn, Food Sovereignty and Autonomy*. The final session of the PPT took place in November 2014, three years after the initial request for a hearing was made.

The PPT was established in 1979 as the successor to the Russell Tribunals on Vietnam (1966–67) and on the Latin American Dictatorships (1974–76). The PPT was created out of the realisation that 'law and justice in many circumstances cannot be entrusted to the State and their institutions.'[7] The PPT's sessions sought to react to the suffering of people 'produced by State and government oppression, but also by private enterprises, banks and international financial institutions'.[8]

The PPT as an ethical non-governmental tribunal 'examines the causes behind the violation of fundamental rights of peoples and determines if these rights have or not been violated'.[9] The PPT sessions are also described as a mechanism for raising awareness of national and international public opinion on rights violations. 'The mission of the Tribunals is *to promote universal and effective respect of fundamental rights of peoples, minorities and individuals; and work for the generation of law that protect those rights*'.[10] In so doing, the tribunals qualify (or characterise) *situations* in legal terms, thereby contributing to the identification of duty and rights holders in relation to situations when these are not apparent, as in the case of human rights violations committed by local authorities to protect the interests of transnational corporations.[11]

By attributing responsibility to particular actors with faces or brand names, these mechanisms of popular litigation have contributed to the questioning of what feminist political economist Suzanne Bergeron theorises as the dominant script of neo-liberal globalisation that is represented as an abstract dominant and unified force/system.[12] The possibility of attributing responsibility has been a central aim of the PPT in Mexico given the context of impunity and violence as the following quote from the *Final Ruling* shows.

[7] TPP Capítulo México [PPT Mexican Chapter], 'Que es el Tribunal Permanente de los Pueblos?' ['What is the Permanent Peoples' Tribunal?'], unpublished, 26 April 2011 (on file with author). See generally Tognoni, Chapter 2 in this volume, and by Fraudatario and Tognoni, Chapter 6 in this volume.

[8] 'Que es el Tribunal Permanente de los Pueblos?', above n. 7.

[9] Ibid.

[10] Ibid. (emphasis added)

[11] Rosalba Icaza, 'Global Europe, guilty! Contesting EU Neo-liberal Governance for Latin America' (2010) 3(12) *Third World Quarterly* 123.

[12] Suzanne Bergeron, *Fragments of Development: Nation, Gender and the Space of Modernity* (University of Michigan Press, 2006) 156–57. See also Icaza, above n. 11.

> In this realm of impunity that is today's Mexico, there are murders with no murderers, torture with no torturers, sexual violence with no abusers, in a constant abdication of responsibility, in which it would seem that the thousands and thousands of massacres, murders and systematic violations of the rights of peoples are always isolated acts or marginal situations rather than true crimes for which the State bears responsibility.[13]

Following the work of feminist decolonial philosopher and popular educator Maria Lugones,[14] I have argued elsewhere that the mere act of questioning dominant discourses and scripts on globalisation is one of the ways in which the PPT contributes to global cognitive or epistemic justice.[15] In short, cognitive or epistemic justice is mainly understood here as necessary to achieve global social justice.[16] To achieve it, one has to deal with the erasure of knowledges and ways of being in the world, including notions and practices of justice outside the nation-state's legality, that have been produced as 'backward', 'traditional', 'other', or 'particular' in relation to a supposedly 'universal' knowledge.[17] More precisely, this paper seeks to explore ways in which the PPT in Mexico is imbricated with Eurocentric modes of legal production but that nonetheless contributes, in a relevant but fragile way, to epistemic justice.

8.3 Indigenous Struggles for Legal Pluralism and Autonomy in Mexico

Contemporary indigenous peoples' struggles in Mexico carry with them a long tradition of resistance against domination and extermination dating back to colonial times. For some, this tradition has influenced and been

[13] TPP Capítulo México [PPT Mexican Chapter], *Final Ruling* [English version], 15 November 2014, http://permanentpeoplestribunal.org/wp-content/uploads/2012/07/SENTENCIA FINAL_MEXICOingles.doc.pdf.

[14] Maria Lugones, 'Structure/Antistructure and agency under oppressions' (1990) 87(10) *Journal of Philosophy* 500–7, and Maria Lugones, *Pilgrimages/Peregrinajes: Theorizing Coalitions Against Multiple Oppressions* (Rowman and Littlefield, 2003).

[15] Icaza, above n. 11.

[16] Boaventura de Sousa Santos, João Arriscado Nunes and Maria Paula Meneses, 'Introduction: Opening up the Canon of Knowledge and Recognition of Difference' in Boaventura de Sousa Santos (ed.), *Another Knowledge Is Possible: Beyond Northern Epistemologies* (Verso, 2007) xix–xxii.

[17] Rosalva Aída Hernández, Rachel Sieder and María Teresa Sierra, 'Introducción' ['Introduction'] in Rosalva Aída Hernández, Rachel Sieder and María Teresa Sierra (eds.), *Justicias indigenas y Estado: violencias contemporaneas* [*Indigenous Justices and the State: Contemporary Violences*] (FLACSO/CIESAS, 2013) 11; Boaventura de Sousa Santos, *The Rise of the Global Left: The World Social Forum and Beyond* (Zed Books, 2006).

influenced by local, national and international long-term shifts of the monocultural state towards a pluricultural (the Mexican case) or a plurinational one (the Bolivian and Ecuadorian case).[18]

In this shifting context, the struggle for legal pluralism and autonomy is a more recent one. In Mexico, as in other countries, the demand of indigenous people for state recognition of their existence and of their right to autonomy coincides with the crisis of the nineteenth-century model of the state as a single nation with a culturally homogeneous population.[19] This crisis marks in some cases a formal end of assimilationist policies towards indigenous populations but not necessarily of welfare policies.

According to López Bárcenas, in the case of Mexico the timeline of indigenous communities' struggle for legal pluralism and autonomy started with demands for state recognition of indigenous people as subjects of rights, to the realisation of human rights as individual rights, followed by demands for the promulgation of minority rights law to more recent demands for collective rights and autonomy.[20] Interestingly, these later demands implied that indigenous peoples in Mexico were recognised as subject of rights, and not mere objects of public welfare, amidst a worldwide (neo) liberalisation trend.[21]

Mexico ratified International of Labour Organization (ILO) Convention No 169[22] in 1990 and two years later, marking the 500th anniversary of the 'Discovery of the Americas', the Federal Constitution of Mexico[23] recognised the existence of indigenous people and the pluricultural nature of the nation. This reformist moment, in all Latin America, will be characterised as a 'new multicultural constitutionalism', one that was compatible with the ongoing neoliberal reforms' emphasis on individual (and/or civil society) responsibility and a smaller state.[24]

Accordingly, this new set of 'legal recognitions' did not include recognition of the collective rights of indigenous persons as belonging to a

[18] Hernández et al., ibid., and Catherine Walsh, 'Development as *Buen Vivir*: Institutional arrangements and (de)colonial entanglements' (2010) 53(1) *Development* 15.

[19] Francisco López Bárcenas, *Autonomía y derechos indígenas en México* [*'Autonomy and Indigenous Rights in Mexico*] (CEIICH-UNAM/ Ediciones Coyoacán, 2005), 9.

[20] Ibid., 7. [21] Ibid.

[22] International Labour Organization Convention (No. 169) concerning Indigenous and Tribal Peoples in Independent Countries, Geneva, 27 June 1989, 1650 UNTS 383, in force 5 September 1991.

[23] Constitution of the United Mexican States, article 2.

[24] Hernández et al., above n. 17; Donna Lee Van Cott, *The Friendly Liquidation of the Past: the Politics of Diversity in Latin America* (University of Pittsburgh Press, 2000) 17.

specific *pueblo* (people). The current status of recognition represents a characterisation of indigenous individuals as members of minorities who need to be integrated into the larger Mexican society.[25]

This is different from the position adopted in other countries in Latin America such as Ecuador and Bolivia, where recent constitutional reforms have meant the recognition of indigenous peoples as subjects of rights and, consequent on this, have granted recognition to the existence in these countries of diverse normative systems. Furthermore, the constitutions of these countries recognise the possibility of exercising rights as individuals or as collectives/communities together with their indigenous systems of justice.[26]

One relevant element that could help us understand the contrasting reformist outcomes of Mexico and Bolivia/Ecuador is the Zapatista uprising.[27] The Mexican state multicultural reformist trend of the 1990s was marked not only by its coherence with ongoing neoliberal trends but also by the war against the indigenous-based Ejercito Zapatista de Liberación Nacional (EZLN, Zapatista National Liberation Army) that declared war against the Mexican state and neoliberalism on 1 January 1994.[28]

National and transnational demonstrations prompted a ceasefire after just ten days of war, and peace negotiations between the EZLN and the Mexican state started. In the forefront of these negotiations was the question of state recognition of collective rights of indigenous peoples and of their autonomy. By 1996, the San Andrés Agreements for Peace had been signed by the Mexican state representatives and the EZLN;[29] these accords included the recognition of the right of indigenous peoples to apply their own judicial systems.[30] However, these agreements were eventually rejected in 2001 by the executive and amended by the legislature, to the extent that the right to self-determination was recognised as already being enjoyed and expressed in the mere existence of the indigenous communities.[31]

[25] López Bárcenas, above n. 19. [26] Walsh, above n. 18.

[27] López Bárcenas, above n. 19.

[28] Bruno Baronnet, Mariana Mora Bayo and Richard Stahler-Sholk (eds.), *Luchas 'muy otras'. Zapatismo y autonomia en las comunidades indigenas de Chiapas* [*Otherwise' Struggles: Zapatism and Autonomy in Chiapas Indigenous Communities*] (Universidad Autonoma Metropolitana, CIESAS, Universidad Autonoma de Chiapas, 2011); Hernández et al., above n. 17.

[29] Acuerdos de San Andrés, 16 February 1996, http://zedillo.presidencia.gob.mx/pages/chiapas/docs/sanandres/acuerdo.html.

[30] Baronnet et al., above n. 28. [31] López Bárcenas, above n. 19, 81.

Due to the state's rejection of the previously agreed San Andres Agreements of 1996, the EZLN embarked on the creation of de facto autonomous territories with their own judicial, political, economic, education and health systems.[32] Up to the early 2000s, the Mexican state not only did not recognise the autonomy of Zapatista territories (named *Caracoles*) but also, for journalist Francisco Pineda and feminist anthropologist Mercedes Oliver, maintained a 'low intensity war' despite the official ceasefire of 1994.[33]

Recent assessments of the experiences of normative, political and security autonomy of the Zapatistas and other indigenous and peasant communities in Mexico note that these emerged as intricately related to two main trends. On one hand, the state's formal recognition mechanisms and technologies have become novel forms of control and surveillance. On the other hand, the state's war on drugs and drive to protect the interests of transnational capital in 'resource' rich territories have come with increasing violence against indigenous communities.[34]

8.4 PPTs and the Coloniality of International Law

In Anglo-Saxon academia, the essay by Gayatri Spivak, 'Can the Subaltern speak?', has been a central reference point for understanding the power of discourse in the subalternisation of difference and more specifically on the role of intellectuals in representing the 'subaltern'.[35] Spivak's ideas constitute a crucial reference point in post-colonial analyses of contemporary forms of epistemic violence.

[32] Ibid.

[33] Francisco Pineda, 'La guerra de baja intensidad' ['The Low Intensity War'] in Andrés Barreda and Ana Esther Ceceña, *Chiapas 2* (Ediciones Era, 1996), 173–95; 'Cara de Guerra: Un Ejercito Federal Mexicano, unos indigenas, un territorio' ['The face of war: One Mexican Federal Army, some indigenous people, one territory'] *CAPISE*, 17 December 2014, http://web.archive.org/web/20160614195843/http://www.capise.org.mx:80/cara-de-guerra-un-ejecito-federal-mexicano-unos-pueblos-indigenas-un-territorio/; Mercedes Olivera Bustamante, 'Acteal: Los efectos de la Guerra de baja intensidad' ['Acteal: The Effects of Low Intensity Warfare'] in Rosalva Aída Hernández Castillo (ed.), *La otra palabra: mujeres y violencia en Chiapas, antes y después de Acteal* [*The Other Word: Women and Violence in Chiapas, before and after Acteal*] (Centro de Investigación y Estudios Superiores en Antropología Social/IWGIA Grupo Internacional de Trabajo sobre Asuntos Indígenas, 2nd edn. 2007) 114.

[34] Hernández et al., above n. 17, 16.

[35] Gayatri Chakravorty Spivak, 'Can the Subaltern Speak?' in Cary Nelson and Lawrence Grossberg (eds.), *Marxism and the Interpretation of Culture* (Macmillan, 1988), 271.

My engagement in this chapter with the contributions of peoples' tribunals to epistemic justice connects with two traditions of critique that belong to a different geo-genealogy[36] to that of post-colonial studies: decolonial thinking[37] and the epistemologies of the South.[38]

In this sense, I am writing from an epistemic location that questions the 'modern' version of 'history' that places the British Empire (or sometimes the French Empire) at the centre of modern/colonial history and that goes back more than five centuries to 1492 when Abya Yala (the Americas) was conquered and the genocide of millions of indigenous peoples and of their knowledges and ways of being in the world took place.[39] This epistemic location acknowledges that modernity has its 'underside', coloniality, and as such it is not just the fortunate product of the Renaissance or the Industrial Revolution.

Modernity/coloniality has been understood as a co-constitutive binomial and a structure of management that operates by controlling the economy and authority (government, politics); knowledge and subjectivities; and

[36] Vázquez explains the relevance for decolonial critique of geo-genealogies to stress the site of enunciation. In his view, a geo-genealogy is a genealogy that acknowledges its situated origin, indicating a relationship to a geographically situated origin: Rolando Vázquez Melken, 'Colonialidad y Relacionalidad' ['Coloniality and Relationality'] in Maria Eugenia Borsani and Pablo Quintero (eds.), *Los desafíos decoloniales de nuestros días: pensar en colectivo* [*The Decolonial Path of Our Times: Thinking Collectively*] (EDUCO/Universidad Nacional de Comahuep, 2014) 173, 178.

[37] Maria Lugones, 'The Coloniality of Gender' in Walter Mignolo and Arturo Escobar (eds.), *Globalization and the Decolonial Option* (Routledge, 2010) 367; Maria Lugones, 'Towards a decolonial feminism' (2010) 4 *Hypatia* 742; Walter D. Mignolo, *Historias locales/diseños globales: Colonialidad, conocimientos subalternos y pensamiento fronterizo* [*Local Histories, Global Lessons: Coloniality, Subaltern Knowledges and Frontier Thinking*] (Ediciones Akal, 2003); Walter Mignolo, 'Dewesternization, Rewesternization and Decoloniality: The Racial Distribution of Capital and Knowledge', public lecture, Centre for the Humanities, University of Utrecht, 13 May 2013; Anibal Quijano, 'Coloniality of power, ethnocentrism, and Latin America' (2000) 1(3) *Nepantla: Views from the South* 533; Vázquez, above n. 36; Rolando Vázquez, 'Translation as ERASURE: Thoughts on modernity's epistemic violence' (2011) 24 *Journal of Historical Sociology* 27; Rolando Vázquez, 'Modernity coloniality and visibility: The politics of time' (2009) 14(4) *Sociological Research Online* 7 www.socresonline.org.uk/14/4/7.html; Catherine Walsh, 'El pluralismo jurídico: el desafío de la interculturalidad' ['Legal pluralism: The challenge of interculturality'] (2012) 133 *Nueva América* 32; Catherine Walsh, 'Shifting the geopolitics of critical knowledge: Decolonial thought and cultural studies "others" in the Andes' (2007) 21 (2–3) *Cultural Studies* 224; and Walsh, above n. 18.

[38] Boaventura de Sousa Santos, *Una epistemología del Sur: La reinvención del conocimiento y la emancipación social* [*An Epistemology of the South: Re-Inventing Knowledge AND Social Emancipation*] (CLACSO y Siglo XXI, 2009); Santos et al., above n. 16.

[39] Mignolo (2003), above n. 37; Quijano, above n. 37.

gender and sexuality.[40] From this perspective the 'coloniality of power' explains that 'the basic and universal social classification of the population of the planet in terms of the idea of 'race' is introduced for the first time with the Conquest of the Americas.'[41] This analysis 'has displayed the heterogeneous and transversal character of the modern/colonial system',[42] counterpoising racial domination to the Eurocentric Marxist theory of class exploitation.

Nonetheless, when modernity/coloniality is understood not only as a co-constitutive binomial but also as two different movements or forms of relationship with reality, it is possible to highlight their different locus of enunciation: the historical movement of modernity as the moment when hegemony and privilege has named reality, for example, the name given to Abya Yala[43] as 'America' after the arrival of Christopher Columbus and the peoples inhabiting her as 'Indians' and more recently 'indigenous' or 'minorities'. Meanwhile, the historical movement of coloniality is understood as the locus from which the negation of realities and worlds otherwise that exceed the dominant modern geo-genealogy of modernity takes place, for example, when normative systems outside or in the margins of the nation-state are denied validity.[44]

From this perspective, modernity is 'the name and narrative that the western civilisation project with totalizing pretensions gives to herself and to the representation of the world' while coloniality is 'not a mere abstraction ... [but] the group of historically concrete practices and forms of exclusion exercised by the modern/colonial project'.[45] In this chapter, I seek to understand concrete practices of epistemic exclusion operating in the PPT Eurocentric modes of legal production as well as whether epistemic justice is possible given such exclusions.

Following these ideas, I understand epistemic justice as taking place when forms of being in and seeing the world, that have been rendered invisible or subalternised by modernity/coloniality, are brought into the public gaze. 'The struggles for epistemic justice seek to break down hierarchies and exclusions related to dominant forms of representing

[40] Mignolo (2003), above n. 37; Quijano, above n. 37. [41] Lugones, above n. 37, 371.
[42] Vázquez, above n. 37, 176.
[43] Abya Yala is the name of what now is called the 'Americas', given by the Kuna indigenous people; it has been used by indigenous peoples' contemporary mobilisations across South America.
[44] Vázquez, above n. 37, 176. [45] Ibid., 175–79.

the world and the imposition of certain historical values, knowledges and views of the world.'[46]

The sessions of the PPT are seen as mechanisms and processes with the potential for contributing to epistemic justice in as much as they break down hierarchies and exclusions related to the plurality of understandings about what is supposed to be justice.[47] An emphasis on the contributions of the PPT sessions to epistemic justice would mean then to pay attention to how they contribute to the visibility of the many ways in which justice is understood and experienced despite the many forms of violence of capitalism and/or state authority.

Following Santos' ideas, Vázquez has argued that the struggles for social justice are struggles for 'political visibility', a term that makes reference to 'bringing the claims for justice into the light of the public' and that 'signals the *close relation* that there is between the *material means of oppression and epistemic discrimination*'.[48] This is a clear attempt to connect oppressions and resistances transcending the explanations of causal relationships based on the all-encompassing power or logic of capitalism. As I observe later in this chapter, this 'intersectional' approach is absent from key PPT documents and statements that explain different forms of violence in Mexico. This absence has the effect of epistemic erasure as notions and practices of justice that do not fit in or exceed the all-encompassing logic of capitalism is silenced in the process of legal translation for the construction of a legal case of 'power deviation' (*desafío de poder*).[49]

8.5 A Decolonial Feminist Perspective on the Permanent Peoples' Tribunal

A feminist critique and expansion of Mignolo and Quijano's understandings of the coloniality of power explains it not only as the intersection of

46 Rosalba Icaza and Rolando Vázquez, 'Social struggles as epistemic struggles' (2013) 44(3) *Development and Change* 683.

47 Icaza, above n. 11.

48 Vázquez (2009), above n. 37 (emphasis added).

49 PPT Mexican Chapter, *Final Ruling*, above n. 13. Power deviation [*Desviación de poder*] is defined as an abnormal situation in a state in which popular representatives abuse their mandate and make use of laws and institutions for particular interests contrary to the public interest. In the case of Mexico, power deviation includes illegal acts and corruption, distortion and destruction of rights and institutions, the acknowledgement of privileges through ad hoc laws and norms and institutions to benefit powerful private interests, as well as to obstruct access to justice for Mexican people, 5–6.

oppressions and power that classifies people according to race but also to the European heterosexual standard.[50]

From this perspective, decolonial feminist theorisations of social resistance to coloniality's intersected oppressions has managed to pose important questions to a supposedly unitary and all-encompassing (capitalist and/or state) power system by bringing to the fore the fragmented characteristic of self-identities and consciousness.[51] Acts of resistance are seen as taking place against multiple sites of oppression and power through multiple identities, consciousness and the fleshy reality of a racialised and subalternised body. In other words, one can be a male Mixe indigenous person belonging to a community of radio communicators, who is actively struggling against local state repression that favours capitalist accumulation by the dispossession of communal lands and racism. At the same time, this activist can make use of some means of the local state's legal system that condemns public disobedience as an illegal act.

Accordingly, the theoretical move that I aim to introduce here stems from situated experiences of multiple intertwined forms of oppression (sexism, classism, racism, heteronormativity and so on) and implies the possibility of challenging modern/colonial totalizing narratives of a unitary system of oppression: capitalism, globalisation, heteronormative patriarchy and so on.[52]

Furthermore, this feminist perspective opens up the possibility of going beyond traditional political-economy paradigms, which conceive of capitalism as an all-encompassing global or world system.[53] From this perspective, social struggles against oppressions are primarily represented as reactions to the structures of (capitalist) oppression, and only secondarily as alternative political practices based on life experiences.[54]

8.6 Dialogues on the PPTs in Mexico: Is It Worthwhile?[55]

With the ideas set out above in mind, I have argued that the PPT's sessions contribute to epistemic justice through practices that allow for

50 Lugones, 'The Coloniality of Gender', above n. 37.

51 Lugones, above n. 14.

52 Lugones, 'Towards a Decolonial Feminism', above n. 37.

53 Ramón Grosfoguel, 'The epistemic decolonial turn: Beyond political-economy paradigms' (2007) 21(2–3) *Cultural Studies* 211.

54 Icaza and Vázquez, above n. 46.

55 This section is called 'Dialogues' to display the exchange of ideas with Mexican academics-activists involved in different forms and extents in the PPT. This is not an arbitrary selection of a name, but a concrete epistemic decision that seeks to avoid the

the political visibility of knowledges (and not only of testimonies of violence) that otherwise would have remained ignored or produced as non-existent.[56] This was specifically to be observed in relation to the Tribunal's sessions on European multinationals and neoliberalism and their hearings in Vienna (2006)[57] and Peru (2008)[58] in which a number of cases related to communities and peoples of indigenous nations and African descent received a great deal of attention in the Tribunal's proceedings, deliberations and rulings. An example of this was the reflections on Andean indigenous conceptions such as *el buen vivir* (the fullness of life) in the final report of that PPT.[59]

However, the contribution of the PPT to epistemic justice is not free from tensions. The tribunals classify social grievances in legal terms through the lens/gaze of international law. This legal qualification or characterisation works as an activity of 'translation', in some cases of incommensurable notions of justice or absence of justice, violence or well-being. This carries the risk of erasing and making invisible what does not fit or seems problematic to attach to a particular rule of international law.[60] This is what has been termed 'translation as epistemic erasure'.[61] In practical terms, this erasure might be subtle and not premeditated, but it has certainly taken the form of selection of 'model cases' due to their relevance in terms of their legal analysis.[62]

This idea – that the PPT's contribution to epistemic justice is not free from tensions such as the risk of legal qualification or characterisation as a form of epistemic erasure – are now the entry point into my analysis of the PPT in Mexico.[63] My exploration started back in 2010 with a brief

term 'fieldwork' but, more importantly, the practice of extracting knowledges of people in the Global South for the benefit of academics, like me, based in the Global North. This political/epistemic/ethical position of collaborative research is elaborated further in da Costa et al., above n. 3; and Icaza, above n. 3.

56 Icaza, above n. 11.

57 Permanent Peoples' Tribunal, *Hearing on Neo-liberal Policies and European Transnational Corporations in Latin America and the Caribbean: Indictment*, Vienna, 10–12 May 2006.

58 Permanent Peoples' Tribunal, *Session on Neo-liberal Policies and European Transnational Corporations in Latin America and the Caribbean: Ruling*, Lima, 13–16 May 2008.

59 Permanent Peoples' Tribunal, *The European Union and Transnational Corporations in Latin America: Policies, Instruments and Actors Complicit in Violations of the Peoples' Rights, Deliberating Session: Judgment*, Madrid, 14–7 May 2010; See also Icaza, above n. 11 and Walsh (2007), above n. 37.

60 Santos et al., above n. 16.

61 Vázquez (2011), above n. 37.

62 Icaza, above n. 11.

63 I am deeply grateful to Gustavo Esteva, Xochitl Leyva and Silvia Marcos for sharing their views on the PPT in Mexico. Of course, all shortcomings and misinterpretations are my responsibility.

conversation I had with a feminist academic-activist closer to the struggles of Zapatista indigenous women about a request that a group of Mexican feminist organisations had to submit to bring the PPT to Mexico to judge the case of femicides. Our main common concern was the extent to which the PPT's (modern/colonial) legalist vocabulary and Eurocentric rationality would allow the coexistence of pluriversal notions of justice beyond an international human rights perspective. After the first pre-hearing of the PPT on *Femicide and Gender Violence* in 2012, we exchanged some ideas and written texts and despite doubts, she participated in the PPT.[64] I remained as a critical supporter based in the Netherlands and followed the PPT developments in the Mexican press, social media and through email conversations with other academics and activists supporting them.

In mid-2013, I had the opportunity to travel to Oaxaca, Mexico, to the Universidad de la Tierra[65] (Land University) and discussed the previous concerns with some of the organisers, participants and a judge of one of the hearings of the PPT sessions in Mexico on *Violence against Corn, Food Sovereignty and Autonomy*.[66] My main question to them was, is it worthwhile to bring the PPT to Mexico amidst the ongoing struggles for the recognition and autonomy of indigenous systems and practices of justice? Just as the feminist academic-activist had, they expressed their hesitations but also their firm commitment to the PPT process.

In the process of writing this chapter, three other questions emerged:

1. In which ways does a [deep] questioning of an all-encompassing state-centric and/or capital-centric narrative of 'a' system of power unveil the limits of universalisms, including 'international human rights law'?
2. Can the PPT's ways of working allow/facilitate/encourage the political visibility of a pluriversality of forms in which life is organised, experienced and ruled in Mexico?

[64] See 'Preaudiencia sobre Feminicidio y Violencia de Género del Tribunal Permanente de los Pueblos' ['Peoples Permanent Tribunal Preliminary Hearing on Femicide and Gender Violence'], press release, 8 March 2012, https://web.archive.org/web/20160426073250/http://www.tppmexico.org/boletin-de-prensa-preaudiencia-sobre-feminicidio-y-violencia-de-genero/.

[65] UNITIERRA OAXACA and Gustavo Leyva are two key references for the post-developmental critique to developmentalism: Universidad de la Tierra, http://unitierra.blogspot.nl/.

[66] 'Pre-Trial Hearing Judgement: PPT Regarding Corn', https://maiznativodeoaxaca.wordpress.com/2015/03/11/1243/.

3. Why is it necessary to reflect on this critique of international human rights in the framework of the PPT to preserve its relevant but fragile contribution to epistemic justice?

Fourth and fifth questions emerged from the series of email exchanges with one key organiser of the PPT who was hesitant about the relevance of my ideas given the context of impunity and violence towards human rights activists in Mexico, and who actually asked me: Is your analysis worthwhile? For whom is it relevant? Therefore, the question mark in the title also aims to highlight that the epistemic position that is taken here starts with a questioning of who has had the power and the right to formulate the questions in the geopolitics of knowledge.[67]

In order to address some elements of these questions, the rest of this paper focuses initially on addressing the first two questions previously mentioned through a textual analysis of the PPT public statements and documents produced by the organisations involved in the proceedings in Mexico. This analysis is conducted in order to understand how the problem of dispossession and violence in Mexico is explained by those who sought the presence of the PPTs in Mexico back in 2011 as a means of popular justice given the context of impunity and violence. In particular, in this section I ask which analytical perspectives are privileged, and what remains silenced, in the process of legal translation for the construction of instances of 'power deviation' as a 'case' to be judged from the perspective of international human rights law.

Then I present alternative ways in which the judges and organisers of the PPT's hearing on *Violence against Corn, Food Sovereignty and Autonomy* paved the way towards some sort of epistemic justice by contributing to the political visibility of a pluriversality of forms that organised life around corn in Mexico.

Finally, I reflect on the limits and perils of universalism in human rights law identified by critical interculturality approaches. Walsh describes critical interculturality as opposed to functional interculturality. The latter is 'an institutional strategy that seeks to promote dialogue, tolerance, coexistence, and inclusion without necessarily addressing the causes of inequality; it makes diversity "functional" to a system'.[68] Meanwhile, a

[67] Geopolitics of knowledge is used here as expressed by Walter Mignolo in the form of questions: 'who, when, why is constructing knowledges?': Walter D. Mignolo, 'Epistemic disobedience, independent thought and decolonial freedom' (2009) 26(7–8) *Theory, Culture & Society* 159, 160.

[68] Walsh, above n. 18, 21.

critical interculturality perspective 'initiates with a profound questioning of the system [of inequality and exclusion] and seeks its major transformation in social, political, epistemic, and existential terms'.[69]

8.6.1 The PPT in Mexico and the Coexistence of Many Forms of Violence

In the General Indictment ('Acusación General') of the PPT Mexican Chapter presented in the general hearing,[70] the current context in Mexico is characterised by the coexistence of different forms of violence. Violence related to drug trafficking and the Mexican state's war against drug traffickers coexist with economic forms of violence that are manifested in huge disparities in levels of income distribution, the state of crisis in the process of social reproduction, the squandering of communal goods and so on. Parallel to this, a rapid trend towards the violent and fast degradation of natural resources through contamination of vast amounts of land, water and soil with industrial and household residual toxins is described.

In the case relating to violence towards corn, this is presented as a top-down process of contamination through genetically modified strains introduced by multinational corporations such as Monsanto, Dupont, Novartis and Aventis, with the active support of the federal and local authorities.[71] Moreover, violence related to *difference* including ethnic, gender and sexual orientation is described as direct forms of physical abuse, such as hate crimes and femicide and more subtle forms of discrimination that include acts of racism, sexism and classism, which lead to the exclusion of vast sectors of the Mexican population from public and private institutions, services and public space.

The General Indictment carefully documents these different forms of violence and describes the context in Mexico as a humanitarian crisis due to the ongoing structural violence.[72] Inspired by what seems to be Galtung's perspective of structural violence,[73] this is presented as mainly a product of processes of neoliberal restructuring expressed in the form

69 Ibid.
70 PPT Mexican Chapter, *Acusación General* ['General Indictment'], unpublished document on file with the author.
71 Ibid. 72 Ibid., 2.
73 Johan Galtung, 'Violence, peace and peace research' (1969) 6(3) *Journal of Peace Research* 167.

of liberalisation, deregulation and privatisation policies. The North American Free Trade Agreement (NAFTA) that entered into force between Canada, Mexico and the United States in 1994 deserves special attention as one of the policies that produces direct forms of violence including the one exercised against collective property of land, means, practices and institutions of popular subsistence, forced displacement of peasants from rural to urban areas and so on.

The main objective of the document is to demonstrate the 'complex causal relationship between the humanitarian and socio-political catastrophe that characterized the country'.[74] In doing so and according to Galtung's views of structural violence as 'avoidable', the document emphasises the 'reiterative, sustained and systematic forms through which the Mexican state has promoted an economic liberalisation policy, trade liberalisation, privatisation, denationalisation of public goods and stabilized inflation' in accordance with the so-called Washington Consensus framework.[75] Moreover, the document argues that the Mexican state adopted various policies which were not democratic or legitimate and which led to negative economic and socio-economic outcomes, with the result that it is the state that bears primary responsibility for the resulting humanitarian disaster.[76]

These voluntary state acts are presented as the causes behind what is conceptualised as *deviation of economic and political power*.[77] This power deviation as specific crime attributed to the Mexican state is characterised/described as 'a crime that unfolds silently and invisibly . . . by its own nature and mechanisms it is a crime that, despite the empirical evidence, seems not to have been perpetrated and hence, those who are responsible appear not to be so.'[78] This is an important qualification of the nature of state power deviation and as such it contributes to a *denaturalisation* of violence in Mexico by displaying the processes, mechanisms, decisions or lack of decisions taken by state actors and institutions as conducive to different forms of violence.

Overall, it is possible to assert that from this document's perspective, violence in Mexico is the product of two decades of neoliberal restructuring and its accompanying logic of modernisation. One can hardly deny that such a view is accurate. However, as will be explained, this perspective silences a radical questioning posed by experiences that have been produced as non-existent by certain narratives about the state, capitalism and power.

[74] *Acusación General*, above n. 70, 4. [75] Ibid. [76] Ibid. [77] Ibid. [78] Ibid. 10.

8.6.2 The Silences and Non-visible Sides

According to the General Indictment, the abuse of economic and state power is an 'abnormal attitude' (*actitud anómala*) through which the state 'makes use of its functions and powers to benefit particular interests which are contrary to and harmful to the general interest that it is supposed to protect'.[79]

This view of the state as a perpetrator of the crime of power deviation as an *abnormal situation* seems to be grounded in a particular view of the state that is blind to the process that founded the modern/colonial Mexican state, one characterised by the systematic exercise of force and violence, genocide, dispossession and predation. This characterisation of the present situation as abnormal is persuasive only if one does not take into consideration the experiences and perspectives of those systematically excluded from the modern/colonial project of nation-state building in Mexico: indigenous people and their communities, women and all those sectors of society not represented by the liberal notion of (male/urban/propertied/heterosexual) citizen. Unfortunately, the view of the state that permeates the document fails to recognise the state as a mechanism of control and violence, of exclusion in the name of 'national' unity and cultural homogenisation.[80] An example is the creation of provinces (*estados*) and municipalities (*municipios*) that divided indigenous peoples in Mexico. This view remains central despite the fact that two of the main cross-cutting topics of the PPT in Mexico were indigenous peoples and their territories and, of course, gender.[81] The General Indictment is also silent on the systematic attempts by the state to control through schooling, health and law those who have been represented as inferior or 'backward' together with their forms of organisation, knowing, being, living and sensing.[82]

Finally, in the PPT's General Indictment, ethnic and gender related discrimination and racism are mostly understood as by-products of systemic or structural logics of capitalist dispossession. These are far from being understood as interconnected forms of oppression. For example,

[79] Ibid., 5.

[80] López Bárcenas, above n. 19; Luis Villoro, *Estado plural, pluralidad de culturas* [*Plural State: Plurality of Cultures*] (Paidos/UNAM, 1998).

[81] *Boletín No. 1 del Tribunal Permanente de los Pueblos Capítulo México 2011–2014*, 26, web.archive.org/web/20141209055400/http://www.tppmexico.org:80/documentos/boletines/.

[82] Icaza, above n. 11; Vázquez (2009), above n. 37; Boaventura de Sousa Santos, *Towards a New Legal Common Sense: Law, Globalization and Emancipation* (Cambridge University Press, 2nd edn., 2002).

when the PPT's General Indictment argues for a criminal case against the Mexican state, it does so through a construction of a hierarchy of causalities in which the structural – read as capitalism and particularly its current over-accumulation crisis – is the key causal force behind everything else. Of course, one can agree with this capital-centric view or not. What matters here is that such a view produces as residual or in the worst case simply renders invisible the complex interrelations between capitalism/racism/sexism/eurocentrism and the violent oppressions that result from these intersections. These are vividly manifested, for example, in acts of physical violence against indigenous women's bodies or in the forced displacement of indigenous communities from their ancestral territories, issues which were central to two of the thematic hearings conducted by the PPT. Interestingly, these were named 'themes' not 'logics' or 'causes' and, as such, are not given the same explanatory power as capitalist over-accumulation to understand the different forms of violence in contemporary Mexico.[83]

8.6.3 The Many Layers of Violence and Resistance

Paradoxically, in the PPT proceedings there was also the possibility of a complex view of the intersections between capitalism/racism/sexism/eurocentrism. This was the case of the PPT thematic preliminary hearing on *Violence against Corn, Food Sovereignty and Autonomy* conducted in San Luis Beltrán, Oaxaca, Mexico on 26–27 April 2013 under the name *Transgenic Contamination of Native Corn.*

In the *dictamen* (ruling)[84] produced by the pre-hearing judges, Camila Montesinos, Joel Aquino and Gustavo Esteva, it is also possible to find many coincidences and continuities in the attribution of the specific crime of power deviation to the Mexican state. The document clearly states in relation to the state's deviation of power, 'we can demonstrate

[83] Thematic hearing on *Femicide and Gender Violence* and thematic hearing on *Violence against Corn, Food Sovereignty and Autonomy.*

[84] Camila Montecinos, Joel Aquino, and Gustavo Esteva, *Dictamen que presentan Camila Montecinos, Joel Aquino y Gustavo Esteva en la Preaudiencia Nacional: Contaminación Transgénica del Maíz Nativo, celebrado en San Luis Beltrán Oaxaca, los días 26 y 27 de abril de 2013* [*Dictamen Maíz*] [*Final Ruling presented by Camila Montesios, Joel Aquino and Gustavo Esteva in the national pre-hearing: Transgenetic Contamination of Native Corn, held in San Luis Beltran Oaxaca on 26 and 27 April, 2013*] [hereafter *Ruling on Corn*] https://maiznativodeoaxaca.wordpress.com/2013/05/22/dictamen-final-de-la-pre audiencia-contaminacion-transgenica-del-maiz-nativooaxaca-26-y-27-de-abril-de-2013/.

with the evidence that we have received [that] it [power] has been misused through new laws and through policies and programs . . . which are clearly against peasants' interests and in favor of corporations.'[85] Furthermore, there is a special emphasis on transgenic contamination as an intentional form of 'power deviation because the state apparatus was used in favor of private interests' and against communities' food sovereignty.[86] The authors of the document conceptualise transgenic contamination as a form of control:

> [T]he invasion with transgenic corn has been prepared by the government at the service of corporations that produced and commercialized it . . . it is mostly a way of controlling the seeds market in Mexico . . . to this end laws have been modified to the benefit of big corporations and to the detriment of small producers, who are then placed at the margins of law when they sell or exchange seeds they produce.[87]

Nonetheless, the document also gives examples of how, for peasants and indigenous communities, the disappearance of corn from Mexican agriculture goes beyond material/economic loss and into the other areas of life: spirituality, history and autonomy. In the document, corn is presented not only as a seed but also 'as an experience', a deeply human(e) experience that shapes how life is lived and organised.[88] This subtle, but nonetheless existing, realisation informs the way in which the crime of power deviation in relation to transgenic contamination is considered: Mexico plays a role as a genetic reservoir of corn as well as the knowledges necessary to keep corn alive.[89] Accordingly, for the authors of the ruling the crux of the problem is that losing native corn in communities means the end of their autonomy and knowledges that have been preserved for centuries.

The authors also pay special attention to evidence of resistance despite oppressive and systemic forms of violence caused by the state's power deviation. For example, they share the following quote: 'Women and men in Oaxaca, we are sowing our corn even against a system that wants to eradicate our Mexican and Oaxaquenio countryside'.[90]

The document also privileges what seems to be the authors' interests in carefully pondering why, against all odds, the culture of communities survives due to the organisation of life that stems from the *milpa* (corn fields): 'among ourselves we ask why does *tequio*[91] survive? Why do

[85] Ibid., 2. [86] Ibid., 4–5. [87] Ibid., 4. [88] Ibid., 3. [89] Ibid., 5. [90] Ibid., 3.
[91] Eds: community volunteer work.

communitarian services survive? Why does the system of *cargos* survive? Why does traditional medicine survive?'[92] There is an acknowledgement that the struggle of indigenous communities for their autonomy, ways of life and government dates back centuries and it is linked to corn.

8.6.4 The Coloniality of Legal Pluralism

A classical notion of legal pluralism defines it as 'the presence in a social field of more than one legal order' and contrasts it with the 'ideology of centralism' in order to debunk the myth of law as a 'unified, exclusive and hierarchical order depending [on] the power of the state'.[93] In this chapter, the notion of legal pluralism is considered from a critical intercultural approach to law and/or legal pluralism as formulated by Vachon and Coll,[94] Esteva and Prakash,[95] Santos[96] and Walsh.[97] According to Walsh, legal pluralism is 'within this same paradigm [hegemonic western thought] and conceived from a pluricultural interpretation of the sphere of justice that highlights separation and opposition of two or more ways of conceiving and practising law, one being the 'ordinary' national norm and the other or others the non-ordinary and hence simply added to the established legal system'.[98]

This 'adding' is often used to make reference to the 'recognition' of *usos y costumbres* (customary law) as rules of 'traditional' orders, which are incorporated as 'normal' national norms. Accordingly, legal pluralism

> seeks to address the problem of legal monism [as] the notion of one single system of rights for all, a principle of the modern uni-national and monocultural State and its normative power to suppress and marginalise difference by establishing one single way of being, knowing and living that is shaped according to the European image and experience.[99]

This is grounded on what Escobar calls a dominant ontology that is based on Western rationalism and focused on '[the] belief in logical truth as the

[92] Ibid., 12.

[93] John Griffiths, 'What is legal pluralism?' (1986) 24 *Journal of Legal Pluralism* 1, 4.

[94] Agustí Nicolau Coll and Robert Vachon, 'Etnicidad y derecho: Un enfoque diatópico y dialogal del estudio y la enseñanza del pluralism jurídico' ['Ethnicity and law: A diatopic and dialogical approach for the study and teaching of legal pluralism'], paper presented at the Instituto de Investigaciones Juridicas de la Universidad Autónoma de México, 17–19 May 2015, www.dhdi.free.fr/recherches/theoriedroit/articles/agustivachon.htm.

[95] Gustavo Esteva and Madhu Suri Prakash, *Grassroots Postmodernism: Remaking the Soil of Cultures* (Zed Books, 1998).

[96] Santos, above n. 82. [97] Walsh (2012), above n. 37. [98] Ibid., 36. [99] Ibid., 33.

only valid (or main) grounds for knowledge about an objective world made up of things that can be known'.[100] From this perspective, a normative system, which is not based on objective knowledge, is disregarded or recognised as non-ordinary.

Therefore, for some 'opening the legal canon' to non-modern/colonial practices and systems of justice could be only an act of inclusion but not one that automatically leads to a rethinking of the monocultural modern/colonial state-centric model of justice.[101]

This is why legal pluralism that does not challenge the racial and modern/colonial structure of the state and its legal field can be seen as part of a rule of law that is accommodated to the multi/pluricultural logic of transnational capitalism and its neoliberal project.[102] From this perspective, this push for an 'integrationist' legal pluralism could be one of the many characteristics of what some conceptualise as 'neoliberal multiculturalism'.[103] In other words, legal pluralism is not in itself a radical or progressive solution to the question of exclusion of diverse notions, systems and practices of justice, but an instrument that might, or not, contribute to fracturing the exclusionary logic of state law.[104]

Therefore, calls for recognition of different systems of justice, including what is called, in a modern/colonial relationship, 'traditional customary law', do not secure a deep transformation of monocultural state-centric notions of justice central to national and international legal systems. Walsh takes the example of the 2007 UN Declaration on the Rights of Indigenous Peoples and highlights that it brings about new recognitions such as

> the intrinsic rights of indigenous peoples that derive from their political, economic, social structures and their cultures, spiritual traditions, history and understanding of life, specially their rights over their lands, territories and resources.[105]

However, the differentiation that this declaration establishes between law and collective systems of life and individual-positivist-rationalist

[100] Arturo Escobar, 'Notes on the Ontology of Design' (unpublished paper, 2012) 16, http://sawyerseminar.ucdavis.edu/files/2012/12/ESCOBAR_Notes-on-the-Ontology-of-Design-Parts-I-II-_-III.pdf.

[101] Coll and Vachon, above n. 93; Santos, above n. 82; Walsh (2012), above n. 37.

[102] Walsh (2012), above n. 37, 33.

[103] Charles Hale, 'Neoliberal multiculturalism: The remaking of cultural rights and racial dominance in Central America' (2005) 28(1) *Political and Legal Anthropology Review (PoLAR)* 10.

[104] Santos, above n. 82.

[105] Walsh (2012) above n. 37, 34.

law and its Eurocentric modern/colonial/capitalist roots should be pondered carefully because 'the firm intention to respect the customs does not always imply the will to take away from them from the action of progress, development and civilisation under the control of the Nation-State'.[106]

This call for careful reflection also becomes relevant in relation to the PPT's legal framework, which includes the Universal Declaration of Human Rights, and the Charter of Economic Rights and Duties of States, and in the case of indigenous people and their territories, ILO Convention No. 169, as well as the non-governmental Universal Declaration of the Rights of Peoples. Overall, these frameworks have made important contributions to the formal recognition of indigenous rights as well as important limitations that lead to epistemic violence as erasure of notions of justice that do not and cannot be translated into this legal language or through the rationality that accompanies it. These legal frameworks are based on one model – individual-positivist-rationalist law – that has 'silenced the validity of plural legal systems which were colonised by hegemonic powers'.[107]

Another limitation that is rarely considered is the way in which these frameworks fail to contribute to the recognition of different places of legal production besides the nation-state.[108] Indeed, law and, particularly, international human rights law contribute to a systematic invisibility of forms of justice that are produced as secondary, non-universal and residual expressions of the latter and that do not necessarily imply or secure equality or equity.[109] This is the case of 'traditional' and 'customary' law, which are conceived as in need of recognition by universal institutions and practices in order to 'exist'. Less has been said about the fact that these normative systems are at the 'margins of state legality',[110] and when recognised by the state, then become part of 'the technology of power, domestication and domination'.[111]

[106] Coll and Vachon, above n. 93, 270. [107] Hernández et al., above n. 17, 18.

[108] Walsh (2012) above n. 37, Hernández et al., above n. 17.

[109] Branwen Gruffydd Jones, 'Introduction: International Relations, Eurocentrism and Imperialism' in Branwen Gruffyyd Jones (ed.), *Decolonizing International Relations* (Rowman and Littlefield, 2006) 1; Willem Assies, 'La oficialización de lo no official: Re-encuentro de dos mundos?' ['The officialisation of the non-official: Re-encounter of two worlds'] (2000) 11(21) *Alteridades* 83, 94 (earlier version quoted by Walsh (2012), above n. 37, 35).

[110] Walsh (2012), above n. 37, 34.

[111] Assies, above n. 108; Hernández et al., above n. 17.

This has been the case in the southern Mexican state of Oaxaca, the place where the PPT hearing on *Violence against Corn, Food Sovereignty and Autonomy* was held. Oaxaca's first local constitution dating from 1825 recognised that the state was composed by all the peoples and parties that previously formed the province with that name.[112] By 1998, the state of Oaxaca recognised that

> indigenous peoples, their communities, linguistic groups and afro-descendant communities were subjects of rights, while the recognized rights included their normative systems and indigenous jurisdiction, together with others that already existed such as bilingual and inter-cultural education, access to justice in State tribunals, to elect authorities through customary electoral system and the free association of municipalities.[113]

However, indigenous jurisdiction and the validity of normative systems have been restricted to minor issues[114] and have recently faced important setbacks due to the Mexican state's war on drugs.[115]

Nonetheless, and against all odds, these normative systems referred to as 'traditional' also 'express centuries of resistance to preserve systems of life rooted in territories'.[116] For example, in Oaxaca indigenous people 'have successfully kept alive their rich diversity of language and culture, while coexisting with their colonizers'.[117]

This resistance for some is an exercise against colonisation and cultural imperialism of the state and its laws, as well as of human rights. For many communities around the world, we are told, human rights are not only alien but also incommensurable with existing notions of justice and well-being. In particular, Esteva and Prakash present a brief description of the notion of justice that is practised in the municipalities of Oaxaca in which sixteen different indigenous peoples communities coexist as an example of this incommensurability:

> [T]heir justice do[es] not, for example, look for punishment when a person violates a shared custom. He or she is perceived as someone in trouble, who needs understanding and help; including the opportunity to offer compensations to the victim of his or her misdemeanour. . . . Rather than confine wrongdoers in jail, many of these communities tie them to trees or confine them to places for a few hours or days with the expressed

112 López Bárcenas, above n. 19, 54. 113 Ibid. 114 Ibid., 55.
115 Hernández et al., above n. 17. 116 Walsh (2012), above n. 37, 34.
117 Esteva and Prakash, above n. 94, 111.

> hope of allowing their passions to calm down. . . . These practices are not conceived as forms of punishment. Instead they offer communal support.[118]

With the previous example, I aim to display the ontological difference that grounds the Zapoteco indigenous community's normative views. This difference is enunciated from a locus that exceeds modern/colonial Western-rationalist-positivist-individualist experience that informs legal pluralist epistemologies and state-centric legal systems proposals.[119]

Against this background of the debate regarding law and legal pluralism, one can consider recent calls for 'humanising human rights' and for 'other grammars of human dignity' that imply 'abandoning the category "human" . . . as [a] globalised localism[]', as the product of racism.[120]

Despite all of this, in the document produced by Montecinos, Aquino and Esteva, a brief but nonetheless important observation for the purposes of this chapter's analysis is made:

> It is important to note that this demand [the return to the rule of law] is presented by [indigenous] communities that have suffered for over 500 years the perverse use of law instruments against themselves, communities that have suffered not only unfair laws, but laws that have ignored and discriminated them, together with corrupted and racist tribunals.[121]

With this observation, these authors remind us of the context in which the struggle for legal pluralism in Mexico is marked by a contentious relationship between state legality and the struggle for indigenous autonomy as a challenge to it: in other words, to consider the violence of coloniality as an inseparable and constitutive underside of modern state legality.

8.7 Final Reflection

After pondering all the previous elements, this final section offers a reflection on, not a closed answer to, the questions of whether the PPTs in Mexico and the present analysis are worthwhile.

118 Ibid. 119 Escobar, above n. 99; Vázquez, above n. 37.

120 Julia Suárez Krabbe, 'Democratising democracy, humanizing human rights: European decolonial social movements and the alternative thinking of alternatives' (2013) 10(3) *Migration Letters* 333, 336, 340.

121 *Ruling on Corn*, above n. 84, 7.

From the PPT protagonists themselves – indigenous peoples' communities and their supporters – who are embarked on the struggle for legal pluralism and autonomy, I have learnt that the tribunals are worthwhile despite their (modern/colonial) legalist vocabulary and Eurocentric rationality. For those who emphasise the PPTs as processes that create opportunities for mutual learning among the participants, these have 'opened a real communicative process that allowed us to be transformed by such experience'.[122] Meanwhile, for others the PPT proceedings are instruments of visibility but little else.[123] This is an important but certainly a modest role.

Moreover, contrary to a superficial observation that could simply characterise the PPTs as another form of modern/colonial imposition of a particular gaze over what is supposed to be justice, well-being, life, dignity or social change, the PPT thematic pre-hearing on *Violence against Corn, Food Sovereignty and Autonomy* seems to point at something more subtle and complex.

As I have indicated before, in the documents produced by this thematic hearing, statements on social media and key conversations held with one of its judges, there exists a fragile but nonetheless highly relevant opening for a *coexistence of notions of justice*. If we follow the notion of resistance developed by Lugones' decolonial feminism, it is possible to understand that the mere visibility of a coexistence of different notions of justice, or an ecology of normative realities following Santos,[124] in itself represents a crack, a fissure in the supposedly all-encompassing and homogenised modern/colonial system of international law in which the PPT operates.

However, the opening to a plurality of notions and practices of justice is not automatically conducive to a rethinking of the ways in which the PPT organisers and participants perceive justice. Nor does it address the ways in which the very existence of non-punitive justice – as the above-mentioned case of Oaxaca illustrates – raises questions about the language, rationality, logics and procedures employed by the PPT with particular attention to its legal translation.

To move towards a critical revision of the universalism of human rights law within the PPT process is a pending and contentious issue

122 PPT Mexican Chapter, *Final Ruling*, above n. 13, 4.

123 'Preaudiencia sobre Feminicidio y Violencia de Género del Tribunal Permanente de los Pueblos', above n. 64.

124 Santos, above n. 82.

given the context of violence against human rights activists and impunity in Mexico. To think and write about this move from the privileged position of Global North academia 'compels us to switch our attention not to what is being said but to who is speaking and what for'.[125] This epistemic position takes the form here of 'written words that uncover the road travelled in a dialogical process' with PPT protagonists in Mexico.[126] This chosen route could be worthwhile only if it contributes to thinking justice *otherwise* in a *relationship* with those at the forefront of the struggles that are taking place in the graveyard that is Mexico today.

125 Mignolo (2013), above n. 37.

126 Icaza, above n. 3, 2.

9

The Biak Massacre Citizens' Tribunal and the Disputed Indonesian Region of West Papua

NICOLA EDWARDS

9.1 Introduction

The Biak Massacre Citizens' Tribunal (the 'Biak Tribunal') was convened at the University of Sydney on 6 July 2013 at the request of the Centre for Peace and Conflict Studies. The tribunal was established to inquire into an atrocity that occurred on 6 July 1998 on the island of Biak, in the disputed Indonesian region of West Papua.[1] The Biak Tribunal is one of hundreds of 'peoples' tribunals' that have been established since the Russell Tribunal in 1967.[2] Of the many dozens of peoples' tribunals that have been convened throughout the world since this time, many have focused on human rights violations in Asia, including several sessions of the Permanent Peoples' Tribunal held in European cities to investigate variously the Indonesian occupation of East Timor, the Chinese occupation of Tibet, the Filipino Moro conflict, human rights violations perpetrated by the Filipino Arroyo regime and the Sri Lankan civil war.[3] There have also been several independent peoples' tribunals convened in Asia, including the Women's International War Crimes Tribunal on Japan's Military Sexual Slavery convened in Tokyo in 2000 and the Kuala Lumpur War Crimes Commission, which was first developed in 2007 to investigate the crimes committed by the United Kingdom and United

[1] West Papua is the name independence activists give to the entire Indonesian half of the island of New Guinea, although officially this comprises the provinces of Papua and West Papua.

[2] This chapter uses the terms 'peoples' tribunal' and 'citizens' tribunal' interchangeably.

[3] Gabrielle Simm and Andrew Byrnes, 'International Peoples' Tribunals in Asia: Political theatre, juridical farce, or meaningful intervention?' (2014) 4 *Asian Journal of International Law* 103, 104, 107.

States in the 2003 war in Iraq.[4] These tribunals adopt legalistic methods and forms in an attempt to address concerns that the participants believe have not been adequately resolved within formal legal systems.

Although such tribunals have no recognised legal authority and no power to enforce their verdicts, many scholars argue that they are nevertheless significant. Blaser contends that '[t]ribunals will contribute to the creation of new norms and a change in how we think about international law.'[5] Writing about the Women's International War Crimes Tribunal, Chinkin is similarly enthusiastic about the importance of peoples' tribunals, arguing that they seek to 'influence the development of international law'.[6] Borowiak also argues that they are important, although according to him this is because they 'draw attention to lacunae within the existing formal accountability structures of global governance'.[7] Similarly, Klinghoffer and Klinghoffer argue that peoples' tribunals self-consciously attempt to 'transform international law' by highlighting the inadequacy of existing standards.[8] Writing specifically about peoples' tribunals in Asia, Simm and Byrnes similarly argue that they 'respond to a perceived gap in official structures of accountability', and perform other important functions, including 'building solidarity and networks, and recording and memorializing otherwise unacknowledged experiences'.[9] In sum, although peoples' tribunals do not deliver legally binding verdicts, scholars have nevertheless considered them to perform a wide variety of significant functions depending on the nature of the tribunal in question.

As it is now some years since the Biak Tribunal published its verdict, it is timely to re-examine this tribunal and to consider what impact, if any, can be attributed to it. This chapter aims to examine the significance of the Biak Tribunal. It evaluates its importance in the broader context of scholarly activism about human rights violations in West Papua. In Section 9.2, the chapter begins by outlining the argument that West Papuans have been denied the right to self-determination and the related

[4] Ibid., 109.

[5] Arthur Blaser, 'How to advance human rights without really trying: An analysis of nongovernmental tribunals' (1992) 14 *Human Rights Quarterly* 339, 365.

[6] Christine Chinkin, 'Peoples' Tribunals: Legitimate or rough justice' (2006) 24 *Windsor Yearbook of Access to Justice* 201, 212.

[7] Craig Borowiak, 'The World Tribunal on Iraq: Citizens' Tribunals and the struggle for accountability' (2008) 30 *New Political Science* 161, 162.

[8] Arthur Jay Klinghoffer and Judith Apter Klinghoffer, *International Citizens' Tribunals: Mobilizing Public Opinion to Advance Human Rights* (Palgrave MacMillan, 2002) 5.

[9] Simm and Byrnes, above n. 3, 103.

scholarly accusations that Indonesia is committing genocide in the region, while Section 9.3 analyses the Biak Tribunal itself, and Section 9.4 proceeds to an evaluation of the tribunal's significance.

9.2 Framing Human Rights Violations in West Papua

Although the Biak Tribunal was convened explicitly in order to examine events which occurred in West Papua in 1998, to understand its significance it is necessary to briefly consider a longer history of the region. Indonesia and West Papua were both part of the Dutch East Indies, but when the Netherlands accepted Indonesian independence in 1949, it retained control of West Papua. The Netherlands argued that West Papuans had a distinct ethnicity, culture, history and religion,[10] and thus qualified for their own self-determination.[11] In contrast, Indonesia argued that self-determination had already been exercised by the entire people of the Dutch East Indies when Indonesia declared independence in 1945 and that continued Dutch control of West Papua was a denial of this right.[12] Fearing the spread of communism in Indonesia, the United States sponsored negotiations between Indonesia and the Netherlands, which culminated in the 1962 New York Agreement.[13] This agreement allowed for the transfer of the administration of West Papua to Indonesia, on a condition that Indonesia later hold an 'act of free choice' to consult West Papuans about whether they 'wish to remain with Indonesia'.[14]

When this vote was held in 1969, only 1,026 specially selected 'consultative assembly' members were allowed to participate.[15] Although they unanimously opted to integrate with Indonesia, Brian May, a correspondent for Agence France-Presse who lived in West Papua during the period, alleges that Indonesian forces attacked some of those who refused

[10] Michla Pomerance, 'Methods of self-determination and the argument of primitiveness' (1974) 12 *Canadian Year Book of International Law* 38, 47.

[11] Antonio Cassese, *Self-Determination of Peoples: A Legal Reappraisal* (Cambridge University Press, 1995) 82.

[12] David Webster, 'Self-determination abandoned: The road to the New York Agreement on West New Guinea (Papua), 1960–62' (2013) 95 *Indonesia* 9, 12.

[13] Ibid.

[14] Agreement between the Republic of Indonesia and the Kingdom of the Netherlands concerning West New Guinea (West Irian), New York, 15 August 1962, 437 UNTS 273, in force 21 September 1962, cited in Eben Kirksey, *Freedom in Entangled Worlds: West Papua and the Architecture of Global Power* (Duke University Press, 2012) 36.

[15] John Saltford, *The United Nations and the Indonesian Takeover of West Papua, 1962–1969: The Anatomy of Betrayal* (Routledge Curzon, 2003) 160.

to support the 'consultative assembly' and forced them to abandon their villages,[16] while members of the assembly were offered monetary incentives[17] in return for supporting Indonesia.[18] Despite an initial protest from Ghana, ultimately the General Assembly approved West Papua's integration with Indonesia in November 1962.[19] West Papua has been internationally recognised as part of Indonesia since this time.

However, West Papuan activists have never accepted the validity of the 'act of free choice' and insist that they have never had the chance to exercise their anti-colonial right to external self-determination.[20] This claim has become stronger over time as the principle of self-determination has crystallised into a rule of international law, according to which the 'act of free choice' would have been invalid. Nevertheless, Indonesia continues to deny that West Papuans have a right to external self-determination and, in an attempt to suppress the independence movement, has perpetrated a plethora of human rights violations up to the present day.[21]

[16] Ibid., citing Brian May, *The Indonesian Tragedy* (Routledge and Kegan Paul, 1978) 192.

[17] Ibid., 193. [18] Ibid., 158–65.

[19] The situation with regard to the implementation of the declaration on the granting of independence to colonial countries and peoples, UN GA Resolution A/5217, UN Doc A/RES/1810(XVII) (17 December 1962); Question of Kenya, GA Res A/5217, UN Doc A/RES/1810(XVII) (17 December 1962); International conference of plenipotentiaries on consular relations, GA Res A/5217, UN Doc A/RES/1810 (XVII) (17 December 1962).

[20] Jennifer Robinson, 'Self-Determination and the Limits of Justice: West Papua and East Timor' in Helen Sykes (ed.), *Future Justice, Sydney: Future Leaders* (Future Leaders, 2010) 168, 178.

[21] See, e.g., Karishma Vaswani, 'Indonesia confirms Papua torture', *BBC News*, 22 October 2010, www.bbc.com/news/world-asia-pacific-11604361; Charlie Hill-Smith, 'It's sheer bloody murder, right on our doorstep', *Sydney Morning Herald*, 8 January 2012, www.smh.com.au/federal-politics/political-opinion/its-sheer-bloody-murder-right-on-our-doorstep-20120107-1ppd2.html#ixzz3hXsBAIGE; Peter Lloyd, 'Indonesian Counter-Terrorist Unit accused of mass killing in disputed Papua province', *ABC News*, 24 May 2013, www.abc.net.au/news/2013-05-24/indonesian-counter-terrorist-unit-accuse-mass-killing-papua/4712070; Marni Cordell, 'Indonesian police open fire on civilians in West Papua', *The Guardian*, 25 September 2013, www.theguardian.com/world/2013/sep/25/indonesian-police-civilians-west-papua; Jenny Denton, 'West Papuans "tortured, terrorised"', *Sydney Morning Herald*, 7 October 2013, www.smh.com.au/world/west-papuans-tortured-terrorised-20131006-2v2ae.html; Ronny Kareni, 'This is how Indonesia treats West Papuans', *New Matilda*, 11 April 2014, https://newmatilda.com/2014/04/11/how-indonesia-treats-west-papuans; Amy McQuire, 'West Papuan independence leader found floating in sack at sea', *New Matilda*, 1 September 2014, https://newmatilda.com/2014/09/01/west-papuan-independence-leader-found-floating-sack-sea; Michael Bachelard, 'Indonesian military and police fire into crowd of West Papuan civilians, killing 5', *Sydney Morning Herald*, 8 December 2014, www.smh.com.au/world/indonesian-military-and-police-fire-into-crowd-of-west-papuan-civilians-killing-5-20141208-122wf0.html#ixzz3hXmnHGV0.

Since 2004, several scholars have alleged that Indonesia's attempt to suppress independence activism in West Papua has involved such egregious and systematic human rights violations that they may amount to genocide.[22] Genocide occurs when any of five prohibited acts – killing members of a group; causing serious bodily or mental harm to members of a group; deliberately inflicting on the group conditions of life calculated to bring about its physical destruction; imposing measures intended to prevent births within the group; or forcibly transferring children of the group to another group – is committed with the special intent to destroy, in whole or in part, a national, ethnical, racial or religious group, as such.[23]

The first substantial scholarly allegation that Indonesia may have committed genocide in West Papua was made in a seventy-eight-page report prepared by an international human rights clinic at Yale Law School in 2004. This report contended that Indonesian security forces had committed a range of acts prohibited under the Genocide Convention – including killing, torture, disappearance and rape – in an attempt to suppress the West Papuan independence movement. The Biak massacre is listed as one such act.[24] While these human rights violations could amount to genocide if accompanied by the requisite *dolus specialis*, the report notes that the inference of special intent is complicated by the Indonesian government's argument that it is not targeting West Papuans as a group, but merely targeting those who support separatism.[25] The report is thus tentative about whether a prima facie case of genocide can be established.

More recently, several scholars affiliated with the Centre for Peace and Conflict Studies at the University of Sydney have similarly alleged that

22 Asian Human Rights Commission, *The Neglected Genocide: Human Rights Abuses Against Papuans in the Central Highlands, 1977–1987* (Asian Human Rights Commission, 2013), www.tapol.org/sites/default/files/sites/default/files/pdfs/NeglectedGenocide AHRC.pdf; Elizabeth Brundige, Winter King, Priyneha Vahali, Stephen Vladeck and Xiang Yuan, *Indonesian Human Rights Abuses in West Papua: Application of the Law of Genocide to the History of Indonesian Rule* (Allard K Lowenstein International Human Rights Clinic Yale Law School, 2004), https://law.yale.edu/system/files/documents/pdf/Intellectual_Life/West_Papua_final_report.pdf; John Wing and Peter King, *Genocide in West Papua? The Role of the Indonesian State Apparatus and a Current Needs Assessment of the Papuan People* (Centre for Peace and Conflict Studies at the University of Sydney, 2005), https://sydney.edu.au/arts/peace_conflict/docs/WestPapuaGenocideRpt05.pdf; Jim Elmslie and Camellia Webb-Gannon, 'Slow-motion genocide: Indonesian rule in West Papua' (2013) 1 *Griffith Journal of Law and Human Dignity* 142, 145.

23 Convention on the Prevention and Punishment of the Crime of Genocide, Paris, 9 December 1948, opened for signature 9 December 1948, 78 UNTS 277, in force 12 January 1951, article 2 (hereafter Genocide Convention).

24 Brundige et al., above n. 22, 44, 63. 25 Ibid., 5.

Indonesia is committing genocide in West Papua, but these claims have been based on less convincing legal reasoning and evidence. A year after the Yale Law School report, John Wing and Peter King, both affiliates of the Centre, produced a report entitled *Genocide in West Papua?*[26] The report documented human rights abuses, neglect and the spread of HIV/AIDS in the region, suggesting that overall these destructive acts and processes amounted to a 'silent genocide'.[27] Although it has been described as the most widely cited and influential analysis of the genocide claim,[28] the report does not even mention the element of special intent, which is vital to establishing the crime of genocide in legal terms. Thus, as McGibbon notes, the report falls short of establishing a prima facie case of genocide, since it 'provides no evidence whatsoever' of the intent to eliminate the West Papuan group.[29]

More recently, Jim Elmslie and Camellia Webb-Gannon – visiting scholars at the Sydney Centre for Peace and Conflict Studies – have argued that the Indonesian military and police forces have been perpetrating a 'slow-motion' genocide in West Papua since 1962.[30] The idea of

26 Wing and King, above n. 22. 27 Ibid., 2.

28 Rodd McGibbon, 'Pitfalls of Papua: Understanding the Conflict and Its Place in Australian-Indonesian Relations' (Lowy Institute for International Policy, 2006) 96, www.lowyinstitute.org/sites/default/files/pubfiles/McGibbon,_Pitfalls_of_Papua_1.pdf; Wing and King, above n. 22, cited in Esther Heidbüchel, *The West Papua Conflict in Indonesia: Actors, Issues and Approaches* (Herrmann J&J-Verlag, 2007) 14; Luis Rodríguez-Piñero Royo, 'Political Participation Systems Applicable to Indigenous People' in Marc Weller (ed.), *Political Participation of Minorities: A Commentary on International Standards and Practice* (Oxford University Press, 2010) 308, 337; David Hill, 'On the Border: Local Media in the Land of Papua' in Krishna Sen and David Hill (eds.), *Politics and the Media in Twenty-First Century Indonesia: Decade of Democracy* (Routledge, 2011) 26, 43; Danilyn Rutherford, *Laughing at Leviathan: Sovereignty and Audience in West Papua* (University of Chicago Press, 2012); Peter King, 'In defence of the Papua sympathisers: A rejoinder to Ed Aspinall' (2006) 25(4) *Policy and Society* 133.

29 McGibbon, above n. 28, 96.

30 Elmslie and Webb-Gannon, above n. 22, 145. While the idea of a 'slow-motion' genocide is not supported by legal precedent, the concept is not unique to West Papuan scholars and activists. The Permanent Peoples' Tribunal on Sri Lanka in 2013 described something similar when it alleged that genocide, as a 'social process' which includes 'the construction of the conditions which make the genocide viable', had been occurring in Sri Lanka from as far back as 1833 and 'reached its climax' between 2008 and 2009: Permanent Peoples' Tribunal, *Session on Sri Lanka and the Tamil People II*, Bremen, 7–10 December 2013, Verdict, 16–17. More recently, one of the judges from the Permanent Peoples' Tribunal on Sri Lanka has adopted a similar concept in an academic analysis, arguing that the Rohingya in Myanmar 'have been subject to a process of slow-burning genocide over the past thirty-five years': Maung Zarni and Alice Cowley 'The slow-burning genocide of Myanmar's Rohingya' (2014) 23 *Pacific Rim Law and Policy Journal*

'slow-motion' genocide is not a legal term, but borrowed from a phrase the West Papuan leader, Clemens Runawery, used to describe the gradual destruction of the indigenous population as a result of transmigration (a policy which involved the state-sponsored migration of Indonesians from densely populated islands to less populated regions, including Papua).[31] Elmslie and Webb-Gannon adapt the phrase to encapsulate their argument that the crime of genocide has gradually been committed by the Indonesian state since 1962. They argue that Indonesia has perpetrated a series of acts prohibited under the Genocide Convention since this time, resulting in the deaths of up to 500,000 Papuans.[32] The Biak massacre is listed as one such prohibited act.[33] Whereas other scholars have found the element of special intent to be problematic, Elmslie and Webb-Gannon argue that the Indonesian government's intent to destroy part of the West Papuan group can be inferred from the fact that the government has an interest in destroying 'those West Papuans who opposed Indonesian rule'.[34] However, to claim that intent can be inferred from Indonesia's desire to destroy the West Papuan independence movement suggests that the target group is in fact a political group, which is not a protected group under the Genocide Convention. Elmslie and Webb-Gannon's article can thus be understood as part of a scholarly activist body of literature which persuasively documents egregious human rights violations in West Papua but lacks the necessary evidence or legal reasoning to make the contentious allegation that such violations amount to genocide – as opposed to crimes against humanity, a possibility that will be discussed further – completely convincing.

This lack of legal rigour is problematic given the particularly provocative implications of the West Papuan genocide allegation. Of course, any accusation of genocide is controversial, as genocide is considered the 'crime of crimes' and conveys such moral condemnation that Mamdani describes it as 'a label to be stuck on your worst enemy'.[35] However, there

683. The International People's Tribunal 1965, which examined the atrocities committed in Indonesia in 1965–66 as part of the suppression of a 'Communist revolt', also adopted an expanded definition of 'genocide' as including acts undertaken with the intent to destroy a political group in whole or in part: see Wieringa, Chapter 5, in this volume. Other peoples' tribunals have taken a more traditional approach: see Byrnes and Simm, Chapter 1, this volume.

[31] Elmslie and Webb-Gannon, above n. 22, 145. [32] Ibid., 148. [33] Ibid., 149.

[34] Ibid., 155.

[35] Mahmood Mamdani, 'The politics of naming: Genocide, civil war, insurgency', (2007) 29(5) *London Review of Books* 5, 8.

are certain perceptions about the crime of genocide that mean that a genocide allegation is particularly provocative when made by a group seeking independence from an existing state. This is because it is sometimes argued that genocide triggers exceptions to the principle of territorial sovereignty.[36] Grodsky argues that it is based on this belief about the legal effects of genocide that three-quarters of the members of the Unrepresented Nations and Peoples Organization (an organisation which represents many independence groups that self-identify as nations but are not accorded a vote in the United Nations) claim to have been the victims of genocide.[37] West Papuans are just one of about thirty members who make this claim.[38] Grodsky is highly critical of these allegations, which he considers to be a calculated part of 'global sympathy campaigns' in which independence activists attempt to play the 'genocide trump card'.[39] This scepticism fails to account for the fact that many groups seek independence precisely because they are persecuted by their home state and may genuinely believe they are the victims of genocide, whether or not this is legally accurate. However, Grodsky makes an important point in highlighting that precisely because accusations of genocide by independence groups are inextricably political, such allegations also tend to be treated with a high degree of scepticism. When measured against this particularly high burden of proof, the accusations about ongoing genocide in West Papua that have been made to

[36] Genocide could trigger an exception to the principle of territorial sovereignty if, as some commentators suggest, there is right to 'remedial secession' in cases where a non-colonial people is severely oppressed. For example, Cassese suggests that 'the contention could be made' that '[e]xtreme and unremitting persecution and the lack of any reasonable prospect for peaceful challenge make secession legitimate': above n. 11, 120. Similarly, Crawford notes tentatively that '[a]t least it is arguable that, in extreme cases of oppression, international law allows remedial secession to discrete peoples within a State': James Crawford, *The Creation of States in International Law* (Oxford University Press, 2nd edn., 2007) 118. Alternatively, it has been suggested that genocide may create an exception to the principle of territorial sovereignty by triggering the 'responsibility to protect': Christian Tomuschat, 'Secession and Self-Determination' in Marcelo Kohen (ed.), *Secession: International Law Perspectives* (Cambridge University Press, 2006) 38–42. See also Donnelly, who argues there is an evolving 'anti-genocide exception to the prohibition of intervention': Jack Donnelly, 'Genocide and humanitarian intervention' (2002) 1 *Journal of Human Rights* 93, 98. These principles remain *lex ferenda* at best.

[37] Brian Grodsky, 'When two ambiguities collide: The use of genocide in self-determination drives' (2012) 14 *Journal of Genocide Research* 1.

[38] Grodsky derived this figure by conducting media and Internet searches for reports about the secessionist groups and found the allegations in the leader's own statements: Ibid., 7.

[39] Ibid., 4.

date – and particularly those which have come from the Centre for Peace and Conflict Studies – have fallen well short of the mark in so far as they claim that the legal elements of the international crime of genocide have been clearly established.[40]

9.3 The Biak Tribunal

It was in the wake of these highly controversial genocide accusations that the Biak Tribunal was convened in 2013 at the request of the Centre for Peace and Conflict Studies to inquire into a single massacre which occurred fifteen years before on the West Papuan island of Biak. The tribunal was open to the public and a video of the proceedings and many of the documents that were adduced as evidence are available on the Biak Massacre Citizens' Tribunal website.[41] The following analysis is based on this online documentation of the tribunal, rather than the physical proceedings, which the author was unable to attend. As explained on the Biak Massacre Citizens' Tribunal website, the Tribunal was coordinated by a committee comprising six Australian academics – including Peter King, Jim Elmslie and Camellia Webb-Gannon of the Centre for Peace and Conflict Studies – and the West Papuan activist, Frederika Korain.[42] It took the form of an inquiry 'in the nature of a coronial inquest' and aimed to determine generally what occurred during the Biak massacre, rather than to charge individuals or the Indonesian state with responsibility for the events. The Tribunal website says nothing more about its aims, but writing after the event, one of the organisers explained that the Tribunal also aimed to encourage Jakarta and the United Nations to 'enact justice for the survivors of the massacre'.[43] Elsewhere, three other

40 Of course, genocide was initially theorised by Raphael Lemkin as encompassing a much broader scope of acts than is contained in the current legal definition, including political, economic and cultural genocide: William Schabas, *Genocide in International Law: The Crime of Crimes* (Cambridge University Press, 2009) 173. While the proposal to include 'political groups' was specifically rejected during the Genocide Convention negotiations, many activists and social scientists use the term 'genocide' to connote the broader concept that was originally conceived by Lemkin.

41 Biak Massacre Citizens' Tribunal, www.biak-tribunal.org.

42 The other committee members were Jason MacLeod, a lecturer in community development at the University of Queensland; Budi Hernawan, an affiliate of the Regulatory Institutions Network at the Australian National University; and Eben Kirksey, a lecturer in anthropology at the University of New South Wales.

43 Jason Macleod, '"Laughing at Leviathan: Sovereignty and Audience in West Papua" by Danilyn Rutherford' (2014) 116(4) *American Anthropologist* 891.

organisers have noted that it similarly aimed to 'allow [the] bloody event and its victims to be appropriately marked on the historical record' and to identify the 'perpetrators and masterminds of the massacre'.[44]

Two well-respected legal professionals served as Counsel Assisting: former New South Wales (NSW) Director of Public Prosecutions, Nicholas Cowdery AM (Member of the Order of Australia), QC (Queen's Counsel), and Gustav Kawer, a West Papuan human rights lawyer.[45] One of the two 'Presiding Jurists' was the Honourable John Dowd AO (Officer of the Order of Australia), QC, who was a former Justice of the Supreme Court of NSW and a former NSW attorney general and current president of the International Commission of Jurists Australia. Keith Suter, a public intellectual and chairperson of the NSW branch of the International Commission of Jurists was appointed as the second 'Presiding Jurist'. In addition, two Australian Senior Counsel – Graham Turnbull SC and Daniel O'Gorman SC – had a role as 'interested parties' and challenged the evidence which was raised in the proceedings as if acting on behalf of the Indonesian government (which had not responded to the invitation to attend) and individuals named in the proceedings as alleged perpetrators, respectively.

9.3.1 The Tribunal Proceedings

Although the Biak Tribunal was convened at the request of the Centre for Peace and Conflict Studies, affiliated academics did not play an active role in the Tribunal itself. The proceedings opened with a twenty-minute introduction by Cowdery QC. He began by locating the Biak massacre within the broader context of the West Papuan struggle for self-determination, arguing that the people of West Papua have never accepted the 'fraudulent act of free choice' and 'continue to agitate for genuine democratic choice'. He explained that the events in Biak occurred in response to a peaceful protest in which the Morning Star flag, a symbol of the West Papuan independence movement, was raised and people occupied the Biak town centre. He alleged that Indonesian troops opened fire on peaceful protesters on the morning of 6 July, after four days of protest. While Cowdery QC explained that it was necessary to

[44] Jim Elmslie, Camellia Webb-Gannon and Peter King, 'West Papua making waves' (2013) 74 *Australian Options* 21.

[45] In Australia, senior barristers (lawyers specialising in advocacy) are referred to as Queen's Counsel (QC) or since 1994, Senior Counsel (SC).

convene the Biak Tribunal to investigate the Biak massacre because calls for a formal inquiry in Indonesia had been ignored, he made no explicit reference to the source of the jurisdiction or legitimacy of the tribunal, or to the many other peoples' tribunals which proceeded it, although they could potentially have been claimed as a source of legitimacy.

Four witnesses gave evidence in the course of the day: Ferry Marisan, who worked for a non-government organisation documenting the massacre immediately after it occurred; Eben Kirksey, who witnessed the events while he was on university exchange (and who was one of the tribunal organisers); Tineke Rumakabu, who claimed to have been kidnapped and tortured by security forces after supporting the protest; and an anonymous witness whose testimony does not appear on the Tribunal website. Although these witnesses were 'sworn in', their evidence was supplemented with several prerecorded video testimonies which were not produced under oath. This included a statement by Philip Karma, who was the leader of the Biak protest and is now in prison in West Papua, and a statement from Octovianus Mote, who was the local bureau chief of the newspaper *Kompas* at the time of the massacre. Two written 'testimonies' were read for the audience: an anonymous 'story' of a family being rescued, and the 'story' of Agus, who witnessed the massacre at the age of twelve. A written statement by Edmund McWilliams, who was serving as Political Counselor in the US Embassy in Jakarta and visited Biak shortly after the massacre, was also read aloud.

Two Australian barristers – Graham Turnbull SC and Daniel O'Gorman SC – were appointed to present 'alternative points of view' on the evidence. While making it clear that he was not acting under instructions, Turnbull SC advanced the kind of arguments which might have been made by the Indonesian government. He noted that much of the 'evidence' heard by the tribunal would be inadmissible in an Australian court. He questioned whether the protests were in fact peaceful, implying that it was lawful for security forces to engage in some use of force for the purpose of self-defence. He suggested that it was 'inappropriate' to talk about the question of self-determination in investigating the Biak massacre and warned that the Presiding Jurists should not reach a conclusion 'based on notions that are coloured by the struggle for West Papuan independence'.

Another 'alternative point of view' was presented by O'Gorman SC, who advanced arguments as if acting on behalf of the individuals who had been directly accused by witnesses in the course of the proceedings. He contended that it was unfair to implicate individuals based on 'evidence' that would not be accepted as such in a court of law and urged that the Presiding Jurists should only make findings about the Biak massacre in general, rather than findings about the culpability of the specific individuals responsible.

The proceedings were closed by Cowdery QC, who suggested what conclusions the Tribunal should reach. He concluded that members of the Indonesian security forces had deliberately killed people who were peacefully protesting to demand their right to self-determination. This massacre occurred after four days of demonstrations, which had allowed the Indonesian authorities ample time to assess the situation. Accordingly, Cowdery QC argued that the decision to surround the demonstrators and fire on them was planned. He noted that after the shooting, many other people were taken to naval vessels and never seen alive again. There was evidence that many had been tortured. Although Cowdery QC did not name any individuals, he noted that the Tribunal had access to reports which identify the senior military officers who were allegedly responsible, so findings could be made about individual liability.[46]

9.3.2 The Tribunal Verdict

The Tribunal verdict was published five months later, on 16 December 2013. This eight-page, unsigned document reaches only three conclusions, which are narrower than those suggested by Cowdery QC. First, military and police forces attacked a peaceful demonstration, leading to 'the deaths and injuries of scores of people and the detention of a further group of the demonstrators'.[47] Secondly, 'a large number' of people were killed by Indonesian security forces, while 'some of the women and girls' were raped and sexually mutilated.[48] Thirdly, the Indonesian government has tried to 'downplay the seriousness of the actions' and has not commenced legal proceedings against any of those individuals responsible.[49] There is no explicit reference to the right to self-determination. The verdict does not name any of the individuals allegedly responsible

[46] Although Cowdery QC did not name any of the accused, the Biak Tribunal website, above n. 41, has published a list of 'Possible Biak Culprits', which names ten individuals and briefly describes their alleged involvement.

[47] *Biak Massacre Citizens' Tribunal Verdict*, 16 December 2013, 2, www.biak-tribunal.org/wp-content/uploads/2013/12/Biak-Tribunal_Final-Verdict_16-December-2013.pdf.

[48] Ibid. [49] Ibid.

for the massacre, despite Cowdery QC's suggestion that the Presiding Jurists had access to sufficient information to do so.

Based on its restrained conclusions, the verdict makes five recommendations. First, the Indonesian government should hold an independent judicial inquiry. Secondly, the Indonesian government should institute criminal proceedings against members of the armed forces and police who may have committed 'crimes and crimes against humanity'.[50] Thirdly, the Australian and US governments, which were responsible for training Indonesian military and naval officers, should pressure the Indonesian government to commence criminal investigations. Fourthly, Indonesian security forces 'should carry out such disciplinary proceedings as are appropriate under Indonesian law'.[51] Finally, the Indonesian government should establish a body to pay damages to those injured.[52]

Remarkably, the verdict is almost devoid of legal sources or legal reasoning. It does not explicitly attempt to explain how the acts it documents might be understood as violations of international law or Indonesian law. In fact, the verdict does not make any direct reference to sources of law at all. Although it recommends that '[a]n investigation should be carried out ... into the ... crimes against humanity which occurred on 6 July 1998', thus implying that at least some of the acts documented amount to crimes against humanity, this concept is not defined.[53] According to the definition in the Rome Statute of the International Criminal Court (Rome Statute), crimes against humanity occur when acts, including torture, rape and persecution, are 'committed as part of a widespread or systematic attack directed against any civilian population, with knowledge of the attack'.[54] The Biak Tribunal documented these kinds of acts and the evidence as summarised by Cowdery QC suggests that the attack was planned. To suggest that the Biak massacre amounted to a crime against humanity for which individual perpetrators can be held individually criminally liable is not implausible on the basis of the Tribunal findings.[55] However, neither the verdict nor the Tribunal proceedings engaged in any explicit legal reasoning in order

[50] This wording is curious, since legally 'crimes and crimes against humanity' is a tautology; it would be more accurate to write 'crimes, including crimes against humanity'.

[51] *Biak Massacre Citizens' Tribunal Verdict*, above n. 47, 2. [52] Ibid. [53] Ibid.

[54] Rome Statute of the International Criminal Court, Rome, 17 July 1998, 2187 UNTS 3, in force 1 July 2002, article 7.

[55] Whether or not specific individuals could be held criminally liable, the actions of the military and police involve violations by Indonesia of its obligations under international human rights law.

to reach this conclusion. Indeed, the reference to 'crimes against humanity' in the verdict is so offhand that it may not even be referring to a legal category but rather a moral condemnation. This means that the Biak Tribunal cannot be understood as an example of a peoples' tribunal that plays an important function in attempting to expand international legal norms, since it eschews legal reasoning processes. However, this does not mean that the Tribunal was insignificant. Having already established in some detail the nature and content of the Biak Tribunal, the final section of this chapter will proceed to an evaluation of the ways in which the tribunal can be considered important.

9.4 Evaluating the Significance of the Biak Tribunal

In evaluating the significance of the Biak Tribunal, it is vital to acknowledge that three years later, none of the tribunal's recommendations have been implemented by the governments to which they were addressed, and no criminal proceedings have been instituted. Eben Kirksey, one of the academics involved in establishing the tribunal, optimistically suggests that 'the government . . . may still investigate and prosecute this case. It is really too soon to tell'.[56] However, the fact is that it was never reasonable to expect the tribunal to result in prosecutions, which are unlikely to occur unless there is a radical change in the political situation. In part this is because there are significant barriers to prosecuting the massacre as a crime against humanity. Indonesia's Human Rights Court Act of 2000 established crimes against humanity as a domestic offence for the first time.[57] Although this statute allows for retroactive prosecution – which would be necessary to apply this new offence to the Biak massacre which occurred in 1998 – retroactive prosecution cannot occur in the permanent human rights courts that were created by the 2000 legislation, but rather would only be permissible in a special ad hoc human rights court.[58] Such a court must be created upon recommendation from Parliament and pursuant to a subsequent Presidential Decree.[59] Neither is likely to be attained at the present time, as there is very little political support for accountability.

[56] Email from Eben Kirksey to author, 10 November 2014.

[57] Undang-Undang Republik Indonesia Nomor 26 Tahun 2000 Tentang Pengadilan Hak Asasi Manusia (hereafter Human Rights Court Act), article 9 (author's translation).

[58] Human Rights Court Act, article 43.

[59] Ibid. Even if such a court was established, prosecution may nevertheless be constitutionally impermissible, since in the *Masykur Abdul Kadir* case the Constitutional Court found

Indeed, even activists' calls for the Indonesian Human Rights Commission (Komnas HAM) to release the findings of its historical investigation into the massacre – the results of which could be made public without any prosecutions necessarily following, as has been the case with its investigation of the 1965 massacres – continue to be ignored.[60] There is no likely prospect of international prosecution either. The Rome Statute had not entered into force in 1998, and at any rate, Indonesia is not a party, so the International Criminal Court has no jurisdiction to prosecute the Biak massacre as a crime against humanity in The Hague.[61] This means prosecution could only be achieved outside Indonesia if one of the accused individuals was to travel to another state which then chose to exercise universal jurisdiction.

Prosecuting the 'ordinary' offences – such as rape and murder – that were committed during the Biak massacre would not require the establishment of an ad hoc human rights court since these were already offences in Indonesian law at the time of their commission. However, there are compelling political reasons why the Indonesian government would be reluctant to do even this. For one thing, the Indonesian state allegedly still uses its security forces to violently suppress West Papuans,[62] so prosecuting security agents for the Biak massacre would mean punishing them for the same kind of acts the state still requires them to commit. Further, and no doubt of greater concern to the Indonesian government, is the problem that officially acknowledging the massacre by prosecuting those individuals responsible could strengthen the West Papuan claim for independence, at least politically if not legally. In light of these broader concerns, it was never realistic to expect that the Biak Tribunal would lead to accountability within Indonesia. The fact that the tribunal did not achieve this goal says little about its efficacy as a peoples' tribunal and does not mean that it was inconsequential.

On the contrary, when assessed in the broader context of scholarly activism about human rights violations in West Papua, the tribunal is significant in several respects. First, certain aspects of the tribunal's design allowed for the examination of the Biak massacre in a way that

that a defendant could not be prosecuted for a crime that did not exist at the time he allegedly committed it: Indonesian Constitutional Court Decision No. 013/PUU-I/2003.

60 Yuliana Lantipo, 'Komnas HAM Didesak Buka Kembali Kasus Biak Berdarah' ['Komnas HAM Urged to Reopen the Biak Massacre Case'], *Tabloidjubi*, 26 February 2015, http://tabloidjubi.com/16/2015/02/26/komnas-ham-didesak-buka-kembali-kasus-biak-berdarah/. See also Wieringa, Chapter 5 in this volume.

61 Rome Statute of the International Criminal Court, above n. 54.

62 See, e.g., the sources referred to above n. 21.

was more credible than the genocide allegations which preceded it. Part of this credibility arose from the tribunal's design as an 'inquest' which focused primarily on the determination of 'facts' about the Biak massacre, rather than on attempting to categorise these 'facts' as amounting to a particular crime. This allowed the tribunal to establish a detailed picture of the Biak massacre in a way that appears more politically neutral than if the proceedings had focused on establishing that the Indonesian government had committed crimes against humanity or genocide. Further, although the Tribunal was generally pro-West Papuan and made occasional mention of self-determination, there was a deliberate attempt to avoid bias by ensuring that a variety of points of view were heard.

In particular, the appointment of Turnbull SC and O'Gorman SC as 'interested individuals' to represent the interests of the Indonesian government and named individuals was effective in making the tribunal at least appear to be attempting to represent both sides. The separation between Cowdery QC, who led the proceedings and made the most wide-ranging accusations as Counsel Assisting, and the Presiding Jurists, who made no mention of self-determination in the tribunal verdict, furthered the appearance of impartiality. Additionally, a great deal of credibility emanated simply from the reputation of the legal professionals who were involved. Together, these features of the tribunal meant that it was able to investigate the Biak massacre in a relatively credible way.

Secondly, although the tribunal was credible in part because it avoided the controversial genocide issue, the record produced in the course of the proceedings could nevertheless be useful for activists seeking to advance this claim elsewhere. Since the Biak massacre is described as one of the prohibited acts of killing which are said to constitute the West Papuan genocide,[63] creating a detailed public record of the Biak massacre potentially strengthens a specific component of this accusation. Indeed, it seems that this is partly why the tribunal was convened. As Jim Elmslie, one of the Tribunal organisers, explained:

> [T]he purpose of the tribunal was to create an official record of the atrocity. ... We thought if we could establish, to a large degree of accuracy, the details of one event, it would be powerful and useful.[64]

[63] See, e.g., Brundige et al., above n. 22, 44, 63.

[64] Elmsie, cited in Marni Cordell, 'West Papuans tortured, killed and dumped at sea, Citizens' Tribunal Hears', *The Guardian*, 13 December 2013, www.theguardian.com/world/2013/dec/13/west-papuans-tortured-killed-and-dumped-at-sea-tribunal-hears.

According to Elmslie, making a record of the Biak massacre constitutes a vital step in the larger task of exposing 'the broader pattern of Indonesian occupation'.[65] There are several components of the documentary record created by the Tribunal which could be used to help support this broader claim. In addition to the Tribunal verdict, there is also the record held on the Biak Massacre Citizens' Tribunal website, which features videos of almost the entire proceedings. Further, the Tribunal was covered in several mainstream media publications (discussed in greater detail in the following paragraphs), thus creating a secondary record. While much of this evidence would be excluded from official criminal prosecutions as hearsay, nevertheless, having such material assembled together and effectively 'accredited' by respected legal experts creates an important record for activist purposes. It is precisely this kind of detailed documentary material that activists need if they are to make a convincing demand that the international community investigate systematic human rights violations – including crimes against humanity or genocide – in West Papua.[66]

Thirdly, the tribunal was important because it attracted significant media coverage about the Biak massacre and human rights violations in West Papua more generally. At least eighteen mainstream media pieces covered the tribunal, including ten articles in Indonesian newspapers,[67]

65 Ibid.

66 Indeed, the Tribunal's findings have been used in this kind of broader campaign. One of the Tribunal organisers, Camellia Webb-Gannon, reports that in March 2015 several Tribunal participants presented the Tribunal evidence to a group of federal Australian politicians as part of a campaign to raise political awareness about human rights violations in West Papua and that the evidence was 'met with a favorable tripartisan reception': Camellia Webb-Gannon, 'Salvaging democracy for West Papuans in the face of Australia-Indonesia obstruction' (2015) 13(45) *Asia-Pacific Journal* 1.

67 Ati Nurbaiti, 'After Geneva "Makar", tolerance and reporting rape', *Jakarta Post*, 14 July 2013, www.thejakartapost.com/news/2013/07/14/view-point-after-geneva-makar-tolerance-and-reporting-rape.html; 'Berita Kematian dari Sydney' ['Reporting death from Sydney'], *Majalah Tempo*, 14 July 2014, http://majalah.tempo.co/konten/2013/07/14/NAS/143036/Berita-Kematian-dari-Sydney/20/favicon.ico; Muhaimin, 'Australia Tekan Indonesia Soal Kasus Papua Barat' ['Australia pressures Indonesia about the West Papua problem'], *Sindonews*, 16 December 2013, http://international.sindonews.com/read/817501/40/australia-tekan-indonesia-soal-kasus-papua-barat; Haris Kurniawan, 'Indonesia Diminta Tak Takut Tekanan Australia' ['Indonesia shouldn't be scared of Australian pressure'], *Sindonews*, 17 December 2013, http://nasional.sindonews.com/read/817606/13/indonesia-diminta-tak-takut-tekanan-australia; Egidius Patnistik, 'Majelis Warga Australia Desak Indonesia Selidiki Pembantaian di Biak' ['An Australian Citizen's Assembly urges Indonesia to investigate the Biak massacre'], *Kompas*, 17 December 2013, http://internasional.kompas.com/read/2013/12/17/0859281/Majelis.Warga.Australia.Desak.Indonesia.Selidiki

three pieces in the Australian media,[68] and two articles from the Melanesian region,[69] as well as coverage in UK[70] and US newspapers[71] and on New Zealand radio.[72] Perhaps the most important of these was an eight-minute feature on the Australian Broadcasting Corporation's *7.30 Report*, a well respected current affairs program which plays on prime time television. This volume of media coverage was an important achievement in itself, since the issue of human rights violations in West Papua is seldom covered in mainstream media, let alone when the violations in question had occurred fifteen years earlier.

Moreover, although peoples' tribunals have often been criticised in media coverage, the reports on the Biak Tribunal were mainly positive, with some pieces even written in such a way as to suggest that the Tribunal was officially sanctioned.[73] A piece about the Tribunal on the

.Pembantaian.di.Biak; Novi Christiastuti Adiputri, 'Pengadilan Australia: TNI Perkosa dan Bunuh Anak-anak Papua Barat 1998' ['Australian Court: TNI raped and killed West Papuan children in 1998'], *DetikNews*, 17 December 2013, http://news.detik.com/read/2013/12/17/095024/2444013/1148/pengadilan-australia-tni-perkosa-dan-bunuh-anak-anak-papua-barat-1998?topnews; 'Kata Wiranto Soal Pengadilan Australia Sebut TNI Bunuh Anak Papua pada 1998' ['Wiranto on the Australian Court that says the TNI killed West Papuans in 1998'], *DetikNews*, 17 December 2013, http://news.detik.com/berita/2444580/kata-wiranto-soal-pengadilan-australia-sebut-tni-bunuh-anak-papua-pada-1998; Benny Mawel, 'Komnas HAM Akan Bawa Kasus Biak Ke Pengadilan Ham Berat' ['Komnas HAM will bring the Biak case to the Human Rights Court'], *Tabloidjubi*, 20 December 2013, https://tabloidjubi.com/16/2013/12/20/komnas-ham-akan-bawa-kasus-biak-ke-pengadilan-ham-berat/ Benny Mawel, 'Tragedi Biak Berdarah, Diadili Di Australia' ['The Biak tragedy is tried in Australia'], *Tabloidjubi*, 5 July 2013, http://tabloidjubi.com/16/2013/07/05/tragedi-biak-berdarah-diadili-di-australia/.

68 Matt Peacock, 'Searching for the truth about a massacre in West Papua', *7.30 Report*, 16 December 2013, www.abc.net.au/7.30/content/2013/s3912701.htm; Alison Bevege, 'Light shed on massacre', *Northern Territory News*, 18 December 2013, 18, www.territorystories.nt.gov.au/bitstream/10070/249251/18/ntn18dec13018x.pdf; Sally Whyte, 'No future for me in West Papua': Activist flees to Australia after "abduction" attempt', *Crikey*, 31 July 2014, www.crikey.com.au/2014/07/31/no-future-for-me-in-west-papua-activist-flees-to-australia-after-abduction-attempt/.

69 'West Papua Case', *Fiji Times*, 19 December 2013; 'Atrocities in West Papua Revealed', *Solomon Star*, 2 June 2014, www.solomonstarnews.com/news/regional/2243-atrocities-in-west-papua-revealed.

70 Cordell, above n. 21.

71 Prodita Sabarini, 'Rights should be part of US "pivot" to Asia', *Boston Globe*, 6 January 2014, www.bostonglobe.com/opinion/2014/01/06/rights-should-part-pivot-asia/RfqI1Ij24ZIwmNMZoXFJIO/story.html.

72 'ICJ calls for official inquiry into Biak massacre', *Radio New Zealand*, 19 December 2013, www.radionz.co.nz/international/pacific-news/231388/icj-calls-for-official-inquiry-into-biak-massacre.

73 For example, Klinghoffer and Klinghoffer note that the media criticised the Russell Tribunal for its impartiality: above n. 8, 7. Falk similarly notes that 'mainstream media

Indonesian website, *Sindonews*, describes it as 'a court in the University of Sydney' which was 'headed by the former attorney general of NSW', without mentioning that this 'court' was convened by civil society and had no legal force.[74] The same article claims that 'Australia is pressuring Indonesia to take responsibility' for the Biak massacre, incorrectly implying that the Tribunal findings were supported by the Australian government. This is despite the fact that neither the Rudd Labor government, in power while the tribunal was held, nor the Abbott Liberal Coalition, which had gained power by the time the verdict was announced, made any public comment on the tribunal.

Similarly representing the Tribunal as if it were an official Australian initiative, an article in Indonesia's most respected newspaper, *Kompas*, describes the Biak Tribunal as an 'Australian Peoples' Tribunal',[75] while an article in *Detik News* describes it as an 'Australian court' inquiring into the 'massacre of Biak citizens'. Also slightly misleading was the coverage on Radio New Zealand entitled, 'ICJ Calls for Official Inquiry into Biak Massacre', which might be read by a lay person as meaning that the International Court of Justice – the primary judicial branch of the United Nations – was demanding an inquiry, rather than two members of the non-government organisation the International Commission of Jurists.[76]

To a large extent these misleading representations can be attributed to mistranslation and a lack of familiarity on the part of journalists with both legal terms and the concept of a peoples' tribunal. Nevertheless, the effect was advantageous for the convenors of the Biak Tribunal because it meant that not only did the proceedings attract media attention but also some of this coverage inadvertently added to the perceived legitimacy of the Tribunal as a legal institution.

It is difficult to assess what effect, if any, the tribunal and the way it was covered by the media has had on the Indonesian government. An article published soon after the Tribunal's verdict claimed that media coverage of the proceedings had caused Komnas HAM to return the case to the list of serious human rights violations it planned to investigate.[77] Almost two years later, in November 2015, Komnas HAM announced

attacked the legitimacy of the Russell initiative, ignored its presentation of evidence ... and scorned its conclusions': Richard A. Falk, 'Keeping Nuremberg Alive' in Giuliano Amato et al. (eds.), *Marxismo, Democrazia e Diritto dei Popoli: Scritti in Onore di Lelio Basso* [*Marxism, Democracy and Peoples' Law: Essays in Honour of Lelio Basso*] (Franco Angeli Editore, 1979), 811, 813.

74 Muhaimin, above n. 67. 75 Patnistik, above n. 67.

76 Radio New Zealand, above n. 72. 77 Mawel, 'Komnas HAM Akan, above n. 67.

that it was establishing a team to 'audit' human rights violations in West Papua from 1969 to the present day, including the Biak massacre.[78] While there are still yet to be any prosecutions, a special team to investigate gross violations of human rights was formally established in 2016, and at the beginning of 2017 the Coordinating Minister for Political, Legal and Security Affairs announced that the government would prioritise investigating five historical cases of gross human rights violations in West Papua, including the Biak massacre.[79] This represents a considerable step forward after fifteen years of official denial that the massacre occurred. Of course, this Komnas HAM investigation is not directly attributable to the public scrutiny caused by the Biak Tribunal alone, but can more plausibly by understood as a result of decades of activists' attempts to draw attention to the plethora of human rights violations that have been perpetrated in West Papua. Nevertheless, the Biak Tribunal was an important initiative within the history of this activism, which by drawing domestic and international media attention to the massacre fifteen years after the event helped make it politically infeasible for the Indonesian government to continue to deny the egregious human rights violations occurring in West Papua.

9.5 Conclusion

This chapter has argued that the Biak Tribunal, when considered within the particular context of scholarly activism about human rights violations in West Papua, was significant in several ways. Admittedly the Tribunal was less ambitious and less grounded in legal analysis than those which have sought to change international legal norms. Nor have any of the tribunal's recommendations been implemented – most importantly, there has been no independent judicial inquiry and the Indonesian government is yet to institute criminal proceedings against any of those responsible. However, following the government's announcement in 2017 that it would prioritise investigating historical human rights abuses in West Papua, including the Biak massacre, the Tribunal's aim

[78] Maria Rita, 'Komnas Bentuk Tim Audit HAM Papua' ['Komnas team to audit Papuan human rights'], *Tempo*, 19 November 2015, http://nasional.tempo.co/read/news/2015/11/19/078720306/komnas-bentuk-tim-audit-ham-papua.

[79] Kristian Erdianto, 'Pemerintah Prioritaskan Penuntasan Lima Kasus Pelanggaran HAM di Papua' ['Government prioritises resolving five instances of human rights violations in Papua'], *Kompas*, 30 January 2017, http://nasional.kompas.com/read/2017/01/30/20540371/pemerintah.prioritaskan.penuntasan.lima.kasus.pelanggaran.ham.di.papua.

of spurring an official investigation into the massacre is now one step closer to being realised. It remains to be seen whether this investigation will result in any more facts about the Biak massacre being revealed to the public, let alone whether it could lead to the prosecutions the Tribunal recommended. Nevertheless, this new investigation is an important development which is at least partly attributable to the cumulative pressure caused by decades of activism on human rights violations in West Papua, including the Biak Tribunal.

Further, the Tribunal has already made some other important contributions. First, aspects of the way the Tribunal was organised – in particular, the adoption of the form of an inquest, the appointment of two Senior Counsel as 'interested individuals' to challenge the evidence and the separation between accusations and verdict – allowed for the realisation of some relatively credible findings about the Biak massacre. Secondly, the tribunal produced an important documentary record that could be used by activists in their more wide-ranging accusations that Indonesia has committed genocide. Thirdly, the decision of the Centre for Peace and Conflict Studies to organise a tribunal was a successful strategy for attracting a significant amount of media attention to a single atrocity which occurred fifteen years before in a conflicted region. Thus, although the Biak Tribunal does not stand out in its form or reasoning when compared to other peoples' tribunals, within the context of West Papuan activism, it was a significant step in an incremental series of efforts which might one day result in justice and accountability for West Papuans.

10

Assessing the Contribution of the Latin American Water Tribunal and Transnational Environmental Law*

BELÉN OLMOS GIUPPONI

10.1 Introduction

Access to water has become a topical issue in the scholarly literature. However, the enforcement of water rights has proved to be a difficult task. Transnational initiatives at the international and regional levels have arisen to enforce specific legislation relating to water resources. Since its inception in 1998, the Latin American Water Tribunal (Tribunal Latinoamericano del Agua) (LAWT or Tribunal)[1] has emerged as a non-governmental body with a multidisciplinary composition and a mandate based on both formal and informal sources of law.[2]

The LAWT's activities are based on international environmental law and relevant environmental principles, namely, the sustainable development principle and the precautionary principle. Within its mandate, the Tribunal is committed to protecting water resources in the region and addresses issues at public hearings such as privatisation of water utilities, mining activities, access to water in indigenous territories and water pollution.[3] The legal framework the Tribunal applies includes relevant international environmental law norms that protect natural resources;

* An earlier version of this chapter was published as Belén Olmos Giupponi, 'Transnational environmental law and grass-root initiatives: The Case of the Latin American Water Tribunal' (2016) 5(1) *Transnational Environmental Law* 145–74.

[1] The LAWT was established in 1998 and, initially, its activities only covered Central America, being originally known as the Central American Water Tribunal and subsequently renamed the Latin American Water Tribunal.

[2] See Ramses Wessel, 'Informal international law-making as a new form of world legislation?' (2011) 8 *International Organizations Law Review* 253. See further Alan Boyle and Christine Chinkin, *The Making of International Law* (Oxford University Press, 2007).

[3] The complaints submitted are available in Spanish on the LAWT website, http://tragua.com/audiencias.

international human rights law (in particular, the 1989 International Labour Organization (ILO) Convention No. 169 concerning Indigenous and Tribal Peoples in Independent Countries[4] and the 2007 United Nations Declaration on the Rights of Indigenous Peoples[5]); and the principles set out in the Latin American Water Declaration.[6]

In this chapter, I analyse the role played by the LAWT in resolving environmental disputes over water resources. The chapter argues that, whereas the traditional model for interstate dispute settlement offers only limited possibilities for redress to non-state actors (mainly individuals and groups), the LAWT provides them with the opportunity to present their demands in a quasi-judicial forum. The chapter also looks at how international environmental law accommodates global civil society approaches as the driving force behind transnational lawmaking processes.[7]

10.2 Introducing the LAWT: Procedure and Theoretical Conceptualisation

From the outset, the LAWT was conceived as an autonomous and independent international forum for environmental justice endowed with the mandate to serve as an alternative justice mechanism. It operates in a manner that is complementary to other formal administrative and judicial bodies to find solutions to water resources-related problems of concern to Latin American citizens, overcoming the 'democratic deficit in water management' and the 'environmental impunity situation'.[8]

10.2.1 LAWT Procedure

The LAWT may receive cases involving allegations of damage or threatened damage to water resources in Latin American states.[9] Social organisations,

[4] Geneva, 27 June 1989, 1650 *UNTS* 383, in force 5 September 1991.

[5] GA Res 61/295, UN Doc A/RES/61/295, 13 September 2007.

[6] LAWT, Declaración Latinoamericana del Agua [Latin American Water Declaration], 1998, http://tragua.com/quienes-somos/declaracion-latinoamericana-del-agua/.

[7] See generally M. J. Warning, *Transnational Public Governance: Networks, Law and Legitimacy* (Palgrave Macmillan, 2009).

[8] Carmen Maganda, 'The Latin American Water Tribunal and the Need for Public Spaces for Social Participation in Water Governance' in Jan Feyen, Kelly Shannon and Matthew Neville (eds.), *Water and Urban Development Paradigms: Towards an Integration of Engineering, Design and Management Approaches* (CRC Press, 2009) 687, 688.

[9] Complaints may also be submitted online: http://tragua.com/denuncias.

community groups and individuals who are aware of practices that threaten the sustainability of water resources in Latin America may forward a motivated complaint grounded on robust scientific evidence.[10] Allegations must thus be supported by compelling scientific evidence that a threat of environmental damage or actual damage to water resources exists.[11] The cases heard by the LAWT concern different water-related disputes: some deal with national disputes (individuals or groups and governments, interregional conflicts), while others involve transboundary cases. There are also cases against private corporations involved in the privatisation of water supplies in various countries.[12] The Tribunal has dealt with more than seventy different cases.[13]

Following the submission of a complaint, the LAWT Scientific and Technical Commission evaluates the application thoroughly and examines the supporting evidence in light of the precautionary principle as embodied in Principle 15 of the Rio Declaration: 'Where there are threats of serious or irreversible damage, lack of full scientific certainty shall not be used as a reason for postponing cost-effective measures to prevent environmental degradation'.[14]

As a general rule, the Scientific and Technical Commission 'selects cases for public hearing that are the most representative and best supported causes in terms of content and coherence' and, in particular, those cases involving actions or projects that 'pose the greatest hazard to the largest population'.[15] The Tribunal can then decide whether to hold a public hearing at which plaintiffs present their case and the defendant

[10] LAWT Statute, a summary of which can be found at http://tragua.com/wp-content/uploads/2012/04/FundamentosTLA.pdf.

[11] Javier Bogantes and Jorine Muiser, *Estrategias erróneas y la vulneración de los sistemas hídricos en América Latina* [*Erroneous Strategies and the Endangering of Water Systems in Latin America*] (LAWT, 2011), 86.

[12] Javier Bogantes, 'Tribunal Latinoamericano del Agua: Una alternativa de justicia' ['The Latin American Water Tribunal: An Alternative Form of Justice'], paper presented at the Workshop on Peoples' Tribunals, Rome, 28–29 September 2013 (author's translation).

[13] As of the end of 2016, the Tribunal had held ten public hearings: Costa Rica (2000 and 2004); Mexico (2006); Guadalajara, Mexico (2007); Guatemala (2008); Istanbul, Turkey (2009); Argentina (2012); Guatemala City (2015); El Salvador (2016). and Mexico Federal District (2016): see http://tragua.com/audiencias.

[14] Rio Declaration on Environment and Development, *Report of the United Nations Conference on Environment and Development*, Rio de Janeiro, A/CONF.151/26 (Vol. I), Annex I, (3–14 June 1992), Principle 15.

[15] Mikita A. Weaver, 'El Agua No Se Vende: Water is not for sale! The Latin American Water Tribunal as a model for advancing access to water' (2011) 11(3) *Pepperdine Dispute Resolution Law Journal* 519, 526.

has the opportunity to respond to the allegations. Once the decision has been made, the LAWT will formally notify the defendant of its entitlement to appear at a public hearing to exercise its right of defence. Even if a case is not selected for the public hearing, 'technical guidance is still provided to the plaintiffs to help them resolve their conflict because the committee has already performed extensive technical analysis'.[16]

During the LAWT public hearings, selected cases are presented before the jurors who make up the Tribunal. The 'jurors' of the LAWT vary from case to case, as they are selected by the Scientific and Technical Commission from a list of experts.[17] The LAWT's composition is interdisciplinary, comprising not only legal experts but also a diverse range of professionals from fields such as history, literature, anthropology, geology and hydrology.[18] The jurors come mainly from Latin American countries, but may also come from other regions as well.

The 'core principles' that govern the proceedings are systemic analysis, ecocentric ethical principles, indirect evidence and inversion of the burden of the proof.[19] At the hearing, plaintiffs and defendants are each allocated thirty minutes in which to present their claim and defence respectively.[20] Witness testify and may be cross-examined for twenty minutes before the jury. The plaintiffs and defendants then have ten minutes in which to submit a summary of their case and their conclusions. The jurors examine the evidence and may question the witnesses. If necessary, the LAWT may arrange a site visit to assess the severity of the situation described in the complaint.

On completion of the proceedings, the jury deliberates in private to reach a verdict and then publicly announces the verdict, which includes recommendations for the settlement of the dispute. Although the LAWT's 'verdicts' are not judgments in any formal sense, they contribute to generating and raising public pressure on states and increasing the 'visibility' of environmental conflicts. Because the hearings are public and the media devote attention to the cases examined, verdicts contribute to the transparency of the disputes. The public hearings receive media attention and

16 Ibid.

17 For a list of members as of 2014, see LAWT, 'Presentación Institucional', 2014, at http://tragua.com/wp-content/uploads/2012/04/ANEXO-I.-PRESENTACION-INSTITUCIONAL.pdf.

18 This list is illustrative; other professions are also represented in the Scientific and Technical Commission: ibid., 9.

19 LAWT, 'Procedural Rules': see LAWT, 'Presentación Institucional', above n. 17.

20 Ibid.

generate debate in society, which helps organise local communities to protect natural resources. Furthermore, the LAWT organises other dissemination and training activities on sustainable water management in local communities and fosters dialogue between the public authorities in charge of water governance and policy making and the users.[21]

10.3 Conceptualising the Role of the LAWT

Several different theoretical frameworks could be applied to theorise the LAWT's functions and role. In this section, I will explore the 'environmental conflicts' approach, the 'human rights' approach and the 'dispute settlement' approach.

The environmental conflicts approach emphasises the role of the LAWT as a public forum for the resolution of socio-environmental conflicts. Relevant elements of this approach are the recognition of the unequal distribution of natural resources and the struggle by communities to gain access to water resources.[22] This analysis is in line with theoretical contributions from authors such as Escobar on political ecology, with a focus on local communities' social struggle to access and control water resources.[23] From a sociological perspective, theories about 'environmental racism' may also play a role in understanding the discrimination suffered by minorities, especially indigenous and afro-descendant communities, in the enjoyment of environmental goods.[24] These tensions are apparent in the various complaints brought before the LAWT. Local and indigenous communities that take part in the proceedings are often those most exposed to the potential harmful effects of activities that interfere with the enjoyment of the right to water.

[21] Ibid.

[22] Luis Suárez Rojas, 'La Comunidad de Carhuancho y Sus Avatares por el Agua: Una Mirada al Bien Común y Las Desigualdades Persistentes en la Sierra Central, Peru' ['The community of Carhuancho and its vicissitudes with water: a look at the interests of the community and persistent inequalities in Sierra Central, Peru'] (2009) 9(2) *Global Jurist* 1, 19.

[23] Arturo Escobar, 'Difference and conflict in the struggle over natural resources: A political ecology framework' (2006) 49(3) *Development* 6. See also Roldan Muradian, Mauricio Folchi and Joan Martinez-Alier, '"Remoteness" and environmental conflicts: Some insights from the political ecology and economic geography of copper' (2004) 7(3) *International Journal of Sustainable Development* 1.

[24] Michael K. Dorsey, 'Environmental (in) justice: Race, poverty and environment' (1998) 22 *Legal Studies Forum* 501, 501. 'Environmental racism' is defined as the discrimination (based on racial or ethnic considerations) in environmental policy making.

Yet, these communities are unable to assert their rights before national courts because of obstacles created by lack of access to justice or legal standing.[25]

Another theoretical lens through which to view the LAWT's function is the human rights approach.[26] The LAWT is committed under its mandate to safeguard the right to water as recognised and protected in international instruments and Latin American constitutions. The starting point for this approach is the General Comment on the Human Right to Water adopted by the United Nations (UN) Committee on Economic, Social and Cultural Rights;[27] similarly, the UN General Assembly has recognised the human right to water and sanitation.[28] More recently, in 2014, the Community of Latin American and Caribbean States (CELAC) adopted the Declaration on the Human Right to Drinking Water and Sanitation.[29]

These developments in international human rights law have informed and impacted national law reforms.[30] Over the last decade, there has been

[25] Adam Davidson-Harden, 'Case 22: Latin American Water Tribunal: Using National and International Law to Form a Basis of Water Ethics' in Adam Davidson-Harden, Susan Spronk, David McDonald and Karen Bakker, *Local Control and Management of our Water Commons: Stories of Rising to the Challenge* (Council of Canadians, 2008) 53, www.ourwatercommons.org/sites/default/files/local-control-management-water-commons_0.pdf.

[26] On the interface between the human rights and the environmental regimes, see P. B. Anand, 'Right to water and access to water: An assessment' (2007) 19 *Journal of International Development* 511; Ramin Pejan, 'The right to water: The road to justiciability' (2004) 36 *George Washington International Law Review* 1181, 1182. See generally Philippe Sands, *Principles of International Environmental Law* (Cambridge University Press, 2nd edn., 2003) 294, 297; and Patricia Birnie, Alan Boyle and Catherine Redgwell, *International Law and the Environment* (Oxford University Press, 2009) 284–85; and Edith Brown Weiss, 'The Evolution of International Water Law' in *Collected Courses of the Hague Academy of International Law*, Vol. 331 (Hague Academy of International Law/Martinus Nijhoff, 2007).

[27] Committee on Economic, Social and Cultural Rights, *General Comment No. 15 (2002): The Right to Water (Arts 11 and 12 of the International Covenant on Economic, Social and Cultural Rights)*, 29th sess., E/C.12/2002/11, 20 January 2003.

[28] GA Res 64/292, A/RES/64/292, 28 July 2010.

[29] Declaración Especial sobre el derecho humano al agua potable y el saneamiento, II CUMBRE Doc. 3.21, 28–29 January 2014, http://celac.cubaminrex.cu/sites/default/files/ficheros/doc_3_21_declaracion_agua_y_saneamiento_espanol.pdf.

[30] See, e.g., the EU-wide legislative initiative 'Right2Water' submitted under the Lisbon Treaty. Consequently, the European Commission issued its Communication on the European Citizens' Initiative, 'Water and Sanitation are a Human Right! Water is a Public Good, not a Commodity!', COM, 2014, 177 final, 19 March 2014, http://ec.europa.eu/citizens-initiative/public/initiatives/successful/details/2012/000003.

a trend towards the recognition of access to water as a human right in Latin America. This recognition has taken various forms. Some countries have revised their constitutions to explicitly embody the right to water: examples include Bolivia, Ecuador and Uruguay.[31] In countries where the right is constitutionally guaranteed, the right is directly enforceable in the courts. At the same time, case law that indirectly recognises the right to water has emerged in other Latin American countries which do not have constitutional protection for access to water. This second group includes such countries as Argentina, Colombia, Mexico and Peru, where the right to water has successfully been made explicit by the courts.[32]

The LAWT seeks to protect the right to water and bases its activities on international human rights instruments.[33] The human right to water is often cited in complaints submitted to the LAWT, particularly, in cases dealing with access by local and indigenous communities to water.[34] In this respect, the Tribunal attempts to guarantee non-discriminatory and affordable access by human beings to safe drinking water by making states comply with their international obligations to respect, protect and implement the right to water.

Finally, the dispute resolution approach seeks to examine the features of the LAWT as an alternative forum for the resolution of disputes over water resources.[35] For some scholars, the LAWT could represent a new alternative in the field of international arbitration.[36] The Tribunal also brings an opportunity to reflect on the nature of international environmental dispute resolution.[37] Sands has emphasised the fragmentation in

[31] Constitution of Bolivia (2009), article 16.I; Constitution of Ecuador (2008), article 12; and Constitution of Uruguay (2004), article 47. The texts of these and other Latin American constitutions may be found at Center for Latin American Studies, University of Georgetown, Political Database of the Americas, 'Constitutions and Comparative Constitutional Study, Constitutions by Country', http://pdba.georgetown.edu/Constitutions/constudies.html.

[32] Belén Olmos Giupponi and Martha C. Paz, 'El Derecho al Agua en la Jurisprudencia Argentina y de la Corte Constitucional Colombiana' ['The right to water in Argentine jurisprduence and the case law of the Colombian Constitutional Court'] (2012) *Diario Juridico El Derecho* 1 (Buenos Aires, Argentina).

[33] LAWT, 'Tratados y Declaraciones' ('Treaties and Declarations'), 2014, http://tragua.com/tratados-y-declaraciones/.

[34] Marco Parriciatu and Francesco Sindico, 'Contours of an Indigenous Peoples' Right to Water in Latin America under International Law' (2012) 1 *International Human Rights Law Review* 211.

[35] Weaver, above n. 15, 528. [36] Ibid., 529.

[37] Cesare Romano, 'International Dispute Settlement' in Daniel Bodansky, Jutta Brunnée and Ellen Hey (eds.), *The Oxford Handbook of International Environmental Law* (Oxford University Press, 2007) 1036, 1054.

international adjudication with regard to environmental issues.[38] Boyle and Harrison have pointed out the main problems of environmental dispute resolution, noting the limited possibilities for non-government organisations (NGOs) to participate in the proceedings as a result of restrictive rules relating to legal standing.[39] In addition, Romano underlines the current features of dispute resolution and highlights the atomisation of litigation at both the domestic and international levels, competing and parallel legal regimes, multiplication of actors and levels and the limits of domestic jurisdictions.[40]

Against this background, one should bear in mind the limitations of 'traditional' dispute settlement mechanisms under international environmental law. They all follow the classical 'interstate' treaty-based models. As a general rule, they do not afford access to private actors (whether individuals or corporations). Therefore, traditional dispute settlement mechanisms do not provide clear-cut solutions for holding corporations liable for environmental damage (as in the cases of Union Carbide in India and Chevron/Texaco in Ecuador).[41]

Interest in the development of environmentally tailored dispute resolution mechanisms has increased recently. Among other initiatives, the Permanent Court of Arbitration (PCA) adopted optional rules for the arbitration and conciliation of disputes relating to natural resources and the environment in 2001–2002,[42] and in 1993 the International Court of Justice (ICJ) instituted a Chamber for Environmental Matters;[43] both mechanisms were restricted to interstate claims. In the international trade realm, panels created at the World Bank (1994), the Inter-American Development Bank (1995) and the Asian Development Bank (1995) allow

[38] Philippe Sands, 'Sustainable Development: Treaty, Custom and the Cross-Fertilization of International Law' in Alan Boyle and David Freestone (eds.), *International Law and Sustainable Development* (Oxford University Press, 1999) 39, 42.

[39] Alan Boyle and James Harrison, 'Judicial settlement of international environmental disputes: Current problems' (2013) 4(2) *Journal of International Dispute Settlement* 245, 258.

[40] Romano, above n. 37, 1055. [41] Ibid., 1053.

[42] *PCA Optional Rules for Arbitration of Disputes Relating to the Environment and/or Natural Resources* (2001) and *PCA Optional Rules for Conciliation of Disputes Relating to the Environment and/or Natural Resources* (2002): PCA, 'Environmental Dispute Resolution', https://pca-cpa.org/en/services/arbitration-services/environmental-dispute-resolution/.

[43] In 1993, the ICJ, acting pursuant to article 26(1) of its Statute, created a Chamber for Environmental Matters, which was reconstituted regularly until 2006, when the Court decided not to hold elections to the Chamber, as no State had ever requested that the Chamber deal with a case. ICJ, 'Chambers and Committees', available at www.icj-cij.org/court/index.php?p1=1&p2=4.

individuals or groups to submit requests for inspection of projects financed by international organisations that may adversely impact the environment.[44] While greater attention has been devoted to the study of these different 'formal' dispute settlement arrangements in environmental law, literature dealing with grass-root initiatives such as the LAWT is scarce.[45]

The following sections examine the features of the LAWT from a 'dispute settlement' approach, emphasizing the key elements featured by the LAWT in light of international environmental law. The analysis focuses on the LAWT as a forum for dispute settlement; it also discusses the LAWT's role in the protection of the human right to water.[46]

10.4 The Main Features of the LAWT under International Environmental Law

10.4.1 Antecedents and the Establishment of the LAWT

Despite its denomination, the LAWT is not an international tribunal in the strict sense. The antecedents to the LAWT are the International Water Tribunals held in Rotterdam in 1983[47] and in Amsterdam in 1992.[48] The main feature of these International Water Tribunals was that they 'took as the culprit in that situation not the states involved, but big private companies which were cited as defendants'.[49]

Both tribunals have laid the groundwork for the creation of the LAWT. The 1983 Rotterdam International Water Tribunal presided over cases regarding environmental damage to the Rhine River basin and helped to reinforce environmental policies and strengthen measures

44 Romano, above n. 37, 1054.

45 Birnie, Boyle and Redgwell, above n. 26, 250–67.

46 Daniel Bodansky, 'Is there an international environmental constitution?' (2009) 16 *Indiana Journal of Global Legal Studies* 565, 576.

47 The International Water Tribunal met in Rotterdam, from 3 to 8 October 1983, to examine the cases of pollution in the Rhine, the North Sea and the Wadden Sea.

48 Ellen Hey and André Nollkaemper, 'The Second International Water Tribunal' (1992) 22(2) *Environmental Policy and Law* 82. The Second International Water Tribunal adopted the Declaration of Amsterdam on 27 June 1991. Maguelonne Dejeant-Pons and Marc Pallemaerts (with Sara Fioravanti) (eds.), *Human Rights and the Environment: Compendium of Instruments and Other International Texts on Individual and Collective Rights Relating to the Environment in the International and European Framework* (Council of Europe Publishing, 2002) 104.

49 José Sette-Camara, 'Pollution of International Rivers' in *Collected Courses of the Hague Academy of International Law*, vol. 186 (Hague Academy of International Law/Martinus Nijhoff, 1984) 119, 146.

against water pollution. Specifically, the Tribunal adopted a Declaration regarding Individual Responsibility for the Protection of the Aquatic Environment.[50] In 1992, the Second International Water Tribunal held a public hearing in Amsterdam at which cases from Asia, Africa, America and Oceania regarding water pollution disputes were presented.[51]

More generally, the history of 'water tribunals' dates back to the Water Court of the Plain of Valencia (*Tribunal de las Aguas de Valencia*).[52] In Latin America, the Brazilian National Water Tribunal, which took place in Florianopolis in 1983,[53] constitutes the immediate model of alternative justice that inspired the creation of the LAWT. In several public hearings, the Brazilian tribunal examined the harmful impacts on water systems in Brazil caused by mining, radioactive and agrochemical pollution and the consequences of dam construction.[54]

Following these institutional precedents, the LAWT was established by NGOs in 1998, initially as the Central American Water Tribunal (CAWT); it extended its activities to cover South America from 2005 and from that time became the LAWT.[55] The essential idea behind its creation was to provide a specialised quasi-judicial forum for citizens and communities in Central America to protect sustainable access to water resources. The LAWT therefore embodies features of a peoples' or citizens' tribunal as a commission of inquiry that seeks another form of accountability outside state-organised structures.[56] In particular, the LAWT offers expert knowledge to deal with alleged violations of environmental norms relating to water resources and to provide recommendations for the resolution of conflicts over water resources.[57]

[50] Ibid. 147. See J. Gerard Peet, *International Water Tribunal Rotterdam 3–8 October 1983: Casebook* (International Water Tribunal Foundation, 1983).

[51] See International Water Tribunal Foundation, *The Second International Water Tribunal: Background and Results 1992–1994 The Casebooks* (International Books, 1994).

[52] The Valencia Water Court represents one of the oldest models of justice that has survived until now. It was recognized as Intangible Cultural Heritage by the UN Educational, Scientific and Cultural Organization (UNESCO) in 2009; further information is available at www.tribunaldelasaguas.org/en.

[53] LAWT, 'Antecedentes' ['Precedents'], http://tragua.com/quienes-somos/fundamentos-vision-mision-objetivos. See also Christian Guy Caubet, 'O Tribunal Da Água' (1994) 18 *GEOSUL* 71.

[54] Caubet, ibid., 85.

[55] See LAWT, 'Quiénes Somos' ['Who We Are'], http://tragua.com/quienes-somos.

[56] These tribunals have been established since the 1960s, although international law scholars have devoted little attention to their contribution so far. However, see Andrew Byrnes and Gabrielle Simm, 'Peoples' Tribunals, international law and the use of force' (2013) 36(2) *University of New South Wales Law Journal* 711, 725.

[57] Weaver, above n. 15, 527.

10.4.2 *The Mandate of the LAWT: Enhancing the Enforcement of Water Law*

Under its mandate, the LAWT is committed to preserving water resources and ensuring access to water as a human right for present and future generations.[58] In carrying out its functions, the Tribunal relies on four pillars: (a) alternative justice to traditional legal mechanisms; (b) environmental security; (c) environmental education and awareness of the protection of water systems; and (d) water security and water governance.[59]

The LAWT represents a landmark in the evolution of 'global environmental law'. As Kotzé indicates in his study on global environmental constitutionalism, a consensus exists among commentators on the various causes of the failure of global environmental law, such as

> the lack of compliance with and enforcement of environmental laws, norms and standards; the lack of, or the inadequate participation of civil society in, governance and law-making processes; a general lack of good governance practices; the continued prevalence of environmental injustice and the lack of access to justice; the lack of legitimacy of the actors and the democratic deficits in decision-making structures; the obstacles presented by state sovereignty, unilateral decision-making, abuse of authority and the serving of self-interests by states; the difficulties of holding private entities such as transnational corporations to account for their environmental wrongs; the lack of core ecological and ethical values.[60]

These challenges to the enforcement of environmental law generally are reproduced and sometimes exacerbated when it comes to water access. The LAWT aims to tackle some of these flaws in the global environmental legal system by (a) increasing transnational action and the coordination of environmental NGOs; (b) helping the organisation of local communities defend their rights; and (c) promoting dialogue between governments, corporations, individuals and communities on the sustainable management of water resources. In sum, as Maganda underlines, 'the LAWT's most important contribution comes from its proceedings that encourage forms of institutional social participation that extend beyond simple protest. ... The tribunal's activities create public space within the context of water management.'[61]

[58] LAWT, 'Quiénes Somos', above n. 55. [59] Ibid.

[60] Louis J. Kotzé, 'Arguing global environmental constitutionalism' (2012) 1(1) *Transnational Environmental Law* 199, 202–3.

[61] Maganda, above n. 8, 689.

10.4.3 Proceedings before the LAWT: Public Interest Litigation and Environmental Ethics

Despite certain similarities with international arbitration, proceedings before the LAWT are different. Firstly, the LAWT's structure and proceedings have a quasi-judicial nature. Secondly, the LAWT is rooted in the tradition of 'tribunals of conscience' whereby hearings are held in public. Thirdly, the LAWT's composition, mandate and legal framework differ from those of an formal arbitration tribunal.

The institutional structure of the LAWT comprises three core bodies: the 'Secretariat', the Scientific and Technical Commission and the jury.[62] The Secretariat, headquartered in San José, Costa Rica, facilitates proceedings, organises hearings and is responsible for all related logistical and financial work.[63] The LAWT also benefits from advice from multiple experts to support its specific tasks, ranging from scientific and technical analysis to communication;[64] the Scientific and Technical Commission stands out particularly in this regard. In addition to ensuring that the complaints and case evidence are scientifically justified, the Commission decides whether to hold a public hearing and chooses the members of the jury, with an eye to ensuring heterogeneity, impartiality and expertise.[65]

During the hearings, organisations such as public institutions, academic professionals and social organisations, which have been invited to participate by the parties, have the opportunity to express their position on the issues. Most of the cases brought before the LAWT have already been decided by domestic tribunals. In such cases the aggrieved parties consider that the national courts have failed to provide appropriate redress, or the government or private corporations have not complied with the rulings.[66] Although the LAWT resolutions (*veredictos*) are not binding on the parties to the dispute,[67] they provide a scientific and technical basis for the settlement of water-related disputes in the region

62 LAWT, 'Organización', in 'Presentación Institucional', above n. 17.

63 Bogantes, above n. 12, 31 (author's translation).

64 LAWT, 'Presentación Institucional', above n. 17. The Tribunal's activities are funded by various international cooperation agencies.

65 LAWT, 'Organización', in ibid.

66 For instance, the case regarding the Atuel basin in Argentina involved two provinces (regions), Mendoza and La Pampa: see WaterLex, 'Tribunal Latinoamericano del Agua, Fundación Chadileuvú c/ Estado Nacional Argentino y Provincia de Mendoza' in *The Human Rights to Water and Sanitation in Courts Worldwide: A Selection of National, Regional and International Case Law* (WaterLex and WASH United, 2014) 281–83.

67 These parties are civil society, basin authorities and institutions in charge of water governance.

10.4.4 Parties to LAWT Proceedings

The applicants are often organisations such as the Latin American Observatory for Environmental Conflicts (OLCA).[68] The main geographical focus of the Tribunal's hearings is Latin America, although during the 2009 World Water Forum in Istanbul (Turkey),[69] a public hearing was held in parallel with the support of the Heinrich Boll Foundation, and cases from other regions were also analysed.[70]

Defendants may be individuals, states/governments or private actors (corporations) that pollute, mismanage or threaten the sustainability of water resources.[71] The various forms of liability that are alleged in the complaints are as follows:

- State responsibility for permitting activities that lead to environmental harm
- Failure by corporations to comply with planning and pollution prevention and control legislation leading to environmental harm
- Failure by the state to control and respond to potential or actual harmful activities carried out by corporations

The LAWT facilitates meetings among the applicants, government authorities and corporate representatives, although it has been difficult to make the latter two appear before the Tribunal. Even so, recent practice shows that government and corporations are becoming more open to dialogue, and representatives from both have appeared and tried to reach an agreement before the LAWT during hearings in Costa Rica, Mexico, Guatemala and Argentina.[72]

[68] The OLCA has contributed towards bringing cases to the LAWT and monitoring compliance with the verdicts

[69] The 5th World Water Forum (WWF) took place in March 2009 in Istanbul: see *Final Report of the 5th World Water Forum* (5th World Water Forum Secretariat, 2009), www.worldwatercouncil.org/fileadmin/world_water_council/documents/world_water_forum_5/WWF5_Final_Report_ENG.pdf.

[70] LAWT, 'Public Hearing Held in Istanbul, Turkey', http://tragua.com/audiencias/audiencia-publica-estambul-2009.

[71] On the role of corporations in compliance with environmental law, see generally Peter Muchlinski, *Multinational Enterprises and the Law* (Oxford University Press, 2007) 537, 546; and Şükrü Özen and Fatma Küskü, 'Corporate environmental citizenship – variation in developing countries: An institutional framework' (2009) 89(2) *Journal of Business Ethics* 297, 302.

[72] Bogantes and Muiser, above n. 11, 88–93.

10.4.5 *LAWT Verdicts and Memoranda of Understanding*

Each decision adopted by the LAWT jury contains a short description of the facts, arguments and parties involved in the dispute, followed by the articulation of relevant legal/ethical standards and their application to the facts. On the basis of the findings, the jurors issue a decision (verdict), which includes recommendations to improve the situation or resolve the legal controversy. These verdicts, despite the name, are not directly enforceable.

In addition to seeking a LAWT verdict, parties to a dispute may sign an *Acuerdo de Intención* (Memorandum of Understanding). The Memorandum is a document that embodies a mutual agreement regarding the protection of water resources as a basic condition for future dialogue and for compliance with the recommendations contained in the relevant verdict. In LAWT hearings in Costa Rica, Mexico, Guatemala and Argentina, local authorities and companies that were parties to some of the disputes reached an agreement and signed such memoranda.[73] The importance of this becomes clear when one realises that in Guatemala in 2008 alone about 40 per cent of cases brought before the jury resulted in the signing of memoranda.[74]

10.4.6 *The Moral Authority of the LAWT in the Settlement of Environmental Disputes over Water Resources*

The principal and laudable goal of the LAWT is to contribute to the settlement of disputes concerning water resources in Latin America.[75] Its activities are based on international environmental law and the principles of harmonious relationship with nature, respect for human dignity and solidarity among people and organisations to protect water resources.[76] According to its mandate, the legitimacy of the Tribunal derives from the moral authority of its verdicts.[77]

[73] Bogantes, above n. 12, 23. [74] Ibid., 25.

[75] However, in Istanbul, the LAWT examined cases of water pollution and degradation affecting other regions.

[76] LAWT, 'Presentación Institucional', above n. 17.

[77] Ibid.; José M. Borrero Navia, 'Fundamentos Ético Jurídicos' ['Ethical and legal fundamentals'], http://tragua.com/wp-content/uploads/2012/04/FUNDAMENTOS-ÉTICO-JURÍDICOS.pdf; Weaver, above n. 15, 525; and Maganda, above n. 8, 688.

The concept of 'legitimacy' in international environmental law has both a sociological and a normative dimension. As Bodansky notes, 'legitimacy concerns the justification of authority; it provides grounds for deferring to another's decision, even in the absence of coercion or rational persuasion.'[78] Borrowing from Bernstein, legitimacy can be defined 'as the acceptance and justification of shared rules by a community'.[79] The LAWT's functions are grounded in the need to overcome the lack of compliance with environmental law, or *crisis de legalidad* as it is referred to in Tribunal documentation.[127] Hence, the very deficit of adequate reaction or legislative and judicial action to enforce environmental laws and to protect water resources provides the impetus to grant standing to citizens to seek alternative redress or 'justice'.[80]

The LAWT's biggest challenge is to reinforce its legitimacy and credibility. To this end, the Secretariat has developed procedural rules according to which the LAWT performs a rigorous scrutiny of complaints in order to ensure impartiality.[81] This is achieved largely through an exhaustive analysis of the scientific quality of the evidence presented in light of the precautionary principle, the sustainable development principle and other principles of environmental ethics.[82]

The LAWT was created by civil society organisations as an ethical tribunal to overcome 'democratic deficits in water management' and the 'environmental impunity situation'.[83] Access to water as a human right was included as a main pillar. It follows that human rights are also embedded in its activities. At the same time, proceedings before the LAWT show specific 'uses' of human rights and certain power relations on social, institutional and discursive dimensions.[84] The demands of

[78] Daniel Bodansky, 'The legitimacy of international governance: A coming challenge for international environmental law?' (1999) 93(3) *American Journal of International Law* 596, 603. See James Nickel and Daniel Magraw, 'Philosophical Issues in International Environmental Law' in Samantha Besson and John Tasioulas (eds.), *The Philosophy of International Law* (Oxford University Press, 2010) 453, 454; and Roger Crisp, 'Ethics and International Environmental Law' in Besson and Tasioulas, *The Philosophy of International Law* 473, 474.

[79] Steven Bernstein, 'Legitimacy in global environmental governance' (2004–5) 1 *Journal of International Law and International Relations* 139, 142.

[80] Romano, above n. 37, 1053.

[81] LAWT, *Manual de Procedimientos del Tribunal Latinoamericano del Agua ['Procedural Manual of the Latin American Water Tribunal']*.

[82] LAWT, 'Presentación Institucional', above n. 17; Borrero Navia, above n. 77.

[83] LAWT, 'Quiénes-Somos', above n. 55.

[84] Maria Backhouse, Jairo Baquero and Sérgio Costa, 'Between Rights and Power Asymmetries: Contemporary Struggles for Land in Brazil and Colombia', Working Paper Series

local communities denote the advent of a transnational system of law redefining the contours of public international law[85] whereby, especially in the field of human rights, civil society is the driving force behind the creation of transnational legal norms.[86]

The LAWT's contribution to the resolution of increasing conflicts over access largely to water could be crucial. By the end of 2016, the Tribunal had received more than 250 complaints and dealt with more than 70 cases.[87] Various infringements have been alleged in the complaints, ranging from water pollution to the construction of dams resulting in reduced access to water.[88] In this regard, the LAWT plays a significant role in increasing the visibility of environmental disputes. Recent environmental studies literature use the concept 'environmental visibility' from an environmental justice perspective to refer to public attentiveness towards relevant environmental problems in specific regions around the world and transparency in environmental management.[89] Increased visibility of environmental disputes concerning water resources is linked to the LAWT's role as an 'environmental justice forum'. At the heart of LAWT proceedings lies the concept that 'the more visible pollution is, the more likely people will organise to do something about it.'[90]

The lack of a sophisticated mechanism to enhance compliance with its decisions is one of the weaknesses of the LAWT. Unlike national and international tribunals, the LAWT has not established its own structured follow-up procedure. Instead, the prevailing party is left to use the publicity of the Tribunal's hearings in their own future advocacy. Despite this limitation, the LAWT plays a remarkable role in raising awareness and contributing to the exertion of pressure on states and corporations to

No. 41, *desiguALdades.net*, 2013, 4–5 www.desigualdades.net/Resources/Working_Paper/41_WP_Backhouse_Baquero_Costa_Online.pdf.

85 Andreas Fischer-Lescano, '"Ex Facto Ius Oritur": Procesos de Escándalo y el Derecho Mundial Emergente' ['"Law arises from fact": Processes of Scandal and Emerging World Law'] (2007) 30 *Doxa, Cuadernos de Filosofía del Derecho* 435. See also Nico Krisch, *Beyond Constitutionalism: The Pluralistic Structure of Post-National Law* (Oxford University Press, 2010).

86 Fischer-Lescano, above n. 85, 435.

87 LAWT, 'Audiencias y Casos' ('Hearings and Cases'), http://tragua.com/audiencias.

88 Ibid.

89 See generally Frances E. Bowen, 'Environmental visibility: A trigger of green organizational response?' (2000) 9(2) *Business Strategy and the Environment* 92; and Frances E. Bowen, *After Greenwashing: Symbolic Corporate Environmentalism and Society* (Cambridge University Press, 2014).

90 Kenneth A. Gould, 'Pollution and perception: Social visibility and local environmental mobilization' (1993) 16(2) *Qualitative Sociology* 157, 158.

comply with the environmental legislation applicable in each case. It should be noted that 'environmental awareness' may be taken for granted in legal systems with a longer environmental tradition, but it is a relatively new phenomenon in Latin America where non-compliance with environmental legislation historically has been high.

The principal manner in which awareness is raised is through the verdicts which may be deployed by NGOs and local organisations to promote the institutional enforcement of legislation.[91] As Bodansky stresses, 'environmental groups typically have a more single-minded focus than governments and hence are more willing to invest in implementation and enforcement measures. . . . They monitor behavior, publicize violations, mobilize public opinion against delinquent states, and provide technical and financial assistance.'[92]

10.4.7 The LAWT as a Legitimate Forum for Alternative Dispute Resolution (ADR)

Compared with domestic or international courts, the LAWT is perceived by the applicants as an environmental justice forum in which both parties receive fair treatment[93] in overcoming environmental injustice – defined as a situation that 'occurs when the redistributed risks generated by pollution control end up disproportionately in low income communities and communities of color'.[94] Fairness is reflected in the special features of the proceedings. Firstly, access for the petitioners to formulate their claims is relatively easy: no strict rules of procedure have to be followed and petitioners are not required to have an attorney. Secondly, evidence is carefully scrutinised by an impartial Scientific and Technical Commission, which can reject evidence that it finds to be contrary to established science.[95] Thirdly, once the complaint is admitted, the respondents are permitted to answer the complaint. Fourthly, during the public hearing,

[91] On the role of NGOs in environmental compliance. see A. Dan Tarlock, 'Role of Non-governmental organizations in the development of international environmental law' (1992) 68 *Chicago-Kent Law Review* 61, 63.

[92] Daniel Bodansky, *The Art and Craft of International Environmental Law* (Harvard University Press, 2010) 234.

[93] Byrnes and Simm, above n. 56, 713.

[94] Richard J. Lazarus, 'Fairness in environmental law' (1997) 27 *Environmental Law* 705, 714.

[95] The members of the Commission are appointed from a list of experts by the Secretariat based on their respective experience; they receive no payment for the tasks performed.

both parties have the opportunity to present their cases publicly.[96] Finally, the LAWT provides a forum for communities to expose environmental problems in a semi-judicial and less formalistic context and to analyse the relationship between sustainable development and social exclusion.[97]

The nature of the LAWT proceedings demonstrates that, with regard to domestic jurisdiction, 'there is an increasing demand for redress and access to justice by non-state entities that (largely) stems from the shortcomings of national legal systems.'[98] However, the remedies available at the international level often preclude individuals and groups from bringing environmental claims. For instance, a number of investor-state arbitration cases before the International Centre for the Settlement of Investment Disputes (ICSID)[99] or under the North American Free Trade Agreement (NAFTA)[100] concern access to water (affected by water privatisation).[101] Access to justice by third parties who claim to represent the public interest before NAFTA and ICSID is quite limited for three main reasons: procedural hurdles for the admission of amicus curiae briefs, economic costs and confidentiality of the NAFTA and ICSID proceedings.[102] Even if the new ICSID procedural rules now allow for amici curiae, the protection granted to individuals and local communities remains limited. Since the focus is on the protection of the foreign investor, the forum does not seem amenable to the settlement of environmental disputes.[103]

In comparison with other alternative adjudicatory bodies and human rights bodies, such as the World Bank panels and the Inter-American Commission and Court of Human Rights, the LAWT offers several

96 Weaver, above n. 15, 523.

97 Scholars have addressed environmental inequalities, their implications and the linkages between poverty on the one hand, and environmental degradation and economic policies on the other: see Backhouse, Baquero and Costa, above n. 84, 4.

98 Romano, above n. 37, 1056.

99 Andreas Kulick, *Global Public Interest in International Investment Law* (Cambridge University Press, 2014) 225–67.

100 North American Free Trade Agreement, San Antonio, 17 December 1992, 32 ILM 289, in force 1 January 1994, www.sice.oas.org/trade/nafta/naftatce.asp.

101 Jorge E. Vinuales, 'Access to water in foreign investment disputes' (2009) 21(4) *Georgetown International Environmental Law Review* 733.

102 'The secret trade courts', *New York Times*, 7 September 2004, www.nytimes.com/2004/09/27/opinion/the-secret-trade-courts.html?_r=0.

103 Andrew de Lotbinière McDougall and Ank Santens, 'ICSID Tribunals apply new rules on amicus curiae' (2007) 22(2) *Mealey's International Arbitration Report* 1.

advantages. The World Bank panels represent a top-down approach that focuses on projects funded by international institutions to the detriment of individual or group demands.[104] The Inter-American human rights institutions have only recently developed a body of case law on environmental issues, given that they are not specialised in environmental issues.[105] In addition, legal standing is more restricted than it is for the LAWT.

10.5 An Evaluation of the LAWT as a Transnational Environmental Dispute Settlement Forum

The LAWT is perceived as an alternative space for environmental justice in the resolution of water conflicts and for the recognition of water as a human right in indigenous territories, incorporating indigenous traditions and customs.[106] In short, the LAWT is more 'user friendly'. As is the case with human rights forums, local remedies must have been exhausted before a party may gain access to the LAWT. The Tribunal's Scientific and Technical Commission accepts cases only if there is sufficient scientific evidence to establish causation between the actions of those accused and the environmental degradation. The compilation of scientific evidence is expensive, but fortunately NGOs and other civil society organisations typically sponsor some of the research, given the public nature of the Tribunal and of the disputes.[107]

[104] The World Bank Inspection Panels were created in 1993: see Steven Herz and Anne Perrault, *Bringing Human Rights Claims to the World Bank Inspection Panel* (Center for International Environmental Law, 2009), www.bicusa.org/wp-content/uploads/2013/01/InspectionPanel_HumanRights.pdf.

[105] See generally Enrique Ulate Chacón, 'La tutela medioambiental en el Sistema Interamericano de Protección de los Derechos Humanos' ['The Environmental Action in the Inter-American System for the Protection of Human Rights'] in Belén Olmos Giupponi (ed.), *Medio ambiente, Cambio Climatico y Derechos Humanos* [*Environment, Climate Change and Human Rights*] (Dike, 2011) 75.

[106] See, e.g., the case before the LAWT regarding the transfer of water from the region of the Cutzamala System to the Valley of Mexico basin (United Mexican States): Patricia Avila-García, 'Water Conflicts and Human Rights in Indigenous Territories of Latin America' in Alberto Garrido and Mordechai Schechter (eds.), *Water for the Americas: Challenges and Opportunities* (Routlege, 2014) 177.

[107] Latin America Solidarity Centre (LASC), 'The Latin American Water Tribunal puts "water polluters on trial"', *Thirsting for Justice – 'Defending the Global Water Commons', Latin America Week*, 15 April 2007, 16, www.developmenteducation.ie/media/documents/Thirsting-for-Justice.pdf.

Some contend that certain features of the LAWT reflect features of arbitration within the alternative dispute resolution (ADR) framework. For instance, Weaver argues that the LAWT has 'developed out of a rich tradition of arbitral bodies'[108] and combines 'various dispute resolution approaches in such a way that the disadvantages and drawbacks of traditional mediation and arbitration are eliminated'.[109] However, this viewpoint overlooks some of the essential features of the proceedings before the LAWT. Firstly, such proceedings constitute public interest litigation; therefore, confidentiality, which is the main feature of arbitration, does not play a role. Secondly, in arbitration the consent of the parties to the dispute to submit it to the tribunal or mediator constitutes the basis of jurisdiction; this is not so in cases before the LAWT. Thirdly, in arbitration proceedings there is a duty to comply with the award, which is enforceable in national courts. For these reasons, it is more accurate to view the LAWT as a forum for mediation that offers the parties an alternative form of resolution of the conflict, while engaging civil society organisations and consultations. As Maganda asserts, 'the body's main innovation lies in the fact that it convenes all the actors in specific cases and attempts to mediate their conflict impartially.'[110]

Indeed, in recent years the LAWT has clearly emerged as a mediator in water conflicts, providing channels to foster dialogue between civil society and public authorities. In this manner, the LAWT has intervened in various mediation processes: it has managed to open channels of mutual understanding in water issues in Huancavelica (Peru) among indigenous communities and local authorities; in El Salvador, including communities opposed to hydroelectric projects and the authorities of environment and energy; and in Mexico, Guatemala and South America.[111]

10.6 The LAWT's Impact on Environmental Law Enforcement

The LAWT's functions in assuring compliance with environmental law can be better understood through the analysis of case studies. In this section, one example of a case brought before the LAWT is discussed to ascertain the impact of its judgments on the resolution of disputes.[112]

108 Weaver, above n .15, 523. 109 Ibid., 528. 110 Maganda, above n. 8, 689.

111 Bogantes, above n. 12, 24.

112 I have analysed a number of other cases in Maria Belén Olmos Giupponi, 'Transnational environmental law and grass-root initiatives: The Case of the Latin American Water Tribunal' (2016) 5(1) *Transnational Environmental Law* 145, 170–73.

The analysis examines the nature of the conflict, the verdict issued by the LAWT and the relation with other 'formal' dispute resolution mechanisms.

10.6.1 *The Construction of the La Parota Dam (Mexico)*

The vast majority of the complaints submitted to the LAWT have originated in Mexico,[113] mainly because of the absence of specialised environmental tribunals in Mexico and the weakness of the rule of law.[114] The high-profile *La Parota* case dealt with the construction of a hydroelectric dam in Mexico with potentially harmful effects for water resources and the environment.[115] The application to the LAWT was one of several initiatives that have been undertaken in Mexico to protect natural resources.[116]

The hydroelectric dam project, La Parota, which was to be built on the river Papagayo, was an infrastructure project carried out by the Federal Electricity Commission (*Comisión Federal de Electricidad* [CFE]) in the state of Guerrero.[117] According to different reports issued by NGOs, this dam would have had severe adverse impacts on strategic environmental resources such as water and the ecosystem and directly displaced around 25,000 people and indirectly affected another 75,000 through the potential environmental harm and the destruction of their livelihoods.[118]

[113] See LAWT, 'Statistics', in Bogantes and Muiser, above n. 11, 86–87.

[114] Octavio Rosas Landa, 'La lucha legal por la justicia hídrica: México en el Tribunal Latinoamericano del Agua' ['The legal struggle for water justice: Mexico before the Latin American Water Tribunal'] (2012) 173 *El Cotidiano* 67, 68, www.elcotidianoenlinea.com.mx/pdf/17308.pdf.

[115] Amnesty International, 'Mexico: Human Rights at risk in La Parota Dam Project', 4 August 2007, AI Index: AMR 41/029/2007, 12, https://www.amnesty.org/download/Documents/AMR410292007ENGLISH.PDF.

[116] Lourdes Romero Navarrete, 'Experiencias de Acción Colectiva Frente a la Problemática Ambiental en México' ['Experiences of collective action in response to environmental problems in Mexico'] (2003) 50 *Revista Mexicana de Ciencias Políticas y Sociales* 157, 167.

[117] Asociación Interamericana para la Defensa del Ambiente (AIDA) [Inter-American Association for the Defence of the Environment], *Informe Grandes Represas en América, ¿Peor el Remedio que la Enfermedad? [Large Dams in the Americas: Is the Cure Worse than the Disease?]* (2009) 94–95, www.aida-americas.org/sites/default/files/InformeAIDA_GrandesRepreseas_BajaRes.pdf.

[118] LAWT, 'Caso: Proyecto hidoeléctirco "La Parota" sobre el río Papagayo en el estado de Guerreero, República Mexicana: Veredicto' ['Verdict on the Case concerning the Hydroelectric Dam Project on the Papagayo River in the State of Guerrero, Mexico'] [*La Parota Verdict*], March 2006, http://tragua.com/wp-content/uploads/2012/04/Caso-La-Parota.pdf.

In 2003, the CFE began the construction of the dam in the territory of the indigenous community of Cacahuatepec.[119] These activities were carried out without consultation with the indigenous communities or representatives of local communities. This resulted in a conflict that involved different actors and gave rise to demonstrations against the construction of the dam. Local communities opposed to the project established the *Consejo de Ejidos y Comunidades Opositores a la presa La Parota* (CECOP, Council of Communes and Communities opposed to the La Parota dam[120]). In 2004, the Ministerial General Directorate of Environmental Impact and Risk conditionally approved the environmental impact assessment for the project. Claimants sought redress before national courts (including administrative review of the ministerial decision by the national agrarian tribunal[121]) and brought the situation to the attention of thematic special rapporteurs of the UN Human Rights Council[122] and the UN Committee on Economic, Social and Cultural Rights.[123] As a result, the UN Special Rapporteur on the Right to Housing issued a statement[124]

[119] Héctor Briseño, 'Opositores a presa La Parota crearán autodefensa en Cacahuatepec, Guerrero' ['Opponents of the La Parota dam will resort to self-defence in Cacahuatepec'], *La Jornada*, 15 January 2014, www.jornada.unam.mx/ultimas/2014/01/15/opositores-a-presa-la-parota-crearan-municipio-con-autodefensas-en-cacahuatepec-7844.html.

[120] Asamblea National de Afectados Ambientales, 'Council of Ejidos and Communities Opposing La Parota Dam', *Asamblea National de Afectados Ambientales*, www.afectadosambientales.org/consejo-de-ejidos-y-comunidades-opositoras-a-la-presa-la-parota-cecop.

[121] The agrarian tribunal has jurisdiction to consider allegedly unconstitutional action: see Marco Vinicio Martínez Guerrero, 'Tribunales Agrarios a veinte años de su creación' ['Agrarian tribunals twenty years after their establishment'] (2012) 50 *Revista de los Tribunales Agrarios* 169, 183–84, www.pa.gob.mx/publica/rev_50/Analisis/tribunales_agrarios.pdf.

[122] Centro Mexicano de Derecho Ambiental (CEMDA) [Mexican Centre for Environmental Law'] and Asociación Interamericana para la Defensa del Ambiente (AIDA), 'Resumen de las ilegalidades cometidas en el Proyecto Hidroeléctrico La Parota, Memorando enviado a los Relatores Especiales de la ONU' ['Summary of illegalities committed in the La Parota hydroelectric project', Memorandum sent to the Special Rapporteurs of the United Nations'], August 2007, http://inicio.ifai.org.mx/ProyectoComunidades/CEMDA-BOLETIN.pdf.

[123] Committee on Economic, Social and Cultural Rights, *Consideration of Reports Submitted by States Parties under Articles 16 and 17 of the Covenant: Concluding Observations on Mexico* [*Mexico Concluding Observations 2006*], E/C.12/MEX/CO/49, 9 June 2006.

[124] UN Commission on Human Rights, 'Statement by Mr Miloon Kothari, Special Rapporteur on adequate housing as a component of the right to an adequate standard of living, to the World Urban Forum III (19–23 June 2006) in Vancouver', http://reliefweb.int/report/zimbabwe/statement-mr-miloon-kothari-special-rapporteur-adequate-housing-component-right.

and, together with the UN Special Rapporteur on Indigenous Peoples, visited the affected area.[125]

At the LAWT hearing in March 2006, local organisations raised a number of environmental issues associated with the construction.[126] The main allegation was that neither the environmental impact assessment nor the authorisation took into account the dangers of damage to water resources or to the local population's public health and quality of life posed by the construction of the dam.[127] The claimants emphasised that the intervention of the authorities had not guaranteed respect for the right to water and other rights at stake. In addition, the violation of the fundamental rights of the affected communities would result in significant social costs arising from the destruction of natural resources. Moreover, they argued that the expropriation of communal lands contravened constitutional principles because the dam would not provide benefits for the inhabitants or contribute to their development.[128] The claimants therefore aimed to guarantee the integrity of indigenous peoples' lands, protect forests and shared water resources, regulate land use and promote actions to improve the quality of life.

Following the conclusion of the hearing the LAWT pronounced its verdict. It determined that construction of the dam violated articles 2 and 27 of the Constitution of the United Mexican States, as well as domestic law provisions on ecological balance and environmental protection, the National Water Act and the Health Act. The LAWT issued recommendations that emphasised the need for a complete and comprehensive assessment of the project, including its environmental, social, economic and cultural impacts.[129] Moreover, it recommended implementing a process for consultation and public participation in the decision-making process relating to major public projects and a mechanism for the resolution of disputes arising from the construction of the dam.[130] The LAWT also specifically proposed the creation of a commission to represent the victims and civil organisations to promote dialogue and a peaceful resolution of the conflict.

[125] Housing and Land Rights Network, 'UN Special Rapporteurs Visit Opponents of La Parota Dam', *Housing and Land Rights Network*, 10 September 2007, http://hlrn.org/news.php?id=q2tt#.WPlxZXosbYI; and 'UN Special Rapporteurs Conclude visit to Mexico', *Housing and Land Rights Network*, 14 September 2007, hlrn.org/news.php?id=pGll#.WPlx4HosbKQ.

[126] The application is summarised in the verdict: *La Parota Verdict*, above n. 118, 1–3.

[127] Ibid. 3. [128] Rosas Landa, above n. 114, 73.

[129] *La Parota Verdict*, above n. 118, 7. [130] Ibid., 8.

Shortly after the LAWT hearing, the UN Committee on Economic, Social and Cultural Rights (CESCR), in its review of the fourth periodic report of Mexico[131] under the International Covenant on Economic, Social and Cultural Rights,[132] also considered the situation. In its concluding observations on the Mexican report, the Committee, referring to the LAWT verdict, expressed its concern about the project, emphasizing that it 'would ... according to the Latin American Water Tribunal, violate the communal land rights of the affected communities, as well as their economic, social and cultural rights'.[133] The Committee recommended that the Mexican government ensure that the peoples and communities affected were 'duly consulted, and that their prior and informed consent is sought, in any decision-making processes related to these projects' and that it should take other appropriate measures to alleviate the impact of the project on these peoples and communities.[134] Initially, the Mexican federal government ignored the LAWT's verdict and the recommendations issued by the CESCR. However, in three decisions adopted between 2006 and 2007, Mexican courts overturned the dam construction permits.[135] Finally, in 2007, the construction of the dam was suspended indefinitely.[136] Subsequent judicial decisions after 2009[137] supported the demands of local communities in their opposition to the project.[138]

131 Economic and Social Council, *Fourth periodic reports submitted by States parties under articles 16 and 17 of the Covenant*, E/C.12/4/Add.16 (25 February 2005).

132 New York, 16 December 1966, 993 UNTS 3, in force 3 January 1976.

133 *Mexico Concluding Observations 2006*, above n. 123, para. 10.

134 Ibid., para. 28.

135 AIDA, above n. 117, 97.

136 Marien Cifuentes Carbonetto, 'El conflicto del proyecto hidroeléctrico represa La Parota' ['The conflict over the La Parota dam hydroelectric project'], Observatorio Latinoamericano de Conflictos Ambientales, 27 September 2007, www.olca.cl/oca/mexico/represas005.htm. See also Committee on Economic, Social and Cultural Rights, *Combined fifth and sixth periodic reports of States parties due in 2012: Mexico*, E/C.12/MEX/5–6, paras. 3–8 and 244 (2016).

137 In April 2011 the Agrarian Tribunal (TUA) 41 ruled in favour of the members of the Council of Ejidos and Communities Opposed to the La Parota Dam (CECOP): see Francisca Meza Carranza, 'Falla el Tua a Favor del Cecop; Declara nula la asamblea de La Concepción' ['The National Agrarian Tribunal rules in favour of CECOP, declares the assembly of La Concepción void'], *La Jornada Guerrero*, 28 April 2011, 1, www.lajornadaguerrero.com.mx/2011/04/28/index.php?section=sociedad&article=007n1soc.

138 Héctor Briseño, 'Diez Años de Resistencia Contra la Presa La Parota' ['Ten years of resistance to the La Parota Dam'], *La Jornada*, 27 December 2013, www.jornada.unam.mx/2013/12/27/estados/028n1est.

The deeper implications of this case relate not only to how local communities could voice their demands but also how they could increase their participation in water management. Specifically, the LAWT provided an institutionalised forum for dialogue to facilitate the parties' mutual understanding.[139] In addition, as a result of the combined pressure from the LAWT, local organisations and international NGOs, the Mexican government decided to halt the project.

10.7 Conclusion

In this chapter, I have argued that the LAWT represents an alternative forum to formal state-based institutions for the settlement of environmental conflicts concerning access to water in Latin America. Although environmental concerns and conflicts related to water resources are not a novelty in Latin America, they have not been addressed in the past with the current level of awareness. Since the LAWT's verdicts are not legally binding, they can not be enforced. However, the verdicts have heightened the visibility of the disputes, and this has helped facilitate compliance with environmental norms. The impact of LAWT verdicts does seem to depend on the 'use' made of them by the parties in subsequent negotiations and advocacy. In the *La Parota* case, for example, the petitioners were at last able to stop the construction of the dam on the basis of the LAWT's recommendations.

A key criticism of the LAWT is that it lacks enforcement powers and, as a result, some disputes are still continuing. This chapter has demonstrated that the LAWT's activities are nonetheless critical as an alternative and effective forum for access to environmental justice in Latin America for three main reasons. Firstly, the LAWT provides the opportunity for claimants to present their cases and provides recommendations for compliance with environmental legislation. The LAWT also facilitates voluntary compliance with water resources legislation and indigenous norms and customs. In this way, the LAWT acts as a mediator recommending compliance with applicable environmental norms and identifying possible ways of resolving the disputes.

Secondly, the LAWT has proved to be an alternative forum to place water issues on the agenda, which contributes to mobilising public opinion. Its proceedings and verdicts raise awareness about water

[139] Maganda, above n. 8, 689.

conflicts in Latin America and thus facilitate public pressure on states and corporate private actors. It increases transparency and environmental visibility in legal procedures, as evidenced in the cases involving approval of the construction of a new hydroelectric dam or permission for the exploitation of mining concessions. Only through the intervention of the LAWT were the affected local communities able to raise their concerns.

Thirdly, traditional water management systems designed by governments adopt a top-down approach without considering the human rights dimension. In contrast, the LAWT offers a bottom-up approach which includes the demands of the various groups in society, such as the local population and indigenous people. This approach represents an alternative to extant fora in which affected groups cannot access justice mechanisms and/or lack legal standing to do so.

In sum, the remarkable activity of the LAWT opens the door to future opportunities to address controversial situations that may arise with regard to access to water where traditional justice mechanisms prove to be ineffective or inadequate.

PART IV

The Future of International Peoples' Tribunals

11

Reflections on the Past and Future of International Peoples' Tribunals

ANDREW BYRNES AND GABRIELLE SIMM

11.1 Introduction

This concluding chapter is structured around three questions against the background of the discussions of selected peoples' tribunals in preceding chapters and in light of some of the broader issues addressed in Chapter 1. The first question is the extent to which the tribunals discussed in this volume are representative of international peoples' tribunals generally. The second question is the relationship between peoples' tribunals, social movements and international law. The third question relates to the nature and extent of the impact of peoples' tribunals on international law and on the states and audiences whom they are trying to convince to take action. In this connection, we also consider alternatives to peoples' tribunals, but conclude that peoples' tribunals often consciously attempt to use international law to benefit those whose perspectives are marginalised and whose voices are often not heard.

11.2 How Representative Is this Collection of Peoples' Tribunals more Generally?

An important issue for us as editors has been the extent to which the peoples' tribunals considered in this volume are representative of peoples' tribunals in general. We have considered this issue in terms of geographic and thematic coverage. In terms of geographic spread, peoples' tribunals are well established in Europe (Tognoni, Simm, Dehm) and Latin America (Tognoni, Fraudatario and Tognoni, Icaza, Olmos Giupponi) and this geographic bias is evident in this collection. This volume includes a strong focus on the Asian continent (Dolgopol, Wieringa, Edwards), but lacks contributions focussing on the Middle East, Africa, North America and the Pacific. Our inability to access scholarship on peoples' tribunals in these areas of the world is partly determined by linguistic limitations, but may also reflect a preference for other forms of activism in these regions. Another explanation is that in South Asia, for instance, we are aware of the popularity of peoples' tribunals but many of these operate at the national level and do not focus on international law.[1]

As to the themes covered, this collection focuses more on issues arising in international criminal law, human rights, environmental justice, the use of force, and state responsibility for mass atrocities. While issues of trade, the international market economy and the role of transnational corporations and international financial institutions are raised, they are not dealt with in the same depth. The increasing importance of climate change and the use of peoples' tribunals to articulate popular protest against adverse environmental impacts of projects and policies means that peoples' tribunals are likely to exert more influence in related areas of international law. In terms of theoretical approaches to the issues discussed, this volume includes several contributions attentive to the problems of peoples' tribunals purporting to represent others (Dolgopol, Icaza). Several chapters are motivated by feminist concerns (Simm, Dolgopol, Icaza), while the need to decolonise international law and inequality in global North–South relations is a focus in indigenous struggles (Icaza) and the discussion of Europe's treatment of migrants (Dehm).

11.3 The Relationship between Peoples' Tribunals, Social Movements and International Law

Although we do not here attempt to articulate a detailed typology of peoples' tribunals, we can propose a spectrum of peoples' tribunals in terms of how closely they adhere to existing institutions, structures and issues dealt with by international law. At one end of that spectrum, we might plot tribunals that, like international criminal tribunals, put on trial individual defendants who are accused of violations of international law and whose focus is a mainly orthodox application of existing positive law to the evidence put before them, albeit within a broader political context of activism around a particular issue. The Tokyo International

[1] See, e.g., Muzaffar Assadi, 'Seed Tribunal: Interrogating farmers' suicides', (21 October–3 November 200035 (43/44)) *Economic and Political Weekly*, 3808–10, and also the Indian People's Tribunal on Environment and Human Rights (IPT) established in 1993 by the Human Rights Law Network: www.iptindia.org/.

Women's Tribunal and the Kuala Lumpur War Crimes Tribunal are prominent examples of such tribunals. However, most peoples' tribunals attempt to interrogate the responsibility of entities like states, international organisations and transnational corporations and may seek to extend international law to do so.

Peoples' tribunals nearly all arise from a political campaign or social movement in which affected groups seek to claim their entitlements under international law and to render the abusers of power accountable within a formal framework bolstered by law. Sometimes the tribunal may be a central part of the broader movement, in other cases it may be just one component of a broader strategy, with the tribunal's verdict providing advocates with another tool to persuade and advance their quest for recognition of and justice for their suffering.

One of the striking aspects of difference between the many tribunals that have taken place is between 'one-off' tribunals and the 'repeat players'. Most modern peoples' tribunals articulate their theoretical and political justification by reference to the tradition that started with the First Russell Tribunal and draw on positive international law (as well as other sources) to ground their grievances. Tribunals that meet only once have a limited opportunity to develop their own 'jurisprudence' to contribute to the evolution of international law and to set out a broader narrative that can evolve over time. By contrast, a body such as the Permanent Peoples' Tribunal (PPT) has a self-referential jurisprudential tradition and has been able to articulate and develop in its hearings overarching theories of power structures and theoretical frameworks over extended periods of time and the hearings of dozens of cases addressing a variety of issues. Another prominent repeat player, the Latin American Water Tribunal, more specialised in its focus, has been able to develop an ethically based practice. Benefitting from its experience over decades in many cases, it has honed its procedures in subsequent cases.

Tribunals that address a specific situation or theme through a small number of sessions within a limited time fall somewhere in between. Examples include the Russell Tribunal on Palestine or the tribunals related to the living wage campaign. Another kind of 'limited series' tribunal may hold a number of national or regional sessions leading to a global tribunal, as did the World Tribunal on Iraq. Other examples are the series of 'courts of women': some have been organised by the same groups over an extended period, with others being organised by various groups with an awareness of and by reference to those other tribunals.

11.3.1 Peoples' Tribunals and the Development of International Law

Some peoples' tribunals see their role as extending beyond the application of existing international law to the critique and transformation of international law. They seek to develop international law in a progressive direction where they consider that it reflects oppressive political or economic power relations.[2] For the most part, this manifests itself in a critique of the neo-liberal international economic order and the international law that underpins it. It focuses on the role of international institutions that set and enforce these policies and states that support and implement them. The role that transnational corporations may play in the violation of human rights (as well as the complicity of home and host states in those violations) has also been a concern of a significant number of peoples' tribunals. One example of a more formalised effort to articulate new (legal) norms is the Charter of Rights against Industrial Hazards[3] that emerged from a series of hearings on environmental hazards held by the PPT.[4]

Peoples' tribunals have also devoted attention to expanding the scope of existing categories of international wrongs. One example is the concept of genocide, defined as an international crime in the Genocide Convention of 1948,[5] and more recently in identical terms in the Statute of the International Criminal Court.[6] That requires the commission of one or more specific actions 'with intent to destroy, in whole or in part, a national, ethnical, racial or religious group, as such'.[7] This international legal definition of genocide is narrower than the practices that many advocates wanted to be included in the treaty at the time of its adoption and narrower than some concepts of genocide employed in

[2] In this context, an understanding of the historical origins of present-day international law has been important. See, e.g., the PPT judgment in its *Session on the Conquest of the Americas and International Law*, para 1.3.

[3] Permanent Peoples' Tribunal on Industrial Hazards and Human Rights, 'Charter of Rights against Industrial Hazards' (1996) 23(4) *Social Justice* 167.

[4] Barbara Dinham, 'Introduction to the "Charter of Rights Against Industrial Hazards": For communities, workers, and protection of their environment' (1996) 23(4) *Social Justice* 164.

[5] Convention on the Prevention and Punishment of the Crime of Genocide 1948, Paris, 9 December 1948, 78 UNTS 277, in force 12 January 1951, art. II.

[6] Rome Statute of the International Criminal Court, opened for signature 17 July 1998, 2187 UNTS 90, in force 1 July 2002, art. 6.

[7] Genocide Convention, art 11; Rome Statute, art 6.

other disciplines such as criminology. Arguments that the Convention definition should include intentional efforts to eliminate sections of the population defined by their political views or a broader notion of cultural genocide were unsuccessful.[8] The PPT has made efforts to promote an expansive reading of the concept of genocide[9] though claims of genocide have not always been upheld by PPT panels.[10] The International Peoples' Tribunal on the events of 1965–66 in Indonesia similarly sought to extend the concept of genocide to the human rights violations it considered.[11]

11.3.2 The Centrality and Role of Victim-Survivors in Peoples' Tribunals

Another feature of peoples' tribunals is the centrality of the perspectives of and roles afforded to the victims-survivors. Theirs is often a role that is greater than merely that of witness, with peoples' tribunals often aiming to restore dignity and acknowledge the agency of victims, at whose initiative peoples' tribunals are usually established.[12] The influence of civil legal systems evident in the International Criminal Court, particularly with the recognition of victims through civil party proceedings and enhanced access to reparations, shows that this perspective is not unique to peoples' tribunals. However, its consistent application to the design of such tribunals and the approach taken to the hearing of evidence and the importance of acknowledging and seeking to provide some redress to victims is a critical component of peoples' tribunals.

Peoples' tribunals may also accuse a broader range of actors than do official institutions, sometimes even intangible defendants such as 'the

[8] William Schabas, 'The Law and Genocide' in Donald Bloxham and Dirk A. Moses (eds.), *Oxford Handbook of Genocide Studies* (Oxford University Press, 2010).

[9] Simona Fraudatario and Gianni Tognoni, 'La definición jurídica y substancial del genocidio a la prueba del encuentro entre el Tribunal Permanente de los Pueblos y las víctimas' ['The legal and substantive definition of genocide tested in the encounter between the Permanent Peoples' Tribunal and victims'], paper presented at the Conferencia Bianual de La International Association of Genocide Scholars, Buenos Aires. www.genocidescholars.org/sites/default/files/document%09%5Bcurrent-page%3A1%5D/documents/IAGS%202011%20Simona%20Fraudatario.pdf.

[10] Ibid. (referring to PPT hearings on the Brazilian Amazon [1990]).

[11] See Wieringa, Chapter 5 in this volume.

[12] See Fraudatario and Tognoni, Chapter 6 in this volume.

world economic system', 'Europe' and 'ourselves'.[13] Peoples' tribunals also permit 'peoples' to accuse corporations of breaches of international law to remedy the lack of legal personality of corporations in international law and the complaint that states too often ignore the wrongs committed by corporations under domestic law. Finally, peoples' tribunals provide a venue for peoples to advocate on behalf of the environment in cases where governments and corporations are accused of placing political gains and profit before environmental concerns.[14]

11.4 The Impact and Usefulness of Peoples' Tribunals

Most peoples' tribunals model themselves on official courts and tribunals, truth commissions and inquiries. Yet peoples' tribunals are not the only form of social activism available to communities seeking redress for human rights violations. So why do many activists choose a legal format of this sort, especially given the lack of formal authority of the tribunals and their verdicts? Alternative means of achieving the aims of spectacle and publicity for a cause are theatre performances (see discussion in Dehm); film, which may also serve as a permanent record of theatre or a tribunal hearing; and posters.[15] Where the correction of omissions from official histories is an objective, archives, books, films, monuments and museums are also possible.[16] Strikes, rallies and protests are other means by which people aggrieved by states, corporations, international organisations and 'the international economic system' make their views known. Given these alternatives, what do organisers hope to achieve through a peoples' tribunal? What impact can it make on the injustice at issue?

While the judgment and 'verdicts' of peoples' tribunals are not binding legal pronouncements, the contributions made by peoples' tribunals are of various types. They can act as a means of publicising information in

[13] See Dehm, Chapter 7 in this volume.

[14] Christopher D. Stone, 'Should trees have standing? Toward legal rights for natural objects' (1972) 45 *Southern California Law Review* 450; Olmos Giupponi, Chapter 10 in this volume.

[15] For example, posters are available of many of the PPT hearings. A documentary film of parts of the proceedings of the 2015 Women's Court: feminist approach to justice is available on YouTube. https://www.youtube.com/watch?v=ePmJfqstB3g.

[16] For example, the Women's active museum on war and peace commemorates the Tokyo Women's Tribunal, http://wam-peace.org/en/aboutus/.

order to support an advocacy campaign, as a 'corrective mechanism through which public intellectuals mobilize world public opinion against powerful countries shielded from sanctions under international law.'[17] Formal findings of accountability invoking accepted law may have a symbolic and political impact and a catalysing effect on advocacy networks.[18] They can also serve as important collections of primary and secondary material that may be useful for formal procedures of inquiry. Equally importantly, they can serve as a solemn recognition of the sufferings of victims and survivors and memorialise 'historical' wrongs.[19]

The impact of peoples' tribunals is often indirect and diffuse, contributing along with other influences to gradual cultural shifts in the development of international law, rather than immediate implementation of a particular tribunal's judgment. As with litigation in official courts, activists who instigate peoples' tribunals may aim to bring evidence into the public domain, to shift public opinion and to assert political pressure. Judgments are usually communicated to governments, international organisations and corporations accused in the proceedings and to the media and non-governmental organizations (NGOs) in order to publicise a particular cause.

Common to all the tribunals, however, is the fact that their findings and recommendations have no formal binding legal status. In this they resemble the findings of the United Nations human rights treaty bodies.

> The Permanent Peoples' Tribunal is an opinion tribunal. Therefore it has neither judicial nor executive power. It may neither give directions nor impose sentences. Its power is twofold. On the one hand, it lies in its appeal to opinion and the links that it makes between the organisations and people who fight for common causes across the world, and on the other, in the juridical work that advances the cause of a more complete and more equitable international law.[20]

[17] Arthur Jay Klinghoffer and Judith Apter Klinghoffer, *International Citizens' Tribunals: Mobilising Public Opinion to Advance Human Rights* (Palgrave, 2002) 5.

[18] Richard Falk, 'Civil society perspectives on humanitarian intervention' (2008) 4(1) *Journal of Civil Society* 3, 11–12.

[19] See Wieringa, Chapter 5 in this volume; Gabrielle Simm, 'The Paris Peoples' Tribunal and the Istanbul war crimes trials: Archives of the Armenian genocide' (2016) 29 *Leiden Journal of International Law* 245.

[20] 'Le Tribunal Permanent des Peuples est un tribunal d'opinion. Il n'a donc aucun pouvoir ni juridique, ni exécutif. Il ne peut imposer des orientations ni faire appliquer des sentences. Sa force est double. Elle réside d'une part dans l'appel qu'il peut faire à l'opinion et dans les liens qu'il permet de tisser entre les organisations et les personnes qui, à travers le monde, combattent pour des causes communes et d'autre part dans le

For some tribunals, this provides a certain freedom being able to make findings on broad issues and recommendations to parties who might never be brought together before the same deliberative body in this way. For others, the lack of formal legal status is a spur to hyperlegalism, as they know that the weight and influence of their findings cannot derive from their formal status, but can only come from the persuasiveness of their reasoning and their evaluation of evidence against clearly established legal standards, to the extent that they wish to persuade based on law.

The Tokyo Women's Tribunal (2000–2001) is perhaps the most pronounced example of such a commitment to a legalistic approach. That tribunal portrayed itself as a reconvening of the post-World War II International Military Tribunal for the Far East, closely following the procedures familiar from modern international criminal proceeding so far as possible. It engaged in a lengthy orthodox legal analysis of the international law issues and the evidence – though not without some innovation and feminist perspectives. While not all aspects of that tribunal's reasons are completely persuasive, there is no doubt that the judgment's thousand or more paragraphs of detailed description, analysis and evaluation represent some fairly assiduous orthodox legal analysis. There are many other instances of this sort, particularly from within the corpus of the hearings of the PPT. The cases relating to Tibet and Timor Leste are but two of the many cases where the tribunal has engaged in what can be described as well-constructed orthodox legal analysis.[21] As the Tokyo Women's Tribunal stated:

> This Tribunal can serve to expose the acts or omissions of the accused to the court of public opinion and thereby, at least, subject the accused to shame. In this way, the Tribunal is similar to the work of scholars and historians, case studies, human rights reports, symposiums, documentary films and other civil society initiatives that publicise historical facts in the absence of any official judicial or legal process.[22]

travail proprement juridique qui fait avancer la cause d'un Droit international plus complet et plus équitable.' François Houtart, 'Introduction' to Proceedings of the Permanent Peoples' Tribunal on Workers' and Consumers' Rights in the Garment Industry, Brussels, 1998, 5 (document on file with authors and translated by the authors).

21 Permanent Peoples' Tribunal, *Session on East Timor*, Lisbon, 19–21 June 1981, and *Session on Tibet*, Strasbourg, 20 November 1992.

22 *The Prosecutors and the Peoples of the Asia-Pacific Region v. Hirohito et al. and the Government of Japan* (PT 2000-1-T) (corrected 31 January 2001), para. 485, https://web.archive.org/web/20051113024358/http://www1.jca.apc.org/vaww-net-japan/english/womenstribunal2000/judgement.html.

Activists may use the evidence presented to, and publicity accompanying, a peoples' tribunal in other legal proceedings and to bolster their negotiating power. For example, the session of the Russell Tribunal on Palestine held in London in 2010 considered that its findings were 'likely to form not only the basis of legal advocacy for years to come, but also legal briefs to national contact points within the OECD system and litigation against some of the named corporations'.[23] At least two such complaints were subsequently filed against companies examined by the Russell Tribunal on Palestine. The first was against CRH, the company whose cement was used to build the wall in the occupied territories, before the Irish National Contact Point (NCP),[24] and the second against G4S before the UK NCP.[25] The complainants argued that each company had failed to observe the Organisation for Economic Co-operation and Development (OECD) Guidelines for Multinational Enterprises.

The complaint before the Irish NCP seems to have proceeded at a glacial pace. The Irish NCP failed for almost two years to respond to regular communications from the complainant, the Ireland Palestine Solidarity Committee (IPSC), and did not undertake an assessment of the complaint. The IPSC complained to the Minister of Jobs, Enterprise and Innovation, within whose department the NCP was located, pointing out that the NCP's failure to act was inconsistent with the OECD Guidelines and requesting him to take steps to ensure the complaint was dealt with in a timely fashion.[26] After some further inconsequential interactions, a complaint to the Irish Attorney General in 2015 and an indication from the NCP in April 2015 that it would start to investigate the complaint, the case was closed in February 2016, without a final statement from the NCP, as CRH had divested from Mashav, the company that provided cement used in the construction of the wall.[27]

23 Frank Barat and Daniel Machover, 'The Russell Tribunal on Palestine' in Chantal Meloni and Gianni Tognoni (eds.), *Is There a Court for Gaza?: A Test Bench for International Justice* (T. M. C. Asser Press, 2012) 527, 538.

24 See *Ireland-Palestine Solidarity Campaign v. CRH*, www.oecdwatch.org/cases/Case_215 and www.ipsc.ie/press-releases/ipsc-submission-irish-department-foreign-affairs-trade-call-input-national-plan-business-human-rights.

25 *Lawyers for Palestinian Human Rights v. G4S*, www.oecdwatch.org/cases/Case_327.

26 Letter from the Ireland Palestine Solidarity Committee to the Minister of Jobs, Enterprise and Innovation, 25 February 2013, www.oecdwatch.org/cases/Case_215/1112/at_download/file.

27 *Ireland-Palestine Solidarity Campaign v. CRH*, www.oecdwatch.org/cases/Case_215.

In the complaint brought against G4S, the UK NCP found that there had not been

> any general failure by the company to respect the human rights of the people on whose behalf the complaint is made or any failure to respect human rights in regard to its own operations but also held that on the basis of the material before it the actions of G4S were not consistent with its obligation under the OECD Guidelines to address adverse human rights impacts a company is linked to by a business relationship.[28]

G4S responded publicly to the NCP's Final Statement drawing attention to the internal measures it had adopted across the company in relation to human rights due diligence.[29] In December 2016 it announced the sale of G4S Israel to FIMIL Opportunity Funds, an Israeli private equity fund.[30]

The 'ethical-moral pressure' of the PPT hearings on transnational corporations in Latin America helped create a more conducive climate for negotiations with corporations.[31] The evidence presented there was used by US trade unions and other organisations to oppose a free trade agreement with Colombia that failed to address issues raised in the hearings.[32] Publicity about the U'wa indigenous community's dispute with oil exploration companies in Colombia added weight to their representations to corporate investors such as JP Morgan and Fidelity Investments who decided not to invest, or sold their shares, in companies party to the dispute.[33] According to organisers and commentators, the Latin American Water Tribunal has produced or contributed to the achievement of practical results in a significant number of its cases.[34]

[28] *Lawyers for Palestinian Human Rights (LPHR) & G4S PLC: Final Statement after Examination of Complaint*, March 2015, www.gov.uk/government/publications/uk-ncp-final-statement-complaint-by-lawyers-for-palestinian-human-rights-against-g4s.

[29] G4S, 'An open approach to addressing human rights complaints', 'Israel', www.g4s.com/en/Social-Responsibility/Safeguarding-our-integrity/An-open-approach-to-addressing-human-rights-complaints.

[30] www.g4s.com/en/Investors/News-and-Presentations/Regulatory-Announcements/2016/12/02/Agreement-reached-on-sale-of-G4S-Israel.

[31] Marco Saguier, 'The Potential of Peoples' Tribunals in Latin America to Pressure TNCs into Adopting Human Rights Responsibilities', Documento de Trabajo No. 41 Area de Relaciones Internacionales FLACSO/Argentina, 2010, 19.

[32] Ibid., 20. [33] Ibid., 20–21.

[34] Carmen Maganda, 'The Latin American Water Tribunal and the Need for Public Spaces for Social Participation in Water Governance' in Jan Feyen, Kelly Shannon and Matthew Neville (eds.), *Water and Urban Development Paradigms: Towards an Integration of Engineering, Design and Management Approaches* (CRC Press, 2009) 687; Mikita A. Weaver, 'El Agua No Se Vende: Water is not for sale! The Latin American Water Tribunal as a model for advancing access to water' (2011) 11(3) *Pepperdine Dispute Resolution Law Journal* 519; Olmos Giupponi, Chapter 10 in this volume.

While governments, corporations and international organisations indicted by peoples' tribunals may adopt an official stance of ignoring them, in some cases, they feel threatened by the publicity generated. The Indonesian government blacklisted an East Timorese activist who appeared at the 1981 hearing of the PPT on East Timor.[35] A Guatemalan trade union leader who had given testimony on labour rights violations at the hearings on Transnational Corporations in Latin America was murdered.[36] It is difficult to prove that the blacklisting and murder were the direct result of participation in peoples' tribunals, yet these events testify to the gravity of the issues at stake. Peoples' tribunals can amplify claims to an extent considered unacceptable by those they accuse.

Governments may also attempt to block peoples' tribunals that they are concerned will criticise them. As noted in Chapter 1, the British and French governments blocked the holding of the First Russell Tribunal on their respective territories out of a desire to avoid public examination and criticism of the United States and their own efforts in the conduct of the Vietnam War.[37] In 1980 the Brazilian military government sought to prevent leading indigenous spokesperson Mario Juruna from attending the Fourth Russell Tribunal on violations of the rights of the indigenous peoples of Latin America by refusing to issue him a passport. Juruna, elected president of the Tribunal by his fellow Tribunal members, successfully challenged the refusal before the Brazilian *Tribunal Superior Federal* and attended the Tribunal (though arriving only on the last day of the hearings).[38]

Occasionally tribunal proceedings do attract attention in domestic politics and governments feel compelled to respond. For example, the Third Russell Tribunal on human rights violations in West Germany (1977–78) was controversial in that country and gave rise to considerable political and public interest. The government of the Federal Republic of Germany (FRG) was required to respond in detail to questions from

[35] Janine Odink, 'The Permanent Peoples' Tribunal' (1993) 11 *Netherlands Quarterly of Human Rights* 229, 231.

[36] Marcelo Saguier, 'Peoples' Tribunals in Latin America' in Darryl Reed, Peter Utting and Ananya Mukherjee-Reed (eds.), *Business Regulation and Non-State Actors: Whose Standards? Whose Development?* (Routledge, 2012), 225, 232.

[37] See Klinghoffer and Klinghoffer, above n. 17, 120–22, 139–. Mehta describes the US efforts to discredit and undermine the First Russell Tribunal: Harish C. Mehta, 'North Vietnam's informal diplomacy with Bertrand Russell: Peace activism and the international war crimes tribunal' (2012) 37 *Peace and Change* 64, 79–84; Binoy Kampmark, 'Citizens' war crimes' tribunals' (2014) 33(2) *Social Alternatives* 5, 7.

[38] Laura R. Graham, 'Quoting Mario Juruna: Linguistic imagery and the transformation of indigenous voice in the Brazilian print press' (2011) 38(1) *American Ethnologist* 164, 169.

members of Parliament. The government went to some trouble to dismiss the Tribunal as associated with leftists and terrorist groups and as engaging in unjustified and baseless allegations of human rights violations by Germany.[39] An internal memorandum prepared by the German Ministry of the Interior claimed that damage to the reputation of the FRG as a democratic state might result from the holding of the Tribunal.[40] Quite apart from this, there was a danger that such an event might stimulate further protests and generate renewed sympathy for terrorists fighting against the state and the potential dangers needed to be addressed.[41] The memorandum considered ways in which the law, or administrative or public information measures, might be deployed to limit the effectiveness and impact of the Tribunal. These included use of the assemblies law to prevent the event, seeking to use the associations law to undermine the local organising committee, a possible ban on political activity under the foreigners law for foreigners living in Germany and the denial of entry to foreigners who wished to travel to Germany to participate in the Tribunal.[42]

Similarly, the Sri Lankan government, although dismissing the PPT session on Sri Lanka held in January 2010 as illegitimate, accused the Tribunal of seeking to influence the results of the then imminent election. It claimed that the Tribunal 'is backward looking and it will not help the important recovery and unification process' and that '[i]n fact the

[39] Antwort der Bundesregierung, 'Russell-Tribunal über die Repressionen in der Bundesrepublik Deutschland', Deutscher Bundestag, 8.Wahlperiode [Response of the Federal Government 'Russell Tribunal on repression in the Federal Republic of Germany', German Bundestag, 8th session], Drucksache 8/1205, 21 November 1977, also reproduced in Freimut Duve and Wolf-Dieter Narr (eds.), *Russell-Tribunal – pro und contra: Dokumente zu einer gefährlichen Kontroverse* [*Russell Tribunal – for and against: Documents from a Dangerous Controversy*] (Rowohlt, 1978), 82; Antwort der Bundesregierung, 'Russell-Tribunal über die Repressionen in der Bundesrepublik Deutschland', Deutscher Bundestag, Drucksache 8/1750, 26 April 1978.

[40] '"Russell-Tribunal" gegen "Represssion in der Bundesrepublik Deustchland"' ['"Russell Tribunal" against "Repression in the Federal Republic of Germany"'], ÖS 2 – 614 300 R/21, VS –NFD, 20 September 1977, reproduced as 'Das Papier des Innenministeriums' ['The memorandum of the Ministry of the Interior'], in Duve and Narr, above n. 39, 96; also available in 'Russell Tribunal zur Situation der Menschenrechte in der Bundesrepublik Deutschland,' *Rundbrief* 9, 26 January 1978, 28, www.mao-projekt.de/BRD/REP/RT/Russell-Tribunal_001.shtml.

[41] Duve and Narr, above n. 39, 99.

[42] Ibid. 99–102. See the critique by Wolf-Dieter-Narr and Uwe Wesel, 'Russell Tribunal: Verschlusssache und nur für den Dienstgebrauch' [Russell Tribunal: Classified information only for official use'] in ibid. 103.

"tribunal" is itself a serious threat to stability of the country. The members of the "tribunal" should be helping Sri Lanka unite and move on at the end of a terrible conflict, not continue to stoke it.'[43]

Attacks from other quarters on peoples' tribunals are less frequent. A prominent recent example has been the attention devoted to the proceedings of the Russell Tribunal on Palestine by the organisation NGO-Monitor (among many other critics of the Tribunal), which engaged in a sustained campaign to challenge and discredit the tribunal, its members and its findings.[44]

The importance of the documentation collected for the purposes of a peoples' tribunal may only become evident years after the tribunal has been held. For example, the archives of the Second Russell Tribunal, held by the Basso Foundation, enjoyed a renewed relevance nearly forty years after the Tribunal took place, when they were digitised and made available to the Brazilian government and community as a contemporary record of the events that were the subject of that tribunal's deliberations.[45]

One consequence of the process of organising a peoples' tribunal may be the creation of networks and linkages between advocacy organisations. While this outcome might not always be anticipated, it is often regarded as one of the most powerful and rewarding aspects of the tribunal process

[43] Government of Sri Lanka, 'Statement on the so-called "Permanent People's Tribunal on Sri Lanka" to be held in Dublin on 14–16 January 2010', Presidential Statement, 14 January 2010, www.info.gov.lk/news_update/Current_Affairs/ca201001/20100115suspicious_political_motivations_of_so_called_peoples_tribunal.htm.

[44] NGO-Monitor, 'Russell Tribunal on Palestine: A Legal Farce and a Total Failure', 10 November 2011, www.ngo-monitor.org/article/the_russell_tribunal_on_palestine_a_legal_farce_and_total_failure. The organisation Fairplay South Africa also organised a Facebook site and Twitter feed 'Russell the Kangaroo' as a vehicle for criticising the work of the Tribunal, www.facebook.com/Russell.the.Kangaroo.

[45] Leticia da Costa Paes, 'O Legado do Tribunal Russell II para o Brasil e para História contemporânia dos Direitos Humanos' ['The Legacy of the Second Russell Tribunal for Brazil and for the contemporary history of human rights'] in *Justiça de Transição, Direitos Humanos e Contracultura* (2014) 8 *Re-Vista*, www.revistavjm.com.br/o-legado-do-tribunal-russell-ii-para-o-brasil-e-para-historia-contemporena-dos-direitos-humanos/; Alberto Filippi, 'O legado de Lelio Basso na América do Sul e seus arquivos de Roma: as particularidades históricas das transições democráticas e a constitucionalização dos novos direitos' ['The legacy of Lelio Basso in South America and his archives in Rome: the history of democratic transition and constitutionalisation of new rights'], *Revista Anistia Política e Justiça de Transição nº 08*, Ministério da Justiça, 2º semestre 2012, 94, www.justica.gov.br/central-de-conteudo/anistia/anexos/2013revistaanistia08.pdf; Fundacão Lelio Basso – ISSOC, 'A digitalização dos fundos do Tribunal Russel II', *Revista Anistia Política e Justiça de Transição* nº 08, Ministério da Justiça, 2º semestre 2012, 438, www.justica.gov.br/central-de-conteudo/anistia/anexos/2013revistaanistia08.pdf.

for its proponents. For example, activists reflecting on the PPT on European Union Transnational Corporations in Latin America noted that, in preparing cases for the Tribunal, they created transnational links between activist groups. The awareness that corporations undertake similar practices in different places created a sense of 'being part of a "transnational community of resistance"'.[46]

11.5 Conclusion: The Future of Peoples' Tribunals

International peoples' tribunals perform a number of valuable functions. Due to their inability to satisfy the criteria that are used to define the ideal form of state-centred court, they are frequently dismissed as illegitimate and ineffectual. A more nuanced approach can see the complexity and importance of these forms of civil society advocacy that aims to highlight inadequacies in the structures, empty promises and hypocrisy of the international legal system. Peoples' tribunals demand that international law and human rights guarantees be developed, interpreted and applied in the interests of peoples rather than of states. They are also a form of recognition and memorialisation of suffering that builds solidarity among victims and survivors of violations of human rights that can offer critique, a sense of connectedness and hope for the prospect of change in the future. As Kampmark has written:[47]

> International citizens' tribunals also suggest a framework of deliberations that broaden the focus of justice. Far from being necessarily parochial expressions of legal sentiment, such tribunals can sharpen issues, focus discussion on salient points, and shed light on matters in a broader way that bypasses self-interested states. Their effectiveness can be gathered from the sheer hostility of critics who would rather dismiss them, but find significant threat in their potency in affecting public opinion. It is precisely in such protests that their effectiveness can be gleaned.

The resort to peoples' tribunals has been a marked feature of civil society activism over the last forty years. That activists continue to deploy this form of resistance and accountability mechanism, despite its lack of formal status, suggests that it offers much more than the critics, who focus primarily on their lack of formal authority, appreciate. Peoples' tribunals continue to offer an attractive option for many groups for

[46] Saguier, above n. 31, 19. [47] Kampmark, above n. 37, 9.

whom there is no 'judge in Berlin' (or Bangalore, Bamako or Beijing) – that is, if their national political and legal systems and the formal inter-state system have failed to recognise the injustices done to them or to provide redress for those wrongs. The continuing enthusiasm for the use of peoples' tribunals evidences a faith in the power of international law to help bring about the acknowledgement of wrongs. At the same time, proponents of peoples' tribunals recognise that international law embodies and perpetuates historical and current structures of power that underpin such violations and that international law also needs to be remade in the interests of peoples and not just nation-states.

SELECT BIBLIOGRAPHY

A The Russell Tribunals

First Russell Tribunal (The War in Vietnam)

Duffett, John (ed.), *Against the Crime of Silence, Proceedings of the International War Crimes Tribunal* (Simon & Schuster, 1970).

Limqueco, Peter, and Peter Weiss (eds.), *Prevent the Crime of Silence: Reports from the Sessions of the International War Crimes Tribunal Founded by Bertrand Russell* (Allen Lane, 1971), www.raetowest.org/vietnam-war-crimes/russell-vietnam-war-crimes-tribunal-1967.html.

Index to archives of First and Second Russell Tribunals, www.fondazionebasso.it/2015/archivio-storico/fondi-archivio/sezione-internazionale/tribunale-russell/.

Second Russell Tribunal (Human rights in Latin America)

Quaderni del Tribunal Russell IIo sul Brasil Cile America Latina, Prima Sessione, Sentenza, April 1974.

First Session (Rome, 30 March–6 April 1974)

Cile, Bolivia, Uruguay: atti della prima sessione del Tribunale Russell II [*Chile, Bolivia, Uruguay: Proceedings of the First Session of the Second Russell Tribunal*], Roma, March–April 1974, 1975, Marsilio, Venezia, Padova.

Tosi, Giuseppe, Guerra Ferreira, and Lucia de Fatima, *Chile, Bolívia e Uruguai, Actas da Primiera Sessão do Tribunal Russell II* [*Chile, Bolivia and Uruguay: Proceedings of the First Session of the Second Russell Tribunal*] (Editora da UFPB, João Pessoa, 2014).

Bertrand Russell Peace Foundation, *Repression in Latin America: A Report on the First session of the Second Russell Tribunal*, Rome, April 1974, (Spokesman Books, 1975).

Second Session (Brussels, 11–18 January 1975)

Le multinazionali in America Latina, Seconda sessione (Bruxelles, gennaio 1975) [*Multinationals in Latin America: Second Session, Brussels, 1975*] (Coines, 1976).

Muñoz, Pedro (ed.), *La violación de los derechos humanos en latinoamérica, documentos del Tribunal Russell II* [*The Violation of Human Rights in Latin America: Documents from the Second Russell Tribunal*] (Editorial Euros, 1976).

Tosi, Giuseppe, Guerra Ferreira, and Lucia de Fatima (eds.), *As multinacionais na America Latina, Tribunal Russell II* [*Multinationals in Latin America: The Second Russell Tribunal*] (Editora da UFPB, João Pessoa, 2014).

(eds.), *Brasil, violação dos direitos humanos, Tribunal Russell II* [*Brazil: Violations of Human Rights, the Second Russell Tribunal*] (Editora da UFPB, João Pessoa, 2014).

(eds.), *Controrivoluzione in America Latina: eversione militare e strumentalizzazione dei sindacati, della cultura, delle chiese* [*Counter-revolution in Latin America: Military Subversion and the Instrumentalisation of Trade Unions, Culture and Churches: The Second Russell Tribunal*] (La pietra, 1976).

(eds.), *Contrarevolução na America Latina, Subversão militar, e instrumentalização dos sindicatos, da cultura, das igrejas, Tribunal Russell II* [*Counter-revolution in Latin America: Military Subversion and the Instrumentalisation of Trade Unions, Culture and Churches: The Second Russell Tribunal*] (João Pessoa, 2014).

Verso la seconda sessione [*Towards the Second Session*], *Quaderni del Tribunale Russell II sul Brasile, Cile, America Latina* (Rome, 1974).

Third Russell Tribunal (Human Rights in the Federal Republic of Germany)

Internationales Russell Tribunal and Internationales Russell Tribunal Deutscher Beirat (eds.), *Zur Situation der Menschenrechte in der Bundesrepublik Deutschland / 3. Internat. Russell-Tribunal* [*On the Situation of Human Rights in the Federal Republic of Germany/The Third International Russell Tribunal*] (Rotbuch-Verlag, 1978).

Fourth Russell Tribunal (The Rights of the Indians of the Americas)

Report of the Fourth Russell Tribunal on the Rights of the Indians of the Americas: Conclusions (Rotterdam, November 1980).

Fifth Russell Tribunal (Human Rights AND Psychiatry)

Russell Tribunal on Human Rights in Psychiatry, Berlin, 30 June–2 July 2001. See 'Russell Tribunal on Human Rights in Psychiatry', Freedom of Thought, last modified 1 October 2001, www.freedom-of-thought.de.

B Sessions of the Permanent Peoples' Tribunal

All the final verdicts or judgements of the PPT's sessions may be found on the website of the Tribunal: http://permanentpeoplestribunal.org/category/jurisprudence/?lang=en. Not all the verdicts are available in English on the PPT website. The titles of all sessions are given here in English:

1. Western Sahara, Brussels, 10–11 November 1979
2. Argentina, Geneva, 3–4 May 1980
3. Eritrea, Milan, 24–26 May 1980
4. The Filipino People and the Bangsa Moro People, Antwerp, 30 October–1 November 1980
5. El Salvador, Mexico, 9–12 February 1981
6. Afghanistan, First Session, Stockholm, 1–3 May 1981
7. East Timor, Lisbon, 19–21 June 1981
8. Zaire, Rotterdam, 18–20 September 1982
9. Afghanistan, Second Session, Paris, 16–20 December 1982
10. Guatemala, Madrid, 21–31 January 1983
11. The Armenian Genocide, Paris, 13–16 April 1984
12. The Interventions of the United States in Nicaragua, Brussels, 5–8 October 1984
13. The Policies of the International Monetary Fund and the World Bank, West Berlin, 26–29 September 1988
14. Puerto-Rico, Barcelona, 27–29 January 1989
15. Permanent Peoples' Tribunal, Session on the Brazilian Amazon, Paris, 12–16 October 1990
16. Impunity for Crimes against Humanity in Latin America, Bogotá, 22–25 April 1991
17. The Conquest of the Americas and International Law, Padua and Venice, 5–8 October 1992
18. Permanent Peoples' Tribunal, Hearing on Industrial Hazards and Human Rights (*Bhopal I*), Bhopal, India, 19–23 October 1992
19. Tibet, 20 November 1992 (revised version, 14 December 1992)
20. The Policies of the International Monetary Fund and the World Bank II, Madrid, 1–3 October 1994

21. Industrial Hazards and Human Rights (*Bhopal II*), London, 28 November–4 December 1994
22. The Right of Asylum in Europe, 8–12 December 1994
23. Former Yugoslavia, First Session, Bern, 17–20 February 1995
24. Violations of the Fundamental Rights of Children and Minors, Trento, 27–29 March; Macerata, 30 March; Naples 1–4 April 1995
25. Former Yugoslavia, Second Session, Barcelona, 7–11 December 1995
26. Chernobyl: Environment, Health and Human Rights, Vienna, 12–15 April 1996
27. Workers' and Consumers' Rights in the Garment Industry, Brussels, 30 April–5 May 1998
28. Violations of the Fundamental Rights of Children and Adolescents in Brazil, São Paulo, 17–19 March 1999
29. Elf-Aquitaine, Paris, 19–21 May 1999
30. Global Corporations and Human Wrongs, 22–25 March 2000, University of Warwick, Coventry, UK
31. International Law and the New Wars, Rome, 14–16 December 2002
32. Human Rights Violations in Algeria, 1992–2004; Paris, 5–8 November 2004
33. Second Session on the Philippines, The Hague, the Netherlands, 21–25 March 2007
34. Transnational Corporations and the Rights of Peoples in Colombia, Colombia, 2006–2008
35. Sri Lanka and the Tamil People I, Trinity College Dublin, 14–16 January 2010
36. The European Union and Transnational Corporations in Latin America: Policies, Instruments and Actors Complicit in Violations of the Peoples' Rights, Deliberating Session, Madrid, 14–17 May 2010
37. Free Trade, Violence, Impunity and People's Rights in Mexico, Mexico, 2011–14
38. Agrochemical Transnational Corporations, Bangalore, 3–6 December 2011
39. Sri Lanka and the Tamil People II, Bremen, 7–10 December 2013
40. Canadian Mining Transnational Corporations, Montreal, 29 May–1 June 2014 (ongoing)
41. Fundamental Rights, Local Community Participation and Megaprojects: From the Lyon-Turin High-speed Rail to the Global reality, Turin-Almese, 5–8 November 2015
42. Living Wage for Asian Garment Workers as Fundamental Human Right (Sri Lanka 2011; Cambodia 2012; India 2012; Indonesia 2014; Sri Lanka 2015)
43. Transnational Corporations in Southern Africa, Manzini, Swaziland, 16–17 August 2016
44. Myanmar's State Crimes against Rohingya, Kachin and other Groups, London, 6–7 March 2017; Kuala Lumpur, 19–22 September 2017

C Publications on Peoples' Tribunals Generally

Akhavan, Payam, 'Is grassroots justice a viable alternative to impunity? The case of the Iran People's Tribunal' (2017) 39(1) *Human Rights Quarterly* 73.

Andersson, Stefan 'A secondary bibliography of the international war crimes tribunal: London, Stockholm and Roskilde' (2011) 31 *Russell: Journal of Bertrand Russell Studies* 167–87 (wide-ranging bibliography of secondary sources in English, Swedish and French).

'International Citizens' Tribunals [review of Arthur Jay Klinghoffer and Judith Apter Klinghoffer, International Citizens' Tribunals]' (2002) 22 *Russell: Journal of Bertrand Russell Studies* 83.

Anthes, Louis, 'Public deliberative drama: The 1934 Mock Trial of Adolf Hitler for "Crimes against Civilization"' (1998) 42 *American Journal of Legal History* 391–410.

Asia Floor Wage Alliance (ed.), *National Peoples' Tribunals on Living Wage for Garment Workers in Asia* (I-mazine, 2014).

Barat, Frank, and Daniel Machover, 'The Russell Tribunal on Palestine', in Chantal Meloni and Gianni Tognoni (eds.), *Is There a Court for Gaza? A Test Bench for International Justice* (T. M. C. Asser Press, 2012), 527–43.

Barreda Andrés (ed.), *La Audiencia final: Sentencia, fiscalias y relatorías – Capitulo México del Tribunal Permanente de los Pueblos (2011–2014)* (Editorial Itaca, 2016).

Baxi, Upendra, *The Future of Human Rights* (Oxford University Press, 2009).

Bimbi, Linda (ed.), *Brasile, violazione dei diritti dell'uomo: Tribunale Russell II* (Feltrinelli, 1975).

(ed.), *Not in My Name: guerra e diritto* (Editori Riuniti, 2003).

Bimbi, Linda, and Gianni Tognoni (eds.), *Speranze e inquietudini di ieri e di oggi. I trent'anni della Dichiarazione Universale del Diritto dei Popoli Popoli* [*Hopes and Concerns of Yesterday and Today: Thirty Years of the Universal Declaration of Peoples' Law*] (EdUP, 2008).

Bjurström, Lena, 'Indonésie: juger l'histoire' ['Indonesia: judging history'] (19 November 2015) 1398 *Politis* 21–22, www.politis.fr/Indonesie-juger-l-histoire,33057.html.

Blaser, Arthur W., 'How to advance human rights without really trying: An analysis of nongovernmental tribunals' (1992) 14 *Human Rights Quarterly* 339–70.

Boehringer, Gill H., 'People's lawyers, people's justice and neoliberal globalization' (2015) 2(4) *Athens Journal of Social Sciences* 275–83.

Bogantes Díaz, Javier, 'Tribunales Éticos: Un acercamiento filosófico y práctico a la justicia ambiental' ['Ethical Tribunals: A Philosophical and Practical Approach to Environmental Justice'], in *Ediciones del Tribunal Latinoamericano del Agua* (Colección Ecología Política, 2012), www.tragua.com/wp-content/uploads/2012/04/tribunales_eticos.pdf.

Borowiak, Craig, 'The World Tribunal on Iraq: Citizens' tribunals and the struggle for accountability' (2008) 30 *New Political Science* 161–86.

Boyle, Mark, and Audrey Kobayashi, 'In the face of epistemic injustices? On the meaning of people-led war crimes tribunals' (2015) 33(4) *Environment and Planning D: Society and Space* 697–713.

Braunig, Marian, 'Von Nürnberg nach Vietnam: Das "Russell Tribunal" von 1967 in Historischen Perspektive' ['From Nuremberg to Vietnam: The "Russell Tribunal" in Historical Perspective'], in Manfred Berg and Philipp Gassert (eds.), *Deutschland und die USA in der internationalen Geschichte des 20. Jahrhunderts: Festschrift für Detlev Junker* [*Germany and the USA in the International History of the 20th Century: Essays in Honour of Detlev Junker*] (Franz Steiner Verlag, 2004), 492–504.

Burnett-Stuart, Matthew, 'Transnational Advocacy Networks as Counter Hegemonic Actors: The Asia Floor Wage Alliance and the Living Wage People's Tribunals', undated, 16–22, www.academia.edu/7276015/The_Asia_Floor_Wage_Alliance_and_the_Living_Wage_Peoples_Tribunals.

Byrnes, Andrew, and Gabrielle Simm, 'Peoples' tribunals, international law and the use of force' (2013) 36 (2) *University of New South Wales Law Journal* 711–42.

Cassese, Antonio, and Jouve Edmond (eds.), *Pour un droit des peuples, Essais sur la Déclaration d'Alger* [*For a Right of Peoples: Essays on the Declaration of Algiers*] (Berger-Levrault, 1978).

Cassese, Antonio, 'The Russell Tribunal', in Antonio Cassese (ed.), *The Oxford Companion to International Criminal Justice* (Oxford University Press, 2009), 497–98.

Caubet, Christian Guy (ed.), *O Tribunal da Água: Casos e Descasos* [*The Water Tribunal: Cases and violations*](Ministério do Meio Ambiente, Fundo Nacional do Meio Ambiente, 1994).

Caubet, Christian Guy, 'O Tribunal Da Água' ['The Water Tribunal'] (1994) 9(18) *GEOSUL* 71–86.

Chantal, Meloni, and Gianni Tognoni (eds.), *Is There a Court for Gaza? A Test Bench for International Justice* (Springer, 2012).

Chinkin, Christine M., 'Women's International Tribunal on Japanese Military Sexual Slavery' (2001) *95 American Journal of International Law* 335–40.

Chinkin, Christine, 'People's Tribunals: Legitimate or rough justice?' (2006) 24(2) *Windsor Yearbook of Access to Justice* 201–20.

Churchill, Ward, Sharon Helen Venne and Lilikalā Kame'eleihiwa, *Islands in Captivity: The Record of the International Tribunal on the Rights of Indigenous Hawaiians* (South End Press, 2004).

Çubukçu, Ayça, 'On cosmopolitan occupations' (2011) 13(3) *Interventions: The International Journal of Postcolonial Studies* 422–42.

da Costa Paes, Leticia, 'O Legado do Tribunal Russell II para o Brasil e para História contemporânia dos Direitos Humanos' [The Legacy of the Second

Russell Tribunal for Brazil and for the Contemporary History of Human Rights], *Justiça de Transição, Direitos Humanos e Contracultura* (2014) 8 *Re-Vista*, www.revistavjm.com.br/o-legado-do-tribunal-russell-ii-para-o-brasil-e-para-historia-contemporena-dos-direitos-humanos/.

Deutsch, Bernard S. et al., *The Case of Civilization against Hitlerism* (R. O. Ballou, 1934).

Davidson-Harden, Adam, 'Case 22: Latin American Water Tribunal: Using National and International Law to Form a Basis of Water Ethics', in Adam Davidson-Harden, Susan Spronk, David McDonald, and Karen Bakker, *Local Control and Management of our Water Commons: Stories of Rising to the Challenge* (Council of Canadians, 2008), 53, www.ourwatercommons.org/sites/default/files/local-control-management-water-commons_0.pdf.

De La Fuente, Lavín, and Juan Hernández Zubizarreta, 'Las empresas transnacionales y el Tribunal Permanente de los Pueblos' ['Transnational Enterprises and the Permanent Peoples' Tribunal', in Pedro Ibarra I Güell y Mercè Cortina I Oriol (eds.), *Recuperando la radicalid: Un encuentro en torno al Análisis Político Crítico* [*Recovering Radicalism: An Engagement with Critical Political Analysis* (Hacer, 2011), 291–307.

Dinham, Barbara, 'Introduction to the "Charter of Rights against Industrial Hazards": For Communities, Workers, and Protection of Their Environment' (1996) 23(4) *Social Justice* 164–66.

Dolgopol, Ustinia, 'The judgement of the Tokyo Women's Tribunal' (2003) 28(5) *Alternative Law Journal* 242.

Dudden, Alexis, '"We came to tell the truth": Reflections on the Tokyo Women's Tribunal' (2001) 33(4) *Critical Asian Studies* 591–602.

Duve, Freimut, and Narr, Wolf-Dieter (eds.), *Russell-Tribunal – pro und contra: Dokumente zu einer gefährlichen Kontroverse* [*Russell Tribunal – For and Against: Documents from a Dangerous Controversy*] (Rowohlt, 1978).

Falk, Richard, 'Keeping Nuremberg Alive', in Giuliano Amato et al. (eds.), *Marxismo, democrazia e diritto dei popoli: Scritti in onore di Lelio Basso* [*Marxism, Democracy and the Rights of Peoples: Essays in Honour of Lelio Basso*] (Franco Angeli Editore, 1979), 811–20.

'War, war crimes, power, and justice: Toward a jurisprudence of conscience' (2012) 10(4) No 3 *Asia-Pacific Journal* 1–16.

'War, war crimes, power, and justice: Toward a jurisprudence of conscience' (2013) 21(3) *Transnational Law & Contemporary Problems* 667–84.

Falk, Richard A., 'World Tribunal on Iraq: Truth, Law and Justice', in Richard A. Falk, *The Costs of War, International Law, the UN, and the World Order after Iraq* (Routledge, 2008), 171–82.

Feierstein, Daniel, *Memorias y Representaciones. Sobre la elaboración del genocidio* [*Memories and Representations: On the Elaboration of Genocide*] (Fondo de Cultura Económica, 2012).

Genocide as a Social Practice: Reorganizing Society under the Nazis and Argentina's Military Juntas (Rutgers University Press, 2014).

Filippi, Alberto, 'O legado de Lelio Basso na América do Sul e seus arquivos de Roma: as particularidades históricas das transições democráticas e a constitucionalização dos novos direitos' ['The Legacy of Lelio Basso in South America and his archives in Rome: Historical details of the democratic and constitutional transition to new rights], *Revista Anistia Política e Justiça de Transição nº 08*, Ministério da Justiça, 2º semestre 2012, 94, www.justica.gov.br/central-de-conteudo/anistia/anexos/2013revistaanistia08.pdf.

Fondazione Internazionale Lelio Basso, *Popoli, minoranze e Stato-nazione: giornate biennali di studio in onore di Lelio Basso* [*Peoples, Minorities and Nation-state: Seminars in Honour of Lelio Basso*] (Fondazione Internazionale Lelio Basso, 1991).

Genocidi/Genocidio [*Genocides/Genocide*](Associazione Nuova Cultura, 1995).

Il diritto all'autodeterminazione dei popoli alle soglie del 2000. Genesi, evoluzione, attualità [*The Right of Peoples to Self-determination at the Turn of the Millenium: Genesis, Evolution, Today*] (Anterem, 1998).

La pace e i diritti fondamentali [*Peace and Fundamental Rights*] (Edup, 2001).

Fraudatario, Simona, 'Le reti di solidarietà per il Tribunale Russell II negli archivi della Fondazione Lelio e Lisli Basso' ['Solidarity Networks of the Second Russell Tribunal in the Archives of the Lelio and Lisli Basso Foundation'], in Giancarlo Monina (ed.), *Memorie di repressione, resistenza e solidarietà in Brasile e in America Latina* [*Memories of Repression, Resistance and Solidarity in Brazil and Latin America*], with a preface by Gianni Tognoni (Ediesse, 2013), 315–60.

Fraudatario, Simona, and Gianni Tognoni, 'La definición jurídica y substancial del genocidio a la prueba del encuentro entre el Tribunal Permanente de los Pueblos y las víctimas' ['Legal and substantive definitions of genocide on trial in the encounter between the Permanent Peoples Tribunal and victims'], paper presented at the Conferencia Bianual de La International Association of Genocide Scholars, Buenos Aires, www.genocidescholars.org/sites/default/files/document%09[current-page%3A1]/documents/IAGS 2011 Simona Fraudatario.pdf.

Fundacão Lelio Basso – ISSOC, 'A digitalização dos fundos do Tribunal Russel II' ['The digitisation of the archives of the Second Russell Tribunal'], *Revista Anistia Política e Justiça de Transição* nº 08, Ministério da Justiça, 2º semestre 2012, 438, www.justica.gov.br/central-de-conteudo/anistia/anexos/2013revistaanistia08.pdf.

Hernández, Raymundo Espinoza, and Andrés Barreda, 'La destrucción de México ante el Tribunal Permanente de los Pueblos' ['The destruction of Mexico before the Permanent Peoples' Tribunal'] (2012) 172 *El Cotidiano* 167–82.

Hey, Ellen, and André Nollkaemper, 'The Second International Water Tribunal' (1992) 22(2) *Environmental Policy and Law* 82–87.

Icaza, Rosalba, 'Global Europe, guilty! Contesting EU neoliberal governance for Latin America and the Caribbean' (2010) 31(1) *Third World Quarterly* 123–39.

Ismaelillo and Robin Wright (eds.), *Native Peoples in Struggle: Cases from the Fourth Russell Tribunal and Other International Forums* (Anthropology Resource Center and Emergency Response International Law, 1982).

Jayasimha, Shreyas, 'Victor's justice, crime of silence and the burden of listening: Judgement of the Tokyo Tribunal 1948, Women's International War Crimes Tribunal 2000 and beyond' (2001) (1) *Law, Social Justice and Global Development*, www2.warwick.ac.uk/fac/soc/law/elj/lgd/2001_1/jayasimha.

Joinet, Louis, 'Les tribunaux d'opinion: Bilan et perspective' ['Opinion tribunals: Assessment and perspective'], in Giuliano Amato et al. (eds.), *Marxismo, democrazia e diritto dei popoli: Scritti in onore di Lelio Basso* (Franco Angeli Editore, 1979), 821–30.

Jouve, Edmond, 'Du tribunal de Nuremberg au Tribunal permanent des peuples' ['From the Nuremberg Tribunal to the Permanent Peoples' Tribunal'] (1981) 46(3) *Politique étrangère* 669–75.

Kampmark, Binoy, 'Citizens' war crimes' tribunals' (2014) 33(2) *Social Alternatives* 5–10.

Kesten, Dietmar and Jürgen Schröder (eds.) '3. Russell-Tribunal über die Situation der Menschenrechte in der BRD (1977–1979): Materialien zur Analyse von Opposition' ['The Third Russell Tribunal on the Situation of Human Rights in the Federal Republic of Germany (1977–1979): Materials for the Analysis of Opposition'], www.mao-projekt.de/BRD/REP/Russell-Tribunal.shtml.

Kim, Puja 'Global civil society remakes history: The Women's International War Crimes Tribunal 2000' (2001) 9(3) *Positions: East Asia Cultures Critique* 611–20.

Kirby, Michael, 'Decision of the Permanent Tribunal of Peoples in its session on Tibet, Strasbourg, France, November 1992' (1994) 68 *Australian Law Journal* 135–42.

Klinghoffer, Arthur Jay, and Judith Apter Klinghoffer, *International Citizens' Tribunals: Mobilising Public Opinion to Advance Human Rights* (Palgrave, 2002).

Knop, Karen, 'The Tokyo Women's Tribunal and the Turn to Fiction', in Fleur Johns, Sundhya Pahuja and Richard Joyce (eds.), *Events: The Force of International Law* (Taylor & Francis, 2011), 145–64.

Landa, Octavio Rosas, 'La lucha legal por la justicia hídrica: México en el Tribunal Latinoamericano del Agua' ['The struggle for water justice: Mexico before the Latin American Water Tribunal'] (2012) 173 *El Cotidiano* 67–79.

Latin America Solidarity Centre (LASC), 'The Latin American Water Tribunal Puts "Water Polluters on Trial"', *Thirsting for Justice – 'Defending the Global*

Water Commons', Latin America Week, 15 April 2007, 16, www.development education.ie/media/documents/Thirsting-for-Justice.pdf.

Libaridian, Gérard (ed.), *A Crime of Silence, The Armenian Genocide: Permanent Peoples' Tribunal* (Zed Books, 1985).

Louvrier, Julien, 'Le Tribunal Russell II pour l'Amérique latine (1973–1976): Mobiliser les intellectuels pour sensibiliser l'opinion publique internationale' ['The Second Russell Tribunal on Latin America: Mobilising intellectuals to influence public opinion]', www.academia.edu/166082/Le_Tribunal_Russell_II_pour_l_Amérique_latine_1973-1976_Mobiliser_les_intellectuels_pour_sensibiliser_l_opinion_publique_internationale.

Maganda, Carmen, 'The Latin American Water Tribunal and the Need for Public Spaces for Social Participation in Water Governance', in Jan Feyen, Kelly Shannon, and Matthew Neville (eds.), *Water and Urban Development Paradigms: Towards an Integration of Engineering, Design and Management Approaches* (CRC Press, 2009) 687–95.

Manfredi, Zachary, 'Pluralizing the History of International Criminal Law: Reconsidering the Russell Tribunal as an Alternative form of Left Legalism', paper delivered at The Rituals of Human Rights' Workshop, Centre for International Governance and Justice, RegNet, Australian National University, Canberra, Australia, 25–27 June 2014, http://regnet.anu.edu.au/research/publications/6124/rituals-human-rights-workshop-working-paper-no-10-pluralizing-history.

Matsui, Yayori, 'Women's International War Crimes Tribunal on Japan's Military Sexual Slavery: Memory, identity, and society' (2001) 19(4) *East Asia* 119–42.

Mehta, Harish C., 'North Vietnam's informal diplomacy with Bertrand Russell: Peace activism and the international war crimes tribunal' (2012) 37 *Peace and Change* 64–94.

Merry, Sally Engle, 'Legal Vernacularization and Ka Ho'okolokolonui Kanaka Maoli, The People's International Tribunal, Hawai'i 1993' (1996) 19 *PoLAR* 67–83.

Moita, Luís, 'Opinion tribunals and the Permanent People's Tribunal' (2015) 6 (1) *JANUS.NET e-journal of International Relations* 30, http://observare.ual.pt/janus.net/images/stories/PDF/vol6_n1/en/en_vol6_n1_art3.pdf.

Mosley, Hugh, 'Third International Russell Tribunal on Civil Liberties in West Germany' (Spring 1978) 14 *New German Critique* 178–84.

Nayar, Jayan, 'A People's Tribunal against the crime of silence?: The politics of judgement and an agenda for people's law' (2001) (2) *Law, Social Justice & Global Development Journal*, www2.warwick.ac.uk/fac/soc/law/elj/lgd/2001_2/nayar/.

'Taking Empire Seriously: Empire's Law, Peoples' Law and the World Tribunal on Iraq', in Amy Bartholomew (ed.), *Empire's Law: The American Imperialist Project and the 'War to Remake the World'* (Pluto Press, 2006) 337–13.

Nishino, Rumiko, 'Le tribunal d'opinion de Tôkyô pour les "femmes de récon-fort"'['The Tokyo opinion tribunal for "comfort women"'] (2009) 58 *Droit et cultures* 75–84, https://droitcultures.revues.org/2079.

Odink, Janine, 'The Permanent Peoples' Tribunal' (1993) 11 *Netherlands Quarterly of Human Rights* 229–32.

Olmos Giupponi, Belén, 'Transnational environmental law and grass-root initiatives: The case of the Latin American Water Tribunal' (2016) 5(1) *Transnational Environmental Law* 145–74.

Otto, Diane, 'Impunity in a Different Register: People's Tribunals and Questions of Judgment, Law and Responsibility', in Karen Engle, Zinaida Miller and D. M. Davis (eds.), *Anti-Impunity and the Human Rights Agenda* (Cambridge University Press, 2016), 291–328.

Otto, Dianne, 'Beyond legal justice: Some personal reflections on people's tribunals, listening and responsibility' (forthcoming) 5(1) *London Review of International Law*, doi.org/10.1093/lril/lrx007.

Parker, Ian, 'Russell Tribunal on Human Rights in Psychiatry and "*Geist gegen Genes*", 30 June–2 July 2001' (2001) 27 *PINS (Psychology in society)* 120–22.

Peet, J. Gerard, *International Water Tribunal Rotterdam 3–8 October 1983: Casebook* (International Water Tribunal Foundation, 1983).

Pepino, Livio (ed.), *Il Tribunale Permanente dei Popoli, le grandi opere e la Val Susa* [*The Permanent Peoples' Tribunal, Major Works and the Susa Valley*] (Edizioni IntraMoenia, 2016).

Permanent Peoples' Tribunal on Industrial Hazards and Human Rights, 'Charter of Rights Against Industrial Hazards' (1996) 23(4) *Social Justice* 167–81.

Pigrau Solé, Antoní, and Simona Fraudatario, (eds.), *Colombia entre violencia y derecho: Implicaciones de una sentencia del Tribunal Permanente de los Pueblos* [*Colombia between Violence and Law: Implications of a Judgment of the Permanent Peoples' Tribunal*] (ediciones Desde Abajo, 2012).

Rigaux, François, 'La conquête de l'Amérique et le droit international' ['The conquest of America and international law'] (1992) 4 *African Journal of International and Comparative Law* 486–91.

(ed.), *Giurisdizione dell'ambiente e diritto delle generazioni future* [*Environmental Jurisdiction and the Rights of Future Generations*] (Fondazione Internazionale Lelio Basso, 1996).

(ed.), *Le concept de peuple* [*The Concept of a People*] (Story-Scientia, 1988).

'Lelio Basso e i tribunali di opinione' ['Lelio Basso and Opinion Tribunals'], in *Lelio Basso e le culture dei diritti* [*Lelio Basso and the Cultures of Law*] (Carocci editore, 2000), 21–31.

(2012), *Il diritto dei popoli e la Carta di Algeri* [*The Rights of Peoples and the Charter of Algiers*] (Edizioni GruppoAbele, 2012).

'L'autodeterminazione nelle sentenze del Tribunal Permanente dei Popoli' ['Self-determination in the Verdicts of the Permanent Peoples' Tribunal'], in Gianni Tognoni (ed.), *Tribunale Permanente dei Popoli: Le Sentenze 1979–98* [*Permanent Peoples' Tribunal: Judgments 1979–1998*] (Casa Editrice Stefanoni, 1998), 747–61.

Rodríguez, Silvia, Laura Pérez and Tomás Saraví, 'Diálogo con Javier Bogantes, Coordinador del Tribunal Centroamericano del Agua' ['Dialogue with Javier Bogantes, Coordinator of the Central American Water Tribunal'] (1999) (5) *Perspectivas rurales* 106–13, www.revistas.una.ac.cr/index.php/perspectivas rurales/article/view/3508.

Romero Navarrete, Lourdes, 'Experiencias de Acción Colectiva Frente a la Problemática Ambiental en México' ['Experiences of collective action in response to environmental problems in Mexico'] (2003) 50 *Revista Mexicana de Ciencias Políticas y Sociales* 157–74.

Rosas Landa, Octavio, 'La lucha legal por la justicia hídrica: México en el Tribunal Latinoamericano del Agua' ['The legal struggle for water justice: Mexico before the Latin American Water Tribunal'] (2012) 173 *El Cotidiano* 67–79, www.elcotidianoenlinea.com.mx/pdf/17308.pdf.

Russell, Diana E. H., and Nicole Van de Ven (eds.), *Crimes against Women: Proceedings of the International Tribunal* (Les Femmes, 1976).

Saguier, Marco, 'The Potential of Peoples' Tribunals in Latin America to Pressure TNCs into Adopting Human Rights Responsibilities', Documento de Trabajo No. 41, Area de Relaciones Internacionales FLACSO/Argentina, 2010.

'Peoples' Tribunals in Latin America', in Darryl Reed, Peter Utting, and Ananya Mukherjee-Reed (eds.), *Business Regulation and Non-State Actors: Whose Standards? Whose Development?* (Routledge, 2012) 225–38.

Sakamoto, Rumi, 'The Women's International War Crimes Tribunal on Japan's Military Sexual Slavery: A legal and feminist approach to the "comfort women' issue"' (2001) 3(1) *New Zealand Journal of Asian Studies* 49–58.

Simm, Gabrielle, and Andrew Byrnes, 'International Peoples' Tribunals in Asia: Political theatre, juridical farce or meaningful intervention?' (2014) 4 *Asian Journal of International Law* 103–24.

Simm, Gabrielle, 'The Paris Peoples' Tribunal and the Istanbul Trials: Archives of the Armenian Genocide' (2016) 29 *Leiden Journal of International Law* 245–68.

Sökmen, Müge Gürsöy (ed.), *World Tribunal on Iraq: Making the Case against War* (Olive Branch Press, 2008).

Suzuki, Shogo, 'Overcoming past wrongs committed by states: Can non-state actors facilitate reconciliation?' (2012) 21 (2) *Social & Legal Studies* 201–13.

Terrell, Fleming, 'Unofficial accountability: A proposal for the Permanent Women's Tribunal on Sexual Violence in Armed Conflict' (2005) 15 *Texas Journal of Women & Law* 107–45.

Tognoni, Gianni (ed.), *Tribunale Permanente dei Popoli, le sentenze, 1979–1991* [*Permanent Peoples' Tribunal: Judgments 1979–1991*] (Giorgio Bertani Editore, 1992).

Tognoni, Gianni, 'Alle radici del Progetto TPP' ['The origins of the PPT project'], in *Permanent Peoples' Tribunal, Tribunale Permanente dei Popoli: Le Sentenze 1979–1998* (Casa Editrice Stefanoni, 1998) i–xi.

(ed.) *Tribunale Permanente dei Popoli: Le Sentenze 1979–1998* [*Permanent Peoples' Tribunal: Judgments 1979–1998*] (Fondazione Lelio Basso / Casa Editrice Stefanoni, 1998).

Tognoni, Gianni, 'La storia del Tribunale Permanente dei Popoli' ['The History of the Permanent Peoples' Tribunal'], in Linda Bimbi and Gianni Tognoni (eds.), *Speranze e inquietudini di ieri e di oggi. I trent'anni della Dichiarazione Universale del Diritto dei Popoli* [*Hopes and Concerns of Yesterday and Today: Thirty Years of the Universal Declaration of Peoples' Law*] (EdUP, 2008), 95–105.

Torell, David, 'Remember the Russell Tribunal?', in Anna Reading and Tamar Katriel (eds.), *Cultural Memories of Nonviolent Struggles: Powerful Times* (Palgrave Macmillan, 2015), 111–27.

Van Drom, Eddy, 'Assessment of the 2000 Tokyo Women's International War Crimes Tribunal on Japan's Military Sexual Slavery' (2011) 46 (2) Hannan University Departmental Bulletin 155-163, http://id.nii.ac.jp/1104/00000344/.

Wantanabe, Mina, 'The People's Tribunal on Comfort Women', Guest Lecture, Office of the Prosecutor, International Criminal Court, 15 May 2013, www.icc-cpi.int/about/otp/Pages/guestLecture.aspx?name=Mina-Watanabe.

WaterLex, 'Tribunal Latinoamericano del Agua, Fundación Chadileuvú c/ Estado Nacional Argentino y Provincia de Mendoza', in *The Human Rights to Water and Sanitation in Courts Worldwide: A Selection of National, Regional and International Case Law* (WaterLex and WASH United, 2014), 281–83.

Weaver, Mikita A., 'El Agua No Se Vende: Water is not for sale! The Latin American Water Tribunal as a model for advancing access to water' (2011) 11(3) *Pepperdine Dispute Resolution Law Journal* 519–45.

Winstanley, Asa, and Frank Barat (eds.), *Corporate Complicity in Israel's Occupation: Evidence from the London Session of the Russell Tribunal on Palestine* (Pluto Press, 2011)

Zubizarreta Hernandez, Juan, *Las empresas transnacionales frente a los derechos humanos: Historia de una asimetría normativa* [*Transnational Corporations and Human Rights: History of a Normative Imbalance*] (Hegoa y OMAL, 2009).

Zunino, Marcos, 'Subversive justice: The Russell Vietnam War Crimes Tribunal and transitional justice' (2016) 10 *International Journal of Transitional Justice* 211–29.

INDEX